CW00525261

THE ESSENTIAL ART OF RATIONAL THINKING

HOW TO UNDERSTAND, AND SURVIVE, OURSELVES, OTHERS AND THE CRAZY AND SOMETIMES HOSTILE WORLD IN WHICH WE LIVE

THROUGH RATIONAL EXAMINATION, EXPLORATION, PERSPECTIVE AND INSIGHT TO GET AHEAD OF THE GAME OF LIFE TO SURVIVE, SUCCEED AND CHANGE EVERYTHING FOR THE BETTER

ADRIAN CARRINGTON

Book composition = 30% popular philosophy, 25% STEM predicated logic, 7% popular psychology, 4% academic psychology, 4% psychiatry, 6% politics, 4% economics, 6% popular science, 2% law, 4% history, 4% culture, 3% religious discussion, 1% mathematics appendix.

Copyright © Adrian Carrington 2019 – Adrian Carrington is identified as the author of this work in accordance with the Copyright, Designs and Patents Act 1988. All rights reserved. No part of this publication may be reproduced, stored in a retrieval system, or transmitted in any form or by any means, electronic, mechanical, photocopying, recording, or otherwise, without the prior permission of the copyright owner.

CONTENTS

Chapters 1 to 6 examines the eradication of depression and anxiety and to develop a higher state of existence, chapter 7 on understanding the worst and the tragedy of others, chapters 8 to 10 on the understanding, survival and optimization of relationships, education and career, chapters 11 to 16 on our wider troubles; economics, politics, dishonesty and culture, when it can go wrong and how we can get wise and change everything for the better, chapters 17 & 18 on how we might thwart conflict and crime through philosophy, chapters 19 & 20 on is our life nihilistic or should we take another look and chapters 21 & 22 on spiritual/psychological inspiration for survival and a better quality of life.

INTRODUCTION

We can only find happiness and self-fulfilment if we thwart that which adds to our misery and dissatisfaction and that compromises our future potential. If we desire to change things for the better then we have no option but to find the courage to seek what is true no matter how unpalatable and painful that may be, it is only then can we start to act on that truth and change things for a better future. If we are unprepared to even look for or accept that which is true then nothing will ever change. It is often so that we do not even know what is in our own best interests, we often do things that may make us feel good but that may have damaging consequences or that may stand in the way of us achieving even greater things.

"Man is born free and everywhere he is in chains." – Jean-Jacques Rousseau
(Philosopher, France 18th century)

Smart Thinking towards Seeking 'Terminal Rational Objectivity' - the Way to a Better Life

Life is rather like standing in a very large room around which there are many doors and behind which are unknown entities. If we were to assume that all of these entities were bad then this would be pathological pessimism but equally if we were to assume that they were all good then that would be pathological optimism. The reality is somewhere between the two but to open all doors would be reckless and could be very damaging to our existence and to open none would be over cautions and might deprive us of a potentially wonderful life.

What do we do; do we take a risk and open a few of these doors in the mad hope that it might turn out OK, much like playing Russian roulette or do we investigate further as to what might be behind each door before we decide what to do, but do we first equip ourselves with a mind that is sufficiently incisive to be able to really understand what is behind the door. All of us, you, me and everyone have opened doors and later on we have regretted it or have kept other doors firmly shut and later have realised, or not, that we had made a huge mistake. The question is which doors should we open and which doors should remain shut.

Have you ever thought about life, what is my purpose, why is my life the way it is, how can I change it, how can I just make it a little better and more fulfilling, maybe you just don't understand why others are as they are, as if we are all in a boat where some refuse to row or might insist on rowing in the wrong direction, all of this points to dissatisfaction or disappointment that we all will encounter through our life's experience? Certainly most of us will desire to find the answers to those questions and if you seek to find those answers through either study or your own reflection, or better still both, then you are probably a budding philosopher. You aspire to find answers that will make your life, and I hope that of all others, better than what it currently is. Finding those answers and being willing to make changes and in a short time your life can change and may even be totally transformed.

Rational thinking exists within the wider domain of philosophy and if we were to ask an academic about this arcane subject they would probably speak in terms of metaphysics, epistemology, the great thinkers of classical Greece of the renaissance and perhaps of Indo-European (syncretic Christian, Buddhist and Hinduist) philosophy, subjects that would appear somewhat remote from the life that we experience and so one wonders why anyone would want to study it. We often also tend to associate philosophy with that which is morose and sometimes thinking too much is not necessarily good for us, but if we look in the right places and with the right application then philosophy can be highly beneficial.

Philosophy is not something confined to the world of theory, the world of the academic corridors, lecture theatres and seminars, it is highly practical, if you can think philosophically you are on the road to thinking smart and you have a good chance of making your life better than what it would otherwise have been.

"Were there none who were discontented with what they have, they would never reach anything better." – Florence Nightingale (Nurse – Crimean War, England 19th century)

Over millennia intellectual minds, and not just philosophers (rational, during the occasional transients of rationality or in total absence of rationality), have mulled over the same questions that we still do today and it is through their collective thinking that we can gain insight into such things as perception, mind, ethics & morality, good & evil, freedom, life & existence, death, immortality, faith, reality, truth, reason, culture, values, rules – an understanding of which gives us the tools from which we can find answers to those questions that our life often presents.

Within all of this you may not directly find the answer to the question that eludes you and that is nevertheless pertinent to your particular need, however just like the subject of mathematics if you understand the underlying principles you have the means, and so the tools, to solve most of your problems by yourself. With rational objective philosophical insight you have the weapons against life's problems and a better position from which to debate a point of view.

I believe it to be a great missed opportunity for us all that through our years in education we would have studied mathematics, reading and writing and otherwise largely what may set us up for life in our career but yet we, other than just a few, will never get to look at philosophy (nor for that matter rational thought) with any degree of seriousness and perhaps the closest that most of us will ever get to studying it is through religion. Religion in itself, if interpreted correctly and that can be seen and applied in its modern context can often, but not necessarily always, reach us in many ways to provide a moral framework and so may bring some form of order where otherwise there may be none and it can give us some sense of purpose and even hope but it does not answer all of our questions and does not always succeed in what it may set out to do.

If we look within our religions do we always find the answers that assuage all of our dissatisfaction and disappointments, if it is our expectation that they should then perhaps we are just asking for too much; religion may answer questions in relation to our specific relationship with God but does not solve all of our problems, if it did then all of those with a religious faith would be devoid of suffering.

If we think about its educational significance then (rational, not all philosophers are) philosophy is enmeshed in, and intrinsically important to, subjects that we are all very familiar with such as law, politics, psychology, sociology, journalism, theology, literary criticism, poetry, music, drama, even business and even military thinking, yes there are even military philosophers. Science may underpin our standards of living through the technology and medicine that we so much depend upon but the fabric, the basic functions, upon which our society is based, has its origins in philosophy and if you were to study any of these aforementioned subjects you would be very well served to have also studied philosophy as it gives you another perspective, another angle from which to look, and in anything having another perspective will yield massively towards our understanding of whatever we are looking at.

To get to the heart of anything that you seek understanding of you cannot do it by looking from just one angle alone, this won't do. Different perspectives can identify where we have misunderstood the subtleties of a subject or where we can gain other vital information that completes what is incomplete in our viewpoint. Philosophy is therefore a much misunderstood and undervalued subject and I believe that we should all invest some time to explore its principles to enable us to live better lives.

"If I could reach from pole to pole, Or grasp the ocean with a span, I would be measured by the soul, The mind is the standard of the man." - From the poem 'False Greatness' by Isaac Watts (Theologian, England 17th/18th century) and famously quoted by Joseph (John) Merrick 'The Elephant Man' (a man of great refinement and a sufferer of Proteus syndrome)

Going Deep on Philosophy (but just this once)

All knowledge and understanding, whatever it is, has universality it has a common theme of reason and logic. Without reason and logic then what we have cannot be valid knowledge or credible understanding. Societies and individuals therefore cannot function without reason or logic. However, much of what we perceive as knowledge and understanding can lack internal debate around what is or what is not valid, just how tenuous are they connected to that which is true and in this light we must remind ourselves of two important esoteric concepts, that of 'metaphysics' and that of 'epistemology' both of which that are intrinsic to the construction of this book, but what actually are these concepts.

Metaphysics is the study, discussion and reasoning of what is fundamental in what is reality, what meaning is there when we explore its depths or beyond, what is its nature, how we can articulate and therefore define what it is, what it is not subject to and whether or not it is no more than an illusion in the eye of the observer, do we perceive what is real or is reality something quite different. Our very existence, our purpose, our identity, our conscious mind, emotions, thoughts, concepts of space and perceived time, our senses, our objects of study are subject to illusion, i.e. that which is distilled within our own minds, and are therefore metaphysical concepts.

We cannot prove with any scientific method but we can aspire, and no more than aspire, to allude to what we believe to be more than just an illusion through the use of logic and reason. What we all know as physics ostensibly explores what is tangible whereas metaphysics explores the intangible and therefore that which we cannot conclusively prove.

Epistemology is the theory of knowledge, how do we arrive at knowing something through objective rationality and not subjective opinion, how do we justify and validate what we believe, how do we distinguish between what we know and what we just think we know, what is the value of empirical evidence, are we able to see multiple causes or can we only see just one, why are we so certain of where to apportion blame or guilt, how can we even know anything with any certainty and what is that certainty. Our cultural beliefs, what we believe to be just, our political views, in understanding the causes of behaviour and the ills of society are all epistemological concepts. Just what is the validity of what we think we know?

The subtleties of these two concepts are way beyond the scope of this book and are subject to a very deep academic understanding of philosophy, its history, its characters, ideas and development. We may have just attempted to define these subjects but you could also say that the very understanding of what metaphysics and epistemology actually are is subject to metaphysical and epistemological discourse, i.e. they cannot be defined without recourse to their own theories, without recourse to themselves – in trying to arrive at valid theories of reality and knowledge we cannot do so without recourse to the theory of reality and knowledge, in essence this is a circular argument. What is the reality of our theory of reality and how do we verify the means of verification of what we believe we know.

Since what is reality leads directly into what is knowledge then perhaps from a simpler viewpoint metaphysics and epistemology are just too entwined for the amateur philosopher to untangle. Perhaps what we have is an inextricably melded construct what we might call 'epistemological-metaphysics'.

Taking this to its conclusion then none of us know anything with any certainty although we are often very certain that we do. Perhaps if we were to question ourselves more in what we think and what we believe as having a considerable element of subjectivity then perhaps the world might be a better place. Being too certain can often be where we make our biggest mistakes. Perhaps we should be a bit more humble about what we think we know and in the way how we interpret the world.

"The most difficult thing in life is to know yourself." – Thales of Miletus
(Philosopher, Greece 7th century BC)

The Purpose of This Book

In our lives there are many roads that we can take, few lead to utopia and many may lead at times to sorrow, regret, anger or something of an existence with just a few moments of delight. Most of us will have to live on our wits just to survive and most of what we get, beyond survival, feels as if it were more to do with luck than skill or so it would seem. Were we born in the right place at the right time within the right environment and right opportunities or does life seem to be a struggle to avoid drowning in debt and day to day survival, an often less than ideal or pleasant job that may feel so because of unpleasant colleagues that despite all of our best efforts we cannot escape and to add to our burden; the experience of countless bad experiences from others, we may also live in an unpleasant environment perhaps one with oppression, crime, grime, poverty or even war. We may feel disappointed with what our heart searches for but never finds.

For all of us, lucky or not, we are constantly bombarded with news of bad trouble somewhere or other. Life for a lot of us is not so bad, though not beyond room for improvement and for some it can be grim. To a greater or lesser extent our life experience is entrained with fear, disappointment, anger, loss with often a lack of purpose other than connecting with our very basic human needs. If none of this was true, then we would all be perfectly happy, without any exceptions, but being honest is that really what our life experience is are there really no places where we can improve our lot.

There will always be the detractors to what I have written who may live in a very fortunate bubble who cannot or will not acknowledge just what a mess this world is in as we say the *"I'm all right Jack attitude"*. If we don't face the facts then we can never fix the problems and we just go on living in an existence that fails to deliver what potential there otherwise could be.

As a species and as an individual we have various options or paths which we can decide to take; we can advocate a utilitarian (as in its virtue is in its usefulness) nihilistic 'dog eat dog' society, a world in which everyone is totally immersed in the self, where there is corruption, manipulation and deceit, a lonely world where no-one cares for one another and so no-one cares for you, we take what we want and we live regardless of the consequences, this is a world of destruction and often of early death. Or we can live in a world where we all put in effort, where we protect those in genuine need, where there is just law, where we are polite, honest and decent a world within which we can all live good lives.

There is no magic formula to get the best out of life but what we can do is to be better equipped in how we deal with it and this is largely down to us being amenable to ideas that can help us survive, this is therefore a book about those ideas. Some might say that *"a little knowledge is dangerous"* but no knowledge is catastrophic and we simply do not have the time to read all the books that we would need to in order to master life but at least what we can do is seek a reasonable working knowledge of what is going on and ideas on how we might begin to tackle our problems. If we are too rigid in what we believe, we are too inflexible, then we are unable to adapt and possibly therefore unable to survive.

If we have absolutely no intention of changing our views then there is no point in reading anything including this book. If you know everything then why read anything but you also can't criticize what you haven't read. To change our life we must first challenge our own beliefs and that may not always be so easy but if you don't do this your life has no chance of ever changing and you will just stay with what you have. So either be prepared to change your perspective or be satisfied with what you have and what you are. You need to ask yourself; has my way of dealing with life brought me total satisfaction but also has it done so without having to do bad things to others.

This book is designed not to challenge what anyone happens to believe, that is for the individual to do themselves, but maybe to offer a different perspective on everything that hopefully replaces the uncertain with reality and that which is negative with that which is positive. Within this we may find hope, we might feel good about life and we might be fired up to work towards a better world for us all. In addition I hope that, even if you don't agree with what is within that at least it gets us talking about the issues that face us so we can somehow work out what we must collectively do. In doing so we need to be open to listening to the views of others, even extreme views may be worth a thought although not necessarily any more than just a thought, thinking the unthinkable can sometimes contribute another angle to precipitate ideas that may contribute to the most optimal solution.

I have always been an advocate of condensing information, that which goes straight to the point, but delivering it with the right pitch so that it can be easily understood, since if your ambition is to convey knowledge, i.e. to teach, then you cannot do so by being on guard about what you know. To this point I have agonised over many months to ensure that this book conveys, hopefully well, what it sets out to do. Not all will agree with what I have written, this can never be possible, I even knew someone once who if you said *"good morning"* to would always reply *"no its not"* and maybe he was right or maybe he just had a bad outlook on things.

What this is saying is that it is OK to have different perspectives but then to perhaps show some willingness to see the other viewpoint too. However, I believe that this book does have another useful perspective in that due to its quite extensive range and detail that in reading it you may have furnished yourself with enough understanding of philosophy to be able to converse well with any degree level 'applied philosophy' student and that also you will have gained some fluency in material that you may had hitherto not read of or contemplated all of which contributes to your articulation of your point of view.

All words encase an idea from which you can explore so much, so just pause for a moment and reflect on the words 'motivation', 'ego', 'reason' and 'good'; if we attempt to deconstruct what these words are trying to convey what is it that is buried deep within their meaning and how does this effect our perception of the world and of ourselves.

If you can become articulate you can gain power to reason not just externally but also within yourself. This is important to me in that even if you have a totally opposing view to mine I would still dearly want you to be able to articulate your view well as I might then get a better opportunity to see things from your side of the argument which may of course hold greater validity than my viewpoint or may not. If you want to persuade someone to see your point of view then don't use the barrel of a gun or shout others down, first apply reason, logic and self-argument to check the validity of your position and then use articulation. You may still be wrong but at least you have articulated your point as best as you can.

This book is for everyone without exception and it aims in its small way to perhaps give some potential to make all of our lives better. This may appear as an ostentatious ambition, it isn't meant to be, but isn't this an ambition worthy of us all to strive for and shouldn't we all be a part of that ambition and that includes you, wherever you are and whatever you do. Whether you be a miner, whom I have the greatest of respect, working in the bowels of the earth, teacher, factory worker, farmer, fisherman, soldier, cleaner of drains, doctor, nurse, builder, engineer, car mechanic, lorry driver, cook, cashier, carer, student, retiree, young or old, whoever you are, you are not forgotten I have you in mind in writing this book and you are all part of making our society a success and in taking the human race onto better things.

> *"The greatest happiness is to know the source of unhappiness."* – Fyodor Dostoyevsky (Novelist, Russia 19th century)

My aim is to take you through a roller-coaster ride into what dramatically affects our feelings of well-being, what suffering (our self-oppression) that we bring upon ourselves and to end up at its close with optimism and enthusiasm to start anew. In the process that which is negative cannot be ignored in our discussion since how can we fix something if we can't discuss it or at least define what it is? Within all that is negative there is the positive to be found and so useful lessons to be learnt. What we should all aim for is to not seek protection, not to refuse to face that which may oppose what we are or what we think, that way we just can't survive the reality of life, but to toughen up to gain resilience and if we can do that then we are in a good position to make the most of what we have.

My Path from Engineering Science to Philosophy

Given the list of its contents you may wonder, what is my 'platform' to have written a book such as this; am I a philosopher (although philosophy is really something that you do not what you study), a psychologist, an evolutionary biologist, a politician, a theologian, a lawyer? I am actually none of these things, my formal study, as I was later to partly regret, was nuclear engineering (a lot of mathematical analysis that for me I became rather sick of and remain so to this day) and since graduating then continued my studies into electronic engineering (a lot of analysis of logic and analogue circuits) and then for my own amusement studied human biology and I have worked in industry for over 35 years – so I am an engineer and I am used to working in dangerous environments where things can blow up and kill; and my colleagues and I would have to dig deep to find all of the reasons as to why this may happen and how we might thwart it from happening - life itself is not so different.

You would be forgiven for failing to see any connection between philosophy and engineering, a connection that is well exemplified by the 5th century BC Greek philosopher Democritus who would lay the early foundations of atomic theory postulating that matter itself can only be divided down to a certain point from which it is irreducible, an idea that my father was to introduce to me 2500 years later and from which, coupled with my fascination of the prospects of atomic power, that my choice of study was eventually decided. Much of science and even engineering, though devoid of philosophy is nevertheless inextricably rooted in philosophical origins and thought, what we imagine today we invent tomorrow. Philosophy, specifically analytical philosophy, is very much rooted in logic and mathematical thought, noting that the philosopher Bertrand Russell was a mathematician - just as philosophy can spawn science, science can also spawn philosophy.

Engineers spend their whole working life using science, mathematics, logic and reason, these being the fundamental requirements of this profession. Engineering is unlike anything else it is totally unforgiving of error of judgment, it is quintessentially rational, it always has to be fully validated, get it wrong and the design just doesn't work - a small error could prove to be catastrophic, it is demanded to meet effectiveness of design and efficiency within the tight design envelopes of what the physics presents.

However, the mindset of the engineer presents new possibilities in solving problems outside of engineering; we can therefore subsume engineering thinking with its distinct analytical concepts into the wider world. Concepts that if something is bad, then more of it will most probably, but not always, make it worse but by how much, that if something is good then more may make it even better but then will reach an optimum point beyond which its benefit declines and then seek to find that optimum point, that for any observable effect we must determine all of its causes, not just some of them and certainly not just one, that a perceived link between a cause and an effect may in reality not exist or may be less relevant than what we may believe, that we contemplate and study the consequences of our actions, and the very worst possible outcomes (politicians never do this), and the deeper consequences beyond and that ill-consideration, a casual attitude, incompetence or worse recklessness can only yield instability and eventual failure.

Engineers obsess about solving problems, often the apparently impossible to solve, such that much of our work is research with the added pressure of working in a commercial environment where get it wrong, and that would be very easy to do, then the costs and even loss of life could be unthinkable.

Though engineers are not experts in philosophy, politics, economics or psychology but despite the millions of these experts we are still up to our ears in political and economic problems, war, crime, mental illnesses etc. – just why is it that we have not eradicated these problems, why does our world remain in such a mess. Perhaps the experts look too close at the detail in that they cannot see the bigger picture, they are in effect complicating things; in essence they 'cannot see the wood for the trees'. It is not that there is any lacking it is perhaps that our population, its rapid cultural change and consequent problems have grown faster than we are able to resolve. Further to this there is a false assumption that we can solve all of our problems with the 'unlimited supply of money' that in reality, unpalatable as it might be, does not and can never exist. It is a daunting task. Many might criticize the endeavours of others to try to sort out the mess but those who criticize can seldom offer any effective alternative solutions.

However, you will see that this book is festooned with quotations by the famous, many of whom are not philosophers but yet they could reach into rational philosophy, they inspire us to look at life just as they did; hence philosophy is available to us all. I do not confine my interest in philosophy to my career experience alone, although oddly enough it has been useful in this capacity, but as I am also something of an eclectic person when it comes to information I have a fascination and a passion for understanding many things, even more so when they don't make sense. I am also an avid, though selective, reader of world history, psychology, biography, world religions and politics, all that can spawn philosophical thought, from which I have not aimed to devour facts but to open my mind to new ways of thinking and I believe the wider, not just the more, you read the closer you may get to the truth.

"I declare after all there is no enjoyment like reading!" – Jane Austin (Novelist, England 18th/19th century)

Engineers are used to dealing with what can go wrong or that can enter instability (control theory) and why, through observation, research, detailed analysis, formulaic interpretation, calculations and dogged determination to what is often difficult to fathom out. With a completely different perspective, as that of an engineer, this presents the possibility of a new way of looking at our life experience that may yield alternative solutions and maybe a few surprises. In saying that the word 'but' comes to mind, however no-one can ever address everything as 100% perfect as 100% complete, nothing is ever complete, the word 'but' is unavoidable and is what takes us from what is imperfect towards greater perfection.

Challenge and rational debate is therefore one of the most useful of human engagements, we grow because we do not all think alike but because we all think differently it is through challenging each other that perhaps we end up closer to what is true. No book that has ever been written can ever be complete can ever

THE ESSENTIAL ART OF RATIONAL THINKING • 11

close out the truth it is perhaps along the path of truth to an end that is forever elusive.

Some may question the validity of a book about philosophy, of sorts, yet written by an engineer (noting that the philosopher Ludwig Wittgenstein was a mechanical/aeronautical engineer) a book about anything but engineering but maybe this book could never be written by anyone who is a philosopher, a theologian, a psychologist or an evolutionary biologist as they all specialise in their respective fields as do any of us. If we were to take the view that we must be an expert in every subject that this book covers then this book could never be written and gone would be its opportunity to convey the collective thinking from all that and those I have read and studied. Much of what I have written is an assembly of developed ideas based upon axioms, existing theory and the plainly obvious it's just a question of opening our eyes and seeing what goes on.

Through fascination to understand human behaviour in all of its variety, observation, experience, instincts, basic principles, to try to get into the minds, feelings, anguish and lives of others - a sort of thought experiment, through my own failures and successes, through what is logical deduction and through a lot of digging, sometimes to places of thought I would rather not go, to converse at length with those who are not always exactly the nicest of people, some who are even extreme, and through having the privilege to know and to have known some of the very wise and through all of this then writing extensive notes over years and many interrupted nights whilst still working in my day job, where I had no option to do other, in the interest of research into the human condition, we can then establish so much without getting too academic about it all otherwise progress would be just too slow for our own good.

"Life is short, opportunity is fleeting, experience treacherous and judgment difficult." – Geoffrey Chaucer (Writer, England 14th century)

Despite extensive enmeshing of accepted theory, we could spend the next ten thousand years collecting supporting data on the blindingly obvious before we put pen to paper but if we all did so then we would remain in the dark ages, besides do we really need any extensive research to tell me for example that if I were to bash my thumb with a hammer that it's going to hurt, I have also thought about a lot of hammers and a lot of thumbs. If we look at the subjects that I have just mentioned then there are many questions to be answered that still elude many experts or that the experts may turn out to have got totally wrong, yes that happens too. If we were to look at a judge they cannot possibly be experts in everything but yet they have to have an ability to walk across different fields of expertise to be able to conduct a trial – if they didn't have this capability then the trial would just seize up. I am just following the lead of the judge.

However, I am also particularly fascinated by what people think and what they have experienced and whenever we look at old photos we should try to imagine what life may these people have had, what stories they could tell, what suffering and what joy they experienced. They may be long gone but they are not forgotten, their existence and what they have done in their lives eternally echoes through time, as it does for us too, and from this we can learn so much. What we do never entirely fades for any of us.

In my life I have encountered some of the most wonderful of mankind but also some of the very worst I have also experienced the highs and I am very familiar with the very darkest of places but then again we all have stories to tell. In the world of engineering opinion does not exist in quite the same way as it does in most other professions, it is either right or it is wrong, it will either work or it won't work, a solution is required to be exact. A culture such as this yields a more objective view especially when coupled with wider and prolific study aimed at precipitating a greater understanding of what is wrong with our world.

A Reflection on Human Achievement

"For I dipt into the future, far as human eye could see, saw the vision of the world and the wonders that would be." – From the poem 'Locksley Hall' by Alfred, Lord Tennyson (Poet, England 19th century)

Before we start I just wanted to reflect for a moment on just how fantastic the human species is in what achievements we have made when we are at our very best. In our short modern history of just a few thousand years we have developed agriculture, we have looked into deep space and developed theories of the universe, through extensive research we construct amazing machines such that we can generate electricity, we can fly to distant places, we can instantly communicate to the other side of our planet, we have mostly defeated communicable disease, we can design complex electronic systems and we can split the atom and harness its energy and our technology is now beyond the furthest reaches of our solar system.

Further to this we have implemented the rule of law to protect our citizens, we construct the most amazing buildings, we write literature and poetry, we carve, we paint, we compose, we philosophise and we have moved on from our primitive thinking. Through hard work and prudence and only through hard work and prudence we have built a society that is more enlightened, more progressive and more advanced than ever before.

Being and living in a constructive culture enables us to enjoy life to see the futility of war and finally turn our backs on causing it, to be more affluent and to make the most of what we have. We are better fed, we are better educated we have better employment and we are safer in this modern world than we have ever been. We find purpose to exist we have hope we have a future.

"The unexamined life is not worth living." – Socrates (Philosopher, Greece 4th/5th century BC)

The human race was very lucky to have Socrates, someone who had dedicated his life in the search of wisdom, truth, happiness and the purification of the soul for which he was to lose his life for doing so. It would seem that even in the search of a better life for all can upset a few with tragic results. If only they had listened to Socrates rather than destroy him they also would have found salvation. They may have killed this great man but he could not be put down for the world would never be the same again, from then on many great thinkers advanced his ideas in the search for enlightening philosophy from which we have all been touched and it is to one of Socrates contemporaries who we shall look at later in greater detail – The Buddha. It is our goal to achieve the ultimate experience of happiness and meaning in our life and to help others in doing so too - this is what we should aim for.

A Note on Nomenclature

Throughout this document I have applied, in terms of strict psychological definition, some injudicious use of the word subconscious. This is deliberate in that from the perspective of those who live outside of academic psychology will associate the 'subconscious' with our self below the surface of our conscious thought, the self that is hidden, the deeper me that I am not even aware of. Strictly speaking this is not 'subconscious' but is our 'unconscious' mind and if you were to sit in on a psychology lecture the word 'unconscious' would be the correct term whereas going by the book the true meaning of 'subconscious' is in actuality the repository of what we have learnt our value system from which our conscious reactions emanate from and which we are very well aware of.

Our 'conscious' mind, that which we are aware of, calls upon our subconscious mind, in essence our knowledge base, to decide upon actions and opinion, however the deeper unconscious mind may introduce bias and influence to the process that we may not be aware of. We may for example consciously decide what is right or what is wrong based upon our subconsciously embedded rules (that may themselves be wrong), rules that we can call upon that we can recite, but we may not be aware of a deeper bias or deeper emotions that may even corrupt our final thinking.

Target Audience

Life's challenges don't start at any specific age and it doesn't end at any specific age either, from the moment we are born to the moment we die we face the challenges of life and the sooner we wise up to life the better. Through our life we pass through various developmental stages of learning but as soon as we are able to grasp the necessary rules of life, ones that mature through our experience, the better. I hear it all the time, the most standard of lamentations, indeed the lamentation of lamentations; *"if only I knew then what I know now"* and the only way how we can get ahead is to read widely from those who have experiences and realisations to share.

When we are young we often view the words of older others; parents, teachers, colleagues, enlightening literature with suspicion and perhaps this is why we become defiant rebels only later to mellow only later to realise. Do the old not understand the young but do the young understand the old, perhaps the answer is in that the old were young once and the young are yet to become old. The truth is we never stop learning. The sooner we get wise and the greater wisdom we acquire from then on the better placed we are to understand life, to survive it and to live it and to live it to the full.

Before We Move On (a soliloquy/something to contemplate)

Ask yourself; do I look back with regret or did I not learn well from my past to succeed better with my future. Did I struggle or is that struggle yet to come. What I had and what is before me is it all bad luck, am I not at least in some way responsible for my past and for my destiny. Did I or do I choose the wrong path, a path too difficult or one too easy, have I or will I reject good opportunities, that others did not or will not, because it was me that would not or will not think wisely. Did I obsess about perfection and so condemned myself to miss out on opportunities? Was I or am I too hung up about standards or the lack of, did I and will I really make the best of what I have or could have, did I lack the skills that I needed or the willingness to acquire those skills. Could I do better do I even have the desire to do so. Am I willing to look within with a cold eye and recognise the need to change?

Of course life's failures may not all be of our own making but it is quite unlikely that it is entirely as a result of the fault of others. In my lifetime I do not have the time to find out all I need to know and to all that I should read but I can at least optimise what I have by looking again at that which is near self-evident, to explore demystified, life critical yet hitherto esoteric knowledge and to seek out new ideas –

it is from here that I shall advance my thinking and advance my life into greater possibilities and into greater opportunities.

Chapter 1

GETTING WISE ON THE SUBJECT OF ANGUISH

(Destruction of the self)

Self-criticism and the courage to admit that we may be wrong can be a wonderful thing; it is a mark of cultivation, it is what motivates us to develop, to become better than what we are, to become whole and to reach our full potential. In some ways it may be our only route to finding sanity but sometimes it can go just too far where we are being unpleasant to our very self.

Why Should I Need To Read This?

How do you feel today, do you feel absolutely fantastic and without any care in the world; are you at a point of what you might describe as sublime happiness or freedom, devoid of any worries whatsoever - a position where it is inconceivable to imagine anything better, a position that cannot be improved upon. You may very well do and good for you. Have you always felt this way, will you feel the same tomorrow, will it remain so over the coming months and years until you finally depart this world; sounds possible but it is improbable, very improbable. The reality is somewhat different unless you are an expert in surviving life, where you are 'coated in Teflon (PTFE)' (a material with non-stick properties) and where you are lucky enough that nothing bad ever happens to you.

In reality what we experience may not be all bad, it seldom is, but neither is it all good; we might describe our life experience as a cocktail of great days, good days, bad days and some days that are just bloody awful. There is evidence everywhere that without exception all of us have anxieties of some form or other and we all experience low mood and on occasions this can feel just too much to bear. Relationships, loneliness, money, work, ill-health, fear, exams, politics, purpose etc. we can't just ignore them they are there and none will be without problems of some form or other.

In truth at times our lives can feel like absolute shit and even if it doesn't much of our time is far from perfect, that gnawing of bad feeling what may often not be as bad as what we may describe as depression but what we may describe as low mood, degraded happiness or just not feeling so great or what you might describe as feeling partially depressed, anxious or in a suppressed anxious state that could be construed as our own destruction of ourselves albeit there are outside forces at work. Before we can move on to the wider issues, as are addressed in this book, in how we might be able to improve our lives we need to address what is bad and what is between us and our ambitions to move on and live our lives well in this context.

"By conquering your mind you conquer the world." - Guru Nanak Dev Ji (Sikh Guru, Pakistan, 15th/16th century)

So if you are suffering from what I prefer to define generically as 'depressive states' and what you may describe as low mood, anxiety, depression or loneliness or even if you feel flooded with misery or despair, you are dogged with impending doom, have some kind of crisis tsunami or have regrets of what you think is a wasted life, well don't worry because we are about to blast the crap out of it, well at least that is what we aim to do. Remember that underneath of all of that torment is the potential for a better and more successful life.

However, it is essential to bear in mind that we are talking here of that which remains within your own capacity to deal with, or what you might describe as a low mood, anything greater than this or that which may be persistent then you must always seek professional help but don't suffer it and don't let it fester, get help fast, the earlier you deal with it the less damage it will do to you. Remember that this book does not and cannot replace professional help. This is a book written around philosophy and no more, if it helps you, then that's great, but do not take exclusive refuge in what is written here alone as you may not find everything you are looking for or all that you may need.

I have ambitions beyond dealing with that most destructive force of depression in all of its flavours, it is my desire to make the world a happier place in some small way to alleviate those transient degraded feelings that we have or where we may feel some vague indescribable parasitic malaise that lives with us. I wish to explore how we might restore that deep core happiness that we have lost or maybe have never had. So even if you happen to feel that this chapter is not for you please read on as you may discover something about yourself that you were unaware of, just maybe you are not as happy as you could be. None of us, without any exception, are totally at ease with our lives, we do not live life to the full as we should do; there is always something gnawing away or about to strike at us.

The way how we feel about ourselves may be because of different causes and may present different symptoms but it is also contagious. If you feel bad you cannot hide it, try as you might, in some way being ill at ease will reveal itself, often subliminally, even a pet can sometimes detect when its owner has low spirits and so can us fellow humans. If we feel bad then others around us will do so too. If you have ever been in a room with someone ebullient and charismatic though not overbearing then they will make you feel good so logic would suggest that being in a room with someone not exactly on good spirits will not do you much good either.

Through this chapter is a vein of belief that a lot, although not all, of our problems are very much concerned with our perception of our world and what goes on around us, therapy cannot change your circumstances though it will teach you how to change your perception of those circumstances and in a broader perspective it will change you, it will change your perspective frame of reference. To find good mood therefore requires the acquisition of certain skills. Much of what we need to do is to change our perspective is to find the right key, the right code, to unlock the door to a new way of looking at our lives – if we can do this we can solve our problems and find happiness and live for the moment without depressive feelings or anxiety for the future or regrets of the past. You will find that once you have found the right key, that the right thoughts having coalesced, then the bad feelings you have will almost instantly collapse and what troubled you can then be put behind you.

"Be happy for this moment, this moment is your life." - Omar Khayyám (Poet, Persia 12th century)

In Understanding Psychopathology through Exploring Our Own Mind

I am an engineer but I do not know everything about engineering, it's impossible to do so, the range of knowledge and infinite application is beyond the mind of any engineer. Some of us may read just one book and believe that we know all there is to know on a subject, but within that book, indeed any book, you will not find all of the answers, you might think you can but you can't. You may read more but you never reach that pot of gold at the end the rainbow, you never quite get there.

I have read much of the Bible but ask me what a particular verse means in its universally applicable context and I simply don't exactly know and if I wanted to do so I would have to discuss with some, not one, seriously well qualified and mentally stable theological scholars and even then they may need to confer with an even higher authority and if that be God then only God will know the exact meaning in all contexts. My favourite song of all time is Bob Dylan's 'My Back Pages' by 'The Byrds' that I must have listened to over a thousand times but ask me what does it mean and I cannot quite tell you, I may be able to recite it but to understand is a very different thing. And while you are at that also check out another of Bob Dylan's songs 'The Times They Are A-Changin' again by 'The Byrds', easier to understand and within which there are some really great thoughts.

No book gives you fixed rules since you cannot find all circumstances of application within, what it gives you is guidance based on what was known at that time, it is then for you to decide what is and what is not right based upon truth not upon hubris or self-interest based morality, and you must hope that you get it right, get it wrong and the consequences upon you and others could be devastating. Psychology is different since we can determine much of how others think, without total reliance upon books or scholars but by observation but also by looking within ourselves since, after all, we are all equipped with the same set of emotions, well almost.

I have read quite a few good books on psychology and psychiatry and I have spent much of forty years thinking hard about these subjects, I have also observed some fairly nasty people do some fairly nasty things to others; some might carry bitterness about such experience I wouldn't since bitterness eats at you it destroys your life, but what I found fascinating was trying to understand what was their motivation what was their pathology and these experiences together with my studies gave me much to think about including about myself, to expand the exploration of my own emotions to that of understanding others in what they have done and are still doing to one another and I could not have done that from reading alone.

Thankfully I think different to them but I can get at how they might have arrived at where they are by exploring my own mind. Our own mind is an accessible work space for us to explore the psychology of others. What is it that is within the mind of someone who believes that they are always right, who will not listen to reason, who can so easily be manipulated, who have crazy notions about being 'superior', who believes that they deserve so much but yet doesn't want to put any effort in to get it, who has pathological envy, who are quick to hate, who are quick to take offence and cause offence, who seeks to make someone else's life a misery, who can kill, who can suddenly explode in anger over nothing, all of which takes place in all theatres of human existence in work, in politics, in war and even in relationships.

These properties are dormant in us all, what Carl Jung would refer to as our 'shadow', and with the right trigger what we are capable of doing could be unimaginable, we just don't know what we are capable of. If we can get to these emotions that are within ourselves and equip ourselves with some intellectual understanding of their nature then it is amazing what we can discover but we have to accept that we cannot find all of the answers to everything.

An Examination of Psychiatry

For all of us throughout our lives we will encounter and will be afflicted by illness or disease however of these there is only one ailment requiring special attention here as it is within the potential for a philosophical cure and this is unhappiness and to its extreme form depression. Of the cruellest of afflictions, an acute and persistent depressive state can be the most awful and furthermore it is difficult to assuage its effects and unless you are very lucky or you are emotionally dysfunctional then you will have encountered this affliction. And if you happen to think that it is of some amusement that anyone can be struck down with this then you could very easily become its next victim since no-one is immune. Indeed at least one in ten of us are affected by a depressive related disorder in any one year and chances are that almost all of us will encounter it at some time in our lives.

A depressive state is essentially an absolute bastard to endure, it tears us apart, and unless it is very severe we do have at least some chance to defeat it or at least degrade its impact through our own actions alone. If it is severe then we need professional help, you might think that running around the garden naked will help but it won't and you might just only give your neighbours something to feel depressed about. A depressive state is an ailment where the cure, or facilitating a cure, can therefore largely be within your control you just need to acquire the ability to do so by acquiring new ways of thinking about your situation and in taking action.

What we are about to discuss is by no means replacing medical treatments for such conditions though is written from the context of its philosophical consideration. Some depressive illnesses are quite intractable and have more complex causes than I can hope to cover here although at least what we are about to discuss may be of help to anyone who is suffering or to even avoid this problem in the first place. If this helps you then I'm very happy that it does.

If, however, that you believe that this doesn't apply to you, that's great, but it may do so in future so it's worth having the tools to deal with it in advance that can also be of benefit even if you are not in a depressive state you may learn how to live life a little better. However, if you are not affected then it is highly likely, wittingly or unwittingly, that you will know someone who is and being knowledgeable of what their suffering feels like then you may feel a bit more compassionate about their situation - some around you may not appear affected, they may even seem chirpy, they may be a brave soul who is just very good at hiding their true feelings. You may also have some immunity, subject to the luck of your particular circumstances in which you find yourself, that you have some innate defences although no defence is absolutely 100% impenetrable so you may still encounter other circumstances in future that can affect or even cripple you, whatever your thoughts may be now.

Albeit we might only encounter a few at any time who we could say are as far as clinically depressed, it is very apparent that a lot of us sit on a scale where we are far from being at ease and so a lot of us can appear flat, in essence that our life experience is not as good as it could be. It may just be a degraded capacity to feeling ebullient or uplifted, to appear blank, a feeling of detachment or indifference, of taking life too seriously or of losing the ability to laugh, of a withered zest for life, having an inclination to assume a worst not best case scenario or other symptoms that may even be barely detectable and although not what you would classify as deeply depressed but neither is this a state of happiness. This is not happiness as it could be as what its potential is. The perspective of this book is therefore not just in addressing depressive states it is also in finding happiness as pure depression and pure happiness are just different ends of the same emotional stick.

Looking tough or in having, what is often false, self-belief in being tough doesn't mean that you are happy and certainly does not give you any immunity from depressive states for in fact anyone with emotional capacity will at some time face difficulties when they question their life purpose and future or face the simple day to day anxieties. So if even tough people can feel this way then there is no need to feel ashamed about feeling the way you do, the way you feel is not so different than having a migraine attack it just hangs around for longer. Perceived toughness in others often belies the truth of what they are experiencing.

It is quite surprising that even extreme depression affects those who you would not imagine; athletes (including heavyweight boxers) to astronauts, rock stars and even comedians. Some careers can be more prone to this problem than others such as where there is some form of social isolation, where the job is mundane, stressful or distressing, unpleasant or where you encounter extremes of contrast such as a performer who then has to return to that lonely hotel room after their act in front of a rapturous audience.

Being successful, famous, of strong determination, even appearing chirpy or having everything to live for does not make you in any way immune. Depression is something of a leveller as it can attack any of us, young or old, rich or poor, famous or the unknown, at any time. Some of the most wonderful people have become casualties to its extreme form and sometimes ending it all in the most extreme act of self-destruction. When the world loses such people we are all worse off. Perhaps they perceived surmountable problems to be insurmountable, perhaps they were unable to bring themselves to talk about it, but if only they could have sought help since there are lots of ways that support can be found when we look, the world is just not as cruel as what might be imagined.

If life just feels too unbearable and it is not simply just an issue of the way how you look at it; then is it not that you are looking at just the one possibility of your life i.e. the one that you are experiencing – could it be that you could start again from nothing and make a success of your life or just walk away from that awful situation and find exciting new possibilities. You may feel that there are reasons to die but there are also plenty of reasons to live, you just need to go and find them. Learn to look beyond what you are suffering, aim for a better life and go and get it. A feeling of a depressive state is a very personal thing but don't forget that you are not alone in feeling like this you are part of a community that is larger than you might just imagine.

Mental illness covers a whole vista of ailments some of which are quite benign and some that are quite malignant and that will detrimentally affect the lives of many of those you encounter. All of these ailments require professional help from psychiatrists and clinical psychologists and are way beyond the scope of this book. However, depression in its various classifications is a most common form of not so much mental illness but mental suffering, i.e. suffering of the mind, and one from which we can all have some idea of describing it and understanding how to beat it from our own personal experiences of it.

I am not schooled in any great capacity in the workings and ailments of the mind, my knowledge of the subject is more practical than theoretical and is through experience, projection, visualisation and observation, I am in this sense fortunate to have had encounters with all sorts of people and have never lived in any particular bubble. Every chance I get I take an interest in others, in how they think, what drives them; the human race really is amazing and there is so much you can learn in taking this interest.

So does a lack of formal knowledge carry any credibility, well yes it does as the psychiatrist may not have had personal experience of wide ranging depression in all of its manifestations, in all of its nuances, and it is not a pre-requisite to have had such experience to becoming a psychiatrist. Perhaps a mind that is 100% healthy might not be best material from which to make psychiatrists as they do say that; *"calm seas do not make great mariners"* (an African proverb).

I am not advocating the re-emergence of the anti-psychiatry movement of the 1960's; where treatment was postulated to contribute to the cause of a problem and where mental illness was perceived to be no more than a natural reaction to circumstances rather than an ailment, although that is a moot point given the extent to which our mind will go in order to 'survive', however from the philosophical perspective is it not better to have experienced something, to have therefore shared something within the same frame of reference of that experience in order to understand what the sufferer is going through and to be able to understand what they are trying to describe instead of trying to understand an experience purely through its clinical terms alone. I could, for example, not be able to understand any description of the colour 'red' unless I have actually seen this colour. Without the experience of seeing it, the description might cause me to imagine an entirely different colour or not being able to imagine anything.

A psychiatrist is also slightly hampered to some extent in that his/her job is too enmeshed in dealing with those in distress and less so with those who are not, they seek to cure the patient but it is outside of their remit to then take the patient to happiness. From this perspective it is useful to observe how people become happy rather than just how to cure those who are distressed and the main objective of this book is for us all to feel happier and to know how to precipitate happiness.

A doctor of the mind is therefore an observer; is outside of the problem, will be empathetic and will be competent in diagnosis and prescription although is not experiencing what his/her patient is experiencing albeit they have substantial insight into what different states of mind may feel like to the patient. It is because of this fact that not always can the medical profession resolve a problem of the mind, it is very much to do with the patient and indeed although psychiatry holds the keys it cannot work well without any effort and willingness from the patient.

Strangely enough though psychiatric problems can sometimes be solved by others who have no medical training though have specific personalities that can inadvertently solve others problems by not just only being there to support but having innate, perhaps you might call common sense, skills that they are not even aware of having. You will later on read about the survivor personality in the chapter on well-being and gain further insight into this concept.

An excellent example that illustrates this point very well is in respect of someone who exhibited a particular symptom of 'Diogenes syndrome' where the victim hoards everything but more so than most of us would but so much so that it was almost impossible to be able to navigate around the house that would present a challenge to even the most able of potholer. So bad was the clutter that this person's home was a danger in that if the house caught fire then there would be no chance of escape. Attempts to solve this problem through a psychologist was to no avail but surprisingly the one who made progress was the local gardener using nothing but, often underrated, common sense and kindness.

Defining 'The Depressive State' (the scourge of humanity)

So what exactly is a depressive state? Well for anyone it is a deeply personal and unique feeling that the English language cannot easily put into words albeit that English is a most wonderfully expressive language. For some of us we may carry pain that feels beyond ever being assuaged and where words cannot reach us. It is difficult to articulate such feelings and the texture of those feelings and what they mean to you, this being particularly more so if in a depressed state. Description is so much easier to put across if we are in an effusive, up-beat mood. So at the very time when it is critically important to articulate how we feel we are incapacitated in our ability to do so.

In all of our linguistic capability of expression of what we think, we are unable to relate exactly any specific emotion or texture of that emotion to another. Our language is highly adept at describing something visual, for example, although the textures of emotions in exactly how we feel are not well catered for. Saying *"I feel depressed"* might mean something quite different to another just as we all know that in a relationship that one person's idea of 'love' may be totally different from yours, one might be rooted in lust or material gain the other one rooted in genuine care, affection, admiration, altruistic feeling and loyalty – maybe this is why we might say that *"a dog is man's best friend"*.

In accordance with the Oxford English Dictionary - Depression is *'a mental condition characterized by feelings of severe despondency and dejection, typically also with feelings of inadequacy and guilt, often accompanied by lack of energy and disturbance of appetite and sleep'*.

Another useful angle on this is from the Chambers Thesaurus – synonyms being: *'dejection, despair, despondency, melancholy, low spirits, unhappiness, sadness, gloom, doldrums, glumness, downheartedness, pessimism, hopelessness, desolation, discouragement.* It is also interesting though to look at the antonyms being: *'cheerfulness, happiness, euphoria'*.

Expanding on this description we would experience: loss of interest, intellectual capacity, awareness, perception of reality and presence of mind, added to the experience of a crippling inability to think straight and thereby inability to rationalize what is really going on, failure to recall, an overwhelming feeling of being a failure, feeling fragile, loss of ability to articulate – in effect we also lose connection with reality of what we actually are and what potential we have, or could have, our imagination is effectively running riot and this is something we need to keep in mind that we are failing to see our life and our potential as it really is.

The understanding in the way of how our mind operates is rather elusive, we vaguely understand the biology of the brain but we don't have much idea of how it is engineered in as much as an electronics engineer can describe how a single entity, a microprocessor, within a computer executes instructions from a memory (a program) to access signals from the outside world then analyses those signals and decides what is to be done. I won't elaborate more as this would engulf the whole chapter. The operation of a microprocessor is very clever though very simplistic it will ask for specific data and then execute some mysteriously programmed instruction (assembler language) from a list of many such as; 'load accumulator', 'disable interrupts' and 'decimal adjust accumulator', however it is nothing on par in cognitive processing power to that of our brain.

With time we will establish at least some idea as to how the brain is engineered, how it operates at the 'program' level but my wild guess is that it may have a perception and processing area, our consciousness, to which all of our memories, subject matter or situation as thought up, collectively our knowledge and that are relevant to what the mind is currently concerned with, that are instantly and simultaneously broadcasted to. Somehow, don't ask me how, but the processing area must then filter out what it needs and somehow assembles that in such a way in order to arrive at an answer such as what do I do or how should I feel.

I don't have any other than wild intuition in this particular thought but what comes to my mind is that if we were to think of a word that has multiple options in your stored memory then we get a sudden abundant burst of ideas or images from which you then select which one requires your further thoughts. This process may be sequential that all of these ideas or images are consecutively not simultaneously presented from our memory but in our perception of time they all seem to appear at once from which we then consciously or is it subconsciously (strictly 'un') decide what next to do with that information and where to take our next thought.

Our mind could be occupied by listening to some sublime music for example but if we were to suddenly break our leg, the mind being wired to know the order of priority, and our brain function will be interrupted by the pain, so much so that we can't ignore it, it is what we might call a 'non-maskable interrupt'. We bring the higher priority to the forefront of our conscious thinking. Where we label the cause of our depression or anxiety as of high importance then its presence will interrupt our thoughts just as would the presence of pain.

This is quite hypothetical although I believe it must be that when the processing part of the brain doesn't receive a response, i.e. we don't have knowledge or experience of that subject, we can either not worry about it, 'so what if I don't know', or the 'processor' keeps requesting broadcasts without receiving them, in effect the brain stutters, possibly outwardly represented as appearing nervous, we have a situation and we don't know what to do but our mind keeps looking within itself for the answer. Or, however that some other thought then subsequently surfaces and where we don't put much importance to what we were trying to solve we then abandon that last thought and everything returns to normal, we move onto things that our brain is able to process.

In depression/anxiety I believe that what happens is that when we place so much importance on a problem, one that we do not have the information to enable us to solve, then the mind cannot move on to the next external stimulus, in effect the mind gets stuck, it is therefore fixated upon a certain point of worry. To resolve this impasse our mind needs to either learn the correct response to the problem either by us digging for an answer or by being given the answer by others, or it must reduce the perceived importance of the problem so we can then stop looking for an answer that isn't there.

It is as if the rate at which we mature in our problem surviving capabilities has a relationship with how we learn how we solve problems through experience and also to learn when we can or must ignore them and not just through gaining confidence with life i.e. confidence does not necessarily suggest that we have survival skills. If our mind cannot do either of these then it will either enter a state of emergency shutdown, a natural defensive reaction in my view, or with time it will learn to cope if the problem, or its importance, have not diminished with time i.e. to survive, as in all survival, the mind will have to adapt.

A depressive state is all pervasive in the mind such that we are almost totally incapacitated in our ability to put our mind on anything else other than the feelings and causes of our depressive state. It is with you when you awake and it gnaws at you all day, your mind cannot focus, it is hard to communicate, you feel you cannot breathe and you generally do not feel well. You could be the most ebullient, positive person but you are flattened, debilitated and the abilities that you possess are compromised, it is as if a clamp has been put upon your personality. Worst of all is that this state begets more of this state it is a cycle of positive feedback, the more you are feeling depressed the more depressed you might become from which you could fall into a perceived crushing abyss. This is all part of its process its natural course but don't worry as there is light at the end of that dark tunnel.

All this being said one thought you must keep mindful of is that you are not, I repeat not, on your own. The very thoughts you are having others do also. Perhaps no-one you talk to has any idea of what is going on in your head however there are those who will understand exactly what you are going through so you are definitely not alone. Feelings of loss of worth, capability and personality are just false feelings, false beliefs, and so your self-worth, capability and personality have not gone, they may just be a bit messed up during the event though they can and will return to full capacity, just give yourself time to heal.

The Perception of Value Added Research - Important

Speaking as a former engineering student, maths that looks complicated is often horrendously difficult, but once you know how to do it, as in anything, it's easy (albeit you will need to study it for years), yes even the difficult stuff. If you know what's really going on in the detail, often something that lecturers fail to adequately allude to, then it's amazing what you can understand – but leave out some critical minor details and the understanding can be completely 'bollocked'.

Now what we have just discussed in the last section presents a very interesting idea in that depression, and for that matter anxiety, are (other than from tragic events) often rooted in the mind not knowing how to deal with a problem, a problem for which we place too much importance and upon which we then agonise. Yet if we deconstruct the thought processes that are engaged in trying to solve a mathematical problem it has exactly the same properties in that: 1) we don't know how to deal with it, at first (I once spent three months trying to solve something), and 2) for which we place a high importance such as our intended career or passing a qualification is dependent upon, yet what is rather odd is that the same process does not, in itself, precipitate anxiety nor a depressive state.

There must be some difference and there is: In the maths scenario we are very aware that the problem presents an opportunity to learn, an opportunity to expand the mind, we are learning something new we are becoming cleverer than we were, our intellect benefitting from this process. In the depression/anxiety scenario we are not aware that the problem presents an opportunity to learn, not aware that we are expanding our mind, not aware that we are learning something new, not aware that we are becoming cleverer, not aware that our intellect is benefitting from this process.

So let's look at this differently – depression/anxiety is often not the natural state that we enter when faced with a problem it is that we somehow select that certain problems will elicit this state because we have decided that the process in itself in dealing with depression/anxiety is of no benefit to us much in the same way that being run over by a bus doesn't exactly do us any good. We can't see any benefit.

Just imagine studying maths for which the outcome of failing the exam would be dire but then add to this the perception that there is no benefit to you in studying it, no benefit to your intellect, no benefit to your cultivation, no benefit to your career, then what, the study of mathematics transmutes from something interesting to something depressing with the added 'bonus' that our motivation to study it is obliterated, motivation that is as important to us as a propulsion system is to an aircraft. Our perception has changed as has our sense of purpose.

If we look at those problems that would depress us, or cause us great anxiety, but with the eye that can now see that the experience of trying to solve the problems that causes us so much pain bring us huge benefit in that with this opportunity to find a solution we learn something new, we are expanding our minds, we are becoming cleverer and our intellect is benefitting, then from this perspective we can see things very differently indeed and in the process find resilience, perhaps a form of resilience that others, bereft of this perspective, do not have.

Perhaps our problems, that might lead us to anxiety or depression, are to be perceived as nothing more than useful intellectual puzzles from which we have the opportunity to gain useful life skills not as something that would do us permanent harm and without any perceivable benefit whatsoever.

The Puzzle That We Must Ignore - Important

Life's problems (career, relationships etc.) always cause us stress; stress is a natural reaction it is a motivator for us to fix things. But what if that stress becomes a (serious) problem in itself, as in a serious threat, in that the anguish that it precipitates exceeds the attention-stress demanded of its cause and isn't your mental health of greatest importance above all else.

In difficult times we may face the terror of waking up in a state of utter perhaps what seems insurmountable mental anguish and misery. Perhaps this is our daily default state despite our positive efforts the day before, what do we do – we can mull over how we can stop this, on what can we do to fix the problem, a problem, that yesterday, the day before, the week before, the month before could not be fixed; rumination won't do you any good and neither will looking the other way hoping that the anguish will miraculously disappear. (It is impossible to solve any problem if we don't understand what is going on, why the problem is there. Without knowing the mechanism of what is causing the anguish then the remedy will not be found. Perhaps we are destructively obsessed by the problem and inadequately focussed upon the solution to seek a solution but not to feel overwhelmed by the problem.)

But here is an opportunity; to instead take a good hard look at why you think that way understanding that what has just been revealed by these feelings is how your mind operates deep down, perhaps the real issue here is a predisposition to negativity even though we may think that we are upbeat, so what is it that is going on deep below the surface.

You dare not ignore the problem since you fear dire consequences if you do and so your anguish continues unabated ever present. What to do? But you must ask yourself this - what if the anguish is doing more harm than the problem, and its consequences, in itself presents. Is the desperate need to secure a job or find a partner etc. in one year anywhere near as important as avoiding the destruction of our mental well-being. We have to be logical about this in that when the destructive anguish far exceeds the importance of the problem, then perhaps we are better off, perhaps a self-preserving imperative, to ignore the problem. If it is so that we attach to the problem to a point that mentally destroys us, then we have just compromised our chances of solving the problem. So perhaps now is the time when complacency might be just the right medicine.

Physical Consequences

Depression, and it's precursor 'anxiety' (more about that later), in their extreme states can be highly disabling resulting in a plethora of physical symptoms such as headaches, migraines, nausea and vomiting, loss of appetite, vertigo, heart palpitations, breathing difficulties, excessive perspiration, panic attack, tremor, loss of sleep, a feeling of collapse, lethargy, etc. and often there remains a dull unpleasant feeling in your head that is constantly reminding you of the state that you are in. It would feel pretty much as if you have been injected with some form of toxin where your energy feels totally exhausted. So bad can this be that 'conversion disorders' can ensue in that a whole range of psychogenic (of psychological origin) physical symptoms such as skin disorders, hair loss, temporary loss of hearing or sight, an inability to speak or move a limb may follow.

Psychological disorder or trauma can easily result in an issue with the mind manifesting itself as an issue with the body. But don't panic - it's all part of the process it's all quite natural to experience these reactions given the circumstances.

Further to this, psychological 'dis-ease' is not something that we can immediately fix it is as if the state that we are in 'latches' within our mind (see appendix I), it is stubborn and immovable. We can stem the flow of blood or relieve the misery of a fracture by immobilizing a broken limb, we can numb pain with powerful drugs almost immediately but psychological misery hangs around, it is as if the depressive state is somehow physically enmeshed within our brain.

The question is how do we find the way to reset the latch, to clear the mind of bad and what are just erroneous thoughts; a cold shower (maybe), an electric shock (seriously, don't go there and I mean don't go there), a system reboot or new software (now there's a thought) or perhaps acupressure applied to the thumb (certainly really worth checking out). However, our mind does have capacity to automatically switch between states, to de-latch. Just as steam can collapse back to a liquid when it hits a cold surface then even saturated depression can suddenly collapse back to a state of contentment or even happiness, all we need is the trigger, the realization of what is really going on and how we are to look at it, i.e. to get a different perspective.

What Causes Those Depressive States?

There are two broad classifications for the causes of depression one of which is 'endogenic'. This form is from within where the cause is unknown, i.e. it is in essence what is called 'idiopathic'. The term 'idiopathic' is a most useful word and has application particularly in medicine and in engineering. In engineering the science is well established although we do encounter what are called intermittent faults in that some problems do not present themselves all of the time and in some cases can be so infrequent that it is not possible to determine a cause from investigation and experimentation, such problems are therefore idiopathic and usually can only be solved by working on a hunch that such and such symptoms are most probably associated with certain causes which can then be resolved.

In medicine, research into the science of human biology continues on and in some areas of research the answers we seek will elude us for a long time, maybe forever, especially when we are trying to understand the mind and specifically the conscious mind, and within that why we may feel different levels of depression without an obvious external cause. Endogenic depression is something way outside of the scope of this book and would therefore require professional help always so don't delay.

However, the second classification of depression is 'reactive' and it is to this subject that we shall discuss. Reactive depression is where our depressive state is related to an outside influence, i.e. it is 'exogenic', or to an event that can be clearly defined or it can be ignited from ill health. We may not immediately know why this causes our current state but we can establish that it is the influence of a depression inducing event that is most likely to be the cause. (Further to this, depression yields a reaction of pervasive pessimism that yields even more depression in a never ending cycle, our perception of reality goes haywire. We lose sight of our real potential, the strengths and qualities that we have we can no longer see albeit that they are still there dormant and ready to return.)

The seed of influence of the event may be in the distant past, it may be happening now or it is yet to come. The cause may be major such as a loss of a loved one, a violent assault, break up of a relationship, being made redundant, a massive lack of self-worth or lack of purpose or could be minor such as encountering road rage or a rude shop assistant or simply as a consequence of chronic boredom. A sound or an aroma that has some connection or association with a bad experience in the past may also evoke the cause as to the way how we feel.

We may imagine that our world should be one absent of these things but it never can be. In all cases though they are equally valid in that a minor cause, although to you or I might seem minor, to some might dramatically damage their perception of the world and in this sense the loss in faith in what we might have of society or in others. From this perspective we have become negative of the world and are rendered unable to see those things that are positive about life.

The major challenges we face through, for example, the loss of a loved one or loss of our job are things we just have to accept and work through, our feelings are quite natural and normal, anyone would feel the same and thankfully these feelings will be overcome, they are essentially normal transients, though sometimes re-occurring experiences in our life which mostly we will cast aside out of necessity, we will get over and move on albeit we may never forget.

It is unfortunate, and largely unavoidable, that our life experience will, from time to time, present quite major problems and this is so for all of us, some more so than others, this is life as it is, it always has been this way and it always will be this way.

But the most pernicious, and perhaps intractable, causes of a depressed state relates to the lack of self-worth, as this is something that will persist and is deep rooted, and also, although not persistent, to our sensitivity that we may have to the behaviour of others, some people are not that nice, and this is something we encounter frequently in life and can therefore have the same debilitating affect upon us.

Unless we have some overwhelming terrible persistent or traumatic event in our life we may have some chance to cure our bad feelings independent of the intervention of others, and this is through an inner strength of possessing natural abilities to cope and survive and that has been consciously and unconsciously constructed in our minds and if we don't have that inner strength then we can acquire it by re-aligning our thinking.

For us humans we are very eclectic in nature, we are unavoidably conditioned, what we encounter and who we encounter influences what we think and how we behave and this includes equipping ourselves with skills to make the most out of our life experience including how to cope, survive and thrive. The question is also; is our enemy ourselves, is it that the way how we think is what is causing us to feel the way we do and should we therefore challenge and even change our own thinking or what we believe.

Fortunately, there are individuals and cultures that are very positive in this respect although there is also the exact opposite in that some of us may be surrounded by that which is unknowingly toxic and our day to day experience may unwittingly be destroying our chances in life and this includes the way how we feel.

Could it be that the negative feelings that you have for life and for others is not at all reality but is a product of bad conditioning by others through which you will be the one to lose unless you can get to see life for what it really is. Beware in that even those who appear to be our friends might just be our ultimate enemies even though their influence on our lives may appear to be immediately beneficial it may not be what it seems.

Before we move on, reflect on this - might it be that we are so acutely pessimistic that our pessimism, by its own strength, strength that is that is imparted by our very selves, can do none other than precipitate failure or are we so optimistic that our optimism can do none other than precipitate success. Whatever our circumstances it is our choice to face these circumstances with optimism or with pessimism – what is before us, and may even be dire and unspeakably unbearable, but we have a better chance of survival and success if we choose the path of optimism.

Chapter 2

EXPLORING THE ROOTS OF MENTAL SUFFERING

(The normal but tortured mind)

What signature negativity underpins our own unique way of looking at the world – are we on the leash of a mind tortured by massive self-deprecation or paranoia, massive inclination to worry, an overwhelming fear of being alone, are we obsessively impatient for change, are we far too tuned into our age, our sensitivity, our despair, our lack of trust in others. It is here that we must recognise our disconnection with reality in that what we perceive may indeed be there right in front of us it is just that we have unwittingly fell into a state of amplifying that perception perhaps even to levels that are impossible to tolerate. That which we feel too much is often that which we have amplified too much and so amplified beyond reality.

As much as life presents problems, that are undoubtedly real and very present, we need to know when our perception has failed us or has even become our worst enemy. Is what we think subject to reality or is it subject to a faulty over amplified perception.

Life is much like playing a game a chess where to win we have to constantly out-think and outflank our opponent. Take a closer look and we find that our opponent is often ourselves since if we can conquer ourselves we can not only deal with our own lives but we can also better manage our interactions with others. If we have mastered the art of the psychology from within, and from without, then we have mastered everything, if we only master one of those this is where we fail.

The 'Anxiety and Worry' Dimension (are things really as bad as we might imagine?)

"I cannot cope with life, my finances, my work or my relationships. I see only destitution, failure, disease, loneliness and despair ahead of me. I cannot stop thinking of what can go wrong in my life and the ensuing myriad of distressing consequences in its conclusion. I have become doom laden. What future have I for I have none."

Unfortunately we live in a world that presents major problems, it always has, it does now and it always will. Much of this is due to the inescapable political backdrop where we fail to tackle what are our national woes. We either completely ignore important issues, do the exact opposite that common sense would demand, or we dither, often because of a fear of causing offence where offence may well be deserved. Furthermore, we are bombarded through the media, a media that in many places of this world are either under duress or by their own craven or extreme political agenda will be complicit in the aim of their governments and who will sensationalize or, the exact opposite, water down the reality of what is going on. We are largely not fed with the truth. This may seem overstated but we are incessantly spoon fed a diet of the precursors to feeling anxious through what is in the news and that is often a distorted world view at that.

In my life I have heard obsessive debate about the threat of nuclear war, economic catastrophe, antibiotic resistant communicable diseases, impending ice-age followed by global warming, terrorism, our fear of our place in this world, irrational ideas on religion and bizarre non-progressive 'progressive' thinking much of which is hyperbole, stupidity or if has any truth at all often never came to fruition. We live in a mad world that is rammed down our throats. Yes we live in a mad world and one I would say is replete with political and societal neurosis. In amongst all this it is a miracle that any of us stay sane.

In addition to the crap from our political class, we are constantly ill at ease, distressed and worried about our mortgage, our career, passing our exams, our children's future, our loved ones, divorce, illness, old-age, death, crime, paying the bills, that not so nice boss or that nightmare neighbour, interpersonal conflict, the selfishness we see in others etc.

It would seem worst of all that those who are elected to serve us, our politicians, mostly, seem to be part of the problem and not part of the solution, and much of the world's problems, that inflict anxiety upon us, filters down from what our governments do or don't do. Is it no wonder that we all suffer from anxiety. If any of them are reading this right now they might be looking for other ways that they can worry us and thus exert some more control over our lives. The easiest way you can control anyone is to give them something to worry about.

"Of past regrets and future fears." – From the poem 'The Rubáiyát' of Omar Khayyám (Poet, Persia 12th century)

The ability to feel anxious about something is built within us for good reason, it is there to bring us to action when needs be and it helps us to develop, it also prevents us from making mistakes and from not exposing ourselves to danger although this feeling needs to be in proportion to our situation, it must not be exaggerated beyond its needs. Anxiety is a necessary defence mechanism but with the volume turned up too high where something that is insignificant can precipitate a feeling of absolute catastrophe.

When we enter the state of actually suffering from anxiety we enter a state of self-perpetuating 'what-if' rather than 'what-is' scenarios (note the 'self' in that it is us who are doing this to ourselves) in that we identify a problem or potential problem and we then allow our mind to be consumed with worry about that problem that ensues in getting wild, and what are improbable, ideas of what could happen next, ideas that perhaps would easily be resolved through at least some luck, correct application of good common sense and other evasive measures.

Sometimes we focus too narrowly upon what may happen in the far off future rather than living in the present moment and dealing with the challenges that we have now. It is a vicious cycle, a chain reaction of thoughts. We can become too introspective of all these things. We can have irrational fears that exaggerate how we feel. Perhaps we need to a bit dismissive of those negative things in our life. Sometimes we worry because we have nothing to worry about and so we are predisposed to worry.

In exploring how run-away anxiety acts upon us then imagine this scenario: if I lose my health, I will lose my job, I will then lose my home, my wife will run off with the kids and I will lose my mind, or; if I fail that exam, I will not be able to go to college, I will not be able to get the career that I wanted and my future looks bleak. Now there is some, and I emphasis some, probability of this complete disaster sequence happening but it is generally too low a probability to waste your time and energy worrying about it and the very act of worrying can be what ruins your life anyway i.e. it is not the circumstances, that actually may not happen, that would ruin your life, you are essentially doing a good job of ruining your life by yourself by worrying too much about what is really quite improbable.

Indeed the worry itself is likely to cause the very thing that you fear as in a self-fulfilling prophecy i.e. if you worry too much about your health you will destroy your health through worrying or if you worry too much about passing that exam you will be unable to think clearly when confronted with those difficult questions ergo you will fail the exam. This is not, however, and I repeat not, about being complacent as some worry is what motivates us to succeed but just don't let the worry get out of proportion.

In this sense if you are a natural worrier then the only thing you need to worry about is the fact that you are a worrier. Once you recognize that you are a predisposed worrier you might realize that you have nothing really to worry about and thereby you stop worrying about it and the less you worry the higher you can perform in what you aim to do. A philosophical client of mine once said that *"a pessimist is an optimist with experience"* – at the time I found that quite amusing and then being a bit of a cynic, and at that time thought that just about sums it up, but is this really true – well No. Life is largely about what you make it to be and about making the most of what you have and to do that you need to stay positive always through whatever life throws at you.

When I undertook an offshore (as in oil rig) survival training course one thought that stuck in my mind ever since was what the instructor had said that *"the pessimists are usually the ones to die first and the optimists will be the ones most likely to survive"*.

Ask yourself, why do some people in what we might consider to be quite miserable circumstances look happy; it is because they don't let anything get them down, they don't attach themselves to what would otherwise worry them, that does not mean to ignore the problem, they stay calm and optimistic and consequently the more you take that perspective on life the less bad things tend to happen to you – I have yet to quite understand exactly why but a resilient attitude seems to deflect bad luck a lot more than I would expect. Be constructive about how to solve your problems and don't let your problems rule and destroy you. You may not conquer all of what you want to but you can at least be able to limit the damage by being constructive.

When I look at professional athletes they don't just win a race by having the fastest legs, they must also have an unassailable focus, desire and drive to win, they won't be running around the track thinking about their mortgage, the rude bus driver that morning or global conflict, they will be totally focused on what they are doing and they have to do so to win. This is not to say that they don't care, they do care, but they have to be totally focused. Clearly there is the inevitable that for example we are all going to die, however I don't worry about that because I can't do anything about it so worrying about it serves me no purpose. I just live life as best as I can and doing what is right for the moment, besides if we worry about death it might be that we are needlessly worrying – death may not be what you think it is.

If we go back to our scenarios above then let us consider rationalizing our worry. Let's assume that you lost your job, well you might not know that in reality you might have been too good for that job and that you deserve better or that actually you hated where you worked so losing that job could open up better career opportunities for what you really want. I've seen this first hand; twice I have been made redundant and on both occasions I have come off with a better job and a few quid in the bank in severance pay and I have seen the same with colleagues. So the trick is not to worry about work but use that energy to do the very best in your role and that can earn you a better job later if needs be.

If we consider failing that exam, is that really so bad, maybe it proves to you that you have skills elsewhere that would lead you to something more suited to you, despite this you could fail your exams and land up as Prime Minister of the UK, I'm sure you would have a good chance of doing a better job.

My career aspirations meant that I needed to pass exams in mathematics, chemistry and physics to proceed onto my chosen studies but what if I had failed these exams. Well I later realized, too late I add, that engineering was not for me, I do reasonably well at it, but it isn't me, and on reflection and with experience of life I might have preferred to have studied law or teaching and had I failed my exams oddly enough this might have driven me in a direction, unbeknown to me at the time, to studying something better for me in the long run.

Like a lot of things that gnaws at us we can overcome anxiety through perceiving things in a different way but if we don't deal with anxiety it can easily morph into a depressive state. To put it simply depression precipitates from simultaneous existence of anxiety and low energy. Some will wrongly assume that anxiety can be assuaged through imbibing substances such as alcohol and drugs, they seek escape. Such actions are folly and dangerous as they lead to destruction of relationships, loss of work, crime that you may only be partially aware of in an intoxicated state and may even lead to your own death or worse that of others. Drugs in particular can seriously ruin your life more so than cancer.

You cannot escape your problems you must face up to them and deal with them, better still avoid making mistakes in the first place by being careful about what you do and what you decide upon. However, what we must do is to de-stress ourselves and then rationalize our situation, calm the mind down and then use logical reasoning about what you feel anxious about. Perhaps we should also lower our expectations of ourselves, we may expect too much of ourselves, so go easy on yourself. Perhaps we are too forward in volunteering, in trying to do things just too well and in not learning to say no, when others around sit back with their feet up – all of which heaps more stress and more anxiety upon us.

Perhaps we look too much into the detail of something; we look for too much meaning instead of just standing back and taking things a bit more casual. Being a workaholic and a perfectionist can be bad for your health and may indicate an underlying insecurity. But perhaps also when we have what seems a formidable task before us that we fail to realize our need to break that task down into smaller steps rather than try to do everything at once i.e. we manage the task rather than let it manage us.

Anxiety can sometimes be based on not only what might happen but what has happened in that something that you were, or thought you were, responsible for, constantly nags at you with guilt. The emotion of guilt is there for a reason, if we didn't have the capacity to feel guilt then we would be devoid of morality. Now it may be so that you have reason to feel guilty, maybe you have done something bad or just stupid, but we all make mistakes yes all of us, and that is for you to resolve, however maybe we are feeling guilty or too guilty when we shouldn't. At times we may have feelings of guilt because it is our natural disposition to always blame ourselves or question ourselves through having an innate overactive moral response.

Some never have feelings of guilt and never question themselves because they are devoid of any capacity for conscience or morality (more of that later). From this we can postulate that the very fact that we feel guilty, hence attesting to us having moral capacity, may suggest that we should not feel guilty on the basis that our guilt may be potentially precipitated from our overactive response rather than from being justifiable from the facts of what has really happened. Further to this, because we might incorrectly feel guilt this might confuse our perception of the facts too and we start to incorrectly justify our feelings of guilt.

Before we leave this subject we need to explore something a lot more sinister and I coin the term here "nitrous oxide supercharged' anxiety' where anxiety, and its consequent depression, can be so bad that you are essentially ill. In this state anxiety has gone bonkers, our normal state to only think of one thing at any one time is overridden so much so that distraction of any form, including even winning the lottery, will not bring any respite or at least its prospect would be perceived as exactly that. Good thoughts, if any that remain or that can be forcibly conjured up, are interlaced with so many more powerful bad thoughts all hitting you at once and that are also seemingly beyond solution.

In essence you have so many problems or have two or more life critical factors bearing down upon you (e.g. have lost or not in a good relationship, without close friends, unemployed, no home of any sort, have serious financial problems, failing health etc.) all of which, that upon inspection, might be resolvable by solving just one of the many problems or some other single underlying issue. In all of this, this nightmare, this firestorm of mental hell, our perception of life is changed to a state that is indescribably unbearable but where does most of this exist - not in reality but in the mind, the reality being no-where near as bad.

Here an inexorable crescendo of terrifying thoughts will surface from the deepest depths of hell, you can hear your inner dialogue saying: *'everything I do is going to fail'* (wrong - it won't so be resolute in your determination to succeed and be patient, even if it may appear so it isn't), *'absolutely everywhere I look it's bad'* (wrong – it isn't, it's just your current state of mind doing this, you just think everything looks bad in reality it's not everything nor anywhere near everything), *'I feel I am going to die'* (wrong again – you're not going to die, that's not reality it's just a thought process of anxiety going to its irrational extremes and no more). You may just easily imagine, with natural but very much less than justifiable fear, that your mental health will suffer permanent damage but perhaps you can identify and isolate the root cause and just put your attention to that alone to resolve, less then to worry about and less of a mountain to climb. But if unresolved and unchecked this could lead to mental collapse and serious consideration of professional help at this time might be a wise move. However, could the cause be biological not psychological where our state of health or fitness can affect the way how and what we think?

In such painful periods it is easy to fall into a dreadful misperception of reality and it is a misperception. The apparent attack upon the self from every angle is a mirage, it is not real it is conjured up in a mind assailed by rank negativity. We allow a chain reaction of negativity to take hold instead of deconstructing what is really going on; it may even be that we are so much drowning in negativity that we even lose the ability to rationally deconstruct what is going on.

If at all possible we must freeze out what worries us and abandon much of what we worry about in effect make life simpler thus more manageable. Take a chisel and carve out those mad bad thoughts that clearly don't make sense that is they don't make sense if you were to look at them with a positive outlook. It cannot be that <u>all</u> things are falling apart it could be perception playing tricks, if not it could just be that there is a single issue that has lit the fuse, a fuse that once extinguished could bring forth a burst of new opportunity a new and optimistic future and your options may not be quite as bad as what you might think.

It is incumbent upon us all to be a little fairer upon ourselves and not take our mind into the valley of hell a valley of what is often self-torture, recognise this and act positively upon it.

The 'Sensitivity to Life' Dimension (is the world so awful everywhere?)

"I feel distressed and shocked through the bad words and actions of others, such incidents hit me like an earthquake they shake my confidence and my perception of this life, I am unable to deal with the aggression or abuse of others, I feel hurt, I constantly feel distressed at what is happening in the world and to my circumstances and what is my daily experience and I am easily offended."

Chances are that you may have had an encounter with a 'prize arsehole' (but even an arsehole may deserve some sympathy, they may be on the edge with so many problems of their own) so ignore their insults, abuse and aggressive behaviour, do not let them command the way how you feel, do not take anything personal, even if you are a victim of a crime. It could also be that you are too focused on things that are not serious but that can evoke melancholy such as the misery of waiting at that lonely railway station on a wet winters night after work rather than focusing your mind on what you will have for dinner that evening.

"Whenever anyone has offended me, I try to raise my soul so high that the offence cannot reach it." – Rene Descartes (Philosopher, France, 17th century)

Being a bit sensitive is not about being a failure it is about being a successful human being of quality who has a capacity to care about others and appreciates the finer things in life and on this basis you should not reproach yourself but you should feel proud of whom you are. A person who does not possess any sensitivity at all is just plain ignorant or a delinquent personality and even tough people are sensitive in some way. Those who are sensitive are those of quality but to those who are deliberately offensive they are just plain scum. However, we need to stay mindful of are we just too fragile or over-sensitive, are we thin skinned, are we too connected or absorbed upon the bad experiences and not enough on the good, are we lacking ability to let it pass by if others lack social skills or are just being unwittingly annoying albeit they may even have good intentions.

The causal factor of our sensitivity may be something very small when we are verbally assaulted, as in made to feel devalued, belittled, threatened or on the receiving end of unjustified or exaggerated reproach, there are a number of perspectives in our value system that are all attacked at once not just one perspective, so it can take a while to recover from the shock of a verbal assault in that the mind will need to make sense of what has happened, to consciously and subconsciously rationalize the event and one by one learn new rules for each perspective in our value system that has been challenged.

To do this takes time since all events including the bad will imprint themselves on your mind; a mathematical problem or how to close off some great symphony takes time to work out just as do our emotions. In essence though our value system does not need to change, all of what we hold dear we can continue to hold dear, although we do become inured to things that would otherwise disturb our well-being.

We learn to know when not to give a damn and to recognize who not to give a damn about, we learn to ignore others stupid or faulty opinions. Indeed learning 'to not give a damn' is one of the most practical psychological defence mechanisms we have so well worth keeping that thought throughout life.

"What doesn't kill you makes your stronger." – Friedrich Nietzsche (Philosopher, Germany 19th century)

The art to overcome sensitivity at the instant of an 'incident' is to recognize that the perpetrator most probably has an emotional problem and so it is they who have a problem not you, in behaving the way that they do they have just 'unzipped their fly' as to what they are. For example: OK we are not all the best drivers in the world and we occasionally make unintentional mistakes but would it be normal and polite not to give some leeway to those who make such mistakes. Ask yourself was my driving deliberately bad, offensively inconsiderate or so incompetent that I should not be driving anyway – probably not.

Those who commit road rage often do so when they, not you, are at fault or they arrogantly and wrongly presume that they have the right of way. If they were to undergo psychiatric evaluation they would most probably be diagnosed with some emotional instability, perhaps even a gross hatred of their life, they are like a child who if it doesn't get what it wants it then 'throws its toys out of the pram'.

You will find that such people have a propensity to tantrums not just in the car but also at work, at home and in any other situation as they have issues of emotional self-control that knows no boundaries. In a car, with a quarter of an inch of steel wrapped around them, they feel protected and superior, and in other settings they will act out their immaturity in other ways; they play mind games, they are intolerant and are over critical of others, they may never have been taught to question themselves, and they have an over inflated view of themselves which unfortunately, in the less discerning of organisations, might even gain them promotion.

Becoming established in rank they see as a licence to behave badly. At work they will often kiss the bosses bum, if the boss, that is, is a willing participant and just doesn't see that he/she is being manipulated, so they can often secure some sense of impunity from their bad behaviour by the way how they seek out favour from above. Maybe you might recognize someone like this? I can guarantee you will know at least one as such.

The art to overcome the effects of sensitivity in the long term is partly through experience and partly through gaining some psychological immunity, a process we all have to go through - I cannot contract chicken pox again as I have gained immunity to it though still had to experience the suffering of it to gain that immunity. However, it is always within your control to rationalize what life throws at you, so you don't have to react every time someone is being offensive, just stand back and rationalize it and you will realize that in front of you stands an idiot who is not worth worrying about and that whatever they say is just a pile of poo.

Always stay polite and show that you are not reacting just talk past their ill manners, as if you hadn't noticed, and this alone may embarrass them as you have shown yourself to be better than them. If they are being seriously or continually offensive then you might need to tell them that you are going to take further action unless they desist but don't let it develop further – find/develop the confidence so that you <u>never</u> put up with anyone's crap.

Often when people are offensive they also do so because of pathological envy (jealousy) and what they do is because they want to bring you down to their level of misery, one also wonders why you are such a focus of their obsession which may point to other problems they may have. Also, when you have bad encounters with others, when you walk away from it close the door on it, don't take it away with you, go home have a beer and chill out and don't go on about it either. They win if you take the frustration away with you, throw it away and they lose.

And don't forget that if you are still waiting at that lonely and inhospitable railway station or walking home on a cold wet winter's night then don't forget to focus on to other more uplifting things. Be prepared to look beyond what is troubling you to that which is good and optimistic, after all bad feelings don't last forever.

The 'Having a Lack of Self-Worth' Dimension (am I really that worthless?)

"I am worthless, I am overwhelmed in self-doubt, I am constantly put down by others, I am incapable of achievement, what I have achieved is of no value to me nor anyone else or to my future, I believe that others do not like me and I do not like myself, I feel hopeless, what is my purpose in this life for I have none."

Healthy functioning of our mind depends on self-esteem, not in tearing yourself apart, through which we have a very positive attitude to ourselves so we therefore have a good perception of what we are without which we can be emotional vulnerable. This is not, however, to be confused with being conceited or consequential through which our self-esteem has become exaggerated that can often be off-putting or even offensive to others in that our confidence has morphed into arrogance and self-delusion and won't exactly win you friends or any respect, though you might think it does. Such individuals might instil fear or disgust in others and might feel good although they are not nice and they are not liked. Self-esteem is therefore the right place to be and not too much and not too little.

Dislikeable people have a malignant and toxic personality and the good news is that if you have low self-worth or low self-esteem it is very probable that you are not a dislikeable person, the problem is that you dislike yourself for reasons that are plainly wrong.

It is true that we can't all have the intelligence or the vision of Newton or Einstein, the imagination of some of the greatest poets or the looks of some Hollywood greats; they may have more brains, insight or looks than us but we might have more of everything else.

There are plenty of good human characteristics such as; appreciation, empathy, kindness, manners, endurance, charity, altruism, honesty, being straight and decent about what you do. You might also have great skills; can you make people laugh, are you a great cook, can you make others feel good about themselves, you can take a lot of hits in life but never do you inflict this on others, maybe you are also a good listener and have time for others. Maybe you are just a good human being and do we really require anything more of you than that, maybe what you are is all that you need to be and no more. Is there anything else beyond that we need to ask for. These are human qualities to be cherished. We all have something to give and something about ourselves that we should seek to realize that we can be proud of. It is what is ordinary about us is what can make us extraordinary.

If you feel that you are a failure this is only because you have not sought, or had the opportunity, to find what you can really do well or have not realized that what you do you actually do do it well, so go easy on yourself and give yourself time, explore life and find your place to be what is right by you. If you are full of self-doubt, or to whatever positive things that you are doing, don't keep doubting yourself even more put an immediate stop to this doubt now. Unless you are some arrogant son of a bitch or where you need to act cautiously then just see doubt as a useless emotion that you can do without. If you are assailed by those who belittle you or your good work then f*** them who are they anyway probably jealous, do they really matter to you - no.

"There is but one cause of failure. And that is man's lack of faith in his true self." –
William James (Psychologist, USA 19th/20th century)

If you don't like how you look you can change that, you can lose weight, get fit, you can improve your health, eat well, moderate caffeine and alcohol, change your hair style, get those teeth fixed, change your wardrobe, polish up that personality and you can easily project a different you but the different you is really the person you are deep down that you just haven't realized until now. OK you may never get to look like some famous actor or actress, few can, so just feel great about you and what you are.

If you lack confidence you need to build on some skills to give yourself some confidence as acquiring skills is at the root of confidence and provides opportunities to confidently connect with others and thereby become a part of a community. You may already have every reason to already feel confident but perhaps you are just a bit too self-effacing, so be a bit more proud of yourself quietly from within.

Try something new and that you would enjoy doing and ideally something with potential to socialise – maybe learn to dance or learn a sport or to play a musical instrument although anything too esoteric I would avoid e.g. Mongolian stamp collecting as this has limited possibility to mix with others, it might interest you but chances are you will not be able to strike up a conversation with the person next to you on the bus on this subject. Read and learn about the world expand upon your experiences. OK, you may never be able to understand Einstein's theory of relativity, few can, but find something that you can achieve within your limits and do well at it, give it your best shot.

You may be knocked back or knocked down but dust yourself off and keep coming back fighting. With the right application in a year from now you could be in a very different place in your life so don't give up and I mean never give up, ever - and for some inspiration just listen to the song 'Try Everything' by Shakira from the film 'Zootropolis' and make sure you remember the words indeed everyone should know these words.

"If you can force your heart and nerve and sinew, to serve your turn long after they are gone" – From the poem 'If' by Rudyard Kipling (Poet, England 19th/20th century)

The 'Loss and Despair' Dimension (is there really no light at the end of the tunnel)

"I am overwhelmed with sadness, I am alone in this world and I am alone in my suffering, those who I have are no longer close or are very far away, I have no-one, those who are near cannot imagine my loss, my situation or my despair, those I have around me do not understand me, the laughter and joy of others only brings me sadness, my pain cannot be assuaged and I feel heavy in any attempts to do so with a fountain of sorrow that assails me, my loss is terminal, what I do have in my life offers me no comfort or respite, I only see death as my solution, I welcome this end, what future have I for I have none."

Ask anyone as to what 'loss and despair' would be associated with and they would invariably reply 'the loss of a loved one' whilst simultaneously thinking of death and many of you reading this who have experienced this would agree although contrary to this conclusion there are manifold reasons and situations to feel this way. So if you are suffering 'loss' (the cause) or 'despair' (the effect) what might surprise you is that you are not as alone as you might imagine and this feeling of not being alone in this emotion, indeed applicable to any emotion, partly assuages the fact that you are experiencing that emotion.

"Adversity and loss, makes a man wise." – Welsh proverb.

The feeling of despair through loss, or failure, is by far one of the worst experiences anyone can suffer and can be quite intractable and if you want to understand just to whom and under what circumstances it occurs then have a look at to whom and under what circumstances do we see suicide. In fact we see suicide for many reasons and across all ages. Often there is lack of anyone to just talk to who has an empathetic capability or where there is, rightly or wrongly perceived, no-one that the victim feels they can open up to or where the victim has become so emotional withdrawn (catatonic) that they cannot be reached.

Despair, as we have said is not just through the loss of a loved one through death, it can be caused through such issues as; divorce, a feeling of being a failure, redundancy at work, financial collapse, being bullied or controlled, through the mind being imprisoned, through seeing the collapse of your society, through major life changing disability, through disfigurement or a false belief of being abnormal, having no real friends or support structure, being shunned, dire poverty, abandonment of hope, feeling unaccepted in a society, where you have loss of trust in others or where the aforementioned 'anxiety' and 'lack of self-worth' (confidence) feelings have become acute.

Whatever life has thrown at you time will heal, and you can come to terms with your suffering, so be patient and understand that it is natural to feel like this and go through this process. It is also very clear that many causes of despair are systematic to your environment and your society and cannot be solved just from reading a book such as this. For I cannot feed my family or fight disease with philosophy, no matter how sublime, though you can at least be resourceful to make the best from what you have. This may also be a time to seek help so go and get it. Even if you cannot solve what confronts you, as this may be intractable, unavoidable or insurmountable, at least ride the storm as best as you can by acquiring skills, support and advice to survive.

I won't say that there is immediately 'light at the end of the tunnel' but there is good chance that you can arrange your life so you can find some light in there, even if at first it's a bit dim, and with time that light will get brighter. If you don't believe this then pause for a thought for those out there who have managed to survive and turn their life around with terrible odds against them and with their newly acquired survival skills have furthermore thrived. It may be hard to accept this but every challenge brings us opportunity to become greater than what we are, so as difficult as it is, look at this experience as an opportunity to learn.

Philosophy of Depression – Critically Important

There is a philosophical position on this that we should explore as another angle of attack on this crippling emotion, besides if you have the emotional capacity to feel in a depressive state you also have the emotional capacity to feel joy as lack of emotional capacity precludes any chance to feel the state of joy. Through our life it is very unlikely that you will not directly experience any of the above as precursors to depressive feelings or as a result of depression precipitated from some life event, if you have not then maybe you are very lucky or just too young to have had much chance to have encountered this, either way you should always be mentally prepared or at least as best prepared as you can be.

At its worst depression can beget a chain reaction of other very bad thoughts; losing your source of income or experiencing a broken relationship can override reality with the false illusion that everything else, and I mean everything else, in your current, immediate and distant future appears to be very bleak. Our future should be mapped out as a list of what we want to, and will, achieve, a set of goals to aim for based on a positive outlook, our aim set on this path and nothing less than this path.

Whatever, your situation, whatever your loss you still have you and just as your good feelings do not last forever then the same can be said of bad feelings too – remember nothing is permanent; life may seem bad but that does not mean that it won't get better. And if you believe that everything is going to turn out negative then maybe you need to question your interpretation of reality.

Life is a series of cycles - we have generally good experiences, if you didn't maybe you had some opportunity to have done so but missed the moment, and then we encounter a bad experience that will pass and onto another good time and so on. Part of our problem in our modern society with modern communications is that it opens the world up to us, no longer do we see our lives from our own localized perspective, we become all too aware of what others have and so therefore all too aware of what we don't and our lives can be crowned with disappointment and regrets of the past. Media presentation of just a few very lucky people often raises our expectations to where we know is most unlikely ever to be met for ourselves.

However, our lives, for all of us, are better than for earlier generations and many of us haven't had it so good so let's be grateful for what we have. Whatever life has served you it would have been a lot worse in the past. We must not look back with regret just make the most of what we have now for now. If we stay fixed with regrets and mulling over the now just too much then we might be forging more of the same for our future – so your fate can be in your hands.

You have survived life so far and probably done some amazing things so use this as a reference point to move forward. Think back on the good times and see that it is possible, and probably so, that you can still experience more of the same. If you have to make adjustments to life, this is what survival is all about - making adjustments. You will have strengths so use them, if you haven't, then seek to acquire them if you can. Realize that there are always others who encounter similar or even worse experiences and not only survive but thrive.

"If you can make one heap of all your winnings and risk it on one turn of pitch and toss, and lose and start again at your beginnings and never breath a word about your loss" – From the poem 'If' by Rudyard Kipling (Poet, England 19th/20th century)

Do we believe everything that we think, every thought an idea that is of course unquestionably right (!!!) or do we challenge what we think and realise that much of what we think may be very far from reality and very much closer to the irrational. What beliefs hold us back and perhaps even ruin our perspective on life, beliefs that we should do none other than dismiss in an instant. Do we think 'I can't' rather than 'I can', that 'I am useless I always screw up' rather than 'I could do better', that 'I never have any luck' rather than 'I can make my life different through my actions and through the way how I think', that 'nothing will change' rather than 'I can make things change but that I also need to stay patient', that 'whatever I do never seems to bring the desired results' rather than 'have I thought through all the possible angles on a solution including the unimaginable and what might appear to be the improbable or even the impossible' (refer to appendix I).

Are we willing, and able, to replace the way how we think, that may so often fail us, with something new something that will work for us not something that will destroy us.

Is all that we see disappointing or can we not see potential for finding satisfaction if we try harder and look harder and that we adopt a different perspective frame of reference one where to yield a positive result demands a positive outlook an 'I am going to succeed and I can succeed' attitude. Hard as it may seem to imagine there really is no such thing as a 'no win scenario' no matter how hellish life may feel; what difficulties we may face we must face them down assiduously hanging onto hope that can never leave us if we never let go and maintaining the view that 'not all of this world is bad'.

Can we engineer the way how we think for us to stay buoyant in the way how we feel such that nothing can ever sink us – we can look at what our mind is thinking and be able to at least suspect that what it thinks is irrational. That we need to be on guard against our hate, envy and paranoia that may often be way beyond justification although may seem to us so easily justifiable. Of critical importance is to not get introspective to allow the mind time to wander around looking for painful thoughts, so keep active, read and take life as an opportunity to learn. Keep thinking at least a bit positive even when you feel you can't, greet with enthusiasm others who you meet and associate with others who have had, or better still are having, the same experience as you.

But of an even higher importance is that faith in ourselves can so easily be lost, and above all things to survive we must have a fierce unshakable and indestructible 1000% faith in what we are and in what we can do; to not doubt this and not question either. Unshakable faith in your-self is the vector to survival and to onward success. Believe in yourself, always.

If you live in a community where the prevailing culture exhibits persecution or antipathy towards what you are, you will be far from alone in that community so work together and form bonds with those who experience the same. It is very unlikely that you will be totally alone in a community for the reasons just mentioned but the community within which you live will not be fully populated by persecutors or those inclined to antipathy, you will find good somewhere. If indeed you are alone and the feelings against you are pervasive then you can either stay silent, attempt to persuade opinion, where it is amenable to do so, or leave that community but only do so if you are certain that this will give you a good outcome. Either way, think about what you are going to do and plan well.

Strangely enough the experience of depressive states has a benefit to us in that if we were to live lives where we never experienced anything other than good luck, getting everything we want and constantly feeling great about ourselves just maybe we would become self-centred, arrogant and conceited.

It is through suffering that we can develop empathy and selflessness it is perhaps an essential experience through to developing us into decent human beings and perhaps prove that we can endure what many others could not. And if we are decent human beings who care for the well-being of others and not just focused on ourselves then our positive interaction with others will be repaid by their positive reaction towards us and for that alone we will have a better perception of our life experience and so will they.

What we may describe as negative thinking has its uses that are essential for our survival. We may prefer a world view that can trust everyone that they do not present any danger and we may delude ourselves in that whatever we decide to do it will always turn out for the better, although not totally impossible is improbable, and if we think in these terms then we expose ourselves to potential harm and so we must look at everything objectively with a cold eye with logic rather than emotion. A mind just too open is a mind open to being abused and it will be.

In what we have just read we need to be mindful that there is a downside. The more we know the more we may become just too aware of and we may then over-diagnose what we believe to be wrong with us. This can be typical of some medical students in that studying human biology as intensively as they must do then they may just start to believe that every little pain is something more and is something to worry about, minds may get carried away in imagination, we start to imagine what isn't there. All of us swing through moods all of the time, this is normal to do so, but if we are low in mood or anxiety our imagination may lead us to believe that we are mentally ill and need treatment.

Here our knowledge of recognition has morphed into introspection we may seek out diagnosis at the slightest whiff of a problem and then demand treatment when it is really quite nothing. Unless it's something needing medical help then for what are just momentary reactions, the ups and downs, to everyday life we would be better to view these as learning experiences rather than something to become too concerned or alarmed about. We may just think we are going out of our minds when it's just a natural reaction to our different and forever changing life situations, if it clearly is something serious or you suspect it is heading that way then you must seek help for sure but just don't become too introspective at the slightest of bad feelings.

But finally if you happen to know someone in this state then if you can find time to talk to them, a conversation that is, then this can make a world of difference. In your perception it may not mean so much but to them it may just give that glimmer of hope where otherwise there would be none and this could be the very thing that changes a perception of a world where no-one cares to a world that seems just not so bad, one worth living in. Perhaps we really do need to think more about others and a bit less about ourselves and perhaps in doing so we might also feel a bit better too.

Chapter 3

RATIONALLY THINKING YOUR WAY OUT OF DESPAIR

(Reconstruction – a new beginning)

Engineering problems are basically intellectual puzzles with complex machines or systems that often require constant innovation and that take the mind beyond that what we already know, we are frequently, as it were, taken into the fascinating world of the unknown. Our mind is just another machine, granted of sorts, that we know less of than we could ever hope to dream but nonetheless is just another puzzle; one that can be probed, modelled, understood and solved if we add more perspectives to the extant multiplicity in our ways of thinking.

This chapter follows on from the last, with the purpose to discuss possible solutions, from different perspectives, to the issues as described therein but its ambition is much more since the intention here is to also have wider application as in to precipitate a happier frame of mind for us all irrespective of whether we feel good or bad about the life that we think we have.

But before we start I would just like to contemplate the word 'purpose' since without purpose our life is without any meaning we wonder why do we even exist. If all other things are aligned do we feel that we have purpose, it is possible that we don't. In absence of any purpose life can be agonising, it is therefore our primary objective to find a purpose to exist where we can see tangible progress in what we do and where we are going. It can never be overstated that to have a sense of purpose is of fundamental and substantial importance to mental health. Often our employment assuages an otherwise feeling of lack of purpose but beyond that or even concurrent with it we must find a reason to live we must find objectives and we must occupy our mind with positive thoughts and actions always, even if we empty our minds at times when we relax we must be purposefully relaxed.

"If you cannot find purpose in life then I instruct you that your purpose is to learn widely and to undertake acts of kindness to others, this is of great service to me." – 'Theoleptic spirituality'

Non-Specific Rationalization (what is the reality? And exiting our defunct philosophy)

We all know that we can often be irrational about what we think but do we realise that fact when we feel in a depressive state or when we are overcome with crippling self-doubt. If we can realise that depression and self-doubt are often very much based upon irrationality of thought then we can easily dismiss these feelings as nothing more than irrational, nothing more than fantasy. If we can realise this very effectively then perhaps the rest of this chapter is superfluous.

We might all need to accept where we are but do we rationalise what is going on. To rationalize is to use logical reasoning to understand to justify and to decide upon a course of action that to do so often requires effort and consideration from different perspectives; we may then look at different options and what their different outcomes may be. We all decide and take actions using our own reasoning to justify what is to be done although have we done so through logical reasoning. Mostly we use gut feeling, we rely, without question, on our conditioning whether it is right or wrong for how would we know whether it is right or wrong.

If we were to apply rationalization to everything we would be debating at every moment and for every action, 'should I have tea or coffee for my mid-morning break today, which one is best for me', this example clearly being something that does not require any logical reasoning otherwise we would become hesitant in everything that we do, we would become indecisive.

However, to rationalize is something that mostly we do not do and some individuals never rationalize, they never think through what is before them in a logical fashion, some may even apply rationalization with twisted logic to justify immoral actions or doing something that is plain stupid for example for their own political agenda. So rationalization does not necessarily have a moral component, I might use it to decide how best to rob a bank without being caught, though devoid of morality its purpose is to determine how I can achieve an objective or in justifying how I behave through the use of logical reasoning.

So rationalization has much wider application than in the subject of this chapter. If we all thought things through but did so using logic, better still coupled with a moral component, we would therefore make the best decisions but with the right consequences.

"No problem can withstand the assault of sustained thinking." – François-Marie Arouet, 'Voltaire' (Writer, France 18th century)

Imagine this; that if we could tease out and define all of the problems that are causing us to feel the way we do, then get to the root as to why they make us feel that way and then give a rating as to the impact that they have upon us, we could then plan how to face these problems, decide what to do about them and in what order. We solve problems by getting to their root cause and everything has a cause with a rational explanation. We could build a strategy. Like some great military commander we have determined the strength of the enemy, what weapons they have, how they are deployed, their methods of deception and where, when and how they are most likely to attack although we can also determine their weaknesses and consequently our plan to attack and defeat them.

This is the effective way to deal with a problem to be constructive about it or alternatively, being destructive, you could 'hit the bottle', piss off everyone close to you, probably take revenge on some innocent bystander or end up in a police cell or worse your own grave. But before you do anything stupid sit down and think it through first with a clear head and don't listen to the advice of idiots, and yes some of your 'best' friends may also be idiots, who may lead you further down the road to your own destruction.

Remember this, that when we are not feeling too great about life and this is especially so if we are consumed with anger and frustration, mostly for very unwittingly irrational reasons, we are vulnerable to manipulation from what may ostensibly be cogent argument of others or perhaps even serious ill intent – so beware.

It is a good idea to keep a journal and write down what problems you have identified at the root cause of how you feel and at the moment that you encounter those feelings, but before we move on to the solution we need to add another component to the rationalization process, something else other than getting to the root of our worries to determine just how they can be resolved and that is to question the validity of what we are thinking.

It is this step that is of fundamental importance because here we challenge what we are thinking, with a cold eye we examine what I am thinking, is it really true? Is it reasonable? Is it logical to think that way? Chances are that much of what you are thinking (our individualised thought morphology) could be invalid, it is just plain wrong or it is an exaggeration of the truth and in doing so you may come to the conclusion that you do not have to find a solution because the problem is not at all what you think it to be.

You probably question yourself a lot but do you also question that your interpretation of the world could be totally wrong or that there are other more valid ways to look at it – it could just be that it is your nature and really nothing else that makes you look at things from a negative angle. Even if your interpretation is correct are the consequences as bad as you may imagine, could it be that far from being confronted with a disaster that in reality what you have before you is a new opportunity. Take another look at things and do so using logical reasoning rather than relying on your emotions and conditioning, you may just find that you have a lot more options than you had initially thought.

"The most fortunate of us, in our journey through life, frequently meet with calamities and misfortunes which may greatly afflict us; and, to fortify our minds against the attacks of these calamities and misfortunes should be one of the principal studies and endeavours of our lives." – Thomas Jefferson (3ʳᵈ President, USA 18ᵗʰ/19ᵗʰ century)

Perhaps one of the most powerful negative perspectives on life could be summed up in the following statement: *"I have reached a point where I do not see any point in life and I can never find answers as to why I am here and what purpose do I have, that my demise is inevitable and I will never know joy."* Grim reading indeed and a load of tosh - this feeling can hit us like a hammer but is nevertheless completely untrue.

Work, our source of income to survive, and a very good reason to get up every morning at the same time is an excellent source of feeling purpose without which the mind can wander into some dark places but our feeling of lack of purpose or prospect of joy is not because there isn't any it is because we have allowed our negativity to drive our feelings into some kind of black pit. Being negative will not precipitate a positive outcome, if we persistently remain negative deep within albeit perhaps developed through some bad experiences, then this negativity can surface. But why is it that other sensitive souls can enjoy life and find purpose?

There is really so much we can enjoy in life and purpose we can find if only we try to look a bit harder. Sitting around moping getting negative and you won't be able to pull yourself out of this pit but look around see the wonderful things in the world, get motivated, find purpose and find joy and then you will see the point of life.

It doesn't take much instinct to know when we are in a depressed state, although some of us are under par emotionally but just accept that this is how we are, this is how our life may be for now, although should it not be better than this, do we not deserve better than being in this state?

What is it that is making us feel like this or that is stopping us from being a happier brighter person than what we project? This is the start of the process to rationalize what is going on, to dig deep to the core of our emotions and discover what it is that may trigger a depressive event, and once we have reached that stage we are on the road to doing something about it. Much, though not all, of what we ultimately find about ourselves requires a re-alignment of our perspectives, as in how we view our world and it is for this reason that a later section engages with this subject.

However, we also have what is to us a lofty world projected through the media that is a myth as few of us live such ideal lives, as the media often portray an ideal that we all wrongly compare our life to, is it any wonder that we feel some sense of failure in comparing ourselves to that which in reality can be largely unattainable. We may endeavour to achieve better for ourselves although at the end of the day we have to accept the life or 'realistic' potential that we have or otherwise we go mad.

It is important to recognize that you cannot rationalize effectively if your depressive state/anxiety is deeply entrenched, you cannot apply logical reasoning or straight thinking when your head is in a spin, confused and overflowing with problems or negative thoughts where emotions rather than your logical abilities takes control. Your ability to rationalize is compromised, it has become faulty, and may even throw up negative thoughts that you may then incorrectly interpret as being logically justified.

The thoughts then justify themselves in such a believable way that what you thought was just a negative thought morphs into a justified negative thought that leads on to more negativity – if that's you at least rationalize this; that those thoughts may seem rational to you but they may be wholly unjustified and absolutely irrational, so don't blame yourself for being that way as this negative loop can be natural for any of us given those circumstances.

If you have an overwhelming abundance of problems that you can't deal with all at once then you need to put them in order of priority and then deal with them one at a time. If you are in an intransigent negative loop you most probably need professional help first but you may find the other ideas presented in this chapter better placed for you at this time.

Rationalization also enables us to take a rational view on our ability, or for that matter inability, to rationalize. If you can't find the energy or ideas to work out a problem, don't give yourself another problem by worrying about that too, just leave it be, park any attempt to deal with it and come back later, just enjoy life instead of wasting time dealing with things that you can't resolve.

If it is something of urgency or that could have dire consequences and that you are in such turmoil that you can't figure it out then get help or if possible to do so at least take a short break and then look at it again later but don't get complacent. But sometimes things can spontaneously fix themselves, after all most things are not permanent, and often too much worry gets in the way of our ability to fix things, our mind may just subconsciously arrive at the answer or we get one of those eureka moments without us trying to force our mind to do so. We can just sleep on it and voila!!

If you have been unsuccessful in solving a problem then don't be too hard on yourself, just accept that you have at least achieved some small step towards fixing your life. Take one step at a time, however do endeavour to progress, do not sit back and do nothing ever, at least take steps in the right direction with an ultimate aim to sort out your life.

Rationalizing the Despair of Age/Ageing (you are not becoming old, you are becoming more wonderful)

Worrying about age can mentally tear us apart indeed it is the obsession to solve our problems in what is perceived to be 'limited time' is that which yields an anxiety that is of greater magnitude than the perceived problem itself. Some may even think that 'I'm getting to the end of a sentence of enduring life, one that we all must endure'. Stop thinking, don't even think for one second on this, instead suspend your mind into a dimension of timelessness and just enjoy life. Don't throw your time away worrying.

"Nostalgia is not like it used to be!" – Source unknown.

As we age we may look back with disappointment at how our lives could have been, instead perhaps we should look back and reflect on just how bad our life could have been and realise just how lucky we are. Some have had it a lot worse than us.

Have you ever felt; 'I'm getting old, my best years are behind me, my aspirations were never realized, they are gone, never again will I have this chance, I look back with regrets, I only see more of the same for my future or perhaps even worse' and we may even obsess about death which despite the cold clinical views of science may not be what we may think so just maybe things are not anywhere near as bad as they seem. A very good reason why we perceive ourselves as old or getting old is based upon perceptions that remain with us from childhood.

Perhaps we look back at our grandparents and remember how they looked at a certain age, an age that you may be fast approaching or have reached, we no doubt perceived them as being old and we keep that perception through life. The truth is; is that our grandparent's generation would have most probably experienced a life far harder than do we and as a result would have aged faster than later generations. So where does that put us; in reality with our better living standards we shall without doubt age at a slower rate and so we can afford to be less worried about age. When you hear 'sixty is the new forty' it is true for those of us lucky enough to experience a reasonably good life with good living standards.

A word of encouragement here is that many 'ageing' celebrities can look incredibly young for their age and some even improve in their attractiveness and it's not all down to the surgeon's knife; if you listen to them in interview they often have a very obvious and highly upbeat attitude it's as if they can never age. It is even possible that you can be physically younger than a person of a lot less years. Remember that a downbeat attitude promotes rapid ageing so stay upbeat and defeat the ageing process and stay young.

The fact is also that you may possess age although that does not mean that you should dwell on the past, you must be diligent in not looking back, the past is the past, it is gone and there is nothing you can do about it. If you dwell on the past, your disappointments, or upon your fears for the future, to what purpose is this – but I can tell you that you are in a club with a very large membership.

What does this lamentation do for you? All it will do is drag you down with your regrets and broken dreams such that you may even become self-consumed with anger and even hate because of such disappointment and fear, it may even destroy your remaining years ahead. However, what your life has given you, even those bad experiences, is that you have had the fortune to have learnt a lot from your experiences, it has brought you to a point of seeking to make some sense of it all, it may have brought you to reading this book it has made you what you are.

You have come to where you are for a reason, fate has brought you here and from here you can change things. Even if your life story is a sad one you can start to turn things around and it really is never too late. And the regrets of our, even lost, past will evaporate into irrelevance once desired change is realised.

Some of us may have had it so good or maybe they didn't, but some of us may have had it a lot worse and never got the chance to live and experience life as you have and to reach this point. You did, so count yourself lucky. Being alive you still have time ahead of you and whatever has happened in your past you still have time to use what you have learnt to invest what time you have remaining for new fantastic experiences and new things to learn. In effect what matters is the point of time from which your life changes from where you will appreciate things more, whereas when you were young, like all of us you may have taken them for granted.

What has happened before you should see as irrelevant, you need to look towards enjoying the future not look back at the past other than to memories that are good ones. Life's good experiences just taste a lot sweeter when we have the advantage of having appreciation that matures with our age. In addition we have learnt what really matters and therefore our latter years can be a lot more efficient in the way how we optimize time from the perspective of how we enjoy our time. You may have thought you enjoyed or believed in something when you were young but in truth that may not always be so, often it was just to conform and to make connections with others and as you get older you can close that door and be true to yourself in what you want to do and so do just that.

Youth has the advantage of having a long life ahead though is less equipped in how to understand and make the most of life whereas those of advancing years, although may not have the advantage of so many decades ahead, do have the benefit of experience and so can better make the most of what they have. Youth, at times, can also be exceedingly traumatic.

No matter how old you are you can seek new experiences, find good people, learn new things and have fun. From a life of hard work you can afford to have some fun and you deserve to. Age is the time where you can really develop what you are. You must never dwell on illness, incapacity or your hair turning into an unfashionable colour, if your hair has decided it's time to run away just think of the money you are saving at the barbers. Never think 'I am old', do not be hung up about your age, you do not have age you will not define yourself by your age and if anyone asks of your age, you can just say *"I don't know I'm not keeping a record"*.

In these modern times, with our better standards of living, people often convincingly look and behave a lot younger than they would from times past, so if needs be, and if you can get away with it, why not lie about your age, if you are sixty redefine yourself as being fifty and believe it, why not just do it, to hell with anything else just make yourself feel younger. This may seem a disconnection from reality, or is it, but does this matter, I often wonder how real reality is anyway, well sometimes I do, so don't worry about it. However, in this, there is one of very few occasions where this form of dishonesty is totally unacceptable and that is it wouldn't be fair to exercise such dishonesty to a prospective partner and it wouldn't be the decent thing to do.

If you think old you will feel old, think young and you can feel young but don't shave off too many years as you may get away with ten or even fifteen years but twenty years might be pushing it a bit unless you can be very convincing. Another perspective on this is that perhaps we should not think of ourselves in terms of age (years) but in terms of our 'wisdom quotient'; this being just a number without thinking that it represents years where the higher you score the better.

In accordance with Carl Jung age was a process of refinement to take us onto greater things where we can find wisdom, meaning and purpose that often eluded us when we were young. Just don't think how long you have remaining on this planet, and if you do why not imagine that you will live a 1,000 years, just think that you have a mission to find the answers to life and it doesn't matter how long it will take but that at least you are on the case. You may not have youth but look at what you have instead, would you want to go back I wouldn't.

You are more defined by what you are, what you do and what you are going to do, think younger, dress younger, stay younger, be younger, keep up with new developments, keep a sense of curiosity, get modern and don't just communicate with those who are your age after all the young can also gain from the benefit of your experience and wisdom, try and communicate on equal terms with those who are younger and whatever you do; do not lament about how much time you might think that you have left for if you do so you are wasting precious time, so you need to live every minute, not die before your 'appointed' time; with application you can make more of the next months or years of your life than others do in a lifetime and don't get crusty either. And one last word of critical advice; don't lament about your age but keep active find an objective and focus on that.

Remember age does not define what we are. Think young stay young. And if death troubles you ignore it one minute worrying about it is one minute lost in feeling alive. And don't start to panic for at least another ten years from where you currently are.

"If you can fill the unforgiving minute with sixty seconds worth of distance run, yours is the earth and everything that's in it" – From the poem 'If' by Rudyard Kipling (Poet, England 19th/20th century)

Seeking Out the Exit

At times we have some real awful experiences that just gets to you, it can remove all hope, change our perception of the world, make you feel that your life is turning to ash, put you in fear for your future, it can destroy your life – for example, a common one I hear, a malevolent boss who is a complete ignorant bully, an insignificant nothing, a non-entity, who rides roughshod over everyone, he/she may have a business imperative, true, he/she may even have some intelligence although is too emotionally stupid or immoral to see the innate value of you to the business and that you need to be looked after and spoken to with respect, a constructive atmosphere is what is required, for a destructive atmosphere is the most devastating of all issues that a business must face. Smash the morale of the staff and you put the wheels of failure into motion.

A good quality, loyal and well-motivated workforce will work well for a business, they will make it a success and they will dig it out of the crap when things are difficult, but quality needs to be found, loyalty needs to be earnt and motivation needs to be nurtured.

Now this is an example, a good one, but not all bosses are like this and indeed some employees can be a pain in the neck, however the point here is that what do we do to relieve ourselves of the miseries caused by such people, people who have a large impact upon our life, that in effect wield some power over it. This could indeed be a boss or another colleague although could also be a spouse, but it is someone you cannot easily avoid, Monday morning and there they are again with their pathetic puffed up ego and truculence and off they go again one more week of shite that I am going to have to tolerate through gritted teeth.

Well unless you are the same as them then you are better than they are, and don't you forget it, but what you must do is not put up with it, do not stand the shit, the more you put up with it the more shit you get, stand up to it and they will have second thoughts about trying to mess with you. Be polite and stand your ground. If they are impolite tell them there and then, you never know it may even change them for the better. Even a total shit of a person may be amenable to reason and they may not even realize just how they are behaving. Try to be an example to them through being of impeccable behaviour.

It is of course possible that they are completely bonkers and might just sack you on a whim so you need to think about what you are dealing with and with some caution, you need to know what latitude and perhaps support from others you have in facing them down. However, if the person in question is totally unapproachable and beyond hope or you just can't take any more through the acid test in 'am I suffering permanent and immutable misery', and this is not just true of a relationship but also of a situation, then you must find the exit sign, you must mobilize to get away or out from this situation and then in doing so look beyond where you currently are, just see the exit sign and the utopia beyond, always keep that image in your mind, remember you are far more important than a rotten marriage or a rotten job.

Do nothing and put up with the misery or get out of it, it's your choice but plan and plan well. If you have the financial means to afford to do so you have the luxury to just walk away from many of the issues that are eating away at your well-being. Weigh up if the risk is less than the most probable reward and if so it's worth contemplating 'jumping ship'. If you do make the leap of faith and leave then just remember to give yourself time to adjust to your new situation and don't worry about things that appear not to work out as it takes time to adjust to change although if it doesn't work out then move on again – you can just think of yourself as a 'day-trader'.

Not all bosses, colleagues or spouses are unpleasant human beings, many are decent people of quality or at least have some commendable qualities – I have known them all. It's all too easy to read the wrong in people, we all do this from time to time and not everyone is what we would like nor are they perfect, but neither are you and neither am I, but perhaps all of us have some innate paranoia that we need to watch out for; we may just be misreading someone, we may wrongly and even obsessively perceive others or their intentions as being bad or that cannot be trusted, we may read threats from something benign, we may read into perceived attacks or apparent insults that others would not see and we may be quick to react with anger to those who we wrongly perceive as enemies who are in fact thinking of our best interests. Just do not jump to rash conclusions.

Challenging Our Interpretation (calibrating out bias and time)

Are you naturally inclined to think negative? Much of what we experience may only be neutral or even slightly positive but our natural inclination might be to add bias - that which is neutral we may perceive as bad and that which is positive we may perceive as neutral. If this is so and you happen to feel negative then maybe what you have before you is not at all negative it's just your natural bias to think that it's negative so just realise this and remove the bias, recalibrate the way how you measure your life.

An addendum to this is also in its time frame in that that which is just transitory and therefore won't hang around for very long we might run away with the idea that it will persist. Our habit might be to define our feelings within the present within the now and this is how we perceive life. Just realise that situations change, things get sorted and those feelings will disappear.

'Orthogonal' Perspective (looking at things from a different angle, ideally 90°)

We put too much trust in how we feel reflecting upon what our situation is which it may not be. Maybe when we feel not so great we should question our ability to perceive what is really going on, maybe it is not as bad as it seems or its consequences will turn out a lot better than we may anticipate. We also make comparisons of our life to what we perceive to be ideal, *"what could my life have been"* I hear you say, we make the fatal mistake of making a comparison to what is out of our reach, as in the very best of what we see as human achievement or success potential.

Would it not be better if we compared our lives to the very worst that life can throw at us and then be more thankful of what we have and then strive to make things better. Just go in search of lives far worse than yours, observe and take note. Our life experience conditions how we think but being able to jump to alternative ways of thinking, and therefore alternative ways of perception, can change our experience and equip us to deal better with what life has landed upon us.

Just some simple experiences or something someone might say may appear nothing to some although to others, at the right time, can yield moments of extreme self-realization and enlightenment. The more we experience these moments the greater we become of ourselves and the better we can live our life.

"Man is fond of counting his troubles, but he does not count his joys." – Fyodor Dostoyevsky (Novelist, Russia 19th century)

I had one such very poignant moment when visiting the war cemeteries at El Alamein in Egypt as it was here that I realized just how lucky I am. On observing the graves one thing that struck me were the ages of those who had lost their lives in fighting tyranny or forced into fighting for tyranny, young men as young as 18 and it would seem few above 25. They died before they could experience life. In a moment I could see that whatever regrets, disappointments and bad experiences that I had had I was still alive and I was lucky to be so; so what have I really got to complain about. I have still the chance to turn my life experience around to enjoy so many things but these young men didn't get that opportunity, they were cut down by the madness of war and for what. We should be eternally grateful that young men and women defend us and stand against tyranny to protect others elsewhere though the cost to the individual can be the ultimate price we can pay.

The dead do not endure the sufferings of life but the living do. But this being said you may have the comfort of a bed or warmth, there are others who don't, you may have friends and there are others who don't have that either. Look again at what you have.

Writing this book has given me opportunity to think through many scenarios and thus rationalize and precipitate ideas to counter our negative issues, my experience at El Alamein gave me one of many ideas and so I would like to share some others with you:

You feel that you are alone and that no-one understands you. Is this so, do you really believe this, do you feel that no-one else out there is feeling like you and cannot possibly understand these feelings that you have. I often sit on the tube (London underground) and surreptitiously observe others, I am curious to know what they are thinking and what their lives are like. Are they all happy, are they all deeply sad, some are lucky and some are not, some can find the strength to fight what life throws at them by being constructive and others can be so broken down by their miseries that they might even take one of many paths of self-destruction whatever that might mean. The answer is that there are others who feel like you and would know exactly how that feeling is.

You feel that you have failed in life, maybe you didn't pass that exam, you find it difficult to get on with others or you do not see any prospects of a good job, a family or a home. Well the news is; that it is OK to fail and it's even OK to come last and failure might open up alternative opportunities to thrive in other ways. Failing that maths exam might seem bad at the time but you will have other talents that would escape the abilities of the best of mathematicians and that may serve up better opportunity for you.

You may admire and envy others having what appears to be a great relationship, however often things are not as they seem in that the impression of a successful relationship could belie the truth that might in reality be a sheer façade or absolute bloody misery. Don't be fooled into thinking that someone who looks happy is happy, it may often be a brave face. Don't look back with regrets thinking I could have had this I could have had that – these thoughts will devour you.

Make the most of what you have and make yourself proud of what you are and what you are aiming for. Some might even think that *"I deserve better than others"* – well what makes you special over others, they may have worked harder than you and sacrificed more to get what they have – just get over it, not all of them are just blessed with exceptionally good luck that you believe that they do not deserve.

Our thoughts shape our perception of reality and what we think is based upon our conditioning that may often be false or bad conditioning and upon the way how we happen to feel at the time. Recognize that what you perceive is not based upon the truth but is based upon how you think or how you have been conditioned to think based upon what has been rammed into your mind by others or through rather odd literature.

Stand back and realize that what you feel is not based on reality, that you feel the way you do because this is how you perceive things rather than what is really going on around you. Ironically, if we are not so nice, as an individual, we may perceive everyone else to be the same, when they are not, and this may make us lose hope through imagining that the rest of the world is equally not so nice just as we are not so nice. You may even be paranoid about the boss having it in for you, however this boss may have a great deal of respect for you and you just don't see it.

To typify this point; some of us worry too much, often about nothing and you can assuage this worrying if you realize that the worrying does not come from reality but emanates from the fact that you are a natural worrier, if you can rationalize this connection then you can defeat this wrong perception. Take another look from a different angle and you may see something quite different so seek perfection in the way how you perceive life.

It may even be that all that you see around, everywhere you look, you can only see bad, but what is around you is not the whole world and is not the whole human race, you may be living in a bubble of apparent insanity outside of which you may find a whole different experience - there are good situations and experiences to encounter and there are good people to find.

Often our distress from a situation is not from the situation itself; it is for the fact that we do not accept the situation just for what it is. Much of our lamentation is that we ruminate, our mind runs amok on ideas on 'why should this happen to me', 'I don't deserve this', 'this is getting me down', we play on things – instead view that it is just a bad experience that you have had the misfortune of, accept it as it is and leave it at that, it is what it is and that's it. Do not take it personal, you were just in the wrong place at the wrong time or even if you are to blame in some way just learn from your mistakes, amend as best as you can and move on. Perhaps we should value more what we have and value less what we want and that anything that we get beyond that is a welcome bonus.

Unless you have perpetrated some deliberate bad act then no matter how miserable that you feel about yourself remember just how special you are and with the right approach and help from others, and this may require professional help if you do not have an effective other means at your disposal, you can sort your life out and start to progress on the right course. With the right effort things can change for the better, however you need to put in that effort and you need to be patient as turning your life around takes time so be patient and go easy on yourself.

Make it your mission that every day is a new day where yesterday's problems may have evaporated, where you can be positive and where you can progress, sometimes you will be knocked back but don't worry as this happens to everyone even the most successful people have bad days so just accept that, so stay assiduously positive. Transcend your mind above whatever bad experience you encounter and bad experiences will just glide off of you without any effect. Get strength from these challenges even enjoy them and learn to endure.

Whatever your life is just keep thinking *"my life is better than what I believe it to be and has more potential than what my mind limits me into thinking"*. Look at your life for what you have, not for what you haven't got. If you have difficulty with this then think of someone who you admire, your hero, real or fictitious, it doesn't matter who, and how would that person handle this situation. And if you feel you would rather be someone else and not you then just realize that there are also a lot of people out there who you would rather not be, so think about that too.

You may have had some bad experiences that have left an awful impression of life on you often that can cripple your outlook, it can destroy any remains you have of positivity that you were clinging onto. You may for example have had a failed relationship you may have been abused or betrayed such that your mind is now imprinted with the idea that you cannot trust anyone. Such a perception of life is very damaging to your recovery although it is totally understandable how you arrived at that perception.

However, nothing what we perceive is quite what it seems; what you experienced was with one individual, maybe a group of individuals or a sequence of such bad experiences with several individuals/groups but this does not translate into the entire human race being equally so. You may therefore want to look at this again and make a more positive translation of these events, maybe the truth is that you cannot trust just some people, not all of them – they are not all bad, or that you have just made a bad choice and this also may not be your fault, we all have chosen badly, believe me. Just don't let bad experiences ruin your outlook on life, just dust yourself down and move on, life is too short to look back on bad experiences.

Although we praise the idea of thinking positively there is the danger that we could land up being disappointed if things didn't turn out as we had hoped, so although you may be positive stay mindful that the outcome may not always be quite as expected. In other words be positive about life although don't expect everything to turn out just fine, often, despite wise choice and great endeavour things can still go wrong.

If it is so that you have what I would describe as a 'crisis tsunami' then your feelings are that your whole world has collapsed, that what you are experiencing is not a depressive state isolated to one cause, to you everything is falling apart. Even then this may only be, and mostly will be, a false perception. It can easily be that a single perception of the world makes you think negative about everything, even paranoid, that you fall into that 'what if' trap that one thing cascades into another like some chain reaction but even this feeling, no matter how awful, can change in a sudden flash of seeing the world in a different way. Just keep searching for the answers to how you feel.

"There's nothing so bad that it couldn't be worse." – Irish proverb.

One last point on this subject is that on a Sunday a lot of us can suffer an attack of the blues, something like a premonition of gloom, here it is again the day before we go back to work or school, and this can ruin our day, just somehow Sundays may not seem as enjoyable and as free as Saturdays. To a lesser extent this can happen with week days tomorrow being yet another day of work. But why don't we just reimagine that our Sunday is just another Saturday and that we won't adhere to the usual Sunday routine, that is also subliminally telling us *"listen its Sunday; time to feel the gloom"*. Let's instead do what we would do on a Saturday but on a Sunday too, fool the mind and let us redefine things much as we could redefine any week day as a Friday. Let's reclaim these days fully for us and not have some thin veil of depression on what is coming tomorrow.

Distraction (bringing the mind onto something else)

If something that you are thinking about troubles you then stop thinking about it.

Depression and anxiety are just states of mind and nothing more than that. In full flight they will take control of your life and can grip you like the jaws of a vice, you will be assailed constantly feeling them eating at you and you will be mulling over what caused all of this. These thoughts only exist because you have given them house room you are in affect feeding this negative state with your energy that you could better use elsewhere. Others will also have these same feelings and thoughts but they probably keep these thoughts 'Pidgeon-holed' and so they direct their thoughts elsewhere, i.e. you think about it but they don't, not because the problem is not there but because they chose to ignore it.

The mind abhors a vacuum, it will ruminate, the fact that the mind is there means that it will go looking for something to think about, ever tried not thinking and you end up thinking about trying not to think! It could be that what you are obsessing yourself about you do so because to do otherwise could bring about a life changing regret or catastrophe and here you need to think clearly and constructively possibly conferring with others who can help.

However, most of what troubles us doesn't fall into this category and so constant rumination, that could be ruining your life experience, has to stop so discipline your mind to stop thinking about it right now, ignore it and do not dwell on the causes of this misery as this will not bring you any solution. In a depressive/anxious state your ability to rationalize and solve problems with a clear head is compromised so maybe you should just concentrate on getting better first and deal with the causes later, unless of course if delaying action on the cause might bring you more misery. If the way how you feel is through illness or disability make the most of what you have as it is your mind that may limit you further not what misfortunes life has brought you alone. Yes it is true that you may have terrible things to deal with though you must do so with the most positive outlook that you can muster so you can make the best of what you have.

Relaxation or meditation might help (especially for stress) but may also be just the thing to make you feel even more depressed or anxious and your mind may just wander back to what is preoccupying you. If relaxation isn't helping maybe you should try the occasional sensory flooding to immerse yourself in loud music, watching an action movie or anything that is powerful enough to keep your mind occupied and concentrated elsewhere, i.e. outside of yourself and away from your problems.

Another angle on this is that you can mentally relive moments step by step from your past, for example you may have experienced some great day one that stands out one where you may have said to yourself *"this is the life"*, just exclude all other thoughts and relive that day. Remember that your mind is only able to think of one thing at any time so keeping your mind totally absorbed and focused elsewhere will shut out those negative thoughts, so be selective in what you think about; something that is ideal to keep your attention from straying. You may even find something to do or think about that can contribute towards the benefit of others and that can simultaneously get your mind off of you.

"The art of being wise is in knowing what to overlook." and *"The greatest weapon against stress is our ability to choose one thought over another."* – William James (Psychologist, USA 19th/20th century)

I'm not the greatest fan of television, a lot of what is on offer is pretty crap, crass and tasteless though when it's at its best it does offer some really useful distractions produced to a high quality (check out 'Inspector Morse') and so can be highly absorbing, so look for something that captures your attention with awe and if its powerful enough you will find yourself absorbed totally and your mind will unwittingly dismiss those crappy thoughts. For me I find gymnastics jaw dropping in its immense skill, as I do with Irish dancing and immensely talented musicians and although documentaries may not necessarily bring awe they can at least ignite our fascination. Distractions such as these will not suddenly solve all of your problems but they do at least give you some urgently needed respite and bit by bit they can contribute to your ultimate repair i.e. the odd pit-stop can allow the engine to cool down.

"If you have a garden and a library, you have everything you need." – Marcus Tullius Cicero (Lawyer, Rome 1st/2nd century BC)

If its stress that's getting to you then perhaps absorb your attention into more sedate activity such as art, astronomy, gardening, joining a choir, visiting the local library or museum or just going for a walk or why not try out Tai Chi.

Being Lethal, Going on the Attack (fighting back)

Depression is an attention seeker, it seeks out and invariably gets your attention and it's hard to resist its demand for attention. Like anything if you don't give it the attention that it seeks then it will get fed up, stop what it's doing and walk away, if not you can always ignore its voice and just tell it where to get off, we can therefore rid ourselves of it by going on the attack but at the same time refusing to listen to its drivel.

"There is a time for war and a time for peace." – The Bible, book of Ecclesiastes (Christianity)

Negative thoughts and the potentially ensuing depressive state of mind overwhelm our positive thoughts, so much so that they command the battlefield, they have the high ground and they have greater strength but that is because we allow this to happen. Those positive things in our mind are still there though have been swamped, and we can get back to them although it will take effort to do so. The negative thoughts are not as pervasive as what we might imagine, they are just a component of your thinking and not the total sum of it; it is so that we just pay them far too much attention and some of us do so more than others. The odds may even appear stacked against you although this does not mean that you cannot overcome the odds.

"Do not yield to misfortunes, but advance more boldly to meet them." – Publius Vergilius Maro, 'Virgil' (Poet, Rome 1st century BC)

A depressive state at its extreme is a very strong emotion and we can get all too passive about it, we let it take control and we let it wear us down. Just as we mobilize our armed forces to fight off our enemies we need to mobilize ourselves to fight negative thoughts – we need to go on the offensive and we need to do so with tenacity and resolve and with the position that we are greater than our negative thoughts. We are not our depression and our depression is not us. Let's just pause to reflect on a central idea on the philosophy of war (from the book 'Vom Kriege' by the German 19th century military philosopher Carl Von Clausewitz) that makes this very simple for us in the idea that the purpose of war is to destroy the enemy's military capacity and will to fight, this is not to bargain, not to negotiate, but to destroy, to wipe out, to erase (Von Clausewitz would have probably have summed that up in his native German as *"aus radieren"* i.e. to wipe out).

We therefore need to take that same position with our negative thoughts in that; we will not accept anything, we are not even going to be reasonable, we are going to take back control, we are going to annihilate, we are going to get tough, we are going to face it and resolve it through conflict. We shall treat our negative thoughts with the contempt that they deserve, we are not going to show any respect so don't be polite, we are going to look upon them as shit and we are going to tell them to 'f*** off'.

Even if a whole bunch of problems hits you at once, then don't wind yourself up, give yourself a stiff talking to and hold the line, stay positive and just think how would a suave calm cool headed secret intelligence service field operative, e.g. James Bond, deal with this, indeed imagine that character jumping inside your skin becoming a part of you where you gain their strengths, self-containment, self-reliance, resilience and even some of their vitality of life.

The greater the strength of our problems the more support and techniques we shall muster to fight them off, we shall be resolute and we shall have fire in our guts to attack this and defeat it and defeat it we will. If you are not suffering from stress and you don't feel energised to be able to get into this mode then you can do so by watching some actions films that 'kick arse' and get you motivated into that fight back mode.

An idea that someone once ran by me was that if your negativity is rooted in bad experiences of certain people who in some way have been grossly unfair to you or have tormented you then you can defeat this by finding an object that you can punch the shit out of and so indulging yourself in releasing bad energy but just don't take that any further than that as that won't do you any good. Don't forget though that wicked people are not happy so their torment is within themselves, there is reason why they are wicked and it isn't a good one, you can move on they can't, they are stuck with themselves and with their own crap.

Ideas you may have picked up from this book, professional help, friends and family are all part of your weapons and so is your strength to overcome this. Not only that but do things that push aside the negativity, do something, stay active, keep the mind occupied, have something to look forward too, if you are well enough exercise and get those endorphins, our natural feel good hormones, moving. If you feel up to it get out and explore, take trips to interesting places, learn something new, defeat negativity by finding some sense of purpose although pace yourself too so as not to burn yourself out in the process by exhausting your energy. It's also a good idea to have a diary to fill with events and so a structure that will give you something to look forward to.

"To strive, to seek to find and not to yield." – From the poem 'Ulysses' by Alfred, Lord Tennyson (Poet, England 19th century)

Last, but not least, never give up, whatever life throws at you, hold the line, be diligent, do not sag back into feeling a failure, keep at it like an athlete running for that Gold medal, nothing will get in your way and you will triumph. No matter how long it takes you, with dedication, perseverance and the will to doggedly never capitulate and you will be amazed at what you can achieve. Rising to the challenge will also build your character along the way. If you are not up to this approach yet then do not worry as you may need to recover in other ways first before you can take this angle on dealing with life.

"Endure the present and watch for better things." – Publius Vergilius Maro, 'Virgil' (Poet, Rome 1ˢᵗ century BC)

Meditation (narrowing our perspective field and then resting the mind)

Our minds are just too busy and maybe we do think too much and allow our minds to ruminate and dwell on a problem that we think we have, have had or are about to have. We probably all think too much about ourselves, our lives, our problems. Continually we may analyse everything; 'why did they say that', 'what did I do to deserve that', 'why should it happen to me', 'how do I solve this problem' – all of this can send you crazy. We may also try to put on a brave face by looking chirpy and even too ebullient trying to fool everyone and hiding how we really feel and this in itself can be very exhausting to us physically, mentally and emotionally. Sometimes we need to switch off and meditation gives us that opportunity.

"Do not dwell in the past, do not dream of the future, concentrate the mind on the present moment." – Gautama Siddhartha, 'The Buddha' (Founder of Buddhism, India circa 500 BC)

The objective of meditation is very simple - it is to clear the mind. Although this chapter also advocates use of sensory flooding, to distract our thoughts elsewhere, if you can master meditation (a form of sensory deprivation) then this can provide equal benefit. There is no strict rule as to when and to whom these two methods would work but I would see that they could complement each other in as much as for each of us at different times one would be more appropriate than the other. Ergo if your mind is not amenable to meditation then perhaps it needs distraction although if it is not amenable to distraction then perhaps what it needs is meditation. So you need to decide what to choose and when but I certainly would not advocate exclusivity in your selection as the stormy waters of our mind in the depression/anxiety spectrum requires sometimes to tack starboard and sometimes to port.

One thing is certain is that raucous laughter, crowds, small talk and disorientation is a distraction though can leave the 'victim' feel drained and can be the very last thing that you could ever need when feeling the way you do especially if you are forcibly and falsely thinking that you are enjoying yourself. People you see laughing, singing and surrounded by friends in the pub can still feel very much more lonely afterwards for the experience. Be honest to yourself about what the experience is really doing to you. Ordinarily this can be great to meet others for a beer and chat about things a bit less serious than 19th century mid European philosophy and to share some jokes but to a mind that is stressed this can be all too much to take.

The idea that a party might blow the webs out of your brain might just do the opposite. Likewise a relaxing holiday can make you feel wound up with nothing of real interest to keep you occupied – although it depends upon the party and what type of holiday we are talking about here. So be cautious of what might be on offer, run the experience through your mind first and if it looks unpalatable just graciously decline. Perhaps what we need is stillness and quiet and to pace things slowly, to slow down in everything we do and this in itself is a much underrated tool in getting to feel better and less stressed.

If meditation, the antithesis to rumination, is the ticket for you then you are in need of quietness and calm without any excitement or chatter and you need to slow right down and not go looking for solutions. Relaxation of the mind gives us some respite from everyday life and its stresses and can help us to unconsciously resolve our problems as often we find solutions to problems without even thinking about them much as our mind assembles the words that we are about to speak, or type!, without full conscious planning of such.

Meditation also precipitates a state of alertness and allows us to focus the mind better. Just as we would immobilize a broken limb to aid its recovery so we would immobilize the mind to do likewise. If we are suffering from burnout or stress through work or relationships then meditation will certainly help to clear the mind.

Meditation requires a quiet environment that is undisturbed, the idea being to empty the mind of thought, not through force but by allowing the mind to empty itself through focusing on something rather mundane and traditionally this would be through observing our breathing. You may choose either: a sitting posture, my preference, standing or lying down, you may even fancy the idea of hugging a beanbag why not it's not that crazy. If the mind wanders just let it return to the focus of meditation, do not force it and be patient in the process and do not fidget, you need to stay reasonably still. We could equally use other means of focus such as visualizing a colour, assuming that we are a cloud floating through the sky or that we are a tank of water, or that we are an atom or anything that is inanimate (even a teapot!! If you are partial to tea), you can choose whatever you like as long as it works for you. You can imagine that your negative thoughts are leaving you and will not return and that positivity is pouring into every fibre of your existence.

If you are feeling very stressed or overcome with loneliness, or you are very consciously alone then I would recommend this: Sit in a comfortable chair, you will also need a footstall, in what is a yoga position, specifically here the 'dandasana' position, your back should be straight and upright and your legs should be horizontal and extended straight out in front of you so they are more or less perpendicular to the body. Now put two or three cushions on your lap and place your arms straight out in front of you as if parallel to your legs though resting on top of the cushions. Use your television as a focal point and watch something that interests you but that cannot cause agitation. Do this for as long as you like and see what happens.

Find opportunity to meditate every day, better still find a mediation group or find a Buddhist monastery as we just do do things better if we are surrounded by like-minded people. Remember this; do not be disappointed if it does not work for you immediately, it is unlikely that it will as it is a skill just like learning to play the violin although fortunately nowhere near as difficult though nevertheless it is a skill that takes time to master well, however like all skills it will pay dividends. If this practice really serves you well then why not continue it further and find time every day in your life to meditate.

One word of warning is as in all things never overdo it as too much meditation may inadvertently make you oversensitive to life in other words stark contrast may have been introduced much in the same way how light appears so much brighter when you have just opened the curtains in the morning.

Isolation (emergency shutdown)

Most of the ideas in this chapter require and involve taking some form of action to get on the road to recovery although sometimes we can be floored so badly from a dreadful experience that we are unable to do anything. It is as if we have shut down and withdrawn from the world, if this is so you probably need professional help. This state may appear alarming though sometimes we just have to walk away from our problems, get under the duvet, hibernate and rest. Essentially just like an aircraft wing if we don't allow ourselves to bend then we shall break. It is as if the body is taking over, to say you have had enough and to go and sit in 'dry dock' for a while whilst repairs can be undertaken. This may even be symptoms of a nervous breakdown but the mind needs to be taken away from where it currently is to effect repair just as pain immobilizes a broken limb for good reason so would a breakdown immobilize our mind. Our biology restricts movement of a broken limb and also restricts the operation of a broken mind.

We can experience even saturated depression where all of the improbably bad circumstances have come at once, in one strike, but even at this lowest point still look for reasons to live, and you will find them, even when you can only think of reasons to die, you may feel hit bad so you need to rest and rest well to help recovery although just stay mindful that probabilities that were against you will later start to come back in your favour.

So isolation may not always be such a bad thing, it is where others can then be marshalled to handle what you cannot, where you can allow some space and serenity for your mind. This is not advocating a one way ticket to the 'Bermuda triangle' but is giving you some time to step out of the melee and find sanctuary. However, others need to understand that this is part of the healing process although need to be mindful of when this might be a little more serious i.e. where you need professional help.

Through this phase you probably don't want or shouldn't have endless advice, hearing others nattering on might just make matters worse the mind needs to be quiet. If anyone is going to talk then it may be better to talk about normal every-day, but positive, things and nothing about what is troubling the person who is in shutdown. In depression people do need others at times to talk to but the last thing they might want to talk about is themselves so just stay mindful of this.

This may be a good time to rest up, slouch about and do as little as possible, but you still need to look after yourself; eat well, drink plenty (not booze that is), sleep well, keep warm and stay comfortable, you may even want to take your mind to a better place, an imaginary island away from it all. In your current state your ability to deal with problems you may have or have had is undermined and forcibly trying to solve your problems on your own will most probably fail. If you can't put your mind to playing a decent game of chess then you cannot bring your mind to solve your life's problems. You need to wait until you recover to a point where you are able to think about dealing with the problems you have.

With these problems partition them in some order of priority, don't try to deal with them all at once, some you may need to think of them as being on the moon, far away that is, you may need to put them in some imaginary box, lock that box and put it under the stairs. Feel confident that you will get better and that this is just a transitory and necessary phase in the path to recovery. And if you have to have time off work, so be it and don't feel guilty about it, it may even indeed be your work that brought you to this place or at least in some way may have contributed to it.

However, do not completely cut yourself off from the world, stay open to others and stay friendly, communicate with others as soon as you feel fit to do so, do not feel a victim (indeed never ever think of yourself as a victim in any circumstances), do not think I will never get better and do not hate the world for what has happened to you. Remember plenty of others have experienced what you have and remember that at some point you will need to re-connect with the world so don't stay isolated for too long.

Positive Interaction with Others

Whenever we encounter others we have a chance to interact and we can use this to our advantage. Imagine this; I go into the local supermarket to buy half a kilo of cheese, pretty mundane stuff, I have two options (I'm not talking about the cheese here), I can talk, possibly even with a blank expression, to the assistant as someone who just follows instructions; cuts cheese, weighs it, bags it, labels it and hands it to me – now this may seem as a meaningful experience to some but really, is it. Let's rewind; the assistant is a human being, just like you, and possibly feeling unrewarded from repetition of serving up cheese all day.

Wouldn't it be nice if you could break their monotony and take this as an opportunity to make someone feel good, by introducing something un-cheese-like into this interaction. What about looking them in the eye, don't gawp though as that might freak them out, and smile, ask some cheese related open question such as *"I'm looking for a smoked cheese what would you recommend"*, they will think, 'oh someone values my opinion and values the knowledge I have of my merchandise' and this will make them feel good and feel valued.

Whilst you are negotiating the other details of the purchase you could engage in, non-ulterior motive, conversation based on an ordinary observation such as, *"there aren't many people in here this evening"*, this is an opening line. Now don't use my line as the assistant might say *"oh you've been reading that book that's talks about chatting up a cheese counter assistant"* and don't pick a subject that is of no relevance to the situation, such as *"what films do you like"*, as that sounds like you are going into unskilled chat up mode and this defeats the purpose here, and make sure you judge the appropriate point to break off from the conversation since keeping it going clearly beyond what is comfortable for the assistant might look a tad weird.

At this stage you might think that I, that's me not you, have lost it, to write such material, however there is something quite important going on here. The purpose of all this is that we all live lives very much and ostensibly alone, your shopping trip didn't benefit you in any way other than to stock up on groceries and didn't benefit the undervalued shop assistant other than the pay-cheque at the end of the month. Is that enough to satisfy us? – Absolutely not. Can we do better? – Absolutely yes.

The point here is that every time we interact with others, including what appears to be mundane everyday life chores we can make others feel a bit better about themselves, by showing interest in them, and this will make us feel good and we will all feel a bit less lonely and you never know what it might lead to, you may land up with more than cheese for dinner you may just end up with the company of someone delightful.

> *"If kindness is sown then kindness you shall receive."* – Maori proverb (New Zealand).

Now you may have the misfortune, conjured up by you in your mind, of thinking that the whole world is against you and that everyone is bad, if you dig deep enough you will realize that this is not at all true. Our planet has a population of seven billion of us humans, are we all bad, do we all only have self-interest. Look around and you will see such wonderful things that some do for others or even just very simple acts of kindness that makes our world feel a better place and those that do do so without any motivation for gain (although some behavioural psychologists will no doubt disagree with me, although would that not sound a bit pessimistic and if it were true then where did the word 'altruism' come from). You can either join that positive approach to life or turn your back on it. It's your choice.

Us humans we need each other, we need human contact, others to talk to and we need close friends but to do so we need to go out and find them, you will not find others if you just sit at home. To make connections with others takes time and the right presentation of you, since if you join a community, a club or some form of religious group it takes time for others to get to know you and to want to know you and for you to become accepted and in some communities and cultures you may find people can be rather reserved so you need to take that into account and not expect instant success, so be patient and try elsewhere if things don't turn out.

Perhaps as an extension to that idea is that we should allocate corners in libraries, museums etc. where we have 'conversation spaces' with set topics for the day to enable people to get talking to 'break the ice' so to speak but to also explore and debate ideas. It is largely a lonely world although we can make it a whole lot better if we act together.

From Thought Management to Tangible and Permanent Results

In researching our condition in life we can find ways that can manage the way how we feel, we may even write ourselves a letter with all of these accumulated ideas one which we can read back to ourselves when needs be, but in essence we have changed our opinion of our circumstances but this is management we need to seek more permanent solutions and this is particularly so where changing our opinion of our circumstances is not enough, and it is not enough, we need to see physical progression not just philosophical progression.

If you are lonely find a good friend at least, if you detest your job find another, if you are bored find interests, if you lack purpose seek purpose out, doing so and you can kill depression/anxiety stone dead permanently. Make changes to your life not just in how you think or in what may occupy your time but in terms of acquiring things that will make a real difference, who knows you may reach a point where you no longer need to consciously engage in philosophical countermeasures, the philosophy that you had laboured over can now become superfluous and perhaps this is my ultimate aim.

The Salutary Benefits of Knowing What Type of Mad We Are - Important

If anyone believes that they are totally sane then there is a very high probability that they are mad and if you believe that you are mad then there is high probability that you are a lot saner than the rest of us and certainly a lot saner than what you might think since it takes a rational mind to recognise madness. Arguably therefore a mind that thinks that it's mad must therefore be sane. But I wouldn't lose any sleep on it for what is 'normality' anyway. Do any of us really know what we are; chances are that what you think you are is probably quite wrong, so now have another look at yourself, but be honest and be fair on yourself, and then try to see what you really are.

I have previously alluded to this in that can any of us claim to be 100% sane, I certainly doubt that I am (I am, or should I say I was, a compulsive rank negative worrier, tortured by insanely stupid predictions, albeit that some of those predictions turn out to be true). But what is sane, we can't define what it is in any absolute scientific sense; there is no test to prove sanity but plenty to prove otherwise. Indeed I might posit the idea that sanity is just another facet of insanity.

Our nuanced departure from sanity is perhaps what makes us more interesting. Appearing too perfect can look all too uninteresting although I must admit that I am bowled over by those who have what I might describe as 'nigh on perfected personalities' who exude effortless charm, manners, unassuming confidence, wisdom and who are genuinely nice, although any discerning psychologist would then spoil the effect and say *"ah yes but what lurks beneath"* indeed what does lurk beneath.

Now I might be going 'off-piste' in psychological terms but I do believe that recognising and even labelling what we are has its merits. In essence don't feel sorry for yourself or depressed about yourself but try to rationalise and accept why you feel in a sorry state or why you might inflict such on others, not based upon your circumstances but upon how your mind operates, in its lighter shades of pathology. In my terms in realising my, not so uncommon, peculiarity of being a compulsive worrier that when I worry I am aware that it is natural for me to be this way and that my worry is not real it is largely rooted in what I am and with this I can see that I need not worry so much. Hence we accept that our distorted view of the world is a <u>distorted</u> view of the world.

Just examining that thought a bit further - taking worry to its extreme and we may become crippled; obsessed in imagining the very worst, and probably improbable, theoretical outcome even based upon the historical bias of bad luck that may bring us to a point of easily giving up on life – this perception <u>NOT</u> being based upon reality but upon crazy thoughts, how we think but with a large dose of error.

Excessive worry, by its own power, may indeed be the very thing that brings about the consequence that we may be so terrified of. Do we even have an unknowingly 'locked in' subconscious <u>and false</u> self-perception of 'being a loser' that repeatedly defeats our attempts to think positive, our ability to move on and our ability to win. What is it that is locked into the substrate of our subconscious mind, what words can describe what that may be? Realise that anxiety is very often based on what is fiction or a wrong assumption of our world in its totality, on what is as we say 'a load of old cobblers'.

And on the subject of bad luck, is this an equally faulty perception in that something you tried had failed not because of bad luck (every failure, and not just some, as being perceived as bad luck) but could it be down to mistakes you had made from which you can learn and from which you can therefore overcome.

Just see the purpose of what I have just mentioned see how it works upon the issue and see how this technique has greater application. If I was unaware of my 'label' then I might believe that in my perceived 'normality' that I really do have something to worry about when in fact I don't. If we look within ourselves and recognise what we are, and you will find that whatever that is it won't be uncommon, then you might manage your feelings and your life a lot better. Perhaps knowing and accepting what you are may have its benefits, you will understand why you are as you are and it may even motivate a desire to change.

In reality we all exist along a line from the insane to the 'nearly' sane and none of us can ever reach the distal ever so elusive end of 100% sanity and I'm not sure that in doing so that it would do us any good. But what we all certainly are is a product of life and where life has taken us and perhaps we should instead look at what good is within us and not worry about never quite being totally sane.

Chapter 4

REINFORCING YOUR SELF-RESILIENCE

(Consolidation)

The Supremacy of Our Subconscious Obsessions - Important

No matter what we try we often return to a set state of how we had felt, we may have read the earlier chapters and believe that we have found the permanent cure to our bad feelings but yet tomorrow is another day and we end up feeling the same. It is as if there is a preordained and immutable 'what I feel like' position buried within our subconscious mind that is with us all of the time, day in day out, our life being perpetually incarcerated in this state, we may also lack faith in ourselves. Whatever we do life doesn't appear to change much, how we feel in the longer term it is, it would appear, only a temporary fix. However, what is it that we return to, can we change whatever is in our subconscious mind that which appears to be a fixed obsessive state.

All of us are obsessed by something or somethings; we may be obsessed with: the 'everything is going to turn out bad' mindset – forever the pessimist and so prone to anxiety/depression, the 'everything will always turn out good' mindset – forever the optimist but who may be unable to perceive danger and thereby are unprepared to deal with it, the 'I am always worried about my health' mindset - the result of which can be self-fulfilling, the 'I am always going to be alone' mindset – and probably will be if you remain negative about it, the 'I am getting old and going to die' mindset – thus degrading our satisfaction with the life we have remaining and that may hasten our death and that of others nearby, all to which is to where our feelings will return.

Some of us might obsess about things other than how we perceive life we may obsess about an addictive and specific subject or activity such as politics, religion, sport, computer games or social media where what remains important to our subconscious mind is the object of that obsession alone and not how we perceive life; we could as it turns out become emotionally sterile. You may just have the worst luck but a mind totally absorbed in say the sport of football may largely be immune to life's difficulties in other words if we place a primary obsession as principal importance then this is to the loss of importance of everything else.

We may selectively change our thoughts within our conscious mind using some distraction or where we consciously change our perspective on how we look at some aspect of life although whatever we do we cannot easily change what is in our subconscious it is stuck with what we are obsessing about. (In its extreme, and a sort of pastiche to our earlier discussion on 'defining the depressive state', in the chapter on the subject of anguish, prolonged toxic subconscious distress, even though we are only dimly consciously aware, can mess us up really bad it's as if our foot is hard down on the 'how do I solve this but can't' peddle.

It would seem rational to look for an answer but what if we can't find the answer then the mind may enter a state of indescribable turmoil and terror, it is here that we must say to ourselves *"ease down, ease down"* and take a break from all of this.) All the good stuff that has been discussed in the earlier chapters is rendered ineffective where we are subconsciously predisposed to having a negative outlook on life. How is it that we can solve this puzzle since at the subconscious level what is fixed we cannot easily change how we think since an obsession is very powerful it is all consuming and cannot easily change, it resists change.

But what if we were to replace it i.e. we were to obsess about something else. What if we recognise that persistence or return of our bad feelings is rooted in our obsessive negative angle on life (fixating on what is bad rather than what is good) one that with enough of our own effort has entered our subconscious mind like some parasite eating away at any potential for a depressed and anxiety free life. What if we could discipline ourselves to only think positive where we only see positive outcomes, and where there are negatives we just view them as an opportunity to learn, what then? Our action here is to diligently force out negative thought, work towards a positive outlook and only to imagine good outcomes and that this is to become our subconscious new me.

If we keep diligent and stick to a disciplined regime of only thinking positive we can replace the negative predisposition with a positive one. If we keep obsessing on anything negative we shall stay with this background of feeling bad no matter what we do to cheer ourselves up. Granted that even with a positive subconscious mind we will still face negative situations, that are external and outside of our control, although we can consciously deal with those situations but knowing that we have a fixed positivity underneath that can never change.

Sustaining Positivity through Attestation (corroborating evidence)

Do we prejudge everything to be negative and think that we are right to do so, do we ever question that we might be wrong. We don't know everything and we don't know the outcomes and can only predict what the outcomes might be if we sit on our backsides and do nothing i.e. that nothing will change. If we do something positive about our lives we have no idea what the outcome will be other than it has a much better chance of turning out more positive than it currently is. Given that, why don't we just assume a healthier position and prejudge things to be not so positive in that we may suffer later unbearable disappointment if things fail but positive enough to at least feel pretty good about where we are and where we might go.

It's so easy to think positive but we can't do it for long, keep thinking positive and it may exhaust us to the point of collapse. Positive thinking is unsustainable but there is a solution. It's no good trying to force positive thought it is a delusion, of sorts, and subconsciously you will know that it is but what if we go digging for reason to feel positive we construct reasons why we should feel positive about what is good in our lives and what is potentially good. Look closely and examine where your efforts are being deployed and where you already are and there will be positives in there, add them up and then you can see reason to feel positive and optimistic about life.

Switching Perspective from the Microscopic to the Wide Angle

Today you may have experienced the most wonderful day that can be imagined, everything is perfect, but then there is an incident where something, though nothing major, goes wrong. It could be that you encountered someone quite nasty, could it be something you hear on the news or is it that you were disappointed in something minor that happened, or didn't happen that you had wanted to happen. These incidents happen all of the time to all of us and it is unlikely that you will go through one week without experiences of such. Yes the world is a 'little' bit mad indeed.

Some of us are tough bastards, who shrug such things off or have learnt to do so in order to survive, but to some of us such an incident can ruin our whole day, it may even colour the way how we perceive the entire human race, its future and our own future. Why can it be that such a small thing has inflicted such damage – it is because we are so focussed on the minute detail of life, we zoom right in on what has gone wrong. Imagine this that in one hour you experience 1 minute of misery and 59 minutes of the sublime, what is your perception of the world as the clock strikes the hour and the cuckoo comes out and does its thing. You might say well its only $1/60^{th}$ crap and $59/60^{th}$ great so on balance a great experience or does that one minute ruin everything. If you are a 'microscopist' then it's time to take out that lens and fit a wide angle one and look at the bigger picture. See the world for what it offers that is good not that which is bad.

Switching Time Frames (ignoring the future, live now)

We have already discussed about looking beyond where we are and instead to the future if our depressive feelings are in the present but what if we are depressed about what we fear is yet to come, our future, we may fear loneliness, a presumption of a failed life ahead, age or even death. There is a very clear and very simple answer to this and that is don't live in the future don't think of the future, just live in the timeframe of now and make the most of it. Instead of thinking 1, 2, 5, 10 or 20 years ahead why not confine your thoughts to the next week or month and no further than that. Get a plan in place of what you are going to do and make it happen make it count. You may sensibly plan for the long term future but in the context of worrying about the future it is this next week or this next month is that is all that matters nothing beyond so live for now.

"Carpe diem." – Latin proverb (to seize the moment to live now).

Taking Preventative Actions

A depressive/anxious state can fall upon us in ways that can bust us up really bad and we cannot completely avoid such feelings no matter how much we have marshalled our arsenal of countermeasures but the more prepared we are the better. You may not be able to stop what is coming but you can mitigate its impact by being prepared, although there are predisposing factors that we unknowingly walk into.

I rarely hear anything good on the news these days, I am dismayed by the stupidity and corruption of politicians (more of that later), to escape it all we might switch on a soap opera and be deluged with such a tale of woe that would make the utter graphic despair of the Dostoyevsky novel 'Crime and Punishment' look positively upbeat, we switch channels to a comedy program that if we are honest lacks any humour and for which we only laugh to be polite or to not look as if we are so thick in that we just don't get it. We dwell on all of this and we are emotionally strained by not being honest to ourselves and in our attempts to feel part of the crowd.

Granted that we do need to stay worldly and wise through current affairs and we need to keep ourselves entertained but addiction to these things is no less destructive than addictions to drugs or say promiscuity – at some point we shall suffer psychological damage. If we have an addiction, this might even include something as ostensibly innocuous as collecting stamps, or something toxic such as all-consuming conceit, obsession towards someone or something or the persistent criticizing of others, and of where we live, do this and we shall never be satisfied with life. Addiction and obsession leads to psychological harm. Be self-disciplined in knowing when to walk away or at least put it down and occupy the mind with other things that can be good for your life.

Ever heard of anyone who behaves like crap to the neighbours or who doesn't keep up with the rent and gets kicked out of their accommodation and then can't figure out why, with the lamest of excuses smashes things or people and can't understand why they then land up in a police cell, is abusive to a partner and can't understand why the partner runs off with someone else, spends money beyond what they earn and lands up in debt and even bankrupt, shows off to their mates in their new car killing a pedestrian in the process, gets 'smashed' on booze every night and can't work out why their liver or life has run up the white flag.

If you do stupid things you will compromise your future, such actions will bite a big fat metaphorical chunk out of your backside, brutal as it is that is a plain fact and you are better off knowing that than being ignorant of it. It is in your interests that I cannot prevaricate on this I am compelled to be brutal on this subject. The simple solution is be sensible with whatever you do, don't keep making excuses for yourself, take responsibility, do not mix with those who will degrade what you could have been and when it comes to spending money on really much other than your home – if you can't afford it save up or go without. Simply if you associate with fools or do stupid things you will suffer harm.

"He who walks with wise men shall become wise, he who walks with fools shall suffer harm." – The Bible, book of Proverbs (Christianity)

If you exude good qualities and think good thoughts you will feel better for it and your outlook on life will be more positive. Just show compassion to others, do not be harsh, be kind, don't go around being constantly over critical of everything, lighten up, have some sense of fun, be a good listener, be grateful for what others do and have done for you and in the society that supports you, be more open to others and do not look down on anyone, always do the decent thing. Do not lie, cheat, abuse, why not do the opposite, be recognized as someone who can be trusted and be that person. Throw away conceit and self-praise and start enjoying life.

Do not be put off by those who have a face of stone or appear aloof as they may be aching for someone to show genuine interest in them, be available to them and open up to them. If they are indignant that you are showing interest in them then don't worry about it, it's their loss. If you meet those who are beyond reach and those who may not be nice people do not be affected by them just carry on undisturbed in the same way that a single rain drop cannot affect the ocean. And keep smiling.

Some of us do not get the luxury of our own refuge and some societies seek to imprison our minds but what we can do, even on a limited budget, is at least make one room in our abode a decent living space as long as it is clean, bright and comfortable this should suffice and it may only cost little more than a tin of paint, nice curtains and a couple of potted plants. If not why not find somewhere where it is safe to go where you can have time to yourself, even if it's short time, it's your time.

Eat well, get plenty of fresh air (on that subject don't forget to regularly ventilate your home), get plenty but not too much sunshine (note that behind glass you are generally safe from UV rays since glass is mostly opaque to ultraviolet light) and do not become addicted to anything or anyone and this includes the internet, texting or someone you might fancy. Improve your social skills and try to get on well with everyone don't put yourself at the centre of your life put others there instead. Build up and keep in contact with a small social circle, in reality we all have just a few close friends which is better than having loads of people who we think of as friends although who are in fact just acquaintances at best and only associate with those who are good.

Avoid too much news, don't do anything stupid, think carefully before you embark on anything; choosing a holiday, a career, what to study, on buying a car or a house, on getting married. Get a skill and be confident, try not to worry too much, loosen up a bit, take life a bit less serious and let your pulse slow down, have fun, fill your life with as much as you can, think positive and don't give too much of a shit about things that don't really matter and find a purpose for your life that is good.

"I joke a lot, not because I am an idiot, but because my life circumstances are so awful. This may irritate some, maybe you too if you had the misfortune to hear one of my jokes, however it is my way to survive and survive I do well. It is just a great shame that I am a better survivor than I am a comedian - You don't get paid for being a survivor." – a quotation from someone I once knew (England 20th century)

Observe others who are the survivors, where nothing bad ever seems to happen to them or if it does they ride it well. What do you see in them? What is their secret to their survival? Could it be that; if we are careful though at the same time just accept things as they are, in essence not giving a shit, setting the importance we place on what is causing our bad experience at 0%, scavenging a situation that is falling apart as in to just extract, as it approaches final collapse, what we need from it and to hell with everything else, in not putting any importance to solving a problem that just can't be solved, in having an outlook that nothing bad will happen – could it be that bad luck is partly attracted by having a negative outlook on life and not just about making bad decisions.

If you have lost someone you love see if you can join up with others in the same situation and as a gathering make time to remember those who have gone, since doing so in this way you will not mourn alone. Never think about dying, it's coming to us all, so why even think about it, never think about age, keep young and keep positive and make the most of every day. Do not let any day pass you without it being positive and in you making effort to make it feel positive.

And every day use positive words even when you don't feel that way. If someone asks you how you are don't enter into a dialogue about everything that's going wrong, unless this is the purpose of the conversation with this person just say *"I feel fantastic"*, or words to that effect, though sound as if you mean it – try not to sound sarcastic or be sarcastic. Oddly enough taking this tack will fool you, and eventually, will make you feel that everything is wonderful and now having a more positive attitude will attract people to you rather than making them want to run away. If you happen to be a negative thinking person then why not take a new approach in imagining and betting on everything turning out to be positive, could it be that thinking positive might make things become exactly that that it may change your fate.

Perhaps an idea is that just as we display messages on electronic road signs and airport information boards that we also display the occasional positive message such as 'today feel good' or 'smile and the world smiles with you' and this might evoke good feelings in everyone, sometimes we need to be reminded just how good life can be.

Whatever advice here, you need to live life you need to give yourself moments of wonder and you need to give yourself treats but more of this is to come at the end of this book as we don't just want to survive life we also want to live it.

If You Don't Change Anything Then Nothing Will Change! (but before anything else change yourself)

"In seeking to change my life I have put in so much effort over so many years and beyond the point of exhaustion and yet nothing seems to change - now I have lost all hope." But within this statement were you selective in where you directed your effort, selective in what you did, selective in whom you sought out and had sought out – now look again at how you feel, is this statement still valid to you.

A good outcome is subject more so to our ability to select, get on and stay on the right path than to endure albeit that endurance is a critical virtue in surviving life. It is within us to believe that strength prevails but ahead of strength is wisdom - knowing where to push is just so much more important than knowing how hard.

If you do not believe that change within the self can bring about change to the life we experience then I really recommend for inspiration that you take a look at Bill

Murray's character (Phil Connors) in the film 'Groundhog Day' and that of Alistair Sim's character (Ebenezer Scrooge) in the film 'A Christmas Carol' - I would still highly recommend these films even if you do believe as the benefit of their scripts has much wider application. Drilling deeper into the perspectives of thoughts, feelings and change I also recommend that you listen and reflect upon a most amazing song 'Another Train' by the English folk singer Pete Morton.

It can be no more unequivocally axiomatic than to state that *"your life will not change if you do not change your life, if you do not look for a new path"*; in effect there is a 100% probability that your life will not change if you do nothing about it, you will therefore need to act and reading this book may be your first step on the path to doing so. If you have made changes and yet things have not changed despite these changes then this is not uncommon. So what do we do, we carry on and if you are on the right path then eventually change will surface. So long as you keep on the right path and that you don't give up in doing so then you will eventually reach your goal so remain patient, your actions are not futile they <u>will</u> yield results.

If you give up your chances have gone from slim to none but even if your chances were slim to start with all will turn out better with the right effort. Your chance in life is largely what you make it. If you want some fantastic inspiration then I recommend the brilliantly acted film 'Educating Rita', if you are about to give up then this film tells you not to and along the way teaches some important life lessons.

Also, you can't run away from a problem, if you do your problem is very likely to follow you unless of course you change. If you are disappointed with life and you do not change anything then you will remain disappointed. You may still feel that your future is looking bleak but making changes in your life with unassailable determination and a new approach, a new you, will change things, you will start to experience new opportunities and with time hopefully some new friendships.

"Be not afraid of going slowly. Be afraid of standing still." – Japanese proverb.

If you prophesize that what happens in your life will be negative then so it will be, if you prophesize that life will be positive then life has a chance of becoming positive. Life can largely turn out to be how you prophesize it to be. Your negative feelings may feel like some crushing abyss, you might have had a lot of bad luck although it can pass on just like catching a cold – sunshine can always follow. You may even feel that you had missed out on life but thinking like this and you will just be missing out even more.

If you believe that you have missed out then why not invent a different narrative of your past life experience a different though positive narrative – **imaginative narrative, past or present, may even surpass the best of possible realities that**

most of us will ever know (just check out the song 'Make Your Own Kind Of Music' by Paloma Faith). Look at those moments in your life that were good and use them as markers, if you haven't any then start on a path to make good moments. Just keep looking beyond where you see yourself and keep your eye on that desired destination and where you can get to.

What you aim for is just to improve your life not go after the holy-grail or that pot of gold at the end of the rainbow. What you need to do is plan but first, park your worries before you embark upon it. Plan, but don't obsess with the planning, beyond where you currently are and work diligently to get to what is beyond where you are i.e. to where you aim to be and give yourself realistic objectives and a sensible time frame such as one, two or five years, plan well and then get moving.

Make a list of your positive and your 'super-positive' attributes (and you will find them), what is great about you, perhaps even include what you don't have and glad that you don't, what you already have going for you, and where you fall short then put together a strategy as to what you intend to do and make sure it happens. In anything it doesn't matter if you can never become the best, few of us can be, what matters is that you strive to improve on what you are. When you feel that you are straying off-course or entering back into the world of negativity, perhaps even from fear or loss of confidence, then look again at your list and just remind yourself of what you really ought to be positive about. Be diligent to act and monitor your progress and keep to plan.

"I was obliged to be industrious. Whoever is equally industrious will succeed equally well." – Johann Sebastian Bach (Composer, Germany 17th/18th century)

No matter what changes you make, how little they may seem day by day, be patient and feel positive about these changes and for the fact that you are making these changes no matter how little they may seem, they are progress towards your ultimate goal.

And On a Philosophical Note (or just looking at things differently)

A low mood is our own personal bespoke reaction to something that we perceive as bad happening in our life, it is a reaction that only we experience and that we cannot easily articulate exactly how we feel or why we feel that way. The very fact that others, although having empathy, can't exactly know what you are experiencing is partly because their reactive systems work different to yours, hence I use the word 'bespoke'. So you and I may experience exactly the same circumstances though we will react to it differently and will therefore feel different too. For example; divorce for one person may identify with loss, to another it may identify with liberation. Perhaps not the best example but you see the principle here. Hence, we can state that; it is not what we experience that makes us feel the way we do but it is from the way we look at that experience.

Taking that thought a bit further, we can imagine that having realized that it is all in my head and in the way my reactive systems have been configured over my lifetime then perhaps I might be able to look at the depressive/anxious episode in a different light. For any challenge, and depression/anxiety is a challenge, not the best of challenges though, we have two options, we can: let it tear us apart and destroy us or we can consider the challenge as an opportunity to learn. Much in the same way as SAS soldiers (the elite of the British army) are put through hell in their training although become better soldiers as a result, so likewise we can become stronger. Not just that but for the very fact that we consciously make the decision that this crap I'm putting up with is actually a useful learning experience makes it a hell of a lot more palatable. We therefore see it as something to achieve with an imaginary graduation ceremony at the end so think of it as your research project as something to learn. Feeling bad about something all of the time is bad, however if you learn from the experience then feeling bad can have its uses.

So stand back and examine what is going on with how you feel and how you are dealing with it, look at it with interest, don't desire for it to leave you too quickly as you will lose this opportunity to learn, if you are learning from it hang on to it for a while, but not for too long and study it. Perhaps instead of feeling depression we should instead study it, we should study ourselves like looking at an 'ice-core' sample, determine why we feel the way we do and from here we can rationalise how we counter those thoughts.

If we can harness this experience in the right way we are better equipped to defeat it in the future, we become inured and we become immune, we gain a self-image that is unassailable. What would once tear us apart just glides past us. If we used to be sensitive to insults now we don't give a shit about them and I don't mean we fool ourselves into thinking we don't give a shit, we actually don't give a shit (i.e. *"it's water off a duck's back"*). Our minds are prepared for anything. We are now becoming one tough bastard trained to handle any negative situation. This is not to say that we have become some hard, psychopathic, unfeeling, unsympathetic automaton, we can still hold onto our human qualities it's just we don't let anything get at us.

Further to this use your humour to see the funny side of things, even black humour helps a lot. For instance; your house may have burnt down so you might say *"well I never did like that front door"*, your hair may have fallen out so you might say *"well I always wanted to lose weight"*. Look for positives within the negative, the more absurd the better. Also, many things that look bad now later they may give you something to laugh about and often can be a source of comedy to others and your resilient humour will even make you appear a more attractive person. Do not look back to the past with regrets; whatever they were, forget them, they've long gone.

A long time ago someone once threw a brick at my head, that might explain a few things!!!, bad as it was at the time having this large swelling lump, that's not my head by the way, but now retelling the story others do seem to find it funny and so do I. So whatever you face now, as you learn, later you will look upon it in an entirely different way, just look at the nuances and exploit them for your own and others amusement if this is at all possible.

If I have a story to tell I notice that where there are bad experiences within or just things that went wrong and that I can pitch with some humour then this seems to get the attention of others, so bad experiences can definitely have their use. If we have had a sad past then conjure up a different narrative for you and for others to believe in and to be entertained by, whatever it is we can find alternative ways to look back upon what we have experienced. What is negative can often become positive and makes our life experiences more interesting. Indeed there are some comedians who exploit this to the full in exaggerating what is unusual about themselves to them they see this as material for their act and we love them all the more for it.

To be able to laugh at one-self is to be able to take life less seriously and to free up the mind in a positive way. Even those things that made us so miserable we can often later look back and laugh at them.

Comedy demands something to go wrong for it to work. It is often so that comedians have had tragedy in their lives and will use this material to their advantage.

"The funniest people are the saddest ones." – Confucius (Philosopher, China circa 500 BC)

So spare a thought for those who may laugh at their misfortune as inside they may still be in agony with it – some just hide their feelings too well instead of letting it out and at times you need to let that dam burst just as you would lance a boil.

Whatever strategies you adopt and use, whether it be something philosophical from this book, from professional help, from ideas you may develop yourself always remember; that you are not alone, that you should not worry because things will change, if not now they will eventually, so stay patient and don't expect everything to change overnight as it seldom does, set yourself reasonable targets that are achievable, do not ever give up and believe unswervingly in yourself that you can overcome all.

To those who are in despair, who may see no future prospects, just work with diligence to overcome and complete what you need to do and believe in yourself even if other don't and prove them wrong and in doing so you will become stronger. If you are trying at something and no matter how hard you try, if it fails, do not worry, maybe you are just trying too hard at it and need some time away from it or maybe you are just trying the wrong thing that isn't for you.

If you are still trying to figure out what life is all about, what is our purpose, don't worry about it – I think this is a question that eludes us all, just get on with life and make the most of every minute. Just strive to make your life and that of others better.

Finally, this chapter and the last two illustrate various ideas in how we might be able to fix ourselves but this perspective cannot solve all problems and just gives the philosophical angle on it all, but if things for you are really difficult you must go and get help and don't be afraid to do so. However, I would like you to think of the ideas in here as analogous to just handing you a paint brush where you are the artist, you are in control of what you paint and how and so you are in control of your destiny, you are free to change your future. Choose what best suits you and what you are going through to best help you overcome your life challenges.

Aftershocks

We all have waves of feeling bad, bad feelings never hits us just once and then goes away for good, but there is one very important point to address and this is not the aftershocks of feeling not so great, as it can take time to rid our minds of the rubbish that has tormented us, but the aftershocks experienced as a result of learning how to cope with those feelings.

What you have read may have helped you to resolve how you had felt, it may even have changed your life a little, what was a low feeling can instantaneously become a high from some point of sudden realization, but the problem will be is that tomorrow the ideas that are poignant to you and your needs, what new philosophical angle you have acquired, will diminish or you may just forget – 'just what was that swish idea I read and now can't recall'. This happens to all of us, we read something and tomorrow it's gone, we have read although we have not absorbed.

You may have felt some eureka moment that has solved your problems and those bad feelings just fell away, but tomorrow those ideas that precipitated this euphoria have dissipated and your mind will return back to your previous state of anguish.

What's more is that you are likely to feel even worse in that you then believe that even with such good ideas you still cannot feel any better, the pill didn't work, hence making the anguish feel to be even more intractable. What we need to be mindful of is that the reason that you feel this way is not because these ideas are ineffective or that your anguish is further beyond resolve than you first thought but it is because you need to enmesh these new ideas, those ideas that did it for you, within your mind, they need to become part of you, a component of how you think. A carpenter cannot make a chair if he has forgotten joinery.

You may need to mark what ideas have hit a note with you, study them, maybe discuss them with others and then commit them to your long term memory. As soon as you feel yourself slipping back to the way how you felt before then revisit these ideas again and again and eventually you will no longer need to revisit them – they will become part of you. Reach that point of realization that your life can and will get better.

None of This Worked (but the harder you try the greater you will become)

There are more questions in life than the word count of any book, ergo there is no one book that can answer all questions.

You may read this and the last two chapters and you may re-read them a million times and yet you may feel no different. So you may feel that what you have read, comprehensive as it may seem, just can't solve you, so therefore you are beyond being solved. However, this is not true this is just a setback and nothing more. There are a myriad of difficulties out there and it would be impossible to write an all-encompassing book and I am by no means an expert in this field.

What I have written may have taken me countless hours but there are others out there who have devoted countless years and even a lifetime to dealing with such issues. They can with great ease transcend and go much further than what this book can offer. Remember that this book is one of many available on these issues, many others that are very specifically tailored to specific problems (see also Bibliography) that I do not have room here to cover adequately if at all. So do not ever give up hope, you can use this book to help provide you with some direction and other books that are more specific to a topic but sometimes we also need expert help.

If you are in torment and you still cannot find a solution, this does not mean there isn't one, you will find that help if you look in the right places and you will find the solution, the answer is out there somewhere, so never ever give up. Go out there and get that help now.

The Time to Act Is Now

What you have just read is insufficient in itself, these are just words, it is now for you to act and don't hang around do it now. A final point is; be patient, things take time and effort but keep mindful of your progress every day how you learn and how you move one step at a time towards your ultimate goal. If you give up you will not have any chance, even if you think it is pointless maybe you will find out that it isn't.

If it helps write 'post-it' notes with ideas that hit a tune with your new way of thinking of what you need to do or of other positive messages that can pull you back from the abyss so let's saddle up and let's get to it, we have work to do.

That Which Is Intractable

The mind may be preoccupied with something that it cannot solve and for which you place too much importance on i.e. that you attribute serious consequences to if you can't find an answer to the problem. Stop thinking and stop thinking right now, stop thinking of the consequences being serious, just look at the problem as no more than an intellectual puzzle such that what is before you is merely a game where the consequences of failure is unimportant. It is not the experience before you but the mind that is doing battle with something that is hard to work out that given time and less anxiety might even just solve itself. With depression much of the enemy is depression itself more than what is causing the depression as it is doing more harm to you and undermining your ability to resolve what you are facing thus heightening your anxiety.

We are locked into depression partly by our own choice we choose to seek a solution through rumination, a solution that often continually eludes us. I am seeking a solution that can't be found and so is there any point in looking any more. Where there is no solution then through choice at some point we need to accept things for what they are and not keep looking for the elusive solution, so switch off and take the opposite path away from ruminating upon the unsolvable and onto coming to terms with what we have.

Chapter 5

FACING DOWN THE HELL OF LONELINESS

(I am alone or am I?)

Loneliness can feel grim and sometimes some of us might do anything to assuage it we may even be susceptible to engaging in relationships that later we may come to regret. Anything may seem better than loneliness when in reality it isn't.

In 1934 the great and stoic U.S. aviator and explorer Admiral Richard Byrd lived for five months in that desolate continent of Antarctica; frostbitten, poisoned, close to death, living in the most miserable of conditions and with no company he survived and was to later write a highly acclaimed book about his experience. In the early 18th century a Scottish sailor Alexander Selkirk was marooned for four years on an uninhabited island in the south pacific, he too survived and was to later become the inspiration for Daniel Defoe's fictional character 'Robinson Crusoe'.

Admiral Byrd and Alexander Selkirk had one thing in common they had the determination to survive they never gave up and in having this quality they then learnt how to survive. The fact is that those who never face challenges can never gain resilience and those who face challenges beyond what they are able to cope with can be destroyed from the experience. However when we face challenges that are within our capability to deal with then those experiences make us more resilient.

So loneliness may seem like shear hell but with the right application it is survivable and in those moments when you resign yourself to thinking it isn't, then just remind yourself of Admiral Byrd and Alexander Selkirk. They managed to survive loneliness and so can you. So let's just remind ourselves of what Nietzsche said about this - *"What doesn't kill you makes you stronger"*.

Defining Loneliness

We are all creatures of contrast sensitivity, it is not so much what we are or what we are experiencing but how what we are or how our experiences compares with others. Our perception is therefore not so much based in entirety upon what we have or do not have but also and with some potency upon what we believe others have or do not have, just reflect on this. This perception affects us on so many levels of how we feel and also on how we act. From the perspective of this chapter, the corollary to this is perhaps that there is sharp contrast between those who feel loneliness who live in a crowded city to those living alone on an island or perhaps even a space station. Both may feel lonely, but the agony of loneliness can feel a lot worse when you might perceive that all about you are those who are not alone and thus who you may perceive, perhaps wrongly, do not feel loneliness.

However, the feeling of loneliness is so rife that none of us are alone in feeling lonely ergo we are not alone.

Our initial thoughts on how we define loneliness is that it is not just a state of being alone; it is a feeling of isolation, of the deafening silence and ever present sadness of having no-one to talk to, of not having anyone close by who cares or, oddly enough, who you know might not care but where the 'non-caring' doesn't even seem to matter as at least it is company of sorts!!! Typically; it is that absence of not having another person living with you who you can communicate with on a level acceptable to your needs, a sort of meeting of minds, in as much that they have a capacity to empathise with what happens to trouble you – *"a trouble shared is a trouble halved"* as we say.

If our mind is fully occupied we can reach a point where we no longer feel lonely so therefore loneliness has some strong relationship to a feeling of boredom, and therein is a clue to finding the solution. Ask yourself when you are fully taken up with some activity, the extreme of which being surviving some disaster, the loneliness you felt seems to leave you for that moment.

We assume that loneliness afflicts those of advancing years mostly from losing a partner or sadly where their children show no interest, though the reality is that you can be struck by it at any age from cradle to grave. A child may feel neglected by its parents or lacks confidence and levity to be able to make friends at school, adolescence can be a particularly bad phase for many and as a result can lead to the onset of a life of drug abuse in the mistaken belief that a drug induced altered state of mind can take them to a better place, the bewilderment of the university prospectus showing contrived photos of students looking happy that may actually belie the full reality, the shock discovery that your partner, to whom you had put such high a value, doesn't really care and so it goes on.

Your feeling of loneliness can be magnified when everyone else appears to be having a good time such as some religious festival (e.g. Christmas) or a wedding where people will gather, except that you don't feel part of it and you might just have that feeling of being abandoned or ignored, you stand there feeling that you just do not fit in and regret accepting the invitation. You may even feel worse being a single person in what is ostensibly a world of couples and this seems to hammer home more so at events where people are supposed to look happy.

However, you are not alone in these feelings as many experience exactly the same and indeed more of us just don't enjoy Christmas, or weddings, than we freely admit, many even hate it. The commercial hijacking of Christmas and surreptitiously promoting of it earlier every year makes it even less attractive to want to be involved and we seem to have long forgotten what its real significance is, if we hadn't had done so then perhaps more would feel included in celebrating the birth of a compassionate faith one in which all are warmly welcomed rather than abandoned right in the middle of our coldest, darkest and perhaps loneliest season. You can often feel better off alone than having to put on a brave face at some celebratory event one in which you must contrive a celebratory mood when in reality you feel quite the opposite.

In such circumstances you can feel a lot better off even feel great when alone with a good book and the company of the neighbour's cat as I discovered on one particular new-year's eve. No party for me I didn't want one but I was better off for it, but for those who did I hope they were better off too. So it follows that some of our worst times can be when we are alone and some of our best times too so perhaps being alone is not always such a bad thing.

"When I get a little money I buy books; and if any is left I buy food and clothes." – Desiderius Erasmus (Philosopher, Holland 15th/16th century)

On the subject of books; a book is like a personal friend, one that talks to us, it is in the visual frame, for added benefit we could read out aloud since a voice, any voice, even our own is better than silence. A television works differently since subconsciously you are aware that the relationship with the television is impersonal it is not one-on-one, but at least you know that others are watching at the same time. The television is not useless it does fill a hole but is perhaps less effective at doing so than a good book; with a good book you can become immersed. These things alone cannot entirely defeat loneliness, nothing can, but at least they can make things more manageable where you can see things from a different viewpoint.

For some of us, being alone can be an imperative in that if you are a writer or a student then having company can severely get in the way of your work, so if that's you; don't worry about being alone, just keep your mind fixed on your work and those meaningful interactions with others can wait until the weekend or perhaps at some time in the future that fits your timetable.

Being alone may also offer you that freedom and chance to find the right partner in life, one that you are not irrevocably tied to within some disastrous intractable relationship, thus you have the chance of finding happiness later. In these respects loneliness has, although possibly not so obviously a latency in its value to our life to becoming a success. So just keep that thought.

Being alone doesn't necessarily make you feel lonely as this depends very much on the way how we perceive our situation – some may not need any company as they may be fully occupied with so many other things or they may be a dogged optimist, some though may have recently experienced the loss of a loved one and it will take time, often months for at least some recovery and to come to terms with and make the necessary adjustments to their life.

Equally, not being alone does not always equate to not feeling lonely – when we see others maybe in the pub, chatting and laughing, this doesn't necessarily mean that they feel that they have meaningful friendships and so they may also feel the grip of loneliness. At work or in the pub you may appear the liveliest most cheerful person but when you walk through your front door the gloomy cloud of loneliness can still fall upon you. To assuage loneliness some may resort to promiscuity, human contact of whatever form may suffice and any contact may be better than none - so goes the philosophy, and are therefore vulnerable to moments of what are essentially short term meaningless relationships, they get short term respite but at potentially terrible cost or regret of the consequences upon their physical and/or mental well-being.

At times perhaps we may feel not exactly lonely but that we very consciously feel that we don't fit in with what we perceive as societal norms: youth, looks, education, experience, confidence, the illusion of happiness, friends (although may not be), socially engaging, our perceived status, our relationship status, our role in society - we denigrate what we are, we perceive ourselves to be different to not feel part of and thus feel that we are missing out.

But it is highly questionable as to what you might describe as the 'vernacular' societal norm, in actuality there is no such thing it is an illusion. OK some of us don't fit into perhaps many social groups and thereby we are just part of another group one perhaps a lot more unique, less easy to find, but nevertheless with many members. Should you therefore not be proud of the fact that you are different and therefore unique where 'to fit in' may just make you feel too conformist too dull too uninteresting. If we were all the same then planet earth would indeed be a very dull place to live.

Do we really want to fit in with that which lacks uniqueness and different texture or can we not feel great about what we are. Why should being shunned matter to us on the basis of our differences, would you really feel happier mixing with those others whom you are rejected by or would it be better to seek out others who are more like you or who are interested in what you are for what you are and not for being the 'societal norm', those who can help you grow not who will bring you down.

It is essential for us to have regular and meaningful daily human interaction without which our mind may run into all sorts of wild and false ideas that can make our life feel difficult and so negative that cannot be solved through the ideas in this book alone. Without any company whatsoever this book is close to useless in trying to combat loneliness.

We need people around us, some more so than others, but it would be difficult to live in total isolation and unless we can forge meaningful relationships and have regular interaction with others who matter to us, and to whom we matter to them, then loneliness has its inevitability. Unfortunately, societies are often very insular; sit on a commuter train into London and how many strangers will you see chatting, virtually none – should it really be like this. This feeling of loneliness of not having anyone you feel close to in the way that you need if mixed with depression can have serious consequences upon your mental well-being and so you need to stay alert to this development.

We can overcome loneliness but it does have a strong presence and so is not so easy to overcome, it takes effort and often so when we can't find the willpower to do anything about it. When you have a partner, even if your relationship is in the proverbial toilet, you are conscious of another living-being being in your home with you and thus you may then not feel lonely, albeit that you may have other more toxic negative emotions and issues to contend with.

How to Eradicate Loneliness

Before anything else the most important thing you should do is to keep active and make the most of your time and in this way you are flooding your mind you are not giving your mind any time to seek out negative thoughts. Even more, often we wrongly cement our sense of purpose exclusively into having a close relationship without which that thus exacerbates our feeling of loneliness, in essence it is the 'elephant in the room'.

It is quite a revelation that total immersion into doing some serious housework (one example of many), as a temporary 'purpose substitute', can dramatically change how you feel at that time – why not try it for yourself in the interests of your own scientific research, see what you can discover. To feel alive and to feel that our life has purpose we must find things to do and what's really important is to find new things to do and new places to visit, also find things to look forward to so your mind can be focussed on that rather than where you are at present. This distracts the mind away from its present state and gives you the feeling that your time on this planet is used well and that you have taken full advantage of every minute and so you will not feel that your life is wasted and just running through your fingers.

If you are dissatisfied or feel unfulfilled in what you already do or in those who you associate with then you have no option but to branch out and do something new perhaps away from your normal social circle. If it's broke you have no option but to change things.

Get on the horse, get out and visit new places, sit back and observe the world not with envy but with curiosity, maybe find some lectures, exhibitions or musical events to attend and don't worry if you are going on your own, you won't be the only one doing so, and don't worry either about getting back a bit late, just live a little and don't feel guilty about it. If it's raining and there's another one of those train strikes and so you have nowhere to go well do some housework, re-arrange the furniture, perhaps move your favourite chair nearer to the window, read lots as in something absorbing and uplifting, study a new subject or you might like to focus your mind on poetry or a jigsaw puzzle, perhaps a game of chess or mah-jongg on the computer but stay occupied with something.

Make a list of what you are going to do, even write a book. Do not get up late and waste too much time in bed with apathy, get up, get out and try new things, overcome that inertia – get out of the; 'can't be bothered what difference would it make' thinking, break that cycle, do positive things, make effort to interact with positive interesting people who might also make you laugh. Do not dismiss anything just go and try it, you might be surprised. If you don't research where to go and don't go out to meet likeminded others then they certainly won't be coming around your place to meet you – so do your research and get out.

However, one word of warning, don't overdo it, don't burn yourself out so you need to keep an eye on how you are making out here. If you just can't face getting out and so back on the horse or you still need quiet times you may need to refer back to the section on meditation in the chapter on thinking your way out of despair.

Realize that it is OK and not abnormal to feel lonely and that you are not alone in the way how you feel. Maybe you are not aware that one in three homes in the UK is single occupancy, and it is becoming all too common not to have any children either, I would bet, and I'm not a betting man, that many of those living with others would envy those living alone as living with others can sometimes be hell.

Part of our problem is with our common human culture in that we are all raised and conditioned with the idea that our ideal future is in having a partner and having children, if we don't fit that mould for whatever reason or we don't achieve this goal we wrongly feel abandoned, rejected and a failure and this makes our loneliness more crushing, more difficult to bear and we then question do I have a future – well all I can say is *"nuts to that"*. Do not listen to this cultural conditioning, you are not a failure for being alone and you certainly do have a future outside of these culturally enforced 'norms'.

"To find me you do not have to know my instruction or follow my words for if you are universally good then you are unwittingly practicing my ways, though you do not know me I know you and you are very dear to me." – 'Theoleptic spirituality'

Being with someone can restrict your freedom and in some cases badly – you can be evicted from the path you naturally need to take for you to feel fulfilled. Being alone gives you full reign on being able to do what you want and to develop yourself such that you have new opportunities that otherwise would not have presented themselves.

You can get fit, expand the mind, learn new social skills, learn to dance, do some voluntary work, join a church or attend a retreat (i.e. in a monastery), join a choir, use the local library, get spiritual, go and get yourself a non-human but loyal companion, a dog or an unselfish cat maybe, and take great care of it and it will take great care of you, get an electric blanket, take time to properly relax (check out 'Elizabethan Serenade' by Ron Goodwin and Enya's 'Only Time') and ideally do some meditation and burn some incense sticks just for effect, give yourself a treat now and then or just enjoy a cup of tea, but most of all get those communication skills working and get talking to others with the charm that you still have deep down within you.

Never ever think to yourself that I am too old or too incapacitated to do any of this, find ways to do so and even if you can't do everything at least let your mind imagine it all for you (gymnastics maybe? why not) and never lose interest in what is happening in the world, even imagine that you are on a journey since we feel less lonely when we are on the move. So enjoy quality time for yourself.

Overcome loneliness by being part of something bigger than yourself, being part of a crowd embarking on the same action at the same time and usually in the same place, such as watching a football match, though personally it doesn't do anything for me – we do, after all, have different interests, helping out at some charity event, being an active member of a political party, why not if you feel strongly about something. Essentially we all have to feel we belong to something and do things for or with others and therefore get to feel wanted by others.

"The deepest principle in human nature is the craving to be appreciated." –
William James (Psychologist, USA 19th/20th century)

Sadly, this need for belonging can make some of the more easily persuaded, who may be vulnerable through lack of any purpose or through being overcome with envy of others, to fall prey to being seduced into joining gangs intent on petty criminality or worse – you may be fooled into thinking that you no longer are alone that you are now part of a 'community' but you are more alone than what you might even imagine because these new found associates care not about you, the smiles the friendly slap on the back, the contrived concern for your welfare, the familial and inappropriate use of and calling to you as 'bro', 'sis', 'brother' or 'sister' (gang language) is not what it seems as they have ill intent for you and your future, to them you are nothing but a pawn in a foolish and dangerous game and their intoxicating influence on you will ultimately lead to your ruin as in prison or death despite the hollow promises of excitement or some mythical reward. So for your own good only seek out and join with others who are doing something constructive with their lives and constructive in what they do.

Do remember though that when you join a group be positive and look positive in order to attract the interest of others. Being positive is very infectious and so is well-mannered charm, don't expect too much, sometimes it just will not work, and don't worry if you are ostracized as some groups can be quite a clique – they may only be able to bring themselves to say 'hello' to you after you've been a member for a good number of years – if this is what they are like then go elsewhere where you will find friendlier faces. It is of course possible that your loneliness is as a consequence of losing trust and faith in humanity or that you are too closed in your ideas of what would make a good friend and, if so, you need to rationalise that this should not apply to all as we are not all the same and you also need to stay open to others to deserve others openness in return, the person you may not realise could be a potentially good friend so don't close doors too early in your assessment of others.

I'm not a particular fan of sport but I have great affinity and interest in watching the London marathon, the Olympic games and the Wimbledon tennis championships because firstly I admire the skill and effort of these athletes, but also for the fact that I am watching along with millions of others at exactly the same time and subliminally I feel part of something bigger, I reiterate this point as I feel it is important enough to do so to feel part of something in some capacity. This may not be your thing but find something that is.

One other thought is that if you do feel you are rattling around in your home and need to feel a constant presence, then leave the television on in the other room to give some background noise and weird as this idea may seem, although may have some subliminal value, is to leave items around your home that clearly look as if they belong to someone else and not you i.e. something that is definitely not yours or clearly doesn't look like yours so as to fool yourself into thinking that someone else is around.

"It gives me great satisfaction to know that you are thinking of me and that I have a place in your heart, if you are thinking of me I am also thinking of you and with great affection." – 'Theoleptic spirituality'

If you have no-one at all or you have no-one to miss then now is the time to do something about it, but as you are reading this book then you do have the gift to be able to read, and to read and to understand can be a foundation for making a better life for you. If you cannot read or write but you have someone who is reading and explaining this to you then you have the gift of a friend, a good teacher or someone who can always find time in the interest of others and that alone presents hope and opportunity for you to make your life better so why not start now. Beyond that you can also enter the world of the infinite, of debating philosophy, perhaps even about some of the ideas within this book, look for doors that can be opened look for opportunity to speak to others, others who are also amenable to do likewise.

Having read all of that we may have circumstances in which we feel that we are in a hellish world of strangers with an impoverished view of humanity, the room you sit in, the noise that is wafting through that window of traffic, of conversations of laughter and the summer sunshine (all so more potent than in winter), can render a contrast that is difficult to bear.

These thoughts bring me to reminisce on the Simon & Garfunkel song 'The Sound of Silence' that perhaps alludes to sounds that convey nihilism and a consequent feeling of isolation to those that listen. But remember this that you need someone and so does everyone else, we all need each other, and perhaps in knowing this we are not so alone and if you do nothing about it if you do not seek out company it will not seek you out, so get out and go searching but do so in the right places for the right results. If none of us were to make the effort then all of us would live a lonely life. The truth is that there are many of us out there, even those you may not believe to be so, who feel desperately lonely, something we could all easily fix if only we would talk more and listen more.

Projecting Happiness Begets Happiness Begets Adoration

Go on the internet and look for photos of the nicest smile that you can find with eyes that are looking directly at the camera and thus looking directly at you, I'm not talking about seeking out physical attraction but just a wholesome image. Look at this image without becoming obsessed by it but soak up the smile for this person is smiling at you. Here is not just a voice at the end of a phone nor a text message that the mind may just subliminally imagine to be no more than a mirage, here before us is a human being confirmed as best can be, by our visual perception. More than anything a smile elicits perhaps the greatest feeling of euphoria. In a lonely world a smile can give us a much wanted lift and if no-one is smiling then find images that do.

It is natural for us to not smile, to even look stern, when we are feeling down (or with some feeling self-important – not a good thing) and the only reaction that can be expected of this is that others will not exactly be inclined to engage with us. The misery that has fallen upon us from feeling lonely has now delivered another blow in that having been deprived of a welcoming face we instantly become less attractive to others - a face that looks miserable might give a false impression that the person behind the face is unpleasant. Not only might we deprive ourselves of company but we are also depriving ourselves of potential opportunities for euphoria. In difficult times you may think it is hard to smile (sometimes it can be impossible) but if you can just try it and think happy, amazing as it sounds, if you smile and think happy you will feel happy, your personality will flourish and you suddenly become someone who others want to get to know. Just listen to that wonderful classic song 'Smile' by Nat King Cole and you will get the picture.

If you have a miserable look hanging on your face get rid of it it's not doing you any good and it might just condemn you to a life of loneliness. Two caveats to this though are don't overdo the smiling you might just look like a clown and don't sit there smiling at others, other than momentarily, before you have engaged in any conversation since you might then be perceived as a bit weird or even threatening.

Chapter 6

ADVANCED STRATEGIES OF WELL-BEING

(Advanced self-progression)

One of the most fascinating works of art, in my mind, is 'The Tower of Babel' by Pieter Bruegel (the elder) one of the lesser well known of the famous artists. As an engineer I find it something of a delight as Bruegel clearly must have had some strong sense of construction techniques on the super-grand scale. His painting depicts man's desire to reach heaven but also to serve his own vanity but in doing so the tower would finally collapse because the structure and its foundations were just too weak to support its intended ambitions.

Within this story there is perhaps an allegorical message in that weak foundations and vanity can lead to our undoing. Our perspective on this is that we too have ambitions, to understand, survive and live life but in doing so we must build upon strong foundations and be wary of our own vanity if we don't do these things we may just destroy that which we had set out to build.

"Calmness, gentleness, silence, self-restraint and purity: these are the disciplines of the mind." – The Bhagavad Gita (Hinduism)

Delusion as A Tool to Well Being and As an Attribute to Positive Thinking

We all see life from our own frame of reference, our own conditioning and life experience, so we never see things as they really are, we just think we do. It is our perception of things, not reality, is what we see and this shapes our life experience. In effect much of what we see of the world is what we project from ourselves and the world will react accordingly.

Whatever we think, good or bad, of anything, of anyone, even of ourselves, we must recognize that we could be wrong, even very wrong. This recognition of this lack of our connection with reality can therefore be useful in that; if our reality doesn't work for us then why not change our way of perceiving things, in essence exercising some self-delusion, mad as that may seem, that may enable us to look upon things in a different though more positive way and that may even be more close to absolute reality than what we might imagine. I can hear the clinical psychologists gasp with incredulity but what is so wrong in replacing what is unreal with something that is also unreal, but better for our perception of life, given that reality is so bloody hard to reach.

Essentially, it is our opinion of our circumstances that governs our perception not the circumstances themselves. Ask why do two people perceive the same thing in two completely different ways and which one of them would be right? In all probability neither of them, however, certainly one will be having the more positive experience.

We all well know that a pessimist has a negative view of the world and an optimist a positive one but a pessimist not only dwells on what is bad but in doing so forgets what is good and an optimist sees only what is good and forgets the bad. The reality is that truth is somewhere between the two but wherever it is don't lose sight of what is good so as to maintain our life's motivation and don't entirely lose sight of what is bad in anticipation of what may threaten our well-being.

Ask yourself. Do I always feel positive? Do I help make others feel positive? Am I constructive as a person? Do I really see the world, myself and others as they really are? Do I need to take stock of how I am in this world, how I view life and how I relate to others and value others?

Our Mind Has Power beyond What We Might Imagine

What we achieve in life is not limited to our abilities - it is very much, though not entirely, limited to what we believe our abilities to be. In this sense we impose our own glass ceiling. If we think we cannot do something then our minds will follow suit, if we believe we can do something we are psychologically set up to achieve this, our minds are 'teleological', we are in effect goal driven. We need goals and we need the right attitude and determination to succeed.

Although we admire great athletes for their skills and physical condition they are also highly tuned psychologically to win. Those who have an 'I'm going to win' attitude will more likely win and will overcome adversity or at least will make the best out of what they have. Thinking I can't do it or I am going to die will more likely result in failure or death. If we examine that point a little closer then why is it that faith healing or placebos can promote recovery or cure, could it be that it is because that we believe that it will work albeit that scientific evidence suggests that there is total absence of any mechanism of effect.

The brain, or should we say what is within it - our mind, does therefore have a much greater impact upon our life condition than what we might possibly imagine and so we should make the most to exploit this property. Think positive and imagine positive outcomes and give yourself a better chance in life in all that you do and in all trials that you have to face.

We could extend this idea to an imagination that we have an ethereal guru (or guardian angel) one who looks over you and who advises you – this you may see as the collective of your life skills or you may see as some form of entity who watches over you, all this requires is for you to activate this entity through your imagination.

Survival Characteristics

We have two options, we can either become over-protective, avoiding life's difficulties and obsess about staying safe and thereby we learn nothing of how to survive or we can toughen up. In a world that is hard and sometimes cruel, then in order to survive we have no option but to be prepared to toughen up, to do otherwise we are heading into a storm that we cannot imagine. Toughen up and survive or do otherwise and perish. If we haven't toughened up in any capacity then our life's experience has taught us nothing.

Our ability to survive depends upon our ability to adapt. If we are unable to adapt we will not survive. Adaptability is rooted in our personality in what are called 'biphasic personality characteristics'. Put simply a survivor orientated mentality does not have a specific personality signature; are they extrovert or introvert, involved or detached, hard working or laid back, conformist or defiant, tough or passive, serious or flippant, sensitive or unfeeling, emotional or calm, etc., they are none of these but they are also all of them, indeed they are very difficult to describe.

Given the fact that they can float between opposite ends of personality traits they can therefore adapt to the circumstances in that they can be one or the other. They can adapt to suit the environment. If we are not wired as a survivor personality; we will be rigid in what we are or what we think, we lose the ability to adapt, we also lose the ability to develop as a person and we will therefore not be adequately equipped when adversity comes.

Survivor personalities also have a number of other interesting characteristics in that they will subconsciously observe others and if they like what they see they will acquire characteristics of that person, they are generally very inquisitive, they are very alert to what is going on around them, they generally don't take things too seriously especially themselves, except when appropriate to do so, they don't have any ego to bruise, they are amenable to abandoning ideas that are not working and they are charismatic - they seek to make others around them feel good and encourage and respect others, they do not have any fixed rules and a very specific characteristic is that they perceive all adverse situations as, even research, opportunities to learn more about life and to grow.

Common among those who have survived the most dreadful of experiences is the idea that the experience although unimaginably bad made them who they are and for this they feel grateful for the experience. A survivor personality will see useful positive learning experiences even within what is a very negative experience and will even look to find humour if this is at all possible – they survive because, despite the odds, they don't resign themselves to a heavy attitude and they remain positive.

If something in your life is falling apart or what you have put your effort to has failed then you must focus onto those things that are going right for you or what you see is your potential for the future, look around the problem and beyond it. If it's your future that's giving you anguish, most probably false anguish at that then don't think too far ahead just live for the moment.

If you are going to survive it's not a question of being, or thinking I am, tough, cold-hearted or detached it is down to acquiring a less rigid approach to life where we are able to throw out what we believe if it isn't working and adapt to our circumstances, to grow, to move on. Being rigid means you are easier to break whereas being adaptable you just bend, adapt and learn. You need to be open to new ideas outside of your traditional way of looking at the world.

As an adjunct to this subject we should also draw our attention to the psycho-linguistic properties of survival – if we speak in negative terms, if we incessantly clack on about negative subjects, if we are too fixed on nothing but our problems we will release stress hormones in not only ourselves but also in others and thereby undermine the chance of feeling good about life thus undermining our physical and mental well-being and you may also be seen as someone who others would prefer to avoid. However, the opposite is also true; use positive words and don't dwell too much on what is negative in the world and you will feel positive, not only that but you will make others feel positive too and will be someone who others will want to engage with, not to avoid, and this will make you feel even more positive.

Remember that whatever life throws at you hold the line, do not give up hope stay optimistic and stay focussed on your goal.

Self-Confidence – The Route to Happiness

Having confidence is to have belief in our abilities, i.e. it relates to our self-perception we have in dealing with situations, therefore in essence we learn something and we then know how to competently deploy that knowledge when it is required to be put into action, we do not have to think about what we do or how we do it, we can go straight in with the solution. The more complex the tasks that face us, the more we have to learn to gain confidence and so the more difficult it is to gain that confidence.

A person may seem lacking in confidence though this can be because of their chosen path in life, e.g. chosen subject of study or career, is something that does not yield up confidence easily. Choose a difficult path and you may just be wracked with a lot of self-doubt for a long time and confidence may seem just too elusive.

Confidence is transferrable in that if you gain confidence in one thing you become more confident and optimistic in gaining other skills and so it becomes far easier to acquire those skills, you also gain the ability to interpolate confidence in a skill that you do not have but that sits somewhere between skills that you have already mastered. Conversely self-doubt, what we would classify as the opposite of confidence, is equally transferrable in that self-doubt in anything can hamper your abilities elsewhere. A lack of skill in say chemistry and you may then decide that you also cannot master mathematics which of course may be totally untrue.

If you are lacking in confidence you must first find some confidence before you take another step, you must find an easy path to gain confidence through taking on less ambitious goals before you attempt something more difficult, aim too high and you may devastate the little confidence that you may have, aim lower and you are on the road to achieving great things.

Gaining confidence, especially with, or even through having, charm and polished manners can also help; you can win over people you can instantly become more attractive as a person and others will want to know you, being full of self-doubt and a lot of people might just walk the other way. Getting too confident can morph into arrogance or perhaps a menacing countenance and the admiration you gained in others can easily turn to disdain or wariness.

Quiet confidence is infectious and can gain others interest in you and in doing so you will gain more confidence it's as if confidence begets more confidence you will feel better about life and you will feel happier for it. However, confidence has another important value in that outwardly looking confident, but importantly also being confident (and appropriately assertive), is also a very good defence mechanism, others will subliminally wonder why is this person looking confident even when threatened, what is it that I don't know about them, I have a knife but do they have a machine gun up their sleeve.

Looking confident shows that nothing phases you that you are able to deal with a lot of things including being challenged, threatened or even attacked, to others you cease looking like a credible target as easy prey to some predator much in the same way that in a game of Poker you must keep your cool from which you can turn a looming disaster into victory.

Since none of us can know everything it is impossible to feel confident in all circumstances, someone who may be skilled at one subject and none other can even become bombastic and can talk with great enthusiasm and confidence about what they do but engage them in another subject and if they have not expanded beyond the borders of their narrow skill range then they will be outside of their comfort zone and then will appear a lot less confident. This is possibly why when a lot of us move job we often look for more of the same and dare not take the plunge into entirely new things. Those who you admire as confident, as they are demonstrably very confident, may be agonisingly crippled at the idea of performing karaoke to even a favourable audience or could never face having to present a lecture to an audience with elements of the hostile and the too quick to criticize.

Remember go out into the world look good, do good, think good and feel good. And if that doesn't work even if you have worked hard to change you then don't worry as such efforts are never lost just keep on course to gain a more confident you. Also remember that if you don't think that you are of any value then most others won't either so stop being negative about you.

The Folly of Me at the Centre of the Universe – The Route to Misery

A strong attachment to 'me', in 'I must have this', 'I deserve this', 'I am entitled to that', 'why must I suffer', 'why must I go without', 'I must succeed', 'I must be above all others', 'I am better than all others' – all of this is a pathological obsession with our own ego. Unbeknown to us is that this sense of self this centring will bring us harm, just imagine not getting what we want, or seeing what we obsessed about fall apart, what will this do in demanding so much and possibly doing so by abandoning what is right and decent but then realising how little we can cope with this.

You might define suffering as a negative property of mind that is in proportion to the difference between what we want and the importance we put upon it and what we get such that expecting too much is likely to bring disappointment and dissatisfaction whereas expecting too little and odds are that you will be very happy with the result. With excessive ego others will perceive that you have little thought for them and so they are very unlikely to want to know you other than in the most superficial of interactions, you may get used just as you would use others. Others will know what you are and know that you are taking them for granted and so their kindness tap, if they have one, will get turned off.

If we are less obsessed with our ego our concept of 'me that matters so much' is replaced with thoughts, feelings and concerns for others then we are elevated from an insect like mentality to that of the greater human attributes such as compassion and altruism that cannot exist within an overpowering sense of self. It is so that the more interest and feeling we have for others and the less concern we have for ourselves the less we notice ourselves and so the less we suffer and so the further we move along that scale of happiness but in the direction where we want to go.

If we only care about ourselves then don't expect other to care about us.

Self-Actualisation

A self-actualised person is one who has achieved full potential and meaning in life. A feeling of satisfaction with oneself based on ego is only a fragile veneer and is not a state of self-actualisation. Full potential does not mean that we have become some renown academic or a celebrity with perhaps, as in some not all cases an ego on the ceiling (conceit), a strong sense of look at me, albeit kept hidden but nevertheless still there and still seeking evermore attention, and meaning of life does not mean that we have a religious belief in that we believe the culture and morality that it imputes transcends us above all others (dogma). Conceit and dogma are properties of delusion and a malignant mentality. Hence being self-actualised is not some false sense of superiority.

So what really is it – perhaps it is more like a state of Buddhist Nirvana in that we have reached a point of equanimity and wisdom where concepts of ego, life and material wealth are seen as unimportant and impermanent, and the loss of which does not precipitate any fear or suffering.

"Those who can sit in equanimity and who are undisturbed by the ever present flow of desires and disappointments and who do no harm to others and have transcended their own minds, they achieve spiritual peace and as such are very special indeed as are those who have taken this path but still strive to achieve it as their end." – 'Theoleptic spirituality'

A self-actualised condition is therefore more of a state of well-being in spiritual, emotional and mental terms in as much that nothing or no-one can disturb this state. It is an advanced state of existence above our basic human needs. You are at a point where you understand how to live life and have reached some point of balance without fear, anger or attachment but remain self-effacing of being in such state. From the religious angle this may be seen as from Hindu Nirvana in feeling a sense of oneness (theoleptic union) with God, whether you are atheist or creationist the analogy is still valid in representing this idea.

Self-actualisation within its definition, as above, would be fine if we were all living a monastic life, for most of us we are not, we live in the real world within which we have obligations, duties to others, bills to pay etc. So in that context does self-actualization have any value? In our experience of life we must achieve the best we can get within the constraints of what we can do from the unique capabilities we have in ourselves, so from this perspective we need to be self-actualised to achieve our full potential, feel purpose and find meaning in our lives through absorbing as much as we can from life's experience, to be focused and undisturbed and living every moment we have and in everything we do we need to give it our best endeavours and through that process we must equip ourselves with a healthy outlook on life being undisturbed by the madness about us.

From putting more in we shall get more out and we are able to live life to the full. The more we achieve (not material acquisition) the more satisfaction we get with life and have greater potential to give to others and contribute to society as a whole.

Getting Back to Nature

In modern literature the archetypal dystopian world is never portrayed with any beauty - one of oceans, blue skies, mountains, rivers, lakes, forests and prairies. 'Dystopia' is our version of hell it must have hard edges, hard materials and hard attitudes, it must elicit a sense of intimidation not that of our wonder, this is the world of overbearing scale, concrete, steel, machines a world of overcrowding and excessive noise where we are all just a number and no more. Just look to the constructivist 'tech-noire' imagery of much science fiction there you will not find anything appealing to the eye or the soul, it must by its own definition be oppressive and disconnected from our natural world.

Our real world is not quite as I describe although it is not completely devoid of such elements out of necessity. Our planet has a very large population and there just wouldn't be room for us to all live in utopic picturesque thatched cottages with a stream and an abundance of trees at the foot of our tranquil gardens and a backdrop of wild flower adorned sweeping hills. Many of us have no option but to live in sprawling cities, great metropolises of concrete that seem to go as far as the eye can see.

Yet we are human we are products of nature we have ability to discern that which is ugly and that which is beautiful that which is dystopian and that which is utopian, we crave for that which is natural we crave for nature. Take us away from nature and we are outside of our natural habitat, however we are adaptable; without the beauty of nature we must fill this void for beauty with that which is made that which is manufactured.

Our aspiration for beauty now must come from manufactured objects that which can cost us dearly – cars, houses, fashion, art, technology – we have in effect compensated for our loss of nature by substitution with what is artificial what is impermanent what is not for free. Perhaps we are evolving into a new species that will come to abhor the natural world. The very idea that we no longer need nature where we can replace it with manufactured distractions is illusory, we can do anything we like but what we do is it at the cost of our own happiness. Do we not crave to look upon a tree rather than a lump of concrete to hear the sound of a river or a bird rather than that of thundering juggernauts and do we not wish to breathe clean air? Do we not wish to feel an individual identity than one of so many such that we just don't count?

But what of the world of concrete are we happy can we ever find happiness. Cities that are well constructed are planned not only for their utilitarian purposes but also along psychological imperatives, they are therefore perhaps less vertical and perhaps more green than they would have otherwise been. In amongst the imperious buildings and arterial highways will be cleverly secreted soft edges – houses with gardens rather than just apartments, tree lined avenues, parks, lakes, riverside walks, cycle paths, areas of wildlife. If the city dweller cannot easily get back to nature then nature must be brought to the city dweller but if this is not possible and this is the life you know then go in search of nature get back to God's creation and just be struck with wonder at it all.

Fear, Uncertainty, Regret and Obsession

Take a moment now to reflect upon how much of our time is dedicated to our thoughts of fear, uncertainty, regret and obsession; the answer will probably indicate that things are not as they should be. Could we not use that largely wasted time productively for better purpose.

Fear - Fear comes about when we have to face something that from our own deduction where we rightly or wrongly perceive can do us harm in some way that we find alarming and for which we do not know how to resolve to a satisfactory end to be able to avoid that harm. Fear may be rational in that someone points a loaded gun at our head and may pull the trigger, hence fear of death, or may be irrational in that if you fail an exam you may fear that your future is in ruins when in reality it isn't. However, fear has its uses apart from knowing when to run from certain rationally deduced danger or if needs be to destroy its capacity to do harm; fear can also be an opportunity to learn, what challenges us what challenges our emotions may present an opportunity to conquer our fear in a process of useful self-development. In essence we can conquer fear by looking at it from a novel perspective in terms of what we can learn from it. To conquer fear is what makes us grow. In conquering fear we can give our confidence something of a boost. If we face the very things that we fear then from the perspective of 'I am learning from this experience' is what can make us to later desire more of what we thought we feared – essentially we get a kick out of the experience. Those who are shy may gain exhilaration at the thought of public speaking those who have a fear of heights may gain exhilaration in climbing mountains. We are not stuck with our fears, our fears mostly can be overcome just look at fear from the perspective of 'what can I learn from this' and then conquer it.

Uncertainty - Nothing is certain therefore everything has an element of uncertainty about it. You could say that the only thing that is certain about certainty is that it is certainly uncertain but where there is uncertainty the face of new opportunity presents itself and indeed what is uncertain may have much greater possibility, possibly beyond our wildest imagination, than that which is certain. Uncertainty is therefore nothing to fear and can be quite the opposite. We often mull over what our future may bring, we base this upon what we know or what we think we know what we have experienced, good and bad from which we predict outcomes based on what we believe to be accurate forecasting. The whole process is reinforced; from how we feel, that may have had influence upon the outcome, 'I thought it would turn out bad and it did', you may have therefore sealed your own fate and from the fact that life doesn't seem to change much although most probably so because you didn't change anything. Given this you might be able to cite various experiences that turned out just as bad as you expected because you had unwittingly put everything in place to bring about such an outcome and thus your negative anticipatory model is validated to be accurate. You use this model again although you have cast certainty, pessimistic certainty, into the outcome. But what if we were to change something do something completely different and do so with a different attitude, in other words not behave as the pessimistic you but behave as the optimistic someone else, someone else who you would like to be. Do this and things will start to change for the good. Out goes the pessimistic old self and in comes the optimistic new you.

Regret – A regret is a mistake that we have elected to take responsibility for where we have feelings of sorrow, self-blame or disappointment in looking back at what we did, hadn't done or could have done but didn't. Regret is not unique to us as an individual and if we look deep enough most of us would have or should have some regret or other. We all have made mistakes but the realisation of regret is a point of enlightenment it gives you that moment when to start changing your life for the better – we have arrived. If you never have any regrets you never get the chance or motivation to change your life for the better to start to live to the full. Once you realise this regret do not dwell on it, what's done is done, you need to move on, you may need to atone for what you have done or at least learn something from it although what you must do above all is learn to not to repeat those regrettable thoughts, actions or inactions. Next time seek to do better. We may regret so much but look to the future, this is where the rest of your life will be and make sure that you use this time wisely and make use of opportune moments when they come.

Obsession – A mind that is obsessed is a mind that is unhealthily fixated, often with hate or desire, upon one thing; it has an idea, or a person, that it cannot let go of; obsession is enthusiasm that has gone right off scale. Every moment is to be absorbed with the subject of our obsession; what we think of, speak of and read of is totally consuming. In this act of total immersion we would have invested so much so that we are too afraid to accept that we may just have wasted so much of our life on what is a false belief – to do so could lead to intolerable regret we must therefore justify our obsession with whatever, rational or irrational, it doesn't matter which. What we have done is that we have imprisoned our mind in what is quite likely to be ridiculous, what is a distortion of reality, what is an illusion, what is either a gross exaggeration of the truth or an utter lie. Obsession is a form of self-hate that we torment ourselves with, we have become our own victim our all-consuming obsession overrides everything else including our ability to think rationally. Truth is to be abandoned in favour of our object and cause of addiction, our source of madness. You may seek out incessant prosaic discussion with others on the subject of your minds imprisonment but you are beyond reason and perhaps for them it would be better to discuss the fact that you are obsessed and why you are so rather than what you are obsessed about. No good can come of obsession. Take away the obsession and what would fill this hole. What would fill this hole is a life that is now free that has potential to succeed not wasted upon something that is plainly wrong, can go nowhere or will lead to ruin. Put your mind elsewhere do something good. Get out of the obsession or stay in a state of perpetual misery it's your choice. If you think back to your investment well it's gone and there is really no point in investing more on what is a lost cause. But if you cannot shake off obsessive (negative) thoughts then find something positive to obsess about to displace that which is negative.

Do Good Don't Do Bad

Do we all know what is good and what is bad; many don't, their view of the world is 'what I want' and 'what I don't want' nothing more and we shall look into the psychiatric make up of such individuals later in greater detail but for the moment let's just explore the good and the bad.

Some may define that what actually is good is 'something that is of benefit to me or to others though is not in detriment to anyone else' (moral form) or 'something that is of benefit to me and mine but that its detriment to others is irrelevant' (amoral form). What we do that is bad we may do deliberately; or through our own ignorance where we didn't know what we were doing, didn't think about what we were doing or didn't have the mental capacity to know what we were doing, what in the legal world is referred to as subjective or objective recklessness.

The action I have just taken or words I have spoken did it harm another might it have harmed another is this something we remind ourselves of? If you advocate doing bad then don't be surprised that what you give out you will be getting back in some form or other, you should in effect expect retaliation. Spouting hate and bile won't make you feel good you might convince yourself that to spout even more will make you feel better - it won't. Whatever you do that is bad be prepared that you will get the same back.

The consequence of being bad is that you isolate yourself from that which is good, at the very least anyone who is genuinely decent won't want to know you, you will become 'persona non grata' to be excluded out of sensible choice. If you need to feel part of something then be part of something that does good don't attach yourself to others who are bad in the hope that at least you have friends, such people will lead you to your eventual ruin.

Imagine a world where everyone, without exception was just pleasant to each other; kind words, truth, good manners and gratitude do not cost anything. Make it your objective that when anyone walks away from you that they feel better about life than when they walked towards you. If we were all like this our world would open up to new possibilities – just imagine what that world would be like.

Dealing with Conflict

An insult delivered from a fool is devoid of any rationality, substance or objective reasoning, it means nothing, and it should mean nothing to you; something that means nothing cannot reach your feelings, to let it do so would be irrational.

If someone delights in making your life a misery, are very easily brought to anger or who are offensive it is they who have the problem not you. Don't let anything or anyone eat at you as they are not worth it. Always keep good manners, do not offend or easily take offence. Stay above it and keep cool. If you encounter this then look for a productive approach, think of yourself as a counsellor rather than a victim, try to find out why they are as they are, what is their persona, what outcome is it that they seek and how do they connect what they seek to how they are behaving i.e. how do they see that their behaviour can bring about what they seek.

If at all possible do not resort to anger, even when you feel it welling up inside, but don't suppress your feeling either as this can make you ill as sometimes we have to let off steam and show others when enough is enough, patience can only be stretched so far and there is only so much anyone can take. But even anger should be delivered with intelligence for a good outcome. If someone insults you don't forget to not 'give a shit' about it – the person doing the insulting is often someone with a problem.

"If you can keep your head when all about you are losing theirs and blaming it on you" – From the poem 'If' by Rudyard Kipling (Poet, England 19th/20th century)

And again don't forget to have the desire for anyone that you encounter to feel better about life after they met you. Good attitudes will be passed on and will grow in our societies and will become part of our human culture. Whatever life throws at you see it as a useful learning experience. Never think, why is this happening to me? Do not look back with regrets just learn and move on.

Inactivity the Psychological Killer - Aspire To Be Better and Make Good Use of Your Time

"Those who are philosophically astute, who possess humility, who are dignified, who seek the truth, who are free from anger, who are untroubled by that which is unpleasant, who are undisturbed from insults, who do not know envy, who have conquered fear, who do not value material pleasures, who are measured in their response, who have self-discipline, who are practitioners of a steady mind, who can assuage loss and loneliness through being mindful, who are devoted to becoming a better person are liberated and have already transcended the self, such a person is a higher being." – 'Theoleptic spirituality'

It is a sign of cultivation to seek to improve what we are. Acquiring a skill outside of work that is socially engaging and good for our health provides huge benefits of well-being. Always keep occupied with something constructive and good, even if that's doing nothing at least do it well, do not spend time ruminating on that or those who are destructive or that which you can never solve.

We are intelligent animals ergo we need intelligent stimulation; without meaningful purpose and constructive use of our time, boredom or worse will ensue. Lying in bed thinking what I am going to do today can result in doing nothing so get ones arse up and make a decision and go and do it, don't mull over it too much just go and do it. Better to have at least done something that might be fruitless, although that could also be fruitful, rather than doing nothing. Be open to ideas and new ways of thinking, take every opportunity to learn but never obsess on anything, as a mind obsessed on anything is incapable of clear rational thought and this can lead us to madness. Have time for everyone and take an interest in everything you encounter.

"If you can fill every minute with sixty seconds worth of distant run" – From the poem 'If' by Rudyard Kipling (Poet, England 19th/20th century)

Don't overdo it - mental work may not necessarily be the cause of our tiredness, tiredness of the mind is largely through mental stress although tiredness of the body is inevitable from too much physical effort. Tiredness is in detriment to our efficiency so take regular breaks to feel restored. Just don't try to do too much.

The Mode of Never Giving Up, Ever (nothing is ever pointless and if you think negative then you <u>will</u> fail)

If we are faced with continued, even relentless, failure we are inclined at some point to 'throw in the towel' (to quit) and there would seem no point in investing any more effort (as we say *"there is no point in flogging a dead horse"*) and there is logic to this, but if this happens too often we might at some point conclude that there is no point in investing any effort in anything, that nothing will ever work, this is the point where we have given up as in seriously given up on life, the result being that we lose all motivation and we end up not doing anything.

All things need time and at some point the dice will fall in your favour and the lower your chances of what you aspire to the more you will need to throw the dice. Throwing the dice less or not throwing the dice at all will not do. When things aren't working your way this is not the time to give up but to instead step up and keep on, so never give up and at some point your dice will hit a double six, just be patient, be positive and be diligent in your quest.

Finding Who You Are

We can all be dissatisfied with what we are - there is always someone else who you might prefer to be who has what you desire but that you haven't got. We can obsess on this but this will destroy our chances of living the life that we have to the best it has to offer. This pitch is a state of self-destruction. After all of our efforts we cannot lament forever of where we have arrived. We might alternatively imagine that we are something that we are not what we might call 'building castles in the air'; we can put up a false self-pretence to impress or to gain what we wrongly believe will be acceptance and in doing so we have to tread with agonising and exhausting caution around this spun fake image. We are substituting what we are with trappings of that which does not exist.

Where does that leave us? If we cannot be honest about what we are and not ashamed of it in any way then we can never be at ease in our life. This thought is perhaps an allusion to the thinking of the psychiatrist R.D.Laing who viewed that our inner stresses (and progression to something of greater concern) were subject to the inner conflict between what we really are and what we project - in effect the collision between our authentic persona and that of our false persona.

We don't need to pretend anything we need to be ourselves and to get people to like us for what is our genuine self. If you have to put on a false front to find acceptance with certain others then it brings into question just how genuine those certain others are. Do we want to live in a world that is false and ingratiating or one where others value you for what you are as a person – which one is preferable? Just be you and it doesn't matter if you are rejected by those who can't see you for what you are – who are they anyway? Always remember that there is no need to stand on ceremony just be yourself be who you really are don't try to project a false image that which you are not. You may need and want to change what you are from within and you may need to acquire or refine your skills to communicate with others but this is a world away from projecting a false you, one that you can never be at ease with.

Adopting a 'Hang Loose' 'Crocodile Dundee' Type Philosophy (be joyful and you will know life)

In the world of the crab lives a most appalling parasitic organism called 'Sacculina'. Sacculina, a slug like organism, burrows into the crabs body and then bit by bit it feeds and then spreads its developing tentacles throughout its victim, the crab remains alive during this ghastly process. So engulfed is the crab that it falls under the control of this disgusting organism.

Our world is much the same in terms of our hang ups, we all do it, yes all of us; perhaps we think too seriously about what we should not and that includes ourselves (those who seek to bring politics into everything should listen here), we regret too much about things that we cannot change and perhaps that we were never fully responsible for, we worry too much about what may not happen or what we might want to happen, we obsess about being successful or about not being a failure, we obsess about what success or failure we already have, we worry about what others might think of us, perhaps we obsess on what we do or what we are.

All of these thoughts are necessary for our survival and our function but we need to keep them in proportion, out of proportion and we may reclassify these thoughts as parasitic, thoughts that pervade our very existence, wake up in the morning and there they are again heavy, all too present and eating away at our life. We are not living life we are dying from within our own soul.

Is it perhaps that our mind sits upon a substrate of the serious, negative, morbid, inward looking, ever searching and even conceited attachment to ourselves (to the 'I') all of which partially relates to what R.D.Laing described as 'ontological insecurity'; the insecurity or discomfort we experience of our very being our very existence, thus undermining our positivity, our hopes and our optimism for our future and for which we most strenuously, even obsessively, seek to preserve our security, precipitating aversion to any risk, afraid to make a mistake or to fail, but at the cost of experiencing the wonder and possibilities of our lives.

Perhaps many of us wish that we could remove this parasite but it is never easy it may be just too entrenched for psychology or philosophy to reach; it is buried deep within and it is not so easy to cast off what destroys our life in the way how we think but at least we should draw some conclusions about how we think, perhaps we should just loosen up, take the brakes off, perhaps we should just take life a lot less seriously. The solution may just be as simple as that. Just imagine having just one year to live what would you do, how would you think, would you have regrets about how you had conducted your life, what you had done or not done, did you even live or were you just waiting for death?

We may not always be able to systematically overcome these things, albeit we may try damned hard to do so and we may believe that a solution may only come about by dogged effort but we are able to open up to just being joyful and this alone can be a cure to our ills. There really are times where we can solve our problems without even trying and there are times when we should let life to just come to us.

Don't ever take anyone or anything and most importantly yourself too seriously. Hang loose have fun and just enjoy life or remain imprisoned within the self. Perhaps we should analyse less and live more and see what happens.

And if our life has reached a point beyond retrieval for which all solution explored by us and any other cannot solve then perhaps this is the time to adopt total immersion into the 'hang loose' philosophy after all what do you have to lose. With all lost there is no point in getting hung up just chill out, go with the flow, perhaps stop resisting and fighting that which is inevitable, let's just say 'f***' to it all and seek to enjoy life for what it is and there are many reasons that life can be enjoyed when you may imagine that all is lost. Taking an ostensibly irrational path can sometimes be the rational thing to do.

When we have lost everything perhaps this is an opportunity to find a new way to live one that may bring something quite amazing. On reflection the life that you had had may not have been so wonderful and perhaps something greater can then be realised, who knows. But let's not forget that whatever you do you must make sure that you do not bring any harm upon others.

Chapter 7

ESSENTIAL PSYCHIATRY THAT WE ALL SHOULD KNOW

(The characterisation of pathological personalities)

Being endowed with a personality that is by some means corrosively pathological and that may often be completely unacceptable to the well-being of others is also damaging to the self. Possessing such characteristics is in no way beneficial to the individual but instead thwarts the potential of what the individual life could be. If you damage other's lives you also damage your own.

Unless you can secrete yourself by choice, or be marooned, i.e. not by choice, on an island devoid of any human life, and despite the loss of human contact can still maintain your sanity, it is very unlikely indeed that you will walk through life and never encounter an individual who will not cause you problems of some form or other, not just from the perspective of just stealing your wallet, or worse, but through actions that cause you mental anguish as a result of what they are, not through mistakes they have made, as we all do, but through what they are or through what is their intent or motivation. For all around we have madness.

Some individuals are unfortunate in that they suffer mental illnesses that to them can be an existence of hell and these we should always show compassion and be willing to help, but some are of a nature that in various manifestations they are at the centre of the world in that it is a 'me-me' attitude and to them the feelings or well-being of others is unimportant. What you may perceive to be your perfect partner, unbeknown to you, could be pathologically self-centred and may be your worst nightmare even though they may present a normal appearance. Your perceived perfect partner may not exactly be perfect in any stretch of the imagination. In reality what they may be is like a coiled venomous snake contained within a cage, but at the right moment for them, but not for you, and that cage will open, this is inevitable.

To survive life we must therefore understand the nature of others; we have to anticipate threats so we have to be able to discern what sometimes can be most difficult to discern. Those who may appear nice may be anything but. The better informed we are the better we can get ahead of the game and avoid those who will inevitably bring us trouble. This being said, we need to be careful that we don't run away with the idea that we are able to diagnose mental illness just from reading this chapter, we are not psychiatrists, we have not spent years studying the human mind, we only seek to have at least some awareness for our own survival nothing more. However, under the eye of the psychiatrist the psychiatric patient may, wittingly or unwittingly, feign an air-brushed image of themselves one which will slip immediately as they leave the clinical setting, so perhaps us non-psychiatrists have an advantage in that we get to see the real them without any adulteration.

What we would describe as the pathological personality, specifically herein what are mostly technically classified as 'cluster 'B' type personalities', is very relevant through various chapters to follow so we must take some time out and study this issue as a prelude of what is to come.

(Contemporary) Asylum Earth

We are all mad but what type of mad are we. Is it at all possible to ever certify anyone as being sane? We may for example reside on a scale of being too sensitive or perhaps just too detached but at what point are we in the right place. Where we need to be should not be set in stone and so needs to move in accordance with what our circumstances demand and this is perhaps a lot closer to the truth.

If you were on a battlefield and the enemy is about to attack then reason may tell you that to kill is madness and ordinarily your reasoning would be correct but if you follow this fundamental rule of reason, and therefore we presume sanity, then this will drastically limit your chances of survival – as they say in the army *"kill or be killed"* or *"if you don't kill him he will kill you"*. You might delude yourself into thinking that I could always try to reason with this enemy but in doing so we may have despatched reality in favour of reason and so have departed from sanity. On this basis what we might like to define as sanity based upon pure reasoning skills is therefore not entirely sane.

Alarmingly the logical conclusion would then suggest that reason is not necessarily reality and therefore not cognisant with the truth. We may believe that in following reason we are following the truth but we may just be following nothing more than our delusions.

In our modern society we are also seeing that what was universally accepted as the truth is now being redefined, we are forging a world of delusion. Something that we could define with absolute certainty, i.e. what it is, can now be redefined as what it believes, must be believed or desires itself to be i.e. something that it is not. This is well illustrated in the 1835 Russian novel 'A Diary of a Madmen and Other Stories' by Nikolai Gogol in which the main character has the delusion that he is the heir to the Spanish throne only to end up in a lunatic asylum.

However, because this is recognized as new and therefore modern thinking in that what something is it isn't then we must conclude that this thinking cannot be any other than 'progressive,' a 'new enlightenment', and progressive thinking must always be adopted without question by the 'progressive' political establishment, it may also win a few more votes at the ballot box this being self-evident from the palpable enthusiasm of the political 'elite'. Worryingly this delusion is infusing through all facets of our society of what we do and what we think, we must live in an imaginary world that is not real.

In our 'modern' world Gogol's character would not be seen to be ill and therefore in need of help but rather that anyone who didn't agree with him would be the ones who would be seen to be ill. It's as if we all have to join in on the delusion. Madness is now the new sanity. Where we should resolve such anomalies we are instead encouraging them, this is the stuff of politics going crazy. What were drawn up as and are irrefutable facts and established linguistics, rules where we know what something is through logical evidence, are now being recast such that we no longer have any idea about anything.

No longer can we independently state what something is using knowledge and wisdom we now have to ask what it believes itself to be or what others might believe it to be, not what it is, this being self-evident in the world of politics. Junk is now art reason is now control a compliment now an insult!!! What's next? It is my view that anyone can think what they like it is their inalienable right to do so and if it makes them feel better about themselves or what they believe then why not, but just don't expect others to join in since it is also their inalienable right to think as they wish to too. If you are ever to think of something that does not fit with what is deemed 'progressive' thinking, albeit often by a large minority of advocates, then you are guilty of a thought crime, if you dare challenge it or you may have rational fear of it then you are guilty of hating it which of course is way off the truth.

In effect free thought is to be forbidden, totalitarianism is back on the agenda. I might like to think of myself as a teddy-bear, that the moon is made of cheese and that Stalin's murder of millions never happened but there is no hatred nor is there any stupidity in anyone suggesting that these things are just not true. All of this will make sense when we later discuss war, politics and particularly truth.

What is 'Illness of the Mind'?

When any of us think of what is madness our mind will often home in on images of the foreboding Victorian asylum with iron barred windows, turreted towers, high walls and an entrance gate that would look as if it were forged in the fires of hell that when closes may never re-open, for those that enter may never leave, a building of overbearing scale with endlessly long corridors, the image being worthy of any gothic horror story. The very thought of such places evokes visceral fear and misery in us all. Within are unfortunate souls who are committed, abandoned, beyond all help, who look vacantly through eyes that convey deep sadness, who wail or just sit in silence, they are beyond reach of communication, their thoughts, for the main, are largely confined to disorder and wild hallucination, reality cannot reach them, there is in some, manifestations of uncontrollable and dangerous manic behaviour, a danger to themselves as well as to others, their minds may have fallen into the deepest darkest abyss of depression, their madness equally racks their bodies as it does their mind.

The suffering is immeasurable, and is often all consuming, and is made no less worse through the 'treatments' of using restraints, straightjackets, manacles and chains, of confining the patient to a cell no better than the worst nightmare of any prison, to ice baths and un-anesthetized electric convulsion therapy, to crude, experimental and spurious brain surgery to powerful drugs that may often remove what remains of the person within.

Such individuals would often be labelled with frightening conditions such as schizophrenia (dementia praecox), paranoid disorders or delusional psychosis that would instil more fear at that time than cholera, tuberculosis or cancer, you might die of these physical ailments but at least your soul would remain intact as some may have imagined.

It is very true that these conditions of the mind existed then and they still exist now and it is also very true that the asylums of the distant and not so distant past were as I have described. It is also very possible that life then being so unimaginably harsh; that the ever present death, disease, war, urbanized poverty, grim living conditions, lack of education and lack of support for those who had fallen out of society, who were alone, who were abused, who were traumatised, without employment and without anyone to care for them may be what had sent them mad, in effect the bridge could no longer take the load and so collapses.

The reality today is far from this description and indeed not all of the past treatment of the 'insane' was as brutal as we might imagine as certain very enlightened philanthropic organisations did try to help and would use methods much as we would today, recognizing that the 'insane' possibly needed no more than a good home, a good environment away from insanitary cities, kindness and people to show a genuine interest in them. Insanity or madness was in effect recognised as an illness that required humanity, care and administering of effective treatment.

If you encounter those who suffer such, just be mindful of these words, as they are deserving of our compassion not of any revulsion or condemnation but you must remain cautious of those where benevolence could place you in a position of danger. Those afflicted with mental suffering are different to most of us only because it is just where their life has brought them, a life of misfortune in some capacity, a life that could take you to the same place, they are driven to where they are through no fault of their own – just remember this. Could it be that mental illness is mostly nothing more than a natural reaction to our circumstances, much as blood clotting agents that get to work when we bleed, where if we did not break down and disconnect from what is real our suffering may perhaps become immeasurably worse or perhaps more permanently damaging in many instances.

However, what is described has very little to do with the intent of this chapter as what is to come is a lot less innocuous, a lot more sinister, and a lot more toxic but worse still is that it is amongst us, it is silent and goes unnoticed until it strikes. This you may feel is hyperbole, why do I even need to know this, chances are it will never effect my life, an incorrect assumption, and I hope you are right but if you are unlucky enough to meet such characters you may not know it until it is too late, until they have ruined your life and I don't want you to fall into that statistic.

This all being said; in a society where we have a better more affluent life, and if not affluent at least in some respects a lot more supportive more comfortable more tolerable, might we see less such need of the psychiatric profession, will we all live happier, stable lives – I think sadly no. As our societal problems of the past abate and our modern living standards take hold we become less inured and without a grounded sense of ourselves we may become more centred upon the self.

The psychiatric conditions of the past may largely, though not entirely, be consigned to history but nature seems to abhor a vacuum and new conditions will emerge. What in the past was inflicted externally upon the self by a harsh life and lack of basic needs is being replaced by what is being inflicted internally by the self through a lack of what we insatiably desire what we feel we must have. We are now in an age where we have become too obsessed with ourselves we demand too much and we expect too much and this cannot be good for our mental well-being.

Psychopath – 'The Monster in the Shadows'

I present a charming, affable, affectionate and reasonable appearance, but I am none of these things, do not be fooled by my smile or my quietly spoken voice, I have impeccable manners, I appear as what you would call normal but I am far from it, very far from it, I am devoid of empathy, I am indifferent to your suffering, I am deceitful, I am irresponsible and reckless, I wear a false mask of respectability for my own advantage, my contrived but false good-nature is for the sole purpose to gain your trust with the aim to manipulate and use you for my own ends, you may even trust me above all others but I am the last person you should trust, I am constantly scheming and playing games, I have no rules only my rules to take what I want and do what I want and to whom I want and I will do it without conscience or remorse and I will do it with impunity, I have no sense of right or wrong, what I want is all that matters, my mind is twisted such that I can easily corrupt the truth to find ways to justify my disgusting actions, I am arrogant, pathologically self-deluded and I look upon all others as stupid though I may hide this well, I am inclined to be easily irritated or offended and I can become aggressive, very aggressive, I am depraved, I am a practitioner of sadism, I can inflict misery, torture and death, I find death fascinating as my desire is to control everything including you and death to me is the ultimate control that one human can inflict upon another, I get easily bored and seek stimulus or significant moments to keep me away from my boredom, I will kill just for being inconvenienced, your life is of no importance, you are just an object to me nothing more, if I can't kill you I must at least gain your submission, I am dangerous beyond belief though no-one knows what I am because I am beyond detection or suspicion, you may alert others to what you suspect of me but no-one will believe you for I am too clever to reveal what I am – I am psychopath.

What is depicted here is a chilling interpretation of the somewhat euphemistically named 'antisocial personality disorder' as is referred to (reference 301.7) in the de-facto benchmark reference book of psychiatry, the 'Diagnostic and Statistical Manual' of the American psychiatric association, otherwise known universally to those who are familiar with this publication as DSM-V i.e. version 5 at the time of writing this book. However, there are other types or combination of types of esoteric aberrations of the mind that in themselves may present suggestion of psychopathy but that are not psychopathic per se, at worst they may lead to a desire to control or to kill but they are not psychopathic in origin.

From this graphic description we might conclude that such deranged individuals are just a few; they are the likes of Heinrich Himmler (chief of German SS in World War 2), Lavrenti Beria (chief of Stalin's secret police), 'Jack the Ripper' (an epithet, identity of whom has never been established) famous for the gruesome Whitechapel (district of the east end of London) murders of 1888, John George Haigh, an epitome of charm and refined manners, (who after killing his victim would consume their blood and then dissolve the body in acid to remove the evidence) and a whole host of other sick murderers and political psychopaths. The reality is that what we may classify as a psychopathic personality is more prevalent than what we might imagine.

Typical of a murderer is that when they kill they do so for financial or sexual reasons and with the very naïve notion that they can avoid capture, which invariably they can't. In the psychopath the primary purpose of murder is from a desire to experience some peculiar exhilaration of control or validation of assumed power over others where one can only presume that there must be some concomitant and distinct dimension of inadequacy. In the more aberrant mind what they do must be performed as some form of statement something so depraved that the inadequate individual can gain attention, albeit with notoriety; infamy morphs into fame and into the recognition that they desire and feel that they deserve. However, not all psychopaths are murderers and not all murderers are psychopaths; they often place themselves in respectable positions in society, even in politics, at work and even in religion.

The infamous 'Jack the Ripper' of 19th century Victorian London would butcher the victim in some purposeful and semi-frenzied manner. The last poor victim was essentially dissected fortunately it is believed post-mortem, with her bowels and organs deliberately and carefully placed as a display around the scene of the murder. Murder was not so much instrumental, as murder often is, here murder is expressive. In the case of 'Jack the Ripper' we are entering another dimension of the psychopathic mind; the disease in the mind is more progressed, for want of a better word. What was it that he was doing and what was he thinking, this is difficult to say if you do not share the same frame of mind.

With introspection within ourselves we cannot reach such levels of pathology to fathom out what could have been going on inside such a twisted mind, we can only guess. The fact that he had to display such depravity with such intensity and deliberate purpose as if this were some work of art, aberrant as it is, might suggest that he was saying *"look at what I can do what power I have"* would this not seem to indicate inadequacy and is this not something we see in some murderer's today albeit perhaps on a lesser scale. It certainly would have been most interesting to have the opportunity to have spoken to this monster to find out just why he did what he did; knowing this and we could at least add another missing piece to the psychiatric jigsaw puzzle.

However, the more such characters are a loser the more inadequate they feel and so the greater they feel compelled to show off their 'craft' and the more shocking and depraved they must serve it up. It is as if the very act of doing something so disgusting to another human being, to essentially not just kill but to torture, to destroy and to mutilate, is some attempt to assuage their inadequacy. Such an act can make the inadequate mind feel powerful albeit they are essentially pathetic and are essentially non-entities, in truth none of them would amount to much they are invariably worthless and failed human beings. In our world they are incapable of being constructive so they must take the opposite path and that is to destroy. In their depraved attempt to prove self-worth and through the extent of their depravity they essentially reveal by themselves greater evidence of their inadequacy.

But could the disturbance of the psychopathic mind be even more than this in that the gross suffering they meter out to their victims is pathologically entwined with a visceral hatred of society; what they had craved in life, and often wrongly believe to have deserved and never got was without any perceived self-responsibility in effect no acceptance that their fate is by their own hand, their own lack of effort or faulty path that they had chosen in their life or just through bad luck. They consequently have bitter hatred of life and will lay the blame on innocent others or by evil others have had their gullible mind convinced that others are to blame. The idea that they may be to blame for their own demise and misery is not within their cognitive range, they don't want it to be – of course, to them it's always someone else's fault.

In the hands of the feckless, who cannot muster the self-motivation or effort to constructive activity and who possess buckets of arrogance, then frustration can lead to hate and hate can lead to a desire to destroy. Their inadequacy prevents them from admitting their actions are for this reason, this would after all expose their inadequacy or their recognition of a failed life, so they will often make up some fake and/or exaggerated excuse that they must find some bogus argument to justify what they have done. For example it might be something like; *"well I stabbed him because of the way that he looked at me"* which of course the victim didn't or *"I stabbed him because he tried to stop me from beating my wife"* which of course the victim was only trying to protect an innocent and thus to prevent an act of evil.

Fortunately, the graphic description above is representative of only the extreme end of the psychopathic type as of the 1% who may possess this condition are mostly unlikely to stalk dark alleys at night seeking out victims to murder in some grotesque fashion but they will nevertheless be in our lives. Perhaps many have the volume turned down in respect of these aforementioned attributes but nevertheless those attributes are still there, there is still a lack of any moral intelligence and such persons are corrosive upon others in relationships, at work, in politics and with whom they may come into contact with at the bus stop.

You may have even just faint suspicions of what someone may be, albeit without any tangible evidence and particularly so where their true self is well hidden, this being not just a phenomenon of the psychopath alone, but at least you will have some idea of how they think and at some point their cloak will drop or you will see where personality seems to be fake, you will see signs or a pattern of behaviour that might confirm what they really are so stay alert. Never jump to a conclusion that because someone appears nice that they necessarily are nice, you need to know them very well and you need to be adept at knowing how these individuals operate. Remember that what a psychopath can't control or succeed with it might want to destroy.

In relationships the psychopath is a disaster in that other than the obvious they cannot reciprocate affection or care for another soul. Because they have this property of desiring control and an ability to exercise control over others they are often wrongly perceived to have leadership skills and so where they seek out promotion they might often get it. The reality is, is that they are often quite incompetent, ineffective, lazy and highly unsuccessful, they might be the thug, the bully or even the recalcitrant, their ability is to deceive others into perceiving there is a capability where there is none, leadership skill where there is pathological authoritarian control (if I can't control myself then I must control others) and affability where there is manipulation. So be on guard and if you happen to know of one have nothing to do with them or at least as little to do with them as you can.

Narcissistic Personality Disorder (NPD) – 'The Other Monster in the Shadows'

Mention this condition to anyone and they may immediately think of Narcissus the character of Greek mythology who fell in love with his own reflection and from that point on could not look away. We might just also imagine someone who is slightly intoxicated in self-admiration for their self-perceived intelligence, for what skills they may have or for their 'elevated' position in society. We may describe such people as vain, conceited, as being aloof, as projecting superiority but would we ever think of them as having a psychiatric condition. This is where the misconception lies as such people you may describe as narcissistic, and maybe they are a big headed pain in the arse with a somewhat unnatural self-perception, but they are not necessarily afflicted with a clinical level narcissistic personality disorder albeit that their narcissistic attributes are definite properties of those with NPD.

Those with NPD, just like those who are just narcissistic, will admire themselves with the tell-tale signs for example of having to be photographed at every opportunity, of constantly being glued to their favourite instrument, the mirror, of having to be admired by others or perhaps spending just far too much time in the fitting room, but this is where narcissism ends and NPD begins for NPD is all this but it is also a lot more and it's the lot more bit that is not so innocuous. What may start out to be or appear to be innocuous descends into something quite seriously toxic, in other words the measure of narcissism goes off the scale.

NPD is a distinct psychiatric disorder (DSM-V reference 301.81) where the love of the self has gone into overdrive, where self-admiration has extended to new limits of an assumption of being the ultimate object to be admired to be envied but the one who must be admired the one who demands to be admired, the one who is special and superior above all others. Indeed so is their preoccupation with what they imagine themselves to be that they feel deserving of attention to the exclusion of all others. If it so happens that you are the focal point of their nigh on tyrannical demand for attention then this must be so to the complete and irrevocable exclusion of all others, you must be the devotee to your sole object of devotion i.e. them. If they do not receive the attention that they feel they deserve and that they demand then this undermines their feeling of superiority.

Tyrannical demand and absolute control are two sides of the same coin. The psychopath seeks control as some form of destructive play with another's feelings or well-being whereas those afflicted with NPD seek control in order to acquire unnatural extremes of devotion from another. Indeed in the narcissistic world the need for control, with purpose to gain devotion, is perhaps greater than any other need even if it puts those needs under threat.

Associated with NPD will be an overbearing arrogance, one for which they will not associate with or will hold utter contempt of others who they perceive to be inferior to them, that mostly being pretty much everyone and they will often delight in describing such others in disparaging terms such as 'stupid' or 'idiot'. Essentially you must possess some form of prowess or prestige to get anywhere near their acceptance into their select social circle but here is the rub; in that being self-perceived as the ultimate in superiority then they will feel threatened by those who they perceive as a being of greater superiority i.e. with NPD it is difficult to get the inferiority/superiority balance about right.

Get close to NPD and you are in for a rough ride, as at first, and just like the psychopath, they may seem, most convincingly the most wonderful person you have ever met, indeed what you have met you may think is too good to be true which of course it is too good to be true. Along the way, over time and as you get closer, if you are their object of their demand for devotion you will start to sense all is not well, there will be signs, things that may be small but of significance such as demands and complaints that start to come in thicker and faster or the signs may be subliminal where your alarms are starting to ring faintly. You ignore all of this as you have been beguiled by what you believe them to be, which of course they are not. If you are not an object of their demand for devotion then you will probably never know what they really are for what is their true pathological self is cloaked with extreme skill.

Once you have been hooked and reeled in like some helpless fish on a line, and what they would see as irrevocably so, then this is when they strike as they will demand, with confidence, an exclusive devotion to them and to them only. What and who else is important to you is blocking their exclusive demands and to prove true devotion to them you are obliged to abandon all of what and who are important to you. If devotion is to be measured as being true then it must be so to complete exclusion of everything else and everyone else without exception. The feelings you have for others are not important they must be consigned to history as anyone else will be recognized as a threat. If you do not succumb to this process this is when hate, pathological hate, suddenly switches on not just to you but also to your 'inconvenient' associates, those who have access to you become objects of their hate.

However, in seeing that they are failing to arrest the interest and feelings you have towards others then their craving for your attention may force them to 'gas-light' in that they will try to turn the table on you - it is now your behaviour, not theirs, that is at fault, that it is you not them who has a psychological problem or they may back-peddle in that they will attempt to cajole you with affection to manipulate and recover a situation that is falling apart, but be prepared for an attack of 'déjà vu' because any change in them will be short lived. It would not be wise to let them charm their way back into your affections.

When they realize that the game is up then their instability goes off the scale, their failure to secure what is an abnormal demand for attention will turn into a campaign of destruction, destruction that is of you. Along the way you will doubt yourself because you will still hold onto perceptions of what you thought they were i.e. from what was perceived before everything turned sour and they will do everything they can to undermine your ability to doubt them but also to lead you down a path to instead doubt yourself.

If you smell something very bad in an association or relationship then get out of it, save yourself. It will be them who will suffer and unlike the psychopath, with whom they share similar traits, they do have feelings, but so what if they do as they would have destroyed you without any care and any conscience because they only really care for one thing and that is themselves. Welcome to the world of the narcissistic personality disorder.

Oppositional Defiance Disorder – 'The Agitator with a Big Mouth'

Naughty children are known for throwing tantrums, they get easily annoyed and they easily cause annoyance and they do so to gain attention or to get their own way and if not firmly addressed this could lead to later social impairments, delinquency (petty crime) and then onto who knows what. It is common amongst children since what is deemed as good behaviour is something that has to be learnt it isn't developed in the womb, we are not born with social protocol pre-programmed. You might imagine that this is therefore a subject of child development and psychology and that is where it should stay.

We would hope that at some point as adults, and that defines us as adults, that we would have moved on and that we would have learnt that which is good and that which is bad in how we and others behave. Not only is this not always so but oddly enough it can be a regressive development in adults who may never have exhibited such behaviour in their childhood.

If we go back to its definition then at some point, most probably, in our early adult life there must have been a trigger where we have not got our own way. It could be that this was precipitated from our own lack of self-development where our ambitions were thwarted by our own inability or lack of effort to function as a socially and work motivated adult and so we may not have found a healthy purpose in our lives. Or perhaps like the child we have an exaggerated sense of our own entitlement, without the will to invest effort, which if thwarted leads to envy, pathological jealousy and then to seething anger. At this point we still have the rational option that is to internalise what has gone wrong, recognise that the blame lies with us and then step on to changing our lives for the better. Alternatively we can externalise our woes and so blame others for what has gone wrong and for what are actually our own mistakes. The ensuing manufactured anger also gives some sense of compensation for the bogus injustices that we can't drop.

Unprepared to own up to our own fault we must then invent ways to justify our anger with reasons that are external to ourselves, reasons that are not there. If reasons are not there, where shall we find them? - the only option is to manufacture reasons for our anger through intentionally perceiving what is nothing as being intentionally hostile a typical example being you are in the pub minding your own business and someone who you don't know walks over and says something like *"were you looking at me"*, they know you weren't but they need to find an excuse to assault you or at least make you feel uncomfortable for their own sick amusement.

Now the anger is out of the bag so how do we deploy it and do so without falling fowl of the rule of law. We can't go out and smash things so what can we do within the rule of law. What can we do indeed? Well what we can do is relentlessly annoy people, we can set out to disturb the peace, we can set out to agitate, we can argue a point that twists logic and takes delusion right off of the edge of the map, we can make veiled threats we can refuse to follow the rules, written or otherwise, upon which an orderly society functions, we may even try to enforce our rules upon others – rules not designed for good purpose but to irritate and we do all of this with either an indignant look or one of smug satisfaction just to embellish the irritating effect even further. One wonders if these types ever listen to themselves.

Perhaps we can just go around being offensive or rude but whatever it is we need to find what annoys others we need to find the touch paper that can ignite annoyance in others but knowing that they are unable to strike back and are unlikely to do so. Furthermore, unlike say for example NPD, it is often not practiced as a solitary activity; to maximise the agitation, the annoyance and so disturbance of the peace then the rule is 'strength in numbers' and if you can find a cause or a gang with a predilection for doing so all the better. However, be careful what you seek because you can keep prodding others with a stick and they do nothing but at some point they might just get ugly and I mean very ugly and you might just regret what you have started.

What we are describing here is classic 'Oppositional Defiance Disorder' another psychiatric disorder referenced to in DSM-V (reference 313.81). Let us not forget that this disorder is for the consumption of the child only and is not for grown up adults.

Absorption within the Self - The Onward March of the Histrionic Personality Disorder

If the world is sliding into ever increasing attention seeking then if the immediate consequences appear irrelevant then what of the secondary effects, that which is going to happen, since not all causes have an immediate effect. We do not know where this may take us we are entering the unknown, could it be yet another exotic manifestation of political extreme that may turn out to be catastrophic for us all, yet another problem to have to deal with. Do we know for sure what might happen?

I am what you might call a people watcher and sitting in a London café with my ears flapping, yes I know I shouldn't but I can't help myself, I am listening in on others, though some do have a predilection to draw attention to themselves. Often we can learn a hell of a lot about human nature by just observing others especially when they are unaware of being observed since if they were aware that would contaminate the results of the experiment. I once knew of someone who claimed fame to starting an argument in a group then would discretely retire from the scene, a sort of 'forward facing backward walk', then would observe what would happen as the crowd argued amongst itself – thankfully I am not that devious.

Getting back to the café was my observation of two youngsters possibly around twenty years old. What I observed is not necessarily toxic to others but unwittingly to them it could very well be, and alarmingly is becoming a growing trend and seemingly a trendy trend at that. Could this be a contagious affectation an intermeshed influence amongst the easily impressed? So here we are not talking about something quite in the same vein as the psychopath or NPD as there is essentially no desire to control, well not in totality, or destroy but the need for attention may have consequences for all in particular dire consequences for the practitioner of HPD.

What is observable is an enforced affectation, one which presents itself of emulating child-like speech that for a child might appear enchanting but from an adult idiotic, an immaturity that is delivered with pride, of being impressionistic with, to them, unequivocal though in reality cursory unsupportable opinions, consequently they could also be easily duped and so lack innate defence from those who would take advantage of them, of excessive use of fashionable phrases or irrational ripostes, of being self-absorbed. Their own attention and that of all others is directed towards themselves, where their self-projection is over played such that it would be more appropriate to the stage rather than over a plate of egg and chips, where there is also manifest over-attachment to physical appearance, there is no room in their world for the less beautiful.

Conversation is shallow, subjective, unchallenging and is unchallenged from whom they acquaint, could it be that group dynamics is at work here. There is some sense of all-knowing self-confidence rather than true deep learning and experiential wisdom, they know everything and are the expert on everything. When they look at one another they do so with some theatrical doe eyed innocence and inappropriate intimacy so much so you might easily imagine that they are flirting. Their perceptions of relationships are perhaps exaggerated beyond reality and their emotional range is extreme, but beware that those who exaggerate are also liable to invent.

Such a personality who seeks attention will also seek activities, a movement or often a cause, often a groundless cause, that will gain attention whether or not they agree with the cause or not doesn't matter, and with their superficial view of the world they probably don't know anyway, what matters is that it is a cause that will get attention to themselves. They will even seek out or invent, imagine or make accusations of problems that do not exist or they will exaggerate something that does exist though may be nothing like as serious as they might like to imagine, they will do anything, sometimes with major inconvenience to others, in order to gain attention.

Is this all something quite OK or am I observing something that is not quite right, again I must refer to DSM-V (here being reference 301.50) because all is not right. You may look at these characteristics as belonging to someone who is just immature and perhaps shakily self-confident but these are characteristics of an individual who must be at the centre of all others attention.

Oddly HPD is something of a modern and increasing phenomenon though its cause is unknown and given the more recent prevalence of this is it therefore possible that they may have experienced parental borne over indulgence or a cosseted lifestyle with increasing affluence that precipitates an over confidence ahead of where they are in their character development as well as a belief of being all deserving and all important, in effect inflated self-importance or worth or could it be their way of compensating for an exact opposite upbringing, this is something we are yet to discover. This in itself can turn a healthy individual into a selfish being but one who is all too easily alarmed or damaged when things go wrong as is what happens so much in life. Perhaps we just need to be aware that children can be often afforded too much (over indulgence) or too little (neglect) attention and this may indeed be no good for their later life prospects but where is the line, at what point do we say that is too much or too little – it's never easy knowing what is best when you are a parent.

"You've never lived until you've almost died. For those who have fought for it, life has a flavour the protected shall never know." – Guy de Maupassant (Writer, France 19th century)

Life is not an easy path to walk it is not some imaginary utopia. Life is more rewarding for the fact that it is not that easy, thus all of our challenges presents opportunity to learn, to grow and to mature but the HPD may never have faced such necessary development and so will be less able to cope when things go wrong. In an artificial world where there is little to challenge us then our chance to develop into beings that are able to handle life's challenges, when they do come and they will, would therefore have been thwarted and this is something you can be sure of.

Such premature self-assured confidence and centring of self-importance comes at a high price. What may have been created could be an incipient NPD or, despite the apparent self-confidence, potentially a fragile being, a sort of porcelain doll, who can all too easily collapse into hysteria or suicidal depression over seemingly insignificant life events. What is a minor hiccup or disappointment to us, to them is exaggerated into a catastrophe, they are unable to emotionally adapt, unable to mature and unable to handle life.

To protect themselves from a harsh world, then they would prefer to ignore that which they see as ugly or pretend that it does not exist so much so that anyone who threatens that perspective with what is the reality of truth must also be ugly and so must be reviled. All what they have attached to is, as in all things, impermanent; looks fade, the teeth of failure will come to bite you, relationships fall apart, hopes are shattered, what we are and what we have we will one day lose, confidence without experience collapses when faced with others who have matured and who will cogently question subjective ill thought through thinking. With their suffocating attention seeking and self-indulgence they possibly will become unlikeable and irritating.

What they are; is not built upon firm foundation, what they have is just a phantom they have not become complete and they may face mental issues later in life that could easily destroy them. It is for a fact that the more we are centred upon ourselves the more we are prone to mental illness, if we centre ourselves upon others needs then we may have a chance to a better happier life. The life of the self-absorbed in the end cannot be a happy one. Confidence and sense of self are important for our survival, but excesses can be intoxicating and addictive and eventually can do us harm so beware.

The Sub-Clinical Antisocial Spectrum Disorder – 'Defective Interpersonal Conduct Disorder'

Most of us conduct ourselves in a good manner we know how to interact with others in a constructive way we do not deliberately seek to offend and we are not offensive we have what you might describe as social intelligence. You might imagine through some application of logic that everyone would want to be so that they would want to be liked and that this would motivate the way how they behave but we all know that this is not always the case. Some are so twisted with misery that their idea of solving their problems is not through seeking to be liked but through seeking to be disliked - this being a highly unhealthy state of mind in which to exist it is a state of self-torture by electing to be unpleasant. Do not let such people affect you in any way do not take it personal what they say, you may study them and may even try to show them a better way but don't let yourself become their victim.

If I was paid a '£' for every time I heard someone being referred to as 'an arsehole', or a 'bastard', then I would be a very rich man, but what is the nature of the arsehole, there are many. Perhaps it could be someone who is drowning in their own self-importance, who is smug, who is inconsiderate, who is too ignorant to show any gratitude, someone who complains incessantly or who tediously goes on and on about some imaginary cause or offence they have taken, who is petulant, someone who seems to get some pleasure to agitate or disrupt, who is defiant, confrontational or bad-tempered, who meets reason with insults, who seeks to humiliate, who is tactless, someone who is excessively fastidious, a demanding, pushy authoritarian bully or who is abusive and nasty, who is easily brought to violence or criticism, someone who has a very tenuous connection with the truth, the habitual polemicist (one who has to deliberately disagree with everything), who is bad mannered, ignorant or jealous or who is just a complete pain in the arse – as you can see the list is almost endless and the list highlights much of the spectrum of social unintelligence.

The list goes on and on and I'm sure you could easily add more to this list, you may also recognise those disturbed enough to hone their skills in such poor conduct. Could it be that these behaviours are representations of an inadequacy, a need for power, or are they rooted in a conscious or subconscious embitterment towards life? This being said none of these characteristics fall into what is a specific psychiatric taxonomy. Look in DSM and you will not find a specific disorder for any of these characteristics although you may find these characteristics, or symptoms as such, individually mentioned as being evident within a disorder, they might be a symptom of a disorder but they are not a disorder in their own right.

In absence of any medical classification, but not to be confused with childhood prevalent 'conduct disorder', would this suggest that these behaviours fall into the realm of what is normal since there isn't any defined psychiatric condition than can be established, after all none of us are perfect. However, this being said; where something deviates quite beyond the normal range, whatever that may be, that is clearly unacceptable behaviour and that causes concerning distress or discomfort to others, then what we have here is a problem. We might not be able to deduce a specific ailment but what we can say is that the problem is 'sub-clinical' i.e. in this context it is not a distinct abnormality with a label but neither is it anywhere near normal.

Compulsion to certain personality traits, that may often be declared with levity as just 'having a difficult personality' but that is clearly destructive is not normal, and in absence of any distinct psychiatric condition is exercised under full control of the perpetrator. In other words they know what they are doing, it may be nature or nurture but they still know what they are doing because they have the cognitive skills to identify the distress caused to others, it may even gratify them that they are causing this distress or that they are universally disliked, some will even take pride in that which in itself speaks volumes. They may also believe that in having some relationship with you, in the widest of definitions, is that which gives them a license to behave as such.

Those who have distinct psychiatric conditions are possibly not in full control of their actions and so in some respect might be exonerated for their actions; they have in legal terms what is called 'diminished responsibility'. To those who do not have the excuse of diminished responsibility then their destructive actions are repugnant and so equally they are repugnant. Why do I not have any compassion for such miscreants; well they are what we all have to live with every day and they consciously inflict misery upon others. In effect out lives are worse because of these individuals. If you were to encounter them you would walk away feeling worse than when you met them. Why do they behave the way they do is it some act of delinquent fun, is it that their life is in the toilet and so they must make others feel equally so, is it that they must punish others for the inadequacy they feel or is it some sadistic thirst for power validated by their ability to make others squirm.

What we do know is that you may be very well justified, with a significant level of confidence, in calling this person 'an arsehole' as what they present is not some stretch of peculiarity from the norm but is something quite wrong in the context of a malign aberration, they exhibit what is quite plainly unacceptable behaviour. The 'arsehole' can now be seen in a psychiatric context i.e. the 'sub-clinical antisocial spectrum disorder'. If, and without bias, you don't like someone and possibly others don't either and that they cause great difficulty to others in terms of what has been described then it is very likely that they deserve the label you give them.

"Being of pleasing nature, being open to reason and truth, to defend those who cannot defend themselves, to help the distressed and to act with exemplary conduct are signs of magnificence, impress this upon others and they will then equally pursue this path." – 'Theoleptic spirituality'

This being said not all arseholes are beyond hope, we are all worth saving if it is possible to do so since how was it that they got to this position in the first place. There might still be chance to turn them around to get them see an alternative way of looking at things and relating to others and if there is at least some vestige of reason in that tortured soul you may have some chance. If you can turn them around that is great you have just rescued someone from their own stupidity and from ruining not only other's lives but theirs too, but don't reproach yourself if you have failed to do so as they are lucky that someone even tried, most wouldn't even bother. So before you resort to anger challenge yourself to see if you can make them into something better than what they are if you can do this then you have done something wonderful.

However, if they are completely fixed in their ways i.e. 'the once an arsehole, always an arsehole' hypothesis then don't take anything from them personally as the real victim is themselves not you, although it may not feel that way. You might just be better off identifying their behaviour as a form of self-humiliation, one that if they had any sense would feel embarrassed to reveal to others – I wouldn't want the world to know if I have a sub-clinical antisocial disorder and I would keep it well hidden, in other words I would have consigned such behaviour to the bin.

The Sub-Clinical Antisocial Spectrum Disorder – 'The Morally Deficient'

You are in a supermarket and someone deliberately runs over your foot with a shopping trolley, deliberate evidently so as you know for certain that they know what they have done and also for the fact that an apology is not forthcoming but also for the fact that they then follow up with a tirade of abuse at you even though it is them at fault but it could also be that the distress that they cause they will find of some amusement, what you may describe as 'delinquency' in a more colloquial sense. Or it could be that it was you who accidentally bumped into them and you being a decent person apologised, but for them that won't do as they will always turn what is a trifling incident into a drama.

Such types will knowingly park in disabled parking bays even though not disabled and then get angry if anyone points this out to them. They suspiciously have some kind of pathological immaturity such that they have irrational emotions that furthermore they lack the self-control to hold in. Now it could be that this is rooted in paranoia or a sense of persecution, maybe this person as we say *"has a chip on their shoulder"* an inadequacy but what we are seeing here is a predisposition to conflict on an assumption that only they matter.

A simple definition or common cause for such people is that they essentially lack any consideration for others or they lack any sense of moral obligation to such things as debt, duty, behaviour and truth. They may also be inclined to petty crime such as theft, vandalism, disturbing the peace or making false claims. At work they would be the one who would repeatedly cheat their employer through slacking, malingering or through bad timekeeping but yet not see that they have done anything wrong, they behave with impunity as it were. If they are cheating their company they are also cheating their colleagues, much in the same way as those who cheat on their taxes or commit benefit fraud are cheating the rest of us.

In essence the whole must suffer because of the theft of a few. What matters to them is themselves they do what they like and they take offence if anyone tells them that what they do is unacceptable. Could it also be that not only do they not have any concern for what they have done wrong but that they even lack any capacity of knowing that they have done wrong, because as I said only they matter, their minds cannot reach beyond the self; they are in effect amoral.

Outside of the manifestation of this behaviour they may even appear quite affable, decent and reasonable but this doesn't detract from what is hidden within, i.e. what is their potential - they are hair triggered one false step and you will be on the receiving end of a mouthful of abuse or at least some exaggerated display of indignation. They have a gross inclination to excuse their own failings, they are a compulsive forger of excuses, whatever they did or whatever they were supposed to do but didn't, they will always find an excuse, an excuse that lacks any truth, and in the process they will attack those who try to point out to them what the truth actually is.

If you have had an experience like this then you have encountered someone who lives in a world of a very narrow view one that is of themselves and who you often will hear as being described in various disparaging terms but this is not our intention here our interest in so far as this discourse is concerned is identification and understanding of what this is.

It is unquestionably so that such individuals have no sense of reason or decency they lack any capacity to question their actions and are devoid of any feelings of guilt, remorse or empathy towards others, they are unable to accept that it is them who are in the wrong, they have a mindset impenetrable to any form of reason - this indeed may be their definition.

If it so happens that something happens to them or they are in some way inconvenienced then they will easily take offence and they will overreact. If you happen to reverse your car into them by accident, 'shit happens', but to them it is never an accident to them you were deliberately trying to kill them as if they sit in some permanent state of heightened paranoia. To them their world is a world of over-exaggeration and constant blame of others never themselves.

This is the human race in its nadir of behaviour but beware such stupid people do stupid things as they have no concept of right or wrong, they have no concept of consequences so steer well clear of them and stay mindful of the fact that they may hide very well just what they are until the day you happen to cross them. You will be very tempted to verbally strike back but these people are devoid of rational thought so it is best to just walk away to do otherwise and there is distinct possibility that they will escalate the situation, even to the unimaginable. Whatever they do, whatever that say never take it personally and do not give them another thought, they are not worth it.

We may like to find some sociological reason or excuse of how they came to be this way, for example parentally/peer group nurtured reactions in wrongly perceiving threats and then wrongly reacting to wrongly perceived threats but in life we cannot keep making excuses for others we all have to face up to our own responsibilities for what we are, as should they.

The Sub-Clinical Antisocial Spectrum Disorder – 'The Pathologically Jealous'

Ever been bullied, you probably have, in its wider context for it manifests itself in many ways – a derogatory remark, unjustified or false complaints made against you, unjustified anger directed at you, being controlled, being ostracised, made a target to be humiliated to be put down, shouted at, spoken to as if you are stupid, denied deserved promotion, denied the pay that you deserve, your property deliberately hidden or damaged, you are threatened, your path is deliberately blocked, a contrived collision, a physical assault – the many overt and covert techniques to make someone feel bad about themselves and about their life.

We might think of all of this as something for the playground; inflicted by a particularly nasty child who does not know how to behave, ergo not all children are as innocent as we might like to imagine and some can commit unspeakable cruelty even murder, the malevolent disturbed mind can exist or develop at a 'tender' age just as it can in later life, often, but not always, as result of bad parenting. What becomes and remains is a contingent of equally nasty adults.

Often, but not always, the husband who bullies his wife (or wife who bullies the husband), the adult who deliberately intimidates or abuses the child, the manager who bullies his/her staff or the colleague/s who bully other colleagues, those who behave appallingly to others who seek to agitate – what a sick world we live in. When green with envy the pathetically inclined amongst us can become red with rage.

A healthy mind may envy another but it can also accept without any issue that others can and are allowed to be more successful, more intelligent, more knowledgeable, more talented, more attractive, more personable, or possess greater wealth and it is able to feel compassion for those who happen to be less fortunate - but the mind that is pathologically jealous or pathologically depraved invariably precipitates the bully. The mind of the bully is unable to tolerate being 2nd or is easily amused by those who they falsely perceive to come 3rd. If you are greater than I then I must seek to make you feel less. In the mind of the bully what would have been envy morphs into pathological jealousy, what would have been compassion morphs into ridicule – thus the irritation and ensuing bad reaction for coming 2nd morphs into a self-enforced reality of being last.

If you are being bullied do not ask what is wrong with you ask yourself what is wrong with them. You are OK but they're not – you have something that they haven't, they covet what you are, they will deny this of course but really it is no more complex than that. If we can't be successful by way of nature or through our own efforts then at least we should strive to be successful in the way how we behave and if we cannot behave in an urbane manner then we are nothing other than a failed human being in its lowest form. A person who lacks any standards of behavior is irrelevant. If you behave like shit then you will be perceived as shit. A bully, in being a bully, reveals to the whole world just what a pathetic failure that they are, they should be pitied rather than feared.

Chapter 8

ON FINDING SUCCESS IN RELATIONSHIPS

(Running the gauntlet)

Deep down within us all, save for a few, there is good to be found, can others see this and are they prepared to see what we really are rather than what is to be seen on the surface. Even some whom we may dislike, or whom we may disagree with their behaviour, perhaps deep within there is something special. How is it that we judge one another, do we look at surface value or do we look for the deeper person within? Are we prone to reject and isolate rather than seek out meaningful friendships that could change our lives and theirs for the better? Do we even bother to look within ourselves to seek out that which is good and project that image or do we project an image that we may wrongly believe best suits our hopes for the future and survival for the present.

"The force that unites the elements to become all things is Love. Love brings together dissimilar elements into a unity, to become a composite thing. Love is the same force that human beings find at work in themselves whenever they feel joy, love and peace." – Empedocles (Philosopher, Greece 5th century BC)

Earlier this year whilst in London my eyes caught the most delightful creature God could ever create, such curves, such beauty, such class, refinement beyond imagination; I was dumb struck, my heart was pounding, my palms were sweating, my legs were shaking, I was overcome with hormones sending me crazy, I was beguiled and smitten, could this be the one I asked myself, it was love at first sight but what to do? Do I go for option 'A'; go and get a stiff drink and pull myself together and forget the whole thing or 'B'; pluck up the courage to go and ask for her name.

What would you do, you are right, I thought what have I got to lose, what the hell, so me being me I decided on option 'B' I decided to go for it. And her name - Her name was Maserati GranTurismo; the most elegant, stylish beast of a car anyone could ever imagine and you would need a lot of imagination.

Could this be love or lust for I had to restrain my passions from going over and licking the bonnet to see if she tasted as good as she looked. It was here that I had to draw the line as at best that would have been impolite at worst I may have been arrested for being a nuisance or a weirdo besides she was some lady and she deserved my respect. I got her name but didn't get that date but I shall get over it. I didn't get to hear her speak but I guess that that 4.2 litre V8 engine must have sounded like the roar of a lion though with the sweetness of an angel singing. She would have long forgotten me but at least I can look back from time to time to cherish that brief moment of joy and know what it must feel like to be in heaven.

Do We Really Need a Relationship (the cost of which could be your freedom)?

We all need relationships of some form; it would be a lonely world without them, the song by Climie Fisher 'Love Changes Everything' expresses this point very well and if you could find the real deal then love may even cure everything. Many of us never do find the real deal although we may be lucky enough to have experienced at least some transients of the real deal where otherwise we must fill our time with other advantageous activities. We need good friends and if we don't have any family maybe good friends will have to do. We have to live with what we have.

However, what we would define as a relationship is that someone special, a partner, someone we may set up home with or maybe to eventually marry, but also who we can count upon for unswerving loyalty with whom we have implicit trust. But not all of us want or need a relationship defined as such therefore this chapter discusses the positions of all, both relationships in general i.e. 'friendship' and a 'relationship' with another.

> *"I am no bird; and no net ensnares me: I am a free human being with an independent will."* – Charlotte Brontë (Novelist, England 19th century)

We live in a world where it is seen as the cultural norm is to have a partner. Our society in some ways demands that we are in a relationship, it is our trans-cultural pressure that if we are not in one then it is perceived by everyone that you are unfortunate or that is there something wrong with you, worse still you also start to adopt this perception yourself. We are programmed from an early age that we must find a partner and therefore if we don't find one then we will feel a failure. This is further reinforced by the media, the idea of the happy couple is projected, even flaunted, everywhere, marriage is the penultimate achievement and having children is seen as the zenith of our existence. This is all sounds very nice for those who have although can make the have nots who crave for someone special to feel a lot worse about their situation.

It is unfortunate and completely unnecessary but we value our life upon comparisons. Our self-image is not fully about what we are but also about what we don't have that others do and this should not be. We base our assumption of our, or others happiness, on whether or not we or they have that someone special. This is completely wrong thinking, you can be very happy on your own and it is not beyond possibility to be very miserable in having a partner. To the have nots do not envy those that have for, unknown to you, they might be envying your freedom.

Even where we have what we might describe as our ideal partner time can change this perception; even if someone doesn't change people can grow apart from one another. This line of thought may appear to advocate indifference to others or indifference to relationships, neither of which is true, what it advocates is the need to be indifferent to not having a relationship. In absence of a relationship perhaps we should seek another scale of success away from the idea of relationships such as personal development and education since it is natural that if we can't find what we want in life we go looking elsewhere for other purposes to exist – we are purpose driven. If we use the relationship scale to measure our life success when we don't have one then our life can feel like a disaster, when in reality it isn't.

Not in a Relationship (just remind yourself of all those who are likewise) – Loneliness Revisited

We are all aware that being alone gives you some major advantages over being in a relationship. For example you have the freedom to do what you want and when you want and that you have no-one who you have to tolerate who could be controlling, abusive, who you find dull, tedious or small minded or just that you simply can't stand anymore and you have greater opportunity for some excitement in life. You may have ideas about a perfect partner who you may have or who you may admire from afar, but what if they were to leave you then what.

The truth is that there is no destined partner for any of us, it is dangerous to think otherwise since you may have placed too much hope in destiny that may not deliver; what we do have are lots of options and if another option came along you might soon forget the last. However from being alone there is also another dimension available to you and that is you can free your mind and your imagination and it is this property that has distinct use in fighting loneliness.

Given the more obvious advantages of being alone that you can read a good book, go and have coffee with a friend or go and visit an art gallery or museum or whatever takes your fancy but when you come home to that empty house you may find this a most difficult thing to face. Most of the time good friends and good books will not assuage your feelings completely and so there are times when this just won't be enough for you. At these times you will crave for another relationship although the idea of entering into a relationship might be the very worst thing to do.

Our cultures often militates for the need to be in a relationship and like with many things in any culture this is just plain wrong. Just as we are feeling lonely we are vulnerable to irrational thinking by choosing the wrong person or sometimes taking reckless actions that could have catastrophic consequences. Our upbringing imputes a preoccupation so strong that our ability to reason is overridden we are vulnerable to making a bad choice. Maybe we should have been raised with a different though innocuous addiction such as learning to play a musical instrument.

Realistically, if you go out looking in desperation you will land up with desperate results so it is better to just do what you enjoy doing and you might just meet someone right for you without forcing anything i.e. the cliché that *"you can find someone when you are not looking for them"* does therefore make some sense. Indeed you are better off not looking better off just to engage people in conversation for what they are as a person not for what you might see as a potential partner, just remember that behind what you see on the surface is a person and often a good one at that.

Coming back to this idea of a novel way to combat loneliness let's cast our minds back to the chapter on well-being and the ideas of why we should make use of delusion and the power of our mind and to the chapter on Buddhism where we shall discuss meditation. If these are useful in the context of well-being so is it not possible that we can then deploy the same weapons when loneliness assails us. Well the answer is why not.

When that gripping feeling of loneliness falls upon us then this is quality time that you can make good use of so don't waste it. If you visualize that a lot of great ideas came about by imagination by someone thinking through scenarios and ideas for which, without quiet periods, would have not come to fruition. To not use the imaginative and explorative capabilities of the mind we would not have any great scientists, philosophers or composers nor would we have any great food to eat. Ideas do not just fall into our heads from some nebulous celestial origin but sometimes requires a lot of thought. Now the challenge here is not for you to attempt to work out how to refine Einstein's theory of relativity but to attempt something that will just change your life.

The trick here is that when we have these 'black dog' moments (a favoured expression of Winston Churchill concerning his recurrent melancholia) then what we do is we meditate but we do something now quite different in meditation. Whereas we normally use meditation to slow the mind down and to empty it; here we use it to project or imagine an alternative experience. We use our imagination to take us to places, circumstances and events where we wish to be, what we wish to do and in the company with whom we wish to be with and the good thing is there is no limit to our imagination and there is no cost involved.

If you can master meditation well, and anyone can with some practice, then you can master this technique of imagination as an extension to meditation. In all applications you can imagine things exactly as you want them to develop, you can imagine the freedom of this using all of your sensory capability – site, sound, aroma, taste and feel, the more detail you can bring to the technique, and do so in real time, the more realistic this will be. It is much like the experience of watching a film, this often being a group activity as a necessity of fully enjoying the experience, only it isn't because in this film you are in it, not observing it but 'actually' in it.

You can take yourself with the most amazing companions on the most amazing holiday experience without the stress of queues at the airport, a disappointing hotel, boredom of what shall we do next and trying to assuage it by going in the same shops you visited yesterday, getting sunburnt, getting pestered by some slimy sales person on the beach who is often trying to sell themselves, and you certainly won't get diarrhoea from ill prepared food. You have possibly seen so many documentaries on foreign places and so many holiday brochures thinking I can't afford to go there and can't get the time off work well being alone means you can tap quality time to yourself and go to these places with just the same experience as actually doing it though without any drawbacks.

If you do not believe this is such a powerful technique then why not try it anyway as it won't cost you anything but remember the great ideas arrived at through imagination we just need to take the process one step further. Also there is scientific evidence that in playing through scenarios in your mind such as taking a particular penalty shot in football or in delivering a presentation can be as effective in improving your abilities as would be through the actual experience.

With this technique you can do what you want and you can build a narrative if you wish such that your mind almost doesn't discriminate between the actual experience and the virtual experience that you have manufactured. However, note the word 'almost' as you also need to keep one foot on the ground and remain mindful that the experience is a manufactured one as in essence if you allow the 'virtual' to be perceived as 'actual' then you have entered the realm of clinical delusion and that can often lead to no good. So long as you remain vigilant in recognizing that the 'virtual' is not the 'actual' afterwards you can stay safe. Used with wisdom imagination will do you no harm and will only enrich your life experience. It will make positive use of those times where otherwise you would feel loneliness tearing away at your soul.

Personality and Humanity the Winning Route to What Makes us Interesting to others (becoming a good catch)

Some years ago my company was audited by a young lady of average looks but yet all of us men were besotted with her but why? The answer was her personality – she was seriously nice, seriously charming and seriously genuine. A great personality to the discerning is a fantastic compensation factor, in the game of attraction, I don't like to use those words but I think you can see what I'm getting at. It may be so that we can't easily change what we are in the sense of the physical self but in the sense of personality there really is no glass ceiling at all but what you want is not a large overpowering personality you need an attractive personality.

"I have for the first time found what I can truly love – I have found you. You are my sympathy – my better self – my good angel – I am bound to you with a strong attachment." – Charlotte Brontë (Novelist, England 19th century)

Do we know what we are what is our personality – do we even have a personality, do we have the best of human qualities or the very worst, would others call us a nice person and if not then why not. Are we even prepared to acknowledge what we are or does that thought even make us angry. Personality and human quality is the key to finding others not just for a relationship but friends too and not only that but improves our everyday experience not just for us but also for all who we encounter.

In how we present ourselves and in what we present ourselves as there is a fine balance in getting it right, too much or too little and things just won't quite work as well as they could have done and if you forcibly balance things as you suspect they should be then your act will be detected as most of us humans are not idiots we can see through what is disingenuous and we can see when we are being manipulated. We are all born with a clean slate and we all learn behaviours from those around us, if that were not so then we would all behave equally through the 'evolutionary process', and we hope that what we learn will serve us well although not always do we have good teachers or good role models.

All what we are, should be what we are, not what we contrive to be. We must therefore like ourselves and others for what we see as positive attributes and this is how we should construct ourselves as decent human beings. What follows should describe what we might want to aspire to be not what we might want to pretend to be.

Unassuming Confidence – We are all attracted to those who display self-confidence but that do so without being arrogant, egotistical or showy. Being arrogant, egotistical and showy changes what could have been a magnetic person into one who is unattractive or even repulsive. Confidence relates to our experience of success and to the abilities that we have and have had put into practice though at the same time being modest about it but also not letting others know that you know you are being modest, in essence modesty if it means anything should not be consciously enacted.

Investing time in skills not only boosts confidence it may also get you a better job. If we are too attached, anxious or seeking to impress then subliminally this might be detected as desperation for the encounter to work; we give the game away that we are not exactly self-confident and you may have just blown your chances, so remain a bit detached but don't overdo it as you may then appear cold and disinterested. If you are someone who has solid foundations of confidence you will appear more self-contained with abilities to give good advice or to fix things, all round you are perceived as a survivor you are the person to go to for when help is needed and this makes you useful, perhaps even indispensable, and therefore perhaps even more attractive. If you can keep a cool head and not panic when others are running around like headless chickens then this shows that you are emotionally mature, you are in control of yourself and are able to deal with difficult situations. You may even be fearless but being too much so and you may appear as if you are a show-off.

We can also enhance our confidence in the way how we dress, what fashion and style we choose - dress looking like a dogs dinner and you will feel likewise, so look good and feel good too but wear required dress in accordance to the occasion/event, if you look out of place you will feel out of place and this will undermine your confidence.

Humour/Smile – A face looking like a miserable Yak is a dead put-off. There is a saying: *"smile and the whole world smiles with you, cry and you will cry alone"*. Look and be approachable, warm and inviting don't look like someone who would scare small children. A frown requires more muscles than does a smile so why not relax back and look like someone worth talking to. If you do get that opportune moment then act immediately before it can go off the boil. Make sure you have eye contact but don't stare, that scares anyone not just small children, you don't want to be regarded as weird.

Being humourless particularly if you also keep ranting on about something is a big turn-off. Having a great sense of humour gives you an entertainment quality although humour is a skill that requires honing. Why is it that we all love a good comedian, we don't know anything about what they are as a person but their humour is what wins through. Did you ever bother to remember that good joke, or comedy sketch, or did you just laugh at it. If you observe what is funny and explore why and then consign these thoughts to memory you will gain an ability to recall, adapt and apply what you have learnt to a myriad of potentially humorous opportunities. Better still if others think you are very slightly mad this gives you more of a 3D image rather than appearing flat and dull. For good humour check out 'Sergeant Bilko', 'Laurel & Hardy', 'Faulty Towers', 'Steptoe & Son' and 'Porridge' and the films 'My Cousin Vinny', 'As Good As It Gets', 'Sister Act' and 'The Good, The Bad and The Ugly'. Jokes can be mad but never tell a joke that is pathetic as you will be perceived equally so and don't ridicule or say anything distasteful as this is in bad taste and you will be seen as foolish or base.

Don't joke too much as you will be perceived as an idiot or immature who no-one can ever take seriously but don't ever take life too serious either and if you can't laugh at yourself you might have missed an excellent joke. If you want to construct your own material don't forget there are two rules to follow: first remember that a joke is a story for which the punch line violates what would make sense but yet at the same time remains somewhat logical and the second rule is don't break the rules.

Charisma - How does anyone feel after they have spoken with you, do they feel depressed, do they feel belittled, do they feel insulted. If this is how you affect others then it is highly unlikely that they will want to associate with you ever and even less chance that they will want to get to know you. You make them feel worse about themselves or worse about what they perceive of life. A person who is charismatic is the exact opposite, no burping please; they make others feel good about themselves, they identify what is good about you and they work on that in a positive way, they will give genuine compliments, they take a genuine interest in you also, they want to make you feel good, you to them are important as a human being.

Now there are those who use what I have just said as techniques to manipulate, it is nothing more than a trick, to them there is an ulterior motive either they want you, your money or they are 'taking the piss' (idiom for 'trying to make you look stupid') although you will get to work out who is genuine and who is not, exaggeration might be a good indicator.

The Paradox of Interest – Charisma is something that wins over others, if others suspect that we don't care we will be perceived as selfish, cold or unfeeling, however it is a most fascinating fact, and that is not beyond logical reasoning, is the irony that where we appear to care more as charisma might recommend we might also be perceived as less interesting and so less attractive. In other words we are trying too hard and so others may then wonder why so the manipulation warning flag will suddenly appear – 'what are you up to what are you after' is what may come to mind. You may also appear as looking desperate or anxious that is detrimental to perceived confidence. Whenever in conversation never appear too interested or not enough just relax and try to take a middle path.

Greater interest is something that becomes more appropriate when we get to know someone but it has to be mutually progressing not unilaterally so, since you may be getting to know someone better but this doesn't necessarily imply that they are interested in furthering the relationship, of any kind. However, this doesn't necessarily suggest that they don't like you it may mean that what they have with you is all that they want for the present time or perhaps beyond - just look for the signs.

Expressiveness/Vivacity – You can present the most interesting material in the most elegant and articulated fashion, the pitch and flow can be 'spot-bollock' (idiom for 'accurate') but if you lack expressiveness you can turn an interesting subject into one where everyone is looking for the exit. Is your voice monotonic is your delivery bereft of any passion or are you lacking in gesticulation, is the person you are talking to looking as if they are about to nod off.

Make an effort, look at least a bit animated, and use positive language unless it is appropriate to use negative language. If you find it difficult to being animated then practice 'blowing raspberries' at yourself in front of the mirror. Be mindful of the fact that the level of interest in what we say is a lot more to do with how we deliver it and from our body language rather than just the words alone. If you are giving a presentation the secret is great preparation and don't read from the slides let the audience do that, you just add the narrative but make sure that you involve the audience so they must interact. If the prospect of giving a presentation is daunting just imagine that the audience are sitting there in the buff. Always perceive a presentation or any encounter for that matter as a useful learning experience.

Spontaneity and Word Flow – Don't get hung up or worried about what you are going to say. What you say should not be in accordance with a detailed rehearsed script or list of elements or phrases, even for job interviews, you may become so focussed on a script that you fail to adequately listen to the other person or worse not letting them speak and therefore fail to respond in accordance to the dynamics of the conversation, your conversation may also sound like reciting a shopping list. Just relax and be yourself. You may have a rough idea of what you might want to talk about e.g. your recent holiday, your visit to the theatre or a book that you are reading but don't 'plan' any deeper than the very basic elements as you will appear distracted.

Detail is fine and is necessary and can even captivate the audience but let the detail flow naturally don't keep thinking I must mention this, this and this or in this way or that way and don't get into too much detail either; I might be interested in your holiday, especially what went wrong is often very interesting to talk about, however I'm not going to be interested in how many flavours of yogurts and what they were that you could have with your breakfast. Conversation must flow and even be allowed to digress far from where you might have intended, listen to what the other person is saying and then respond appropriately and don't drive the conversation back to your preferred path until the current topic of conversation is at its end point, be mindful that your 'preferred path' may be inhibiting, so you should know when it's the right time to change topics.

If you are on a date don't think at all about having to convey everything about you, it's not an interview, let the conversation take its natural course. Conversation is not all about facts not at all, it's also about what you have experienced, what you have observed, what you think, how you feel and about how you bring in the other person in that you are interested in what the other person is thinking. When you ask questions try to use 'open' rather than 'closed' questions such as those beginning with what, how and why such that would elicit a complex answer rather than a question that can only be answered with a simple 'yes' or 'no' e.g. don't ask *"do you like films"* instead ask *"what sort of films do you like"* and if you're the one doing the answering don't just real off a list of films or genres that appeal to you but also say why, perhaps also referring to some interesting scenes or quotes especially something with meaning or that is funny.

Reading the Other Person but also Listen – An 'ex' once told me that *"she didn't want any flowers for Valentine's day"*, when she said that *"she didn't want any flowers"* I thought she meant that she didn't want any flowers – big mistake. You have a pet although narrow subject; this could be stamp collecting in the 17th century, knitting, handbags, steam locomotives or the aerodynamics of penguin flippers. To you it's fascinating so much so that every time you speak your conversation gravitates towards this subject.

Are you able and willing to recognise that others may not be in the slightest bit interested in what you love to wax on about they may appear to be so but are they just being polite. Your subject may not even be so narrow, as I describe, but it may be too heavy going or soporific for the person sitting across the table from you so beware of particularly politics and religion, your aim to interest them in these subjects might just do the exact opposite. What to you is so fascinating may cause others to climb up the wall with boredom. Be sensitive to others interest span and speak in a language that they understand so don't try to use anything like 'abstruse metaphysical antidisestablishmentarian socio-economic esoteric obfuscations' or similar no don't do that, it may sound clever but it isn't it's just confusing. Know when to change subjects and try to take interest in what others say as the art of conversation is also to be a good listener too and that alone is extremely important.

Don't talk at others talk to them and don't dominate the centre ground of the conversation, i.e. incessantly jabbering on about yourself, you need to want them to raise their subjects of interest too and be genuinely interested in what they say, work on what they are passionate about. A conversation does require two people in it not just yourself and someone else who must only listen and not speak. Try to be casual and easy going such that you are not too serious about things unless where it is appropriate to do so.

Feelings – A word that defines humanity at its very best is 'altruism' – i.e. to put another's interest before your own; if you think of the New York fire department crews who on the infamous date of 9/11 ascended the stairs of the burning twin towers all who risked and many who lost their lives to try, in vain, to save others is an act deserving of the utmost respect of us all; what they did was the sacrifice of themselves for a noble cause. What they did they did not do for personal gain but to help innocent others who were in peril, they knew this and they knew the risks but yet they took those risks. Such actions represent humanity at its very best a quality that would make God proud of what He/She had created.

A friend, that is a good friend, is someone who has genuine concern for you and your well-being, are you therefore someone who others can go to when they need help, and who can perceive when you are needed without them having to say so. A good friend is effective at helping you when you face difficulties and they give you support without any motivation for gain of any sort.

Good Manners – Probably the biggest turn off for others to want to know you is concerning the subject of manners. Being impolite doesn't gain you any sympathy to you or your views and will only cause to antagonise. You won't be liked. Manners cost us nothing yet everywhere we see violation of this quality – it is as if some are predisposed to being rude, offensive or ungrateful all of the time. Lack of manners is counterproductive for all including the one unfortunate enough to possess such behaviour.

Lacking social intelligence as in being offensive, rude, obstinate or surly, failing to show appreciation, or as is becoming typical in the modern world, being unable to construct a polite email, shows humanity at its most base. Conversely, those of good manners make our whole life experience so much better we feel appreciated and we feel we live in a civilised world not one populated by brutes. We can't always be on top form and there are those who try our patience, so sometimes we will slip, however we should endeavour to maintain our standards of behaviour.

But how do we define good manners well let's have a go at what defines impeccable manners. Impeccable manners is in showing respect for all, to be effortlessly charming, to show gratitude and sincerity, that if you do not agree with another's view point you do not act like a spoilt child and get angry, you do not easily take offence and you do not set out to cause offence, that you know when to apologise, you listen to what others have to say with respect not to shout them down, you have emotional self-control. If you show good manners others will follow suit and those who you might have otherwise turned into an enemy could become your friend.

Some may see manners as a weakness but who is the greater person of the two I ask the one without or the one with. Of the two which one has elevated themselves to greater refinement? The one lacking manners will be the unsuccessful human being although they will not recognise this.

Sincerity – We may be all of the things above but are we real are we genuine are we sincere. Do others see us as someone who is honest who can be trusted who doesn't have some hidden agenda. If we are not the genuine article then all of the above collapses, we may appear to be all sorts of things but without being genuine then we are nothing more than an illusion. We are fake we are nothing.

Compatibility – A flat battery won't get a car moving and lethargy certainly is a hindrance to any chance of firing up a relationship - we must therefore exude a sense of at least some energy to look at all appealing, we need to at least look something like a live wire of sorts but just don't overdo the volts. I have sat in quite a few presentations where the energy is there but the pitch and ease of delivery isn't and you land up having to prop your eyelids open with tooth picks to stay awake, indeed your self-enforcement of staying awake could be what is causing you to nod off.

We can be everything and perhaps a very good catch but do we match someone, do we resonate with them. What we are in how we are we cannot change, we have a defined personality one which fits well with some but not with others and we all have different standards or values. In other words people are attracted to others who are like themselves and this includes personality, so if it happens that you get a rejection don't worry about it, they may not realise what they have lost, or of course they may be just unavailable (although might still find you somewhat interesting), but hey who cares, do you, should you, does it really matter.

Personality is something which you can change but why should you, since what you are is what makes you special, it's what makes you unique, so why should you change for someone else. We may want to improve what we are but we should only change if it's our desire to do so for ourselves, not to change to please someone else. If they are so different to you, that they are just not interested then so be it, you can move on elsewhere and find someone who is a better match to what you are, someone who you can resonate with and so light up each other's world.

You may be all of the above and still be unsuccessful in finding friends or that someone special and to complicate things further is that we are all are attracted to different characteristics, we don't all go for the same thing or in the same proportions and perhaps this is something we should question of ourselves in what do we actually go for and is that really good for me. The reality is slightly more complex than having an engaging personality as we shall discuss and at the end of the day you need to find others who share your interests but more importantly they must share your values. Try as you may, to engage with someone who you would like the company of and you may just get nowhere, if so don't try any more – right intention wrong target so look elsewhere. What you want in life may not be what they want since we are all different – different interests, different values and that's it. You may desire for someone's company but be honest with yourself is that person really right for you.

Opening Doors Finding Friends (and don't worry about rejection a salesman never does)

With our ego at work we can become more preoccupied with the quantity rather than the quality of our friends and this may have even gotten in the way of making a good friend. I have heard people boast that they have 100, 200 even 300 friends, most probably acquaintances through social media so it would seem, in reality they are probably more alone than what you might imagine. Is it not better to have just a couple of really good friends who really care about you and likewise who you care about and where genuine interest is manifest by each having a good knowledge of the other; their history, current events, problems and personality. Good friends are those who you can rely on who you know you can call upon for help who are enthusiastic to meet up for a chat with no strings attached and who will want to phone you to know how things are going when they also know you are going through a difficult time.

It's a sad fact that, in circumstances not entirely of our making, that some of us cannot find anyone who we can call a close friend – this is particularly prevalent in cities where a lack of community or where isolating cultures exists, where it is the norm not to talk to neighbours or where you may be perceived as odd if you happen to strike up a conversation with a complete stranger. In effect we, all of us, are responsible for societies where none seem to find any time for anyone yet oddly we all crave human interaction for ourselves.

It would seem that what we want is also what we don't want. We are aching for others to talk to us but if they did that wouldn't fit with the cultural norm and so should be condemned. There are too many walls too many barriers to human interaction - perhaps we are too cautious, we have lost faith or trust in humanity; or could it be that we have an exaggerated paranoia of what might happen? In protecting our own space we might inadvertently be manufacturing our own misery.

These walls often also exist even where we are best placed to meet others such as through friends or at our workplace both that should be fertile ground for making connections and who knows what. Unless we possess fantastic social skills and have massive opportunity to mingle we may just be looking for a very long time to make good friends.

And if you were to ask me what is the technique in how you can make connections I simply don't know the magic formula, but my thoughts on this are just be yourself, don't be anxious in any way, at least look like a personality that others would want to engage in conversation with and find ways to 'break the ice', a brief 'uncontrived' encounter but that is also urbane could also do wonders. Maybe all you need to do is say 'hi' or 'how's things'. Or if it's someone you know maybe ask them for a small favour as oddly enough being asked a favour can subconsciously elicit a good feeling in the other person about you, noting that we are enticed by feelings by emotions but not by logical deduction – we are therefore attracted to someone not based upon reasoning but based upon how we feel.

However, this being said, if you are in a social setting with potential opportunity then if you sit in the corner of the room looking and feeling glum and wracked with negativity then it is very unlikely that anyone will want to make conversation with you. You will go home feeling worse than when you arrived and it's your fault. OK perhaps the occasion might turn out dud anyway but if you don't speculate you don't accumulate so why not talk to anyone after all they are human too and would no doubt like to chat even if that's as far as it goes. Show interest in another as a person not as a potential mate, so don't ignore anyone just because you don't fancy them.

Being togged up in your finest feathers won't do anything for you unless you engage with others and in particular if you don't engage that positive but not 'in your face' personality then you won't get anywhere. To up your chances of success you need to be selective of venue so if you seek someone who is sensitive and into the arts then going to a mud-wrestling match is very unlikely to bear fruit.

Don't forget that there are lots of quality people out there who are alone like you you just need to make the effort to meet them. But also don't forget that you need to look for the right moment to pounce, choosing the wrong moment to approach someone who you would like to chat to and everything could be blown permanently, so synchronisation through observing when is it best to move is the key but if you can connect through working on some common project, cause, or skill acquisition, for example that brings you into close co-operation, i.e. to get to know each other, then this can be a good place to start.

True friendship is never sought, it shouldn't be, it just happens although there is nothing wrong in wanting someone's company and in our rather unfriendly, but in reality potentially friendly, world if someone happens to detect that you would like the pleasure of their company they might just switch off and that might be their loss not yours. You must never give the game away just be friendly with them and see how it goes but don't get hung up about it, don't expect and don't get desperate. Find out what their interests are and if you do get on really well ask them if they might like to join you at an event or an exhibition and if they say no then don't let any disappointment show and don't make a big thing of it, let them do the asking next time.

Never let your mind mull over how suitable someone is for you just make sure you talk to everyone including them, this widens your options and makes you look more laid back about things, if something happens it happens if it doesn't it doesn't and that's all there is to it.

So how in the hell do we break this cycle living in a lonely world where we all would like good friends but yet are too much on guard to let the few opportune moments we have to bear fruit. It's so simple we just need to get out of this mind set of reluctance, we need to drop our guard a bit and talk to others in all sorts of circumstances and importantly let them talk to you instead of looking at them with contempt as if they are someone you can't trust. Granted some need to be treated with circumspection but not all, if you think otherwise you are not being fair on them and you are not being fair on yourself. You may have just lost a chance of meeting a wonderful person and you didn't even know it you didn't even give them the chance.

Just also remember that not everyone may be ebullient and fascinating at first perhaps they are a bit shy or going through a bad patch so don't turn a 'cold hard shoulder' to them, your friendship could be a wonderful thing to them that might bring them to a good place and could win you the friendship of someone who is shy but perhaps very genuine. Gushing people, who we are often attracted to, are not always necessarily the best friends and are not always genuine just remember that, but even those who appear extrovert may in reality feel very much alone. Just be there for everyone.

Modern Expectations Gone Wrong (I might not believe in barriers but I won't fraternise!!!)

You could be the most wonderful person in all manners but fall short in some way of another's lofty expectations and you may feel that ice-cold unfriendliness akin to a polar bear that's just been taken out the freezer and that also happens to be sucking on an iced lolly. You may have no romantic desire for this person at all, you might just be being friendly, but they might like to think that you do and so in their view you should be blanked - their loss not yours. Unless it is deserved, rejection is in no way an insult it is often a compliment.

In the modern world we are bombarded with images of perfection mostly through film, television, magazines and sales brochures. If you are lucky enough to have such looks and figure you may qualify to appear, most of us don't make the grade. Having been selected then the hordes of make-up artists, fashion designers and airbrush operatives will go to work. The perfection that is to be delivered for visual consumption must transcend that which is naturally available. If only my hairdresser could do with my face what she can do with my hair I lament. However, this obsessive compulsion with perfection has raised the expectations of some of what is demanded of a partner in the looks department.

Some of us have also become introspective of our own appearance too, what would have been considered as normal and is normal is now wrongly perceived as not normal enough to the extent that it may be perceived as abnormal, the emergence of the conditions of anorexia and body dysmorphic disorder and the insatiable demand for ever more cosmetic surgery are proof enough here.

If we were to have lived over a century ago most of us would have had a brutal life; work was invariably physical and hard, accommodation, food and healthcare would have been of a very poor standard, people would be broken at a relatively early age so you would age quick and die early. These living conditions would have lowered expectations because what you don't know about you do not crave for and so you are more satisfied with what you have. An excellent example of this is where the tiny and isolated country of Bhutan discovered the television long after most of the rest of us. Bhutan, a predominantly Buddhist society, was renowned for its happiness and for the fact that its communities were so close; then came the television. Instead of interacting with each other the Bhutanese are more often now glued to that electronic box in the corner of the room that reminds them what they are not and what they don't have, the consequences of which is that they are now less happy than they were, as are we all.

The less we know of other's lives the less we expect of our own and so the more we know of others, the more we must have for ourselves, in a sense we have all become demanding, although equally more miserable, more miserable for the fact that we will never achieve what we aspire to have nor realise what we actually need. The problem is that once we have acquired this perspective we cannot shake it off, it becomes an immutable property of the way how we think. Even if we were to take ourselves to a retreat in some monastery deep in the Himalayas our memories of these images persist and it would take great skill and effort to overcome this perspective.

The modern world also affords us better work and softer options with a better standard of living and this with better education gives us a sense of confidence in ourselves, even overconfidence, and with that confidence our expectations will extend to even greater heights. It is with this backdrop that we have expected too much in relationships, we believe that we somehow deserve the best no matter how ugly our personality is. For some of us, no longer would we even consider anyone who is just 95% of what we would desire in a person, no this is not good enough 'for me I want 100%'. Is it then any wonder that so many of us live alone or have broken relationships?

So many demand too much that they cannot look at someone holistically in so much as does that person have decency, compassion, kindness, honour, good nature, personality, are hard-working and loyal – that is no longer enough, some will demand that they have 100% in looks, salary, prestige, the house, the car, the bank balance and that the partner will do exactly what they want upon command. The relationship that is utilitarian based i.e. that adds up the gains using a real or virtual spreadsheet, where the first date is perceived to be more like an interview, may be designed so to assert ego (a bad move), and the relationship, in actuality a business arrangement, is doomed.

"Don't marry for money; you can borrow it cheaper." – Scottish proverb.

We need to be a lot more grounded and realise that absolute perfection is unobtainable, it does not exist. In seeking perfection all you will find is disappointment. If you find what you believe to be 100% perfection you will gradually start to find fault and you will never be satisfied with what you have, your relationship will fail and if you don't wise up to reality you will just repeat this mistake. If you want to make a good relationship then you need to look at the person as a whole and think about what is in their heart, what is their true motivation. We need to compromise, on what we want, for what we really need.

If you still believe this is wrong and that you do deserve absolute perfection then go and look at yourself, are you really that perfect too. You may just be looking for a very long time and never reach your goal – for all of us our biological clocks are going 'tick-tock' we are heading from youth and towards old age and we are not immortal. Those who feel such high entitlement are thus amongst the most conceited of our species and do not realise that very few will like them, all relationships they have will be superficial and they will condemn themselves to an eventual life of loneliness for at some time their looks will leave them and those they seek will judge them just as they judged others i.e. unattractive, in their terms. Our ego can indeed be our worst enemy.

Making Connections

It is an odd thing that as our population increases as our planet gets more and more crowded we all seem to be moving further apart. The concept of community seems to be failing. This is a property of modern society where we have all become isolated; no- one wants to talk to you but do you also want to talk to them, we seem embarrassed about doing so, our world has become clinical where we identify ourselves by our success defined through our career or wealth not for what we are as a person. Or is it that we have become wittingly or unwittingly disillusioned with society and so have become perhaps a little too much over cautious.

This issue is a facet and a failing of modern culture with distinct prevalence in cities, where the imagination that with more people would therefore present greater social opportunity, but where the opposite is what is closer to reality, although can also be due to insular cultural precursors whereby other cultures are not insular but only too willing to engage with and welcome strangers.

Some who are only looking within their life though not beyond may disagree with me and I would dearly love to hear that everyone disagrees although the reality is that I see single people all over the place – why would anyone want to visit a museum, art gallery, cinema or to go shopping alone, surely these experiences are so much better shared. I sit on the tube (London underground) and in casually looking at others I think of how many of them will be going home to an empty apartment and perhaps a microwave dinner for one and who would prefer not to.

So where do we go to make connections even if it's not a friendship it's someone else you can share a few moments with so where do we go? You may make some endeavours with your best you on offer, since a miserable countenance won't get you anywhere, and you might still get ignored but not because of you, it isn't your fault. You could be the nicest and the most amazing person in the room and no-one will approach you and will never know what opportunity that they had missed. Never lose heart if this is how you see the world because the truth is that everywhere you will go where you will encounter unfriendly people can also be the very same places where you will find friendly people too. However, you do need to have some selectivity so don't go to places for the sole pretext of meeting people, go to places that interest you as it is there that you can find like-minded others where you at least have some chance of having something in common and therefore some chance to make meaningful contact.

Finding friends is a game of patience, so don't expect immediate results as things take time, however with well-honed people skills you can win over others and make those connections for sure. Just be mindful that others are quite wary depending on their culture. If you want to up your chances then joining a church, a club or volunteering puts you in regular contact with others who will get to know you and you them and here is a good chance if there ever was one.

Attraction and Getting Wise with Our Hormones

If you ever get the chance then take a look at Leonardo da Vinci's painting 'A Portrait of Ginevra de' Benci' a very fine looking woman (with that certain 'je ne sais quoi'), one who I could perhaps fall madly in love with but yet I don't know this woman, I don't know anything about her. Now I am no expert in art but what is interesting is that as typical of da Vinci's work is that her face has a subtle degree of ambiguity in that it is difficult to discern as to whether Ginevra is happy or sad, friendly or aloof.

Is it that Leonardo was playing mischievous games with us by skilfully drafting 'anatomical dissonance' to invoke some sort of cognitive confusion or was he just bereft of the artistic skills to enable portrayal of drama, realism and passion that are so apparent in the works of Caravaggio. Well that's my theory. Da Vinci was no idiot and given his immense skills he would have been well aware of how our minds can be confused in what they see and therefore in what they perceive.

We can usually get a pretty good idea of what a person is within just one minute of talking to them, not only through what they say but in how they express themselves and through subliminal facial indications that give away what they are and what is their motivation, we already have the hardware to do this. Communication doesn't just depend on the instruments of speech and the emanating sounds from within, but also on our physical presentation; what is the face, the posture and the hands saying to us.

The amount of brain activity (the homunculus) concerned with facial movements is very significant for a reason, our face communicates how we feel and can communicate such things as when we are being friendly, dishonest or a threat, where there is manifest disparity between the sonic and the visual, the words may say one thing the face something else. A person with facial paralysis may say that they are fine but in reality they may feel sad and to the outside world it is hard to therefore know this reality, the face could have revealed the true emotion.

Take the face away from the communication process and the communication process is significantly compromised. However, when we are attracted to someone then their appealing facial characteristics may override our ability to discern, we may for example suspect that this person is as dishonest as can be but physical attraction can run havoc with our ability to discriminate of that which is good and of that which is bad.

"Love is a canvas furnished by nature and embroidered with imagination." –
François-Marie Arouet, 'Voltaire' (Writer, France 18th century)

The 19th century Italian criminologist Cesare Lombroso deduced that certain facial characteristics suggest or relate to being predisposed to crime. You could detect a criminal from their appearance, anything odd in their looks and they might have been condemned. However, Lombroso's theory was found to be not entirely correct, your appearance may raise suspicions about what you are although you might just be the polar opposite but Lombroso wasn't entirely wrong either so in some although not all cases there is partial correlation between how we look and our inclination to crime.

Just as we cannot easily attribute facial characteristics to bad behaviour, neither can we do so for good behaviour either - what we perceive in someone from what we see can be completely wrong. See a handsome or pretty face with a nice smile and personality and we might deduce that this person is honourable, kind, of good temperament and reliable but we don't know them nor do we know their history; how would we know that they are not the complete opposite of what we perceive, indeed what appears to be a saint could be a psychopath. Indeed there have been murderers who have fooled their victim into thinking that they are a saint.

Psychopaths are not all committed to an asylum or a psychiatric hospital, they walk amongst us as do others who we would certainly not classify as insane, in current definitions of insanity, though who are nonetheless not exactly very nice people.

The problem with us is the effect that a person who we find attractive and who we know is attracted to us engages our hormones, the intoxicating chemicals of love, that cause various emotions to run through our cranium and says *"this is the one"*, *"I am destined to be with this person"*, we do not even have any strength to resist this and this is particularly heightened if we might feel alone. Essentially 'love' has seized our minds like the jaws of a vice. Our, what perhaps should be classed as 'type 'A' illegal drug' hormones, drives our rational thinking into being fatally overridden, we are defenceless.

We are so stupefied and smitten that not only are we incapable of rational thought we have also become deaf to the ringing of alarm bells going off in our heads when we consciously or subliminally see something that is not right. The police have a great nose for this, they have to, but the rest of us don't. In effect we only see what we want to see, and what we don't know we fill in the blanks from our own belief of what we believe to be our ideal person. In a fleeting moment we will construct a mental image of someone that in reality may be very far from the truth.

The idea of 'love at first sight' is a fallacy and a dangerous fallacy at that. Those trusted friends can see it but you can't, you might even be tipped off by friends of the object of your affection as to exactly what you are getting involved with but it's to no avail you are not listening. To put it blunt you could be in deep shit and you don't even know it or if you do you choose to ignore it. So ignore this at your peril, even the slightest suspicion be on guard, ignoring it is a rather like driving a car with dodgy brakes, the consequences could leave you emotionally, physically and financially destroyed and might even compromise what support you already have elsewhere.

Hormones are funny things, what in some can turn from a feeling of euphoria, a sense of feeling arrival or a purpose with the world, of having a companion and a bond with someone really special and that may include the more obsessive, and potentially dangerous, feelings of infatuation and being 'joined at the hip' can morph into indescribable hurt, disappointment, loss of faith in humanity and hatred, a hatred so bad that it is off the scale, when you have been shit on or fooled and realize that what you thought you had was in fact nothing but a mirage. The person you thought you knew never really existed.

I do not wish to 'pour cold water' over the potential of romance, many relationships can turn out to be great and why not so good luck to those who have something special and great, however you must choose a partner wisely and get to know them well over time so you must not let your hormones override your rational thought. If something doesn't seem right it is because it is not right and so don't find yourself in the position where you are constantly making excuses for a toxic partner. Painful as it may be to you, if you ignore what is happening you most probably are putting off the inevitable, for which the damage to you will be much greater and you may have lost good years in your life that could have been used productively to finding someone else who would be right for you.

This may sound ominous but not being cognizant of how our emotions can act against our best interests may bring you failure after failure in relationships and at great cost to you. Remember too that divorce is costlier than marriage and avoiding this truth may cost you dearly. So expensive is divorce that I use it as a frame of reference to bring levity to all other calamities that may happen, if I have a friend who laments that his/her car is a dud and has cost a fortune to repair, it looks somewhat less of a problem if I relate to it in context to the costs of a divorce.

"If you cannot get what you desire then desire what you find." – Arabic proverb.

The other consideration here is that do not be bowled over by looks, some of the nicest people are perhaps not so great in this department although underneath the warmth of their soul shines through and a good heart can make someone ordinary look extraordinary and certainly a better catch all round. Just look at others holistically, as in the whole package, don't think 'oh they are not enough of this or that' after all are you that perfect.

Toxic Relationships

Unconsciously do we all have some propensity to choose bad rather than good; is it that we see 'good' as dull and 'bad' as exciting, maybe we do. Now I don't want to go deep drilling into psychoanalysis but perhaps the very thing that we look for is the very opposite of what is in our best interests to have. Perhaps we should reflect on what is it that attracts us to another and realise that maybe we are making bad choices because our preconceived ideas or culture, of what makes an ideal partner, is completely wrong. We have to think outside of the box of the irrational and realise that good doesn't necessarily mean boring and that bad could lead us to tragedy rather than to a life of adventure and fun. Look again at what stands before you, what is the reality, just where are the dangers.

Ever had a 'friend' who seems to delight in what goes wrong for you, who doesn't compliment you, who likes to make you feel bad or bad about yourself who cannot bring themselves to share your joy at something you have succeeded at or that new car you have just bought. An excellent word that aptly describes such a characteristic is 'Schadenfreude' what is literally translated from its native German as 'the pleasure of having done harm'.

If you have a friend who is a practitioner of Schadenfreude, a sort of smiling assassin, they are best not known they may even behave in this way because they are too envious of you or even pathologically jealous, either way it is an inexcusable behaviour – if you know of anyone like this it is perhaps best that you do not know them any more as they will only make you miserable – if a friend does you no good in this way then they are no friend so just be rid of them. Don't call them don't return their messages make sure that you are no longer available, if you have to say it for what it is so be it just be rid of them. At their very worst such a friend may take the damage to higher levels to lead you astray into drugs, reckless behaviour or crime or even worse and perhaps all done so deliberately.

Friends can make your life or they can destroy it, choose badly and you might regret it badly. Your friend may not be a Schadenfreude type one who deliberately seeks to bring you misfortune or that they delight in your misfortune but they nevertheless cause you grief, they have a different issue and that is they use you, their concept of friendship is utilitarian, you to them are useful when they need you but as for you; you don't count for anything.

Do you have a friend who often asks for money and then you have difficulty in getting it back, who only calls you when they need a favour but who doesn't call you when they know you are in need, do you do them favours and never get anything in return albeit you don't expect or ask for anything in return. The solution is the same as with the Schadenfreude type, just be rid of it.

These aforementioned types may seem not too good but let's now get onto the real nightmares where you have encountered or worse still set up home with someone in possession of a pathological personality. In particular you may land in a relationship with a psychopathic or narcissistic personality and you are not aware of it not until it's too late and then you see the toxicity, malevolence, coldness, abuse and hate. Love turns to hate. This raises the question, do we really know anyone, perhaps we do but as they say 'love is blind' so just keep your eyes open and certainly observe your instincts if your instincts feel something isn't right then most probably it isn't.

Look out for any signs that something is awry look also for how they behave towards others especially those who are subordinate to them in some way. If they treat the waiter, the petrol pump attendant or those who report to them at work like shit this will be how they will end up treating you. Malevolent personalities often lack any respect for others, those who are deserving of respect that is, and lack any consideration or empathy for others feelings.

Being in a relationship can not only harm you it can destroy you and the earlier you recognise what you have before you the better. As soon as your nose starts smelling something seriously bad it's time to get out. Our problem is that we all tend to fall back on what we originally thought of someone, the person who in actuality never existed, what existed was phony an illusion a fake. You will keep reminding yourself of the good what you had seen in them, good that was soon to evaporate after you have been caught, in their mind, as irrevocably in their net. Further to this we are often trapped by our emotional investment; you may have known the subject of your trouble for so long, done so many things together and travelled to so many places with many good memories and indeed they may have been mutually felt to be good times but this is irrelevant, what matters is what they are.

If you invested in a business that goes sour and that you know cannot be retrieved do you invest more of your money and effort or do you decide to 'throw in the towel' (idiom for 'to give up') at some point reality has to be faced and this is no different with relationships. OK you have invested time and emotion into the relationship but you must for your own sake be clinical about it, awful as it is, if you carry on you are just throwing in more emotional investment in the hope that others will change which, to be honest, it is highly likely that they won't. Is this person deserving of your effort most probably not, would they extend you the same benevolence, again most probably not.

You may baulk at the idea of leaving a relationship for fear of being alone but if it is your decision to stay with it you may have condemned yourself to a life of certain misery, staying put and you might just get more and even increasing abuse not less, whereas there is still chance that you may find someone else, perhaps not very quickly, but someone who you are worthy of although with some risk of having to endure loneliness but loneliness that is quite possibly infinitely better than living with a nightmare. Just imagine you are on a sinking ship that is certain to sink but the lifeboats are of questionable seaworthiness do you take a chance or go down with a sinking ship it's a simple as that but just 'don't jump from the frying pan into the fire'.

After you have done the deed and waved the trouble goodbye and good riddance you might then feel aftershocks of regret, you forget the bad things and only remember the good things, you may even start to blame yourself you might feel guilt thinking about your ex partners potential dire situation – don't think any of this, we should be prepared to measure others on what is the worst they are capable of doing. Evil is not measured from what good we have done but what evil we have done. Hitler may have kissed babies whilst simultaneously overseeing the murder of millions so is he good or is he bad.

Whatever bad has happened see it as an opportunity to learn, put it down to experience. There are a lot of bad people out there and you may experience this more than once, however don't let that colour your view of the world since there are also a lot of good people too it's just that you have been unlucky.

Never forget this that whatever we think, good or bad, of anyone, even of ourselves, we must recognize that we could be wrong, even very wrong and the consequences could be catastrophic. Stay alert look for signs of what isn't right, if you find any it's time to wave bye-bye.

The Root of Causes of Broken Relationships

"By all means marry, if you get a good partner, you'll become happy; if you get a bad one you'll become a philosopher." – 'gender neutralised' quotation of Socrates (Philosopher, Greece 4th/5th century BC)

If you have been crapped on in a relationship then welcome to the 'I've been crapped on in a relationship' club, I think you will find it has many members so you are in no way alone.

In accordance with contract law for a contract to be valid requires, amongst other things, what is referred to legally as 'consensus ad idem' or what we would call 'a meeting of minds'. A meeting of minds can fail in three ways: 'misrepresentation', 'duress' and 'undue influence' for which the existence of any of these elements could invalidate a contract; you may have signed up to something legally binding but where there isn't a meeting of minds then the contract is no longer binding it has become void.

Drilling down further on this: 'misrepresentation' is where you have been sold something that is not what it is represented to be i.e. it is fake, 'duress' is where you are forced against your will, usually by threat, into doing something and a more subtle form of 'duress', i.e. 'undue influence', is where you have been persuaded, often by someone who you may trust (legally referred to as a 'fiduciary relationship'), into doing something that you might not otherwise have done. Contract law is based upon what is reasonable and fair. When we examine this aspect of contract law it presents two very useful considerations that directly relate to common causes of relationship failure, these being misrepresentation and duress.

Misrepresentation, 'the fake' we are all very well aware of they are everywhere but duress is a special case where you may very well know the shortcomings of who you enter into a contract of marriage with but that you have no choice owing to some 'cultural' coercion of your community where it would be perceived as 'dishonourable' to decline. This is despite the distinct lack of honour of forcing someone against their will and then allowing them to be subjected to a life of misery so where is the honour in that I can't see any can you, although we can only hope that such cultural practices will end with more enlightened thinking and an understanding that no person can ever be considered as property and without free will. No-one can 'own' anyone else to do so is a disgrace to any concept of honour.

Let us now return to the more general problem of misrepresentation. The person we meet may not be the same person who we engage in a serious relationship with, just think back to that first date; you perhaps had very good thoughts of what this person is all about. You might have concluded that they are charming, kind, unselfish, stable, 'un-possessive' and decent they may in fact be none of these and this is coupled with the fact that the word 'love' doesn't have a specific meaning it is open to wide interpretation, it is a 'spectral colloquialism' where your idea of love can be quite different from theirs. What you thought was your soul-mate your ideal partner could later turn out to be a person you despise.

You may delude yourself into thinking that you can change them for the better, you can't, this is a pipe dream, they are what they are with or without the sticking plasters and many who behave badly do so because they do not know any other way, it's how they are and it's how they will always be. Furthermore, they may be a lot worse than this - could they be someone who is driven with gleaming eyes upon the most obvious example and reason for divorce - money. What is it about you that attracts them to you could it be your bank balance or that nice house or just because of your looks alone where all of your other qualities are somehow missed. Now I don't blame anyone looking for stability and for someone who has a work ethic and at least some ambition as these are good character traits that happen to inadvertently bring some wealth too, but money for money's sake is a different ball game it is a game of the exploitative parasite the game of what you might call legalised crime when it enters the stage of 'legalised' divorce settlements.

If the person who you thought that you had entered into a relationship with is in actuality a personality fraud or who has a hidden agenda, in that you don't matter but it is what you have that matters, then the seeds of a failing relationship are sown.

I have heard people say *"oh they've changed"* – it is most probably so that they didn't although not improbable; what they did is that they either knowingly or unknowingly, to you and to themselves, had misrepresented what they are and what they were looking for. When you get closer to these types they either disappoint you, abuse, complain, seek to control, demand, will be on the lookout for a better deal, have expectations of entitlement that incessantly ratchets up or should you happen to be hit with misfortune such as ill health, disability or loss of your income or for that matter fading looks they won't stay around to help you out as their marriage vows might suggest they will instead dump you like a tonne of bricks.

You may have heard all the good words what they would do if you fell on hard times but never forget that 'a verbal contract is not worth the paper it's written on'. This may seem a cynical indictment of relationships but I say all of this with a heavy heart since most of us live in some hope of finding that ideal mate although seldom is it easy to do so if we, or our wise friends (advice), are really discerning about who we should and should not date using rational reasons rather than stock ideas of what is and what is not for me.

"Do not judge by appearance. A rich heart may be under a poor coat." – Scottish proverb.

However, don't let that put you off as there are so many genuinely decent people who don't have personality issues or hidden agendas but just be a little cautious and if you hear anything, see anything or smell anything that doesn't look so great then take heed of the warning signs. My advice is to look for someone of quality of high standards above all else – you might not initially see them as your ideal match although later you might come to realise just what you have and just how lucky you are. If you have the illusion that this is my perfect partner but yet they don't want to know you then they are not right for you and what you may have read into them you may have got entirely wrong anyway simple as that – so it's no loss.

The Loss and Recovery of Trust and Hope - Important

Those who have experienced loss or deprivation are often more appreciative of what they gain. Others who we may perceive as being happy in the relationship department may not be as happy as what we may imagine since they may be unaware of just how lucky they are. You can see it but they can't. Whatever you have, others may not, and for this you should feel lucky.

Loss of trust can lead to a total collapse of confidence in humanity, which to be honest is a bit unfair on us all - we are not all the same. Perpetuating a visceral distrust in all others does us no good, we must identify reality; who can we trust and who we can't. If it is so that we expect too much in the way of the behaviour of others then consequently we will also expect too much in the way of our own behaviour; urbane and cultivated as that may be this can be a disaster; we will judge (often unfairly) too much, perceive too pessimistically, never have any trust in anyone and will feel very alone, very paranoid and very nihilistic about life.

Whether with the mad, the bad or the ill-suited, not necessarily with any fault, the collapse of a supposedly meaningful relationship can be traumatic and where you have invested a belief of unquestionable trust or longevity of relationship then the trauma can feel like earth-shattering indescribable hell. The experience can redefine your perception of life and humanity, you may even imagine that humanity no longer and possibly never did exist that we all live like maggots eating away at a carcass where we only have concern for ourselves. Your intuition your belief in others has failed you. Your faith has been lost.

The consequences may be that you give up on living the life you believed in and you then think why not join the maggots – from now on I shall be self-serving without any sense of conscience, morality or even reason to ever be polite to anyone again after all they are only wretched humans. Your trauma triggers an irrational misanthropy. But you may still persevere with hope and hang onto your values and your humanity in the hope that things will change, however it remains a possibility that all what has happened to you could happen again and if it does then you might really give up on humanity. You may even develop a bitter outlook and perhaps with a fear of being rejected you may then end up ignoring the person who you are interested in, thinking 'I won't give them the pleasure' and what you may have just done is rejected your-self and your future - the other person will just go and find someone else without ever knowing how you had felt about them. This is quite understandable to have these feelings.

This is all very vivid but it is also very wrong. Get hit enough times and your perception can change for the worse (bordering on paranoia) even though what you had experienced was just bad luck or perhaps bad judgment. What you had lost was not what you thought you had lost, your ability to discern did not let you down it just wasn't perceptive enough it was not perfect and that is so for all of us. What has happened to you was just bad luck that can even repeat itself without difficulty since it's very easy to be bitten more than once. However, not all of the human race is the same, the walls that you have built will not only protect you from bad experiences and bad people but will also hold back any chances of good experiences or of making connections with good people.

Whatever happens don't lose trust in all of humanity and don't presume that you will never find happiness just look in the right places, gain knowledge not bitterness and be and remain what you are with your values. Never give up on humanity and eventually luck can turn your way with the right use of effort and wisdom. With some luck, a compass and effort it is not beyond hope to find someone who is your ideal partner, but give up and you will never find them. If you can't persevere if you can't be bothered then you condemn yourself to a lonely existence.

And perhaps a lesson in the dynamics of life, not just for this chapter but for all others, is that we can keep searching and keep trying and we do not see any result. Despite our efforts things can often appear unresponsive and unsuccessful, we impatiently crave an indicator a sign of things moving in the direction we desire and still nothing, we might then resign ourselves to the idea that nothing will ever happen, but when things do change they do so when we least expect and the change can be very rapid indeed. From having nothing to having everything may not always be a gradual process with obvious noticeable progression of success since life often presents change in sudden massive steps and without warning, just what is it that could be around the corner, around which we cannot see.

Some things we cannot succeed with, ever, but some things we can and the things that we can we must never assume that all is lost when the desired outcome has not yet arrived; who knows what tomorrow or what next year may bring. But in the apparent long wait our motivation may take some serious bashing so to keep our motivation charged then perhaps we should imagine that what we want we already have at least is some fashion.

But further to this, and again of wider relevance than just this chapter, concerns our intuition. Albeit that we may reflect on what has just been said our intuition can often demolish what we may think, not always necessarily bad although not always necessarily good either. We may have arrived at a pessimistic view from the lack of desirable or even desperate tangible and identifiable progress and our intuition may conjure up a probabilistic thought of 'ah yes but' in other words we don't believe that positive change can ever occur based upon previous outcomes that wrongly define what we suspect to be our future outcomes. Our intuition has brought us back to a rather pessimistic position. However, intuition is often wrong, I can even recall occasions where my intuition has failed me badly, even very badly.

We may ask: why would our future outcomes be any different than our past and there is one massive reason why and the word is enlightenment – if it is so that we have gained some wisdom/realisation/life changing experience then we are different, we have changed such that our future cannot be quite the same as our past. When we examine our intuitive thoughts did our intuition by itself factor in that we have changed in how we think and so if we have changed so shall our potential circumstances – just wait and be patient.

Beating the Odds - Important

Helicopters relentlessly leave Aberdeen airport like bees departing the hive, they are heading to massive oil rigs, but if one happens to ditch in the North Sea in mid-winter the passengers and crew won't last long, hypothermia will kill them, most are gone in two minutes (although hypothermia is not a bad way to die); but with a survival suit they will survive for at least 48 hours, time enough for a rescue mission.

Statistical evidence, and our 'intuition', tells us that for most of us, once having crossed the threshold of middle age, we are considerably less likely to find a suitable partner and very unlikely to ever having a family - we are ostensibly condemned to a life of loneliness and misery, our future might be looking pretty bleak indeed. That's a typical scenario with the all too typical resignation to this state, morale collapses and we then capitulate. But what if we decided to do something about it having honed our social skills, image and how we think and we make the effort to socialise in the right places and with the right people, what then, because in effect we have just invested in a survival suit and thereby massively changed the odds of survival and of future success. Statistics may suggest that we can only last two minutes but with knowing what to do and how then two minutes can become 48 hours. We can beat the odds, not just by a little but by a lot, by doing something but also in thinking carefully on what needs to be done and on then acting upon it. Those who can't swim drown, those who can swim reach the shore and if we can all swim, we can all reach the shore.

Chapter 9

ON FINDING SUCCESS IN OUR EDUCATION

(In exploration of the far reaching mind, learning to think for your-self)

The most precious gift a parent can give a child is to nurture good manners and gratitude, a sense of what is right and what is wrong, to not take themselves or life just too seriously, to be able to independently survive, to be objective and to be able to identify when they are being manipulated, to have a sense of duty to others, to act responsibly and to accept responsibility for their actions, to do their best, to be educated and to understand life and how to make the most of it.

"It was the best of times it was the worst of times, it was the age of wisdom it was the age of foolishness." – Charles Dickens (Novelist, England 19th century)

It is possible to be very clever and very stupid at the same time. You can sound very well informed on a subject but you must be prepared to look at it from every perspective and with an open mind, it is only then that you will really begin to understand it. You must therefore be amenable to discard all what you have learnt if you were to discover that you were wrong. At the very least every conversation every book every thought and every experience must alter what you believe, even a little, if it doesn't then education and the truth is beyond your reach.

The truth is, is that none of us know very much at all with any great certainty and that includes you and me but yet it is so interesting how dismissive we are of others views, is that through intellectual hubris or is it that we just don't like that which is true, truth that is that we are unwilling to face.

The Experience of Study

Education is not meant to make us feel comfortable, quite the opposite, it is meant for learning; how can we study psychology without looking into the disturbed mind perhaps even our own, mathematics without facing the stress of its extreme complexity, medicine without those gruesome anatomy laboratories, history without the brutality of war, politics without understanding its corrupting elements, law without the depravity of sickening crime, engineering without the intimidation and danger of gigantic machines and physics without the hard cold facts of our universe. Life is hard and so education must be presented without limits such that we are equipped for the unforgiving and harsh but most fascinating world of work. Where we overcome our fears we start to see greater purpose in what we do, fear is a necessary evil that we all have to face without which we cannot develop.

Speaking as an engineering student of the 1970s/80s we were stuffing our heads full of difficult mathematics and physics, we had stacks of books and lecture notes to study, incomprehensible lectures to attend, perhaps in some places often delivered remiss of any observable passion for the subject or for the students being taught, then to another dreary room another dreary lecture in the labyrinthine dimly lit corridors of large sometimes depressing buildings, this would be followed by countless hours in the bowels of the library trying to find the book, chapter and paragraph or mathematical treatise (no internet then) to explain, with marginally less obscurity, what had eluded us all earlier that day.

To fill the rest of our busy day we would work in the various test tube, instrument and machine laden laboratories, trying to connect the theories and mathematical formulas that we had derived to the physical world, the world of thermodynamics, high voltage electrical systems, operational amplifiers, process chemistry, nuclear metallurgy, reactor physics and advanced integral and differential calculus within which lay the esoteric gone exotic subjects such as the (tables of) thermo-physical properties of steam, cavity resonator physics, xenon tilt instability, cylindrical harmonics and the Greek alphabet. The world of engineering is indeed more mysterious than what we might imagine.

"Consider it pure joy, my brothers, whenever you face trials of many kinds, because you know that the testing of your faith develops perseverance. Perseverance must finish its work so that you may become mature and complete, not lacking anything." – The Bible, book of James I (Christianity)

Our study was relentless it would continue on; month upon month, year upon year, more lectures, more brain bashing, more despair, culminating in a load of year end three hour exams so terrifying and fiendish that I often wondered if they were deliberately designed to thwart our chances of passing, just to pass you had to be good and you had to be self-disciplined. It was hard and your effort was not a 9 till 5 affair, your evenings and much of your weekends had no option but to be sacrificed upon the academic altar. The academic institutions would want you, as their alumni, to represent them for their prestige and for their excellent standards, you had to be a credit to them, if you were not good enough they wouldn't want to hand you a degree for the sake of pass rate statistics to attract applicants, you were to be cast aside, no piece of paper for you to say I graduated from this institution. This was the world of the engineering student and a lot of other students as I remember it then. Perhaps the experience, if it didn't destroy us, would develop us into something greater than what we were and perhaps back then we did not realize just how.

"Without perseverance talent is a barren bed." – Welsh proverb.

Now I don't remember so much of what I had learnt then, it was long ago, but I do remember the feelings of gut-wrenching loneliness living in a very small and very grim room in a very big city and of the despair of not knowing if my efforts had really any point and of the fools who told me that they didn't, it was only many years later did I realize that I was wrong and so were they. So you must always see some purpose and elegance in your studies, even if you can't see one there is one; even the paper upon which this book is printed would never come to be without the actions, ideas, observation and research of someone having intellectual curiosity.

And some advice to anyone in such circumstances is; study in the library not in your room it's so much easier to be surrounded by others even if you don't interact with them since loneliness has a vice like grip that makes study even harder to deal with, and secondly; do not commit to your study as your sole 'raison d'etre'; you must seek out and find the time to join social groups, you must do something other than your study, you must interact with others.

Without human contact it can become increasingly difficult to be in a mind receptive to study or for that matter to motivate ourselves into doing anything. If only I had realised this then then my experience of university would have been a better one (I might have achieved a few more 'A's and 'B's and less 'C's), so perhaps what I had felt then was my fault, it was down to me in not recognizing what I had and how lucky I was. In the end what I did gain from my university experience did me some good I just didn't realize it at the time.

Academic collaboration is extremely useful, actually essential, between students, to collectively try to make sense of that which is so difficult to make sense of, to connect that which is unconnected and to fill the chasms of missing information. But a word of warning is that ostensibly out of our need to seek and maintain human contact, and maybe friendship, just beware of sharing with others too much of what you have discovered with your own diligence unless it is well traded, i.e. is such a transaction equitable in the way that you may help one another, for in this context, if what you give is a lot greater than what you receive then one day you may be applying for the same job and you might had inadvertently given your fellow, but less diligent, student the edge over you. This may seem mean, but it isn't, it's a cruel world and we have to see when we cross the line into being too open with our generosity.

I was once asked by a colleague if I could offer up my third year research project, from years past, to a student friend of his who hadn't undertaken any research to submit for his final year evaluation and that I would do so as he was a really nice guy and had run out of time. Not only was this unethical, it's cheating and to me how nice he was didn't cut any ice, besides a person who is nice doesn't cheat others out of their deserved opportunities through being dishonest. If he wanted to graduate then he should earn his degree, with effort, just as anyone else would. So you can guess my answer to his request and it doesn't have three letters as was the same response from everyone else he had asked.

Many may have graduated with a feeling of achievement, which of course it is, though some of us felt worse for the experience. Over the years of study we had become 'experts', so we thought, in a field that was difficult to acquire but it came at a heavy price. Under a regime of the hard degree and perhaps not such nice an environment many of us would lose out on experiencing life. Some may argue otherwise but maybe they never realized what they had missed out on and maybe they still don't. We would have academic knowledge, some of us thinking that knowledge but not just any knowledge but our knowledge and our knowledge only was all you needed to be able to understand absolutely everything, it was as if it were some intellectual franchise that we were party to.

We were all young then, we were full of ideas on everything and many would bounce these ideas off of one another, yet we only really knew what we had learnt within an institution, our vision of the world was narrow and inexperienced. We may have learnt how we could successfully fly to the moon, to cut into flesh and remove tumours, to understand how we think, our history and our life existence but this is not everything.

We had in effect received an education though we were not educated, we were not cultivated, although some with heaps of self-confidence might have thought they were, we would need to catch up on such simple things as common sense, the world of work and the concept that just maybe our viewpoint could be wrong, whereas most, although not all, of those who did not attend university are already well on the way to graduating in these departments. As graduates we could catch up by first seeing that we have potential to catch up and secondly that we must abandon the idea that we are 'dead on balls' accurate with the ideas we have of anything not related to our academic studies. We must effectively come to realize that because some of us may have had huge confidence in what we had studied does not necessarily suggest that we are universally enlightened and all-knowing.

"If I see further than other men it is because I stand on the shoulders of giants." - Isaac Newton (Physicist/Mathematician, England 17th/18th century)

If we hold onto the view that we can interpret the world through a mind closed in upon our core academic expertise that we believe teaches us everything that we need to know (it doesn't), that has not been developed or being given opportunity to experience beyond its academic confines and that we only associate with those of the same kind, i.e. more students or lecturers, then we fail to release ourselves from the shackles of our slot orientated limited reasoning. To learn, to become educated, we must look beyond our academic siblings, we must expand our perceptive field to 360°, we must take an interest and examine everything in our world, we must strive to understand different perspectives and not dismiss them as meaningless, we must mix amongst others from all walks of life – just maybe then we will get a better idea of reaching the enlightenment of true learning.

"The greatest scholars are not usually the wisest people." - Geoffrey Chaucer
(Poet, England 14th century)

You may discover the most amazing things from the most unexpected places and people – you may find, if you look with open eyes, that great philosophy can be had not just from some professor of this quite elevating subject but also from those very far removed from academic study. Just be prepared to be surprised and be open to listen to everyone whoever they are. There are people out there with some very clever ideas who didn't necessarily receive a university education and often have learnt much through having to survive a hard life - as I say an education does not necessarily make you educated. There are indeed a lot of talented people out there so be very careful in how you measure others besides we all have something unique to us, something others have that you may not.

Perhaps the first step on the road to becoming educated is to question what we ourselves and our select social group thinks, often what we vociferate with unswerving lack of self-doubt can still be totally wrong, although for social, political and cultural reasons we may be afraid to admit it for fear of being outcast from our social group, for fear of condemnation or accused of being unrefined or worse. We are sometimes afraid to look at the facts as the facts may be unpleasant and unpalatable to hear, but facts are facts and that is that. Is it not the purpose of an education to intelligently debate and research to arrive at what is the truth no matter how unpalatable it may be? If we do not widen our perspective and we ignore the truth then we really are in trouble.

School – Our First Rung on the Educational Ladder

Like many of us I didn't enjoy school too much and we all tend to pillory the whole experience but like it or not education has changed our lives it has brought us from ignorance to the light if it is used well. Education has taught us to read and to write, something I hold as amongst the most wonderful things that the human race has bestowed upon itself and we have learnt the fundamentals of mathematics. With these skills we can read of our history, good, bad and often not entirely connected with the truth, how our societies are made up from different cultures and religions and we can start to understand the natural world, that of science the world of biology, chemistry and physics and we explore the universe, we can create wonderful things and we can cultivate what we are.

Our school years prepares us for an education on life because school and for that matter university is not the end of our education it is the beginning of our education. And when we have more or less worked it out, if we actually get there, we are often approaching our dissolution; our time on planet earth must come to its end. *"If I only knew then what I do now"* is one of the regrets often uttered by those of us in the latter stages of our life.

If we were to look at our teachers of the somewhat distant, now past, times, some were sadists and bullies, you could see the excitement in their eyes to intimidate, what I often wondered was some fetish to resort to administration of corporal punishment, i.e. the cane, albeit some of us dearly deserved it, the intent to destroy confidence where it existed or thwart its development where it didn't. I often wondered if these bastards were hand-picked at interview by deliberation – I can hear it now Q. *"why do you want to become a teacher"*, A. *"because I loathe children and I would like to beat the crap out of them"*, Interviewer reply *"you sound perfect for the role, when can you start"*.

Some were seriously puffed up with their own ego and some would hate the very thought that you might have ambitions to exceed what they had achieved and would do everything to talk you down and if you fell behind in your subject you were left behind. Some would not only talk down to children but they would also do the same to adults too. Many of us would bear the consequences of such teaching standards for the rest of our lives, our 'glass ceilings' would be lowered through their incompetence, neglect and yes foul play.

This being said there were a lot of teachers who were excellent, in fact beyond excellent, who were firm but fair, who were hard working, imaginative and devoted to the success of their students, who showed immeasurable enthusiasm for their subject and instilled the same in their students and essentially could teach a subject well, not all can, they would encourage and nurture interest where otherwise there would be none. To attend one of their lessons would be pure joy an epiphany, what they did for you was priceless, they gave you a future to realize your potential where otherwise there would be none.

Our school experience and that of the teaching we have encountered is intrinsic to what becomes of us in later life. I can relate to this so well as in my third year at secondary school I just didn't get maths; all those 'x's' and 'y's'!!!, without which I could not be where I am today, although sometimes do wonder where that exactly is, but then I had the greatest fortune to encounter the most wonderful maths teacher and a great woman in my fourth year, she had a fearsome reputation but wow was she a brilliant teacher and only then with her efforts, and mine now they were fired up, did I begin to understand this mysterious subject and then to begin to succeed in it.

Had I not had met this wonderful person where would I be today I ask. Such great examples do a lot more than teach a subject, they impress strengths and virtues on their students, intangible to their subject though very tangible in the wider perspective of what we need to know in life. What we had learnt from them has shaped the very way how we behave, specifically to show respect to all and to have patience. Having a great teacher is like winning the lottery since what we are and what we become cannot be bought with money it requires great people to instil good values upon us; in essence we have received an education in life. Money might buy fancy cars but it cannot buy what we are or what we need to become.

So an important lesson here is that what you understand and what you do not understand, what you are enthused by and what you are not enthused by is not subject to your limitations alone, it depends upon who taught you. It is also often the case that being bottom of the class and the slowest at a subject does not make you a dunce, none of us are really that at all – just think of a car, which one can win a race, the one with the highest acceleration though low top speed or the one with the lowest acceleration though higher top speed. The more pedantic amongst you will posit that it depends upon the length of the race but I think my point is made nonetheless.

I have encountered characters who are; quick to learn, and brag about it but who have a very low glass ceiling, those who may be a genius at one subject and brag about that but crap at the rest and those who may be great at all subjects and again brag but they may woefully lack good manners or the cultivation of self-effacement. I was once reasonably O.K. at maths not because of any innate genius, I haven't any, but because of great teachers plus some bloody hard work. So if you excel at something, just be a bit more tolerant at those who don't, maybe you are not so clever and they just didn't get the opportunities that you had had.

"Better indeed is knowledge than mechanical practice. Better than knowledge is meditation. But better still is surrender of attachment to results, because there follows immediate peace." – The Bhagavad Gita (Hinduism)

If you want to learn and lack the confidence don't let anything get in your way though you must stay realistic in what you can achieve without destroying yourself in the process – most things even the most complex can often be conquered if you have the will, the aptitude and can handle the effort. And if you fail, it doesn't matter, there is something out there that you will be good at and you just need to find out what it is. In my last year at school I failed my English exam and yet here I am writing a book so there is always plenty of hope for us all.

Where Our Confidence Is Our Enemy (the purpose of debate is to find the truth not to prove that we are right)

"The aim of education should be to teach us rather how to think, than what to think." – James Beattie (Philosopher, Scotland 18th/19th century)

If we are educated about the very point of education, then education has taught us, or at least it should do, in how we must think not what we must think and this is where education has its dark side where we allow ourselves to be inculcated to what is erroneous thinking by others who may impress us with their education though who are in reality ignorant or who claim to have an answer to our problems though who in fact just manipulate us for their own, sometimes malevolent, ends. We need to seek independence of thought, we need to have the intellectual capacity and intellectual courage to make up our own minds or we shall be slaves to the ideas of others. If in debate we find ourselves agreeing with everything from one side of the argument then we are not being serious, courageous or independent as not all sides of a debate are completely without some truth or at least without need to be examined.

"It is beyond a doubt that all our knowledge begins with experience." – Immanuel Kant (Philosopher, Germany 18th/19th century)

Modern schooling instils confidence in its students whereas in the past confidence would likely be battered out of you but the problem is that confidence without experience can be a serious drawback. I can sit in a library for a millennia and read every book on a select group of subjects and I acquire confidence in as much that I become confident in me not just in what I have studied, I begin to believe that I am 'all-knowing', 'all-wise', and in the process I possibly become 'all-disliked' and so prone to rejection in job interviews, but the world of bookish learning and discussion amongst equally book absorbed individuals is that they lack experience and they lack latitude of thought. When I say experience I do not mean age – I have met the odd character with the classic 'time-served, I know better than anyone else, attitude', ignore them they are usually idiots who have possibly only one year of experience repeated thirty times not thirty years of real diverse and deep experience as they may claim and they often know a lot less than they pretend.

"I do not think sir that you have any right to command me merely because you are older than I or because you have seen more of the world than I have; your claim to superiority depends on the use you have made of your time and experience." –
Charlotte Brontë (Novelist, England 19th century)

It is so that truly experienced people don't go around shouting about it and they don't talk down to those who are less experienced. It is one thing I can't stand is the 'oh don't you know that' attitude; well there was a time when they didn't know that either so they should shut up and behave themselves, they just might be talking to someone who knows a lot more than them about everything else. However, there are also those who deride education that it is not needed, but where would we be without it, for all of the major advances in all fields, that have taken us from the medieval to the modern world, is through men and women who are prepared to sacrifice their time to research and to understand. In the context of the professional world, a formal education is essential, it does actually mean something, you cannot become a surgeon without first qualifying as a doctor and you cannot become a barrister without first qualifying as a lawyer.

We may look at someone and presume to know what their job entails and for any career; but we don't know what we don't know, and we certainly don't know when what they do can become unimaginably complicated that will demand huge skill, knowledge and experience that we are not even dimly aware of. Most things are a lot more complicated than they look.

"The cleverest of all, in my opinion, is the man who calls themselves a fool at least once a month." – Fyodor Dostoyevsky (Novelist, Russia 19th century)

"It is the mark of an educated mind to be able to entertain a thought without accepting it." – Aristotle (Philosopher, Greece 4th century BC)

From a few books that I clutch to my bosom and from discussion with my fellow students can I acquire the skill of detecting; when I am being duped such as someone trying to sell me a used car with a blown cylinder head gasket, someone being of despicable character though they may appear to all as convincingly most pleasant, a dishonest or incompetent political point of view or from someone who says that they are in need when they are not, can I distinguish between those who can't and those who won't, can I see that which is hidden from view or what moves with stealth, can I see when less than diligent academic consideration is tainted with bias, can I acquire a skill of assimilating all positions of an argument rather than just my own narrow cursory perspective and seeing things for what they really are not what I might like to think they are, can I see that what I believe to be good or bad may be anything but, can I see that to survive I must not be rigid about what I think, do I know when, and when not, to tolerate what is intolerable, do I really know anything about money - how it is made and how it must and must not be spent, do I know when it is best to leave things be or when things are best left unsaid, can I be modest about what I am, have I the courage to face the truth and speak up for it even at the risk of condemnation from those who are close to me, do I know how to communicate well in that I also must show respect for others and give them a chance to speak, do I have the capacity to be endearing to all, do I know how to survive what life will throw at me, do I care for others and do I realise, despite my education, just how little I know.

"If you understand everything then you must be misinformed." – Japanese proverb.

In engineering and indeed every human activity what is done best is not just based on learning, though academic learning is essential, it is also based upon common sense, i.e. through truth that is self-evident and therefore does not need proof, upon instinct and even a wild hunch and yes making mistakes, none of which are gleaned from burying your head in a book but in actually experiencing life in the raw. None of these skills can be purchased through an education, it is as if education is the first step to wisdom though there is still a long way to go and an awful lot of experiences to encounter, people to meet, more than just one perspective to look at and time to mature how we can think cogently and independently to arrive at enlightened thinking.

It can often be the perception of being educated through receiving an education that can lead to massive self-confidence albeit that that education has not made the individual educated. An assumption of intellectual superiority where to look upon others as intellectually inferior is none other than 'intellectual racism' and is no less disgusting than any other form of racism. Sometimes the more confident we are the more we should question ourselves at least a little, to do otherwise can lead to making some very bad critical life choices.

"The greatest deception men suffer is from their own opinions." – Leonardo Da Vinci (Artist, Italy 15th/16th century)

A 'Gestalt entity' is where the whole is greater than the sum of its parts, therefore we can only ever arrive at the truth through where we disagree where there are different perspectives, ideas and opinions (dialectic engagement) and from here we can go beyond what we think we know and we can develop new and great ideas. If it were that we all agreed on absolutely everything that we all had exactly the same perception the same thinking then a Gestalt entity could never exist since the sum of all the parts could never be greater than itself under such conditions. If one person is unable to solve a problem, then two of the same who also think the same and the problem will remain unsolved.

It is through entertaining the idea of disagreement that we intellectually progress, this is what university is all about and should be about. I have a very good friend who has a completely different political view than mine that fires up some really interesting discussions whenever we meet, not where I get him to agree with all what I say, I don't want that, what I'm looking for is for him to blow holes in my point of view, I want to know where I might be wrong and I want to reach the truth. The consequences are always the same, we always walk away remaining the best of friends but where we had both changed our point of view, we both could see something that we didn't before – this is progress.

"A man may learn wisdom even from a foe." – Aristophanes (Playwright, Greece 4th/5th century BC)

It is a manifestly educated position to see that it is not uneducated to have a different view, but it is uneducated to stifle the view of others (totalitarianism by stealth) just because we happen to not agree with them, besides, unbeknown to us, it could be our view that is wrong. In essence we all have freedom to have our own opinion but encased within that idea is that we are all then free to have a different opinion and I find it absolutely astonishing that some of our species cannot see this as being so obvious and need to be reminded of such particularly when they have such high esteem of their own intellect.

An educated mind is one that listens, decomposes, rationally enquires and from dialogue and consensus learns from what others have to say no matter how disagreeable their words may seem and this is something that the great man Socrates would have advocated. Even what may have been uttered by those who are evil we can learn from, we can, in the academic context at least, gain greater insight of the world and also of ourselves. All must be given a platform and all must be listened to, this doesn't mean we have to agree or even sympathise, we should at least listen and you never know you might even experience one of those 'I never thought of that' moments and then see the world in a different way. Remember, that even if you believe someone is doing something stupid they may just be doing something quite clever though you just can't see it – they may be just a lot more discerning than you might imagine.

If free speech is prohibited then we would only have silence in its place without challenge to our world, challenge without which the human race would have never progressed. Without free speech what next; would then freedom to think fall under the same axe or an Orwellian/Zamyatin hell. To debate sensibly no matter what it is, is the fuel for our development besides by looking at the same thing from different perspectives only then can we have scholarly understanding.

"All truth passes through three stages. First, it is ridiculed. Second, it is violently opposed. Third, it is accepted as being self-evident." – Arthur Schopenhauer
(Philosopher, Germany 18th/19th century)

If you believe that debate or perspective must be confined to that which everyone finds to be acceptable and inoffensive then you have missed the whole point of what debate is all about. In the 17th century, Galileo, a very brave man, who dared to challenge the self-deluded and evil Inquisition on the idea that the earth was not at the centre of the universe was forced to recant under threat of death, and no doubt torture, but who was it that was right in the end. In 19th century London no-one would listen to the physician John Snow about his ideas on cholera epidemics, he was right too (check out the brilliant book 'The Medical Detective' by Sandra Hempel, I couldn't put it down). What of those who warned of the threat of Hitler and those who didn't have the courage to listen for fear of causing offence or awakening a monster that would inevitably awake anyway. If you are violently opposed to something where you are not even prepared to listen you may just be very wrong indeed.

Even with years of education we may still know only very little, and a mind closed to at least listening to the views of others will never understand anything. If we have intelligence we should also be aware of our limits i.e. we should have some idea of also what we do not know and where we should engage the ears and not the mouth. Self-appointment to an assumption of omniscience and to believe ourselves to be universally right is nothing more than an achievement of an uneducated mind and if in debate that we resort to constant interruption, raising our voices, aggression or hysteria then we do so because we have lost the argument and to lose control of oneself this way is a sign of the uneducated, a behaviour you may expect of a three year old in a tantrum but not that of an adult.

We should hear out the other persons point of view, let them speak, but if what you hear is not designed for logical debate but to deliberately agitate or invoke acts of evil, where all manner of reasoning and logic falls on deaf ears, then it is time to walk away, not to resort to anything confrontational, just walk away and leave it be.

Being Selective Of What We Choose To Learn

"Chance favours the prepared mind." – Louis Pasteur (Microbiologist, France 19th century)

Back in my days as a student if you could get a university place, few did, you might receive a grant since very few in comparison to today's youngsters would be interested in an academic based career and the thought of years of study, so the state, the economy, could afford to support those few with ambitions to study the essential 'non-imaginary' academic subjects that the state needed for the state to function. A state cannot function without doctors, bacteriologists, engineers, chemists, teachers, lawyers and a whole host of other professions of merit to a modern society. The idea that education (a desire but with ensuing cost) is a human right was never debated; education was supplied out of national necessity.

And on the question of its human rights perspective it isn't that either; it is a human right to be treated fairly by others and to not be forced in what you think (a freedom), since title of this authority rests with none other than the individual, this right being enabled by nation and by law, though none of these things cost anything, they are not subject to economic capacity as are desires or demands of what we desire. If economic capacity can afford higher education for all, and education that often is without any imperative state functioning merits, then so be it, but if it can't it can't and that's it. This being said I find it bewildering where a state does not at least financially assist students, not just undergraduates here, who study subjects that are critical to the operation of a modern society though are perhaps of comparatively limited financial reward and so less attractive as a profession.

"An ignorant people, is the blind instrument of its own destruction." – Simon Bolivar (Politician, South America 19th/20th century)

Universities were designed to largely churn out people with these valuable skills but also to supply the humanities (formerly referred to as 'the arts'), our cultural base, e.g. history, literature, music, art (art that is, that is not devoid of skilful execution), classics, philosophy etc., to provide for an enlightened society without which we would be ignorant, ignorant that is of culture, we would in effect be devoid of cultural refinement, refinement that cannot be supplied from say a medical or engineering education, as I must admit my formal engineering education has not in any way culturally refined what I am.

Roll forward thirty years to today and we have a very different system in which governments have ambitions for as many as 50% of our young to have acquired a degree often that are neither science nor traditional humanities based although they may claim some tenuous connection with. Does this not seem odd as we are now producing many more graduates than there are available careers requiring a degree, despite the greater demand for skills in the modern world, and often now in subjects that do not present any academic challenge and therefore often have very limited career potential.

Some courses are heavily over supplied in that unless you are very careful of the subject you choose, and from what institution, that you will have an extremely high risk of never getting onto your desired career ladder or for that matter will not acquire transferrable skills where you can at least gain access to some other professional path that you might fancy.

Remember also that a building does not become a university by sticking a badge on it, what is important is what is going on inside; what is being taught, to what depth and difficulty and how it is being tested. It is a fact that better universities attract considerably better future pay and career prospects for the graduate. This may seem unpalatable though it is nevertheless the truth and the more we are prepared to face the truth the better we can survive.

Some of us may have high ambitions but we need to get real, we need to look at five years of study (if we include 'A' levels, the common prerequisite to studying for a degree) for which you will accumulate a considerable debt. So whatever you want to do you need to give it the cold eye, be hard headed and ask yourself; what I intend to study and where I intend to study will this give me a solid professional background, what are my realistic chances of getting into the career for which I have aspirations and will that career pay a living wage that is also sufficient to pay off my debt. The piece of paper (the certificate – the legal instrument of evidence of your qualification), the letters (B.Sc.(Hons), MA etc.) the ceremonials are meaningless to you unless value has been added, i.e. you have gained a mind that is incisive, enlightened and far reaching.

An investment in a poor education is not an investment, you need to look at your investment just as a shrewd experienced business entrepreneur would; question yourself - will this investment be of tangible benefit to me, will it bring in a return. Chances are that if you are looking to study what are called STEM subjects (science, technology, engineering and maths and I would include medicine), these being hard subjects, and further do so in an institution of good reputation, then you have a very good chance of finding prospective employers who will want to talk to you.

As I am typing this I know for sure that it is the STEM subjects, most specifically the medical and engineering sciences, that are at the top of the UK employment prospects list and I have to admit to you, as you will note, that where apt I have made some 'surreptitious', or not so, attempts to promote these subjects within this book. However, be sure that the course you might sign up for is what it says it is since some institutions might market a degree that is only tenuously related to the subject e.g. a mechanical engineering degree that lacks any mechanical engineering. So if you take a soft option or something that is oversubscribed compared to national demand then you are limiting your prospects.

"If parents work while their children take it easy, their grandchildren will end up begging." – Japanese proverb.

You need to remember two things in that; governments want to reduce their unemployment statistic and they can do this by lowering the bar on university intake and/or expanding degrees into what are not serious academic subjects and here's the rub they get you to pay for it and that a university in today's climate is a business, a business that must sell its merchandise, its courses, in order to survive i.e. it must get bums on seats. This in itself doesn't sound too far short of a scam, where for your money, you may not have received, as is expressed in law, 'equal consideration', you may have not received commensurate value in education to your capital outlay.

Now in defence it might be said that you entered the arrangement willingly, however was there any 'undue influence' were you therefore incorrectly advised or even blatantly lied to; does the course fail to satisfy 'implied terms of contract' where what you received was not as would be reasonable to expect. If you sat 'a degree in knitting' (!!!) and in three years were given one lecture, a pair of knitting needles and a project to knit a pair of mittens and asked to pay full university tuition fees to do so you might have a very good case. This is a legal minefield but if I had spent ~£30K (tuition fees) on a load of crap I would be wanting my money back, my degree would be invalidated naturally but at least I could invest that cash into some study that is of use to my future.

If I am a lecturer in a low career yield or even quite bizarre subject, am I going to tell you that there is little prospect of you getting into your chosen career but to do otherwise might throw up legal challenges in breach of implied terms as mentioned, but if I am lecturer in a high career yield subject well I need not utter a word and let you explore the job market for yourself. Let the market sell the course not the course sell the market, which may be a disappointing market at that.

Remember, that you might like to believe that you are investing in your future when in actuality you are just investing in your future debt so you must be circumspect with your choice. As I write this there is a grim statistic for graduates (UK) that 56% cannot find jobs where a degree is required and the figure is a lot worse if you are seeking to use what you have learnt, consequently supply and demand has driven graduate wages down over the last few years. And if politicians offer to pay off your debt for you for whatever you have studied, where will the money come from, no doubt from tax rises on your future earnings or a raid on your pension since debt does not miraculously disappear it has to be paid off at some time. Such offer is nothing more than a ploy to gain your patronage at the ballot box. Remember nothing is free.

I would dearly love to see free higher education for all but what would we have to sacrifice to pay for it; maybe free healthcare, maybe welfare benefits, some might say we could cut defence spending but that would be foolish in a world that presents so many dangers. But education can also be gleaned outside of the institution of the university in all sorts of non-residential required subjects, one where laboratories are not required, just visit your local bookshop or if you have limited budget visit the local library. A book doesn't cost much more than a packet of cigarettes and if you don't like the book I suppose you could always try smoking it (bad idea) and it might not give you cancer either.

So it is very easy indeed to acquire knowledge without spending vast sums of money. However, there is a route to reducing student debt and that is to hot-wire our economy with more world class manufacturing and services and investing what economic surplus, if we have any, in science and technology, something that requires more of us to consider STEM subjects as a career path since science and technology is something that we excel at in the UK and that is not common across all nations around the globe.

However, you may for example have your eyes set on a career in media, one that pays very well indeed, and the university you approach will talk up what they have to offer and how through them you will realize your ambitions, *"yes do apply for one of our courses and in five years you will be some great metropolitan, not just provincial - we are talking metropolitan, newspaper journalist or national television reporter"* – does this sound realistic to you.

You need to look at what they are not saying like how many thousands of others are, like you, studying the same subject, what is the uptake of those graduates into their intended profession and something else they won't tell you, or I should say ask you, is; *"do you have connections within your intended career path"* for society is not as egalitarian as you might like to think. A relative or friend in the right place can make all the difference. Life doesn't easily present opportunities equally, so you need to be driven and you need to be thinking ahead of the game.

You also need to beware of courses that take something of very limited academic scope and 'do it to death'; you may for example become an expert in the 'composition of spoon bill platypus poo' that won't easily find you a job, it will be limited in transferrable skills and it is unlikely, but not beyond all possibility, to contribute to your understanding of the world. Another angle on this is the job focussed efficacy of the transferrable skill, for example, a degree in drama could be fantastic for giving polished presentations but presentations always end in a Q&A session that requires the presenter to have an incisive knowledge of the subject being presented, hence the drama graduate may give an excellent presentation on say pharmaceuticals but would flounder during Q&A often in front of a highly informed audience.

In the hard nose world of business floundering gains very little sympathy, if you present on a subject you are expected to know it inside out. Likewise, what is not an education the academic alchemist may cogently redefine as education, you may have just learnt something that is really nothing; it has in effect no application or cultural value. The question is; does the qualification give you a skill that you can trade or an intense ability to understand the world which may precipitate other types of employment prospects or does it, just by its own sake, give you access to particular careers that just require any degree, if not then don't sign up to it unless you can afford to be without a job and are just doing it for its interest value.

Like it or not the wrong subject, the wrong university, qualification based upon course work rather than end of year rigorous exams and a lack of 'heredity' (connections) and you won't be reading the news at 10, you might just get yourself a job stacking shelves and to add to your economic misery you will be saddled with a not exactly small debt.

An unwise choice and you could end up being perceived by hard-nose potential employers as not being the genuine article, just like Pluto's demotion to a dwarf planet, a bad choice and you could be demoted to some kind of 'semi-graduate' status, you have a certificate but you do not have any high yield skills and employers are very well aware of this. However, mistake or not, whatever you have studied all is not lost, you can work with what you have, you can find some way to use it as a platform to get on the ladder, to move onto and extend into other things, to stretch your mind further or to start again so you can ultimately succeed and in doing this you will be all the more wiser for the experience.

If this seems daunting to having to effectively start over again just be mindful that in many professions such as engineering, law and medicine career education continues for life, you never stop having to study and I don't just mean experience on the job I mean serious academic study. Yes life is not all easy but for that reason it becomes more rewarding.

Remember that, to learn and on whatever subject whatever it is, it is never completely wasted, in some way, tangibly or intangibly, it may benefit you. Another angle on this is that STEM subjects, despite their career advantage can also have a major drawback in that; what does incessant studying of mathematics, dissecting cadavers or far too many hours with your head in books do to the mind, some may not emerge better for the experience some may become detached from the rest of what life has to offer and enter a world that is very narrow and without the benefit of the arts, what the mind may gain the soul may lose. To become educated don't just study hard on what you do but also keep your perspective wide and not just on academic material either.

If your considered opinion is that the odds are not good for your desired choice of learning and if you do not desire or have the aptitude to study for some hard though very employable option then perhaps university is not for you. If you have aptitude and drive you do not need a degree to succeed in life, many people may not have a degree but they can find well paid fulfilling careers and they can also cultivate themselves in what they do and what they are. Unfortunately, we now have a society that measures success on whether or not you made it to university – what it should be doing is asking; do you have a fulfilling life, do you enjoy what you do and do you earn enough to live reasonably well.

To add to this perspective is that many with university degrees who work in their chosen field may earn a lot less than what they may have done if they had not studied a degree, their career may indeed pay disproportionately low compared to the effort invested, they may experience a lot more stress in their chosen career or later in life they may get to hate what they do. To fail does not always mean that you haven't won; winning may yet still come so just be patient.

So What Career Path Should I Take?

Perhaps we are all biased on this very question, ask a dentist if he enjoys his job one may say; it pays well, the job is very secure, the hours are easy, I enjoy meeting people, I wouldn't want to work on any particular task for more than an hour, I am my own boss and I love the surgical challenges, another might say; I spend most of my career imprisoned in one room, some of my patients incessantly complain or are plain rude, I spend my entire day looking into a hole often with rotten teeth smiling back at me and a rotten breath to boot, I'm constantly facing blood, saliva and pus and I am stressed knowing the problems I may cause the patient and the litigation if I make a mistake.

Ask an engineer, one might say the job is very interesting I get to manage projects, meet clients, manage teams, undertake design calculations, solve complex problems, use computers a lot, write software, design and see amazing things, work on large projects that may last anything up to five years or more, I love learning new subjects and there is huge opportunity to learn, I get out a lot, I also get to teach others and I give the odd sales presentation or lecture, another might say; well given the length of study it's not that well paid for what it is, I've studied for five years solid and I now have to put in years more of study, I'm not my own boss, I don't like visiting harsh 'tech-noire' highly industrialised installations, my job can sometimes be dangerous, I am under huge pressure to solve seemingly insurmountable technical challenges, becoming an expert in a particular field will thwart my ambitions to move into another that I would prefer, deadlines can be so stressful.

Clearly before you embark on a career path, whether or not this is academic, you need to know a lot about what you are signing up for after all you are going to be stuck with it for certainly forty, maybe fifty, years of your life that's if the job doesn't destroy you or your soul along the way. There is always possibility that you can change jobs later in life using your transferrable skills only but for complete change of profession it is very unlikely that you could do so. Unfortunately when we must decide we are at our most vulnerable to make a wrong choice, we are young, had we the experience of life, like with a lot of things we would realize a lot more about what is good, what is not good and what is a bad decision.

We might just decide on a career path based upon what our parents did, on something that if we had the benefit of experience we would realise would not suit our personality or that the environment would not be appealing, on a whim of what fascinates the hell out of you now, but what of later where fascination can wear out, believe me it can, or what the overstretched careers teachers advised based on cursory evaluation. Like someone falsely convicted of murder being handed a life sentence based on less than diligent application of the law you could just equally be committed to a life sentence of misery at work through an equally less than diligent application of advice or of your own research.

Choice of a life career is a major decision and unfortunately there are a lot of careers that many of us would not want to do, or we may wrongly think we don't want to do though surprisingly that may be a lot more appealing than what we imagined and there are careers that many want to do though may turn out to be a disappointment. A lot of the young generation is put off for example, from engineering because there is a gulf of misunderstanding, this being a particular phenomenon in the UK, as to what this profession offers.

Whatever we do we need to be clinical and realistic about what we are, what are our capabilities (be realistic), what might our future capabilities be (be positive but realistic), ask yourself; do I enjoy practical things or those that are theoretical or academic, what environment would I enjoy, office or on a construction site, am I or might I become outgoing or introvert, do I seek adventure or a quiet life, what would excite me or what would bore me, am I ambitious or not and what promotion prospects are there, and clearly salary is an important factor but to get the most out of life do not get too hung up with salary, you could become very wealthy but also very miserable.

Choose what you would enjoy though make sure that salary prospects are sufficient for a reasonably comfortable life, a life that you want. Whatever you do you need to choose something that has realistic probability of success – you need to choose a route that will get you into employment and more so keep you in employment until you retire. This decision is a greater issue that faces the young today than it did in the past owing to far greater movement of people and manufacturing around our planet, and therefore ensuing far greater competition and thereby impact upon remuneration for jobs, this being evident where one nation has far greater economic, as in salary (average S), enticement than another, a sort of what you might call 'employment osmosis' is inevitable. This is a known economic fact that we need to be aware of.

In completely open systems then nett migration will largely be unidirectional as in from the poorer country to the richer in terms of people (p) being $\partial p(t+\Delta t)/\partial t = \mathcal{F}_P(-\Delta S(t))$, from worker supply and demand $S = S_{P \to 0}[=\mathcal{F}_{S1}(GDP/P)] - \mathcal{F}_{S2}(P)$ (P = population) and from the richer country to the poorer in terms of manufacturing being $\partial M(t+\Delta t)/\partial t = \mathcal{F}_M(+\Delta S(t))$. From the perspective of manufacturing this can ensure a supply of cheaper goods to the richer countries and also lifts the poorer countries out of poverty (more on this later when we discuss economics in the chapter on understanding money) but at the loss of lower skilled jobs. From the perspective of movement of people this will benefit the poorer nation's citizens in their search for jobs and it is for these reasons that you need to be very mindful of and very serious about what you choose to do.

As in all things there are advantages and disadvantages but to get the balance right depends upon invoking tight management of this process but the moral here is that the greater the competition for the job that you want then the more you will need to strive to get it, the harder you will need to work, perhaps the lower will need to be your pay expectations but most important is in what you choose as a career. Movement of what will mostly be cheaper labour is logically great for business (and so upward wealth distillation) and resolves a nation's critical skill shortages though can asset strip the donor nation of its essential and critical dependency skills and therefore to some extent its future but also makes life harder for the graduate or for that matter anyone looking for a job or an apprenticeship in the wealthier nation and with greater globalization we can only see/are seeing salaries falling in the wealthier nations and particularly at the lower end of the salary scale.

All of this points to an interesting conclusion; in that total free movement, counter to our immediate intuition, serves a pure capitalist not a pure socialist construct and so advocates of such philosophy are not therefore socialist but capitalist.

So the important point here is that we need to stay mindful with an eye on the strength of the global competition, not that just within the nation, and what markets demand, so choose wisely, for what is best for you to survive this competition. Make a mistake here and you may live to regret it.

Self-Discipline (we fight to win not to lose) – The Key to Success in Everything - Important

Life is often hard and sometimes it can be unimaginably cruel, we can face unbelievable opposition (though for what reasons), we may imagine or wind ourselves up into thinking that failure is therefore our only destiny, we can just wimp out and succumb, accepting degraded success and degraded prospects and we can react in the most undisciplined manner to what we face.

Granted that life may not always present opportunity and it's very easy for those who have opportunity served up to them to question or even ridicule the failure of others. But one thing is for sure is that without self-discipline of any kind we are unlikely to achieve anything, overcome life's challenges or ever reach our desires. What appears insurmountable we have irrevocably defined as insurmountable beyond any doubt - if therefore you think you can't succeed then you never will, not because you can't (actually you can) but because you think you can't. The question is 'can you triumph in the face of overwhelming odds'.

Victory in battle requires for combatants to be equipped with appropriate strategy, support and supplies, weapons, skills, fitness, a willingness to fight and self-discipline. Life is just another combat mission and if you desire to really make a success of anything that you do or that you seek then above all other things you need to be self-disciplined, as 'cool as a cucumber' (unperturbed by anything), you need to be unfailingly determined, you need to identify the purpose of your aims and you need to be prepared to invest incredible effort perhaps even beyond the threshold of pain and even beyond what may seem like relentless and intolerable failure or odds.

Can you do this, do you even want to do this - you may have no option to do so in order to survive. Can you transcend what you are and become a 'skyhighatrist' (not the drug dealing variety) – to ignore and to conquer negativity, self-doubt, fear and our own inclinations to capitulation. Being all too relaxed and you will not win you will not achieve what you want in life in anything. If though you are prepared to do the other thing then you have just dramatically upped your chances of success and who knows where that may take you. Snap to it and make possible that which seems just so impossible.

Anxiety Risk in the Search for Perfection

Not just applicable to the approach to study is that we should not obsess on the detail and lose valuable time missing the bigger picture. We may for example become too engrossed in a subject with the idea that we are expanding the mind into greater understanding, and this may not always be so. OK we may know something small very well but we are failing to understand the wider world a world that requires us all to be expansive in our interest to become educated to acquire a mind that can really think. Once we have established why something is true do we really need to remember why, should we at this point become more concerned with how we apply this truth in how this knowledge can improve the world.

There are times when detail must be examined and times when it must not and if we obsess on the detail all of the time then we may condition our mind to be inclined to anxiety. In the real post-university world we have to accept lack of perfection; perfection beyond utility costs is therefore not commercially sensible and can yield indescribable anxiety. What costs us more, at all levels, incessant obsessive detail or being prepared to even guess, using what we know, and even make mistakes to probe for a solution and then look at the detail where appropriate. We should be prepared to look more so from above the problem not from below. That which lacks perfection may just be as perfect as needs be.

Chapter 10

ON FINDING SUCCESS IN OUR CAREER

(Work – the stage of giants and of fools)

In the realm of the vast majority of us, the members of the socially intelligent, work could be a most wonderfully productive experience where we all do our bit, help each other and where we enthuse one another to work to the collective good of the business and the community of our co-workers. It is here in the working environment that we find much of our purpose in life, for some it may even be their reason to live, and also where we often find much of our disillusionment. It is through having work or having some equivalent purpose that we are elevated above boredom and out of despair. This perfected working environment is the ideal. Not all are the antithesis of this ideal but few are really very close to it. But what possibilities would there be for us, our businesses and our economy if we could aspire for such an ideal.

In what you are about to read you may sense some belligerence on my behalf but I have seen what work can do to people and what people do at work from both the employee and management perspective and you may also need me to tell you how you feel without any impediment. If I were to sanitise it some would be very disappointed that I had and perhaps might feel adrift without any hope of ever seeing change, some things just demand to be described exactly as they are. The psychological games and dishonesty that can take place within the workplace is not only bad for the employees but it's also devastating for the business.

The assumption that you work your employees into the ground and instil fear to get the best out of them is the thinking of the idiotic. Unimaginable ignorance that exists on so many operating levels of work needs to be replaced with decency, duty and common sense. This failing is not everywhere but it is prevalent enough to warrant this chapter's existence.

"Abandon hope, all ye who enter here." – Durante degli Alighieri, 'Dante' (Poet, Italy 13th/14th century)

In my near four decades of work I have met with the very best and the very worst, bosses, colleagues, suppliers and clients alike. I have met idiots who think that they are very clever, the highly capable who lack confidence, those who are lazy but think they are overworked and those who are overworked though who are always prepared to do more and help others, the bad who others are fooled into thinking that they are good but in reality are no better than a sewer rat, and the good who are made to look bad by those of evil intent.

Work for some of us can be a highly rewarding experience but to get to that point there are a lot of factors that need to be aligned and that can only be achieved through having good employers who do the right thing and choose the right people. Unfortunately this is not always so and so many of us have to endure a daily experience where we walk into our place of work feeling quite sane though perhaps apprehensive but then leave at the end of the day feeling mentally ill with the only hope of recovery through shutting the door on what has just happened only for the same to be repeated tomorrow.

A Licence to Behaving Badly and a Digression into Linguistics

Psychology students study a whole range subjects pertaining to mental illnesses, in how the mind operates and in behavioural peculiarities, both normal and abnormal, and if they are amongst the lucky few who can land a job as a clinical psychologist and so really get to grips with understanding human behaviour then they will gain greater insight into understating such things as personality development and classification, neuroplasticity (the ability of the brain to adapt), lycanthropy (werewolf psychosis), intermittent explosive disorder (having an inclination to disproportionate aggressive impulses) and fundamental attribution error (where we may wrongly attribute blame to an individual, or ourselves, rather than to the circumstances or visa-versa) all of which are fascinating and really well worth some study.

Without going deep through practical experience then the psychology student may just not recognise when all is not right. Even the trained eye can very easily fail to identify when someone has a psychopathic personality disorder. Being an expert in anything doesn't equate with having total infallibility.

In the working environment there is plenty of opportunity to observe human interactions, good and bad, and I have had my ears bent countless times by those complaining about others. So, the place of work offers an abundance of fascinating practical insight into human psychology since work is where many of our human species feel that they have licence to behave as they wish, believing that there are no consequences in doing so. To them work is a stage where they can act out their unacceptable and even disgraceful behavioural peculiarities.

Work can be the unrestrained playground of the socially unintelligent. Behave the same in any other environment and you might just get arrested for doing so, perhaps even thumped and you may well have deserved it. Precipitation of such can be particularly so where there is a lacking of effective senior management, where there is a conceited self-inflated sense of authority over others or where there is a work culture that is too tolerant or even excuses such behaviours and I have seen it all. Now if you keep your eyes open and invest in a few good hours down the library or the internet it is amazing what you can discover about humanity, so the place of work can be fertile ground for the fledging psychologist to equip themselves with some ability to recognise those who may have personality issues.

Now being in possession of language without limits brings us huge benefits, it enables us to articulate all of what we think - noting that thought or feeling is not subject to language alone that facilitates our comprehension about what is going on around us. However, words are often used incorrectly and there is a fad to even use pejorative terms to describe others as what they are actually not, we have thereby corrupted the purity of linguistic definition, we have used the wrong word, although conversely words also give us immense power to articulate and the less limited be our vocabulary the greater that power.

Let's assume for example that we redact the word 'psychopath' from our vocabulary, now without this word we are also deprived of its accurate definition and without accurate definition we cannot identify the sum of the parts that constitute what a psychopath is. We may suspect that someone is psychopathic but without the existence of this word therein a detailed definition and so identification of psychopathy becomes tricky, we won't know what tick boxes are required to confirm or that might otherwise invalidate our suspicions.

Words when used correctly, gives us an ability to recognise and to define where otherwise it would be difficult or even impossible to do so. We have gained the ability to not only articulate what something is, or isn't, but also to construct ideas and we have gained ability to communicate, conceptualise and create what are fundamental precursors to the development of scientific entities and their ensuing technological developments; without language we would have remained technologically in the Neolithic age.

Surprisingly, there is so much going on in a work environment that for many of us the art to articulate has very particular importance. The ability to articulate but also in being honest and tactful is through which many of our work problems can be circumvented with the added benefit of becoming more effective and hopefully more rewarded in our role.

The Purpose of Work

If we didn't work, if no-one worked we would have nothing, there would be no food, no housing, no technology, no medical care, no law, no anything we would be reduced to the level of an animal just seeking out food and shelter to survive and our lifespan would be seriously limited. It is because we and others are prepared to do so much and what often can be quite difficult or unpleasant that we live the life that we do. Productive work turns what would be chaotic into that which is structured where there is order.

Animals mostly possess the same senses as do we, however we have something else that they don't and that differentiates us massively from the animal kingdom; we have relatively high intelligence and we have dexterity way beyond that of any animal, the proportion of the human brain used to operate our hands being so substantial attests to this fact, and so as a species we are very advanced. With intelligence we are able to think up ideas and with dexterity we have the ability to make things, and with the two together we were able to have created complex things such as steam engines and turbines, internal combustion engines, generators and electricity, we were able to make not just simple tools but machines.

With machines and power we are all able to experience a better life one where the machine takes the strain. Our abilities also opens up the possibility to an even better life experience; just imagine that not so long ago we didn't have penicillin, anaesthetics, air travel, the mobile phone or the internet, all this is down to human creativity and effort. Wealth as we may describe is not what money we have but what we can do with it and modern living provides all of these things that can be bought that are made by or provided by others and it is our contribution to do likewise. We all work we all become wealthier we all live better lives.

"Deprived of meaningful work, men and women lose their reason for existence; they go stark, raving mad." – Fyodor Dostoyevsky (Novelist, Russia 19th century)

However, the assumption that work is for wealth and wealth alone is not entirely correct since work also provides something else, it satisfies the human desire for having a purpose with the additional bonus to interact with so many others hence to socialise. We humans are purpose driven. Just imagine how you feel when you have achieved something; you have passed an exam, you have painted the fence, knitted a pair of gloves, fixed the car, invented something, produced some clever spreadsheet, how does that feel, but how would you feel if you did nothing where you either don't have any employment or that all that was required is provided for by machines. Deprived of purpose, a reason to exist, not can be, but is psychological hell; something that <u>must</u> be urgently addressed.

We cannot live for need and pleasure alone we need purpose we need to feel a reason to exist that is external to our own direct needs. Idleness is possibly one of the most destructive of problems in our societies, we are more miserable when we are idle, misery that we can either internalise with depression or externalise by often smashing things including people.

This being said our human mind is very astute into knowing that which is meaningful purpose and that which is artificial; the mind after all requires meaningful purpose to be in a state of well-being. Artificial purpose, that which is manufactured to do none other than to keep us occupied, doesn't do us any good; the mind can discern when we are engaged in doing something that is of no use and therefore no purpose i.e. we are just filling time. What would you prefer to do; help in building a bridge by moving essential materials into position or move slabs of concrete and girders from one place to another and then back again and then continually repeat this process. Building a bridge gives you some sense of pride that *"I contributed to the construction of a bridge"*, moving stuff from 'A' to 'B' and then back to 'A' and you will feel quite miserable in not having achieved anything.

But there is also something else at work here and that is repetition. Imagine that you are doing something really useful that you are working in a factory building a specific product, you might be welding two pieces of metal together at a rate of several hundred per hour (I've actually done this so know it well), what you are doing is useful but it's also torture because the operation is simple and so doesn't require any thinking, you are stuck in one location and that what you produce lacks any sense of awe or beauty. I might be a technician working in a factory assembling jet engines but jet engines are incredibly complex machines, that possibly take weeks to build, plus they are awesome to look at, even the smaller ones, so here any of us would feel a sense of pride and intense interest in what we do.

The corollary of all of this is that we all need meaningful work or purpose to maintain our sanity and that work must not be too simple compared to the potential of the human mind, too repetitive or unnecessarily bureaucratic and it must give us some challenge where we have input into what we are doing where we have at least some sense of control.

If we were to go back in time, and not so far either, then many of us would feel we were doing something productive, however, our misery in many cases, other than in the artisan class, would be as a result of the simplicity of the task and its repetitiveness. In our more advanced modern world one with so much high technology and decision making should we not all feel bursting with a sense of purpose. Sadly this is not the case since as we have become more productive using computers, machines and now robots what are a lot of us to do. We have solved that one by creating jobs that don't actually do anything, if we can't find productive work then we can create 'red tape' and we can create jobs just to artificially maintain low unemployment figures so as not to raise any awkward questions.

This is so apparent that governments and even industries, subject to government regulations, have swathes of jobs that are of no benefit. Some are so unsure about what their job actually means that they sit there all day looking at spreadsheets that don't actually do anything or they attend meetings that discuss what was discussed at the previous meeting in a never ending cycle. This may keep unemployment figures down but this is a con trick that has serious drawbacks in competitiveness in the world market, reduced productivity and increases mental health problems from its ensuing misery of meaningless employ.

The Experience of Work

It's Monday morning again and its 6:30am, off goes that infernal bloody alarm clock with that same tune that you associate with nothing other than another day at work. Where did the weekend go again, it's gone in what seems like the blink of an eye. Some of us are very lucky, we may have substantial job satisfaction and interest, we may love our job and indeed many do and come Monday we can't wait to get at it, it is as if work is what we live for but for many work can be a sheer misery, akin to having to empty a Rhinoceros's potty, a combination of long hours, poor pay, that inflicts overbearing physical and/or mental stress, boredom, dreadful even dangerous conditions and ill-treatment where you are constantly ordered around, monitored and reproached for the slightest of reasons by managers who often are in reality more interested in their own sadistic ego than in the company's success. You may just imagine that you are driven like a machine being driven to its destruction.

The upside of this, if you are lucky, is that maybe you receive a nice fat pay cheque every month, you experience great comradery (more so where you work in danger and so depend upon one another) where you build implicit trust and close relationships with your colleagues, where the work is interesting, where the company is well-organised and un-bureaucratic, where your employer genuinely cares about you the individual, that you have a great boss and a great atmosphere, all of which gets the best out of the staff.

"Beware of the bareness of a busy life." – Socrates (Philosopher, Greece 4th/5th century BC)

But like the machine we have an optimum operating curve. If we require too little performance then we can undermine enthusiasm and interest and so motivation will be lost. As we increase our demand for performance our performance increases but at some point it will reach a yield point in that if we demand too much performance then we invoke so much physical strain or anxiety that the machine or human will break down, we undermine mental performance, ability to focus on the task and we compromise decision making capabilities, what we might describe as a 'bash and smash culture'.

Under high stress people just can't think straight and so their performance is compromised. The actual performance against the demand for performance is essentially an inverted 'U' shaped curve (it has many applications). A clever boss will know where the optimal performance demand point is in order to get the best for the organisation, since the organisation's performance guarantees better job security and perhaps better bonuses all round, though at the same time keeping the workforce happy. Good performance is not brought about by whipping the staff but by recruiting the best people, by recognising and rewarded their efforts, by systematically forging an excellent work place and culture, by making people feel important to the operation and to provide assistance, training and support where it is needed but also knowing when not to do so. Quite simply behave decently to a well selected workforce and you cannot fail.

Benign and Malignant Absorption

One of the most arrogant people, whom I have ever known, had an inclination to disagree and even argue with everyone on any subject, despite not knowing their arse from their elbow, whatever you were to say the response would always be *"I don't agree"* not to politely respond with something like *"I have a slightly different view on that"* or *"I have some alternative conclusions"* thus expressing at least some respect for what the other person is saying. Their self-perception was one of having an opinion superior above all others, often so with overt display of assumed authority and some embarrassing degree of impoliteness or aloofness – this in their view being of absolute necessity to present a superiority that actually is fictitious in the extreme.

With stratospheric hubris this person would always remind us that they were *"fully qualified"*. I was curious to find out here exactly what was meant by 'fully qualified' and about the length of a course that can lead to knowing absolutely bloody everything. As it turned out the answer was 'one day', yes you read that right 'one day'!!! Arrogance really is a strange thing and served this person in the most predictable of manners – they were hated by everyone. Someone once said to me that *"they wouldn't piss in this person's ear if their head was on fire"*. Now I'm not the world's no.1 expert on idioms but that remark didn't exactly sound like an expression of love.

Thankfully most colleagues you will meet are really good people, I even worked in one company that was pretty shit and when I got to speak to others it turned out that they were basically decent very hard working people who were just as dismayed at the company as I was. Needless to say I didn't stay and no-one else stayed around very long either. However, there are always a few who you might describe as characters akin to a variant of the major arcana of the Tarot cards – the tyrant (the bully), the high priest or priestess (the conceited or who have never worked anywhere else and who show incredulity that you don't know something that they do, well they would wouldn't they and often obfuscate in sharing information or a sad character who has some pride in knowing nothing other than the company but yet nothing about life), the fool (the idiot, one who keeps asking too many questions but for deliberate annoyance, one lacking in any magnificence or has behavioural issues), the sloth (the lazy git who could do with some tabasco sauce down their pants to get them moving), those with two faces (untrustworthy or the cloying sycophantic). To be fair though are we being fair on them as often we can get it wrong and we do not really see what is going on in there including our own shortcomings, so are we prepared to be honest and even so with what we are ourselves.

For all of us though does your job control your life in that you define yourself not by what you think but by what job you do. It's a common problem, we all do it, someone asks what are you and we all tend to think of our job perhaps so as this takes up much of our lives even when we are not at work, we are therefore placing too much importance upon it. If we are thinking about work when we are not being paid to think about it we have also become pathologically absorbed it's as if we have volunteered our own imprisonment.

Life is too short to think constantly of work and if you do then you need to recalibrate how you think, perhaps you have family, friends, other interests and aspirations these being your currency for finding purpose outside of work. To free the mind and feel alive then your work should be confined to the place of work not your entire mind and existence. If you were to die worrying about work what would you get from work - a wreath, so is the worry and the obsession worth it?

'Nasty' Jobs Are Performed By Unpleasant People Aren't They?

It's a harsh world and some of us have to do unpleasant things that in many ways would not be perceived as nice, yes some have to apprehend and arrest criminals, destroy an enemy when our nation is threatened or attacked, slaughter animals for meat in an abattoir, pull fish from our oceans, use pesticides and chemical fertilisers on the land to yield affordable food for an overpopulated planet, pollute the atmosphere to provide electricity, we have to 'rape' our planet, by mining and drilling, to extract minerals for fuel and for the manufacture of essential equipment, chemicals and drugs. Yes indeed some of us are very uncouth in doing such 'dreadful' things. But if we didn't do it then who would? Would you?

Some of us live in a sanitized world in that what we do is that we do not in any way damage our planet or the life that lives upon it, but actually we do, none of us can be without this guilt and we might believe that we can make some life adjustments to expunge our guilt but we can't do that either and if we did then we wouldn't survive. If we extrapolate this thinking then we humans are parasites feeding off of planet earth. You may bitterly complain about industry; our polluting power stations, the mining of coal and the drilling for oil but can you live up to this moral perspective by going without manufactured goods and food, communications systems, drugs, electricity, heating, clean water, transport systems, can you live in a tent with nothing, how long would you survive. Do you ever think of the dangers and harsh conditions often that those workers experience to bring you such basic comforts, can you imagine their hardships.

Can you also live in a society where there is no rule of law where there is no-one prepared to put their lives between you and someone who would do you harm? It would be fantasy to suggest that we could live wholesome lives without all of this but the alternative is to live in the middle ages and I do not believe that any of us are tough enough to do so and if we were we would have to accept an average lifespan of perhaps only 35 years, is that something we can live with and can we live with its ensuing poverty.

Those who do 'nasty' things do so because they give us all the life that we want and what we often demand, a life that let's face it we could not live without, so perhaps these 'unpleasant' people are not so unpleasant after all, they sacrifice their safety for ours.

The Boss, the Employee and Even Some Customers

I was very lucky when I landed my first job, my boss was a decent, hard-working and very clever man who didn't push anyone he pulled them along with him; I never heard a bad word about him from anyone except from someone above him who was just a slimy scum-bag. Save for that one odious character we would have all followed him anywhere even through the gates of hell that was the respect and devotion to this man. Since then I have had some great bosses and also some awful ones who you could say fall well within sub-clinical or even clinical pathology, the same I can say of some staff too.

The most amazing colleagues are not those who project their ego, they are the ones who work hard, know a lot but don't show it and who get on with others, they are unassuming, effective and free from bullshit, to them their status is irrelevant, position does not go to their head, but it is what they contribute that is of relevance.

"If your actions inspire others to dream more, learn more, do more and become more, you are a leader." – John Quincy Adams (6th President, USA 18th/19th century)

The qualities of a good boss are in many ways no different to what makes a good employee though with a few extra angles in that they should be hard-working and prepared to do their duties themselves and not feign ignorance of those duties, intelligent enough to have excellent anticipation, to make the right decisions and infrastructural innovations, that they have an excellent understanding of the company products, services, market, clients, structure, processes and operations, are honest and well-mannered and they should be able to get on well with their staff and the managers above them, they should also have leadership qualities in that they are able to handle any problem that is thrown at their department and do so with firmness but also sensitivity.

"There is nothing noble about being superior to some other men. True nobility is being superior to your previous self." – Indian proverb.

A bad manager uses the very worst of psychology, they demotivate rather than motivate they are toxic to the company and they can rapidly destroy what others have invested years of effort to build up. A bad manager is the antithesis of all of the above (last paragraph), they lean on staff constantly demanding a performance that they themselves could not deliver, are utilitarian, have a habit of avoiding issues or responsibilities, could not play a decent game of chess as they can only think one move ahead this being disastrous in running a business, are too lazy to marshal the evidence and data required to make a well-considered opinion, often like to sadistically berate the conscientious where they still won't be satisfied with your work even if you cut your own head off and offered it to them on a silver plate, when suits them only pretend to or have only scant knowledge of what the company does or how it operates, have no control over their mouth or do not choose their words with any care, despite everything else they may have they have a grade 'F' in manners, are thuggish in behaviour and so do not have any respect for anyone, are ego driven and wear their rank like a badge although in reality are 'a paper tiger', have a visceral hatred for any member of the staff who happens to know more than they do which is often so with very little difficulty, they have a very tenuous connection with the truth, they are morally corrupt, are incompetent to handle any situation with any finesse only resorting to bullying demands and are totally unable and unwilling to undertake the roles that their staff perform but yet are on their staff like a rash or they may be some of the above but just vacillating and ineffective.

Some are so disturbed that they will constantly seek or if that fails invent something to complain about ('stress merchants') or question as to why you did 'A' and not 'B' and had you had done 'B' they would have complained why you didn't do 'A' so you can never win with such idiots. They will even shout, intimidate, throw things, play mind games and such behaviour is, to put it crudely, 'excrement', a behaviour that is designed to break you into quivering servitude to feed their ego – in effect what we have here is emotional instability, the psychological makeup is rotten, such managers preside over 'a house of straw' that will easily blow apart. Bosses who behave this way may not be aware but their staff will have some very unkind things to say about them perhaps more so after reading the chapter on psychiatry, indeed some bosses, and to be fair some employees too, do have pathological personalities. I have heard excoriating remarks about some managers so much so that you could strip paint with it, behind their backs they are ridiculed and spoken of using expletives that I can't even spell and the ones who they might think might like them often detest them the most.

Of course there are always the cringingly obsequious sycophants (a pleonasm I know but couldn't resist it) – the quintessential toady; who like a poodle hangs around the boss like a fly around a cow's rear end, who will seek in vain to find a surgeon who would be willing to sew their lips to the boss's bum. But to be fair the toady does have some special and unique skills such as being the company informant by snitching on colleagues, is morally weak, will agree with total conviction to whatever the boss says (morality and truth being an irrelevance), will do anything no matter how low to satisfy the political depravities of the boss – hence they have a stupidity rating of 10 and a likeability rating of 0.

Degrees of Effectiveness

You could be standing on the Titanic knocking back your last gin & tonic, the freezing waters are lapping at your feet and about to swallow you up but you are determined to survive and so you get into action to do so, however standing next to you is an official, a particularly humourless and small minded one (what we would refer to as a 'boring bastard'), who seems to be more interested in discussing what colour should we paint the funnels, even though the ship is going down, and about forms that should be properly filled in with simultaneous display of undeserved deference to this stupidity – 'no forms and I'm not going to launch the lifeboats in the name of the following procedure'. One thought comes to mind 'get a life'. This official is so pumped up with self-importance, *"I have a job to do"*, that albeit that the ship is sinking and lives will be lost it is of no concern, procedure must always come first, and indeed this type of person will even frustrate the desperate efforts of others to survive.

We live in a world where some cannot or will not distinguish between 'the big fish from the small' – they follow rules without question in all circumstances (although a rule should not be completely discarded because of some exceptions of its efficacy). Where circumstances demand, as in the Titanic scenario, I would shoot the official and throw him overboard; his life must be sacrificed if it deliberately thwarts the saving of so many others and mine too for that matter.

Now rule and structure does have its place, without rules and process there would be chaos, but rules are not sacrosanct, if a rule doesn't work well, then change it or bin it. The personality just described who follows rules unquestionably, and with devotional obsession, and who refuses to acknowledge fault within doesn't actually do anything productive, does not contribute any value to an operation and is therefore ineffective. Further to this excesses in bureaucratic, administrative or management infrastructure and a company is effectively choking itself to death – just watch the film 'The Secret of My Success' and you will get the idea. As we have become more and more efficient in productivity thanks to the machine and the computer our operating efficiency has collapsed in a world where competitors are eager to wipe you off the face of the earth. Such inefficiency undermines survival in a competitive market. Obvious you would think, but yet I have seen this everywhere, obvious yes but is anything done about it, often not.

In the past jobs seemed to have an obvious need; you could understand what everyone did by very obvious job titles, today job titles are obscure, possibly hiding lack of any necessity, we have invented work and governments, national and local, with vast tax revenues and a blind eye turned to that eye-watering debt will invent even more non-jobs. There are so many things that need to be done so why can we not employ those in non-jobs in something that would be of benefit to business and to the nation. We have all sorts of shortages but seem unwilling to fill them; this doesn't make any business or economic sense.

If you ever visit the British Museum (in London) you will find a lot of Greek vases. Now you could do one of three things you could just look at a vase and get some idea of its visual qualities so you will know how to recognise a Greek vase, you could read the description and get some idea of its age, where it was found, its purpose, what it was made of and how it was made but you may also want to discover more you might just want to know what was the life experience of the potter what was the history of ancient Greece at the time that the pot was thrown you may even be fired up to sign up for a course on classical history.

This example is an analogy of how we work or how we need to work. You could classify jobs in terms of those that require you to just do something, those that require you to know something about what the product or service does and those that require you to know how to design or concoct the product or service and on occasions those that require you to know why you are doing it. If I relate this to my erstwhile employ in the field of electronics then what you will see is that there are those who build circuit boards, those who test them, those who know how to fix them when they fail and then there are those who design them, so in the electronics industry here is its technical hierarchy from production worker through to technician through to engineer.

At each level this is very much akin to the Greek vase and herein is an important point in that to seek promotion to seek a merit rise (do your research, be realistic and don't be shy about what you deserve and why) then you open up your chances the closer you study the vase, you learn more about what the company does and what are its products and services. The more interest that you take in your job the more interesting it will become and the more indispensable you will become to your employer. If you are only prepared to do what you are paid for then your promotion and pay prospects are limited. But if you do a lot more, you put in a lot more effort and it is so that your employer is not forthcoming in appropriate reward then your invaluable skills and work efforts will be of interest to others who will reward you.

If it happens to be that you were offered a job based on your qualifications then just remember that the qualification is the start to a career since to develop it you will need to learn a lot of good stuff about how you apply that knowledge to what the company does and what it wants from you. If your thoughts are that you don't intend to learn any more then you will not succeed in your place of work, qualifications alone are just not enough.

Many of us would like to just turn up for work do the work, leave at the end of the shift and get paid. Some are workaholics who work damned hard, are not always rewarded that well but are highly productive and some might do extra hours without pay who feel obliged to do our bit for 'king and country' but there are also those who 'showboat' who must be seen by the boss to do the extra hours or who will gleefully boast to colleagues about their efforts, but those efforts are not really there. In my career I have seen it all and I have also seen those few who do exactly as I describe, possibly due to fear of being canned or is it sycophancy, either way what they are doing is 40 hours or less, yes less, of effort in a week strung out to look like 80. I even knew one guy who to be honest none of us had a clue about what he did, he didn't seem to do f*** all except annoy everyone and display his contempt that we all 'worked' less hours than he did. Little did he know that we knew what was really going on, you may ask did he get fired well no because he was always on the boss's leg, if anyone were to get fired it might more likely be someone who actually worked hard, didn't boast about it and had principles.

'Yes men' are invariably useless since a boss needs to know exactly what to do and needs others who are prepared to inform reality and advise where the chosen path may be wrong, a 'yes man' doesn't do this they just acquiesce even when the consequences could be fatal. For the boss to survive the last thing he or she needs is someone who agrees with everything when it is clearly wrong.

Some Thoughts on Getting That Coveted Job (and don't think about what you can't do, think about what you can)

For many the interview is a dreaded experience, even though you may not imagine such you may later find out that you are better than the person sitting opposite you (yes we all have weaknesses, that's all of us) and that's not uncommon, so all you can do is prepare as best as you can, make sure that what's on your CV is honest in that you can elaborate in detail of what is within, that you have some good questions to ask about what they do and how they do it, after all this could be a useful opportunity to learn if nothing else, but also probe for snippets of information about the character and culture of the company and what your future boss's personality might be, that you appear confident and focussed but not arrogant, that you can convince them just how great you are through your experiences and for what you can do for them but at the same time you do not talk big so don't ever say something like *"as I'm very clever"* (you may think that but you may not be and that statement smacks of appalling arrogance) or that *"I don't like to come second"* (grandiose platitudes of exaggeration spewing from one's cakehole), that you don't exhibit any desperation to get an offer (if you do they will wonder why, perhaps no-one wants this candidate so why should we), that you stay relaxed, but not comatose, and perceive the interview more like a semi-formal chat rather than an exam or interrogation and that you look like someone that the person across the table would want to work with i.e. they will like you and if they like you they will see you as an asset to the business and lastly don't forget their name (people feel recognised if you remember their name).

You could be hard-working, well qualified, competent, appear as an obvious fountain of ideas, and enthusiastic (don't overdo it though as this would appear as insincere) but if the interviewer doesn't like you, especially so if you were to express political agitation or anarchistic inclinations then you won't have 'a cat in hells chance' (zero chance) of getting an offer.

However, what I have just elucidated is not completely so since different jobs demand different personalities, for example a miner will have a lot more in common with a soldier, a car mechanic, a chemical plant worker or a fireman than they would with a social worker who may have a lot more in common with a nurse, a teacher, a psychologist or a HR (personnel) manager. Even within apparent allied careers there are different demands; a car salesman would need to have a different approach, different skills and so possible different personality than that of a salesman employed in a civil engineering company engaged in major capital projects.

The question is what careers might match your personality and what personality is the potential employer looking for. If you don't have the personality don't give up since personality can also be fluid in the same way as any skill, you can gain more qualifications so why can't you set out to gain more confidence and why not gain better human skills too such as greater empathy and affability. It's not always easy to change but change is open to all of us. But just remember a personality mismatch and your work experience might just be a miserable one.

And a word for the employer: you may look for candidates who you believe must technically fit what you are looking for, they are to be an <u>exact</u> match and to recruit any other might be a leap of faith a place you fear to go. Consider this; would you rather have an exact match though mediocre worker or a candidate who may not be the best of matches but who has acres of aptitude and within a short time would turn out to be an exceptionally invaluable asset and a great support to you? When looking at CVs be sure to look again and don't dismiss candidates with great potential just because they don't have the very specific skills that in short time they could easily acquire. On another note just remember that those who have disabilities have had to endure and tenaciously overcome perhaps great difficulties, they have overcome what a lot of those without disabilities could not, on this basis a disabled person is much greater than what you might imagine and should be given due consideration on that thought. Disabled does not mean unable it may often mean very able indeed.

Political Savvy - The Ladder to Promotion

You may have an illusion that through hard work, gaining skills in abundance, through acquiring extensive knowledge of the company operation, products and services, through polished and affable engagement with other staff and clients, adopting tact and decency, through capability of responsibility and right action, through insight that you would be an ideal worker someone who deserves promotion and who will massively contribute into lifting the company to greater heights, in effect promotion through merit but you could be far from what is true, even very far.

The reality can be far different as promotion may only come to those who are political operators. It pays to know what is going on in any business, how it operates, what is its culture, even though you may not be a political animal keep those ears sharp know what is happening and know who has and who does not have the patronage of the management above, know who you can trust and those who you can't, know if the company may be in financial difficulties so you can be ahead of the game – it pays to always know what is going on.

Political operators can be remiss of any of the aforementioned fine attributes of a model employee indeed may possess none of them but they know that to work their way to the top there is an easy route that they can arse kiss their way to the executive table or alternatively demonstrate a willingness to do what can only be described as despicable. They may not even be that at all but promotion can go to some people's head where a perceived nice person can upon promotion turn into an egotistical amoral monster.

To get up that ladder they don't need merit they need a simple formula to know who to talk to, how to talk to, when to talk to and in what subject to talk about, to laugh at the boss's jokes, to drive the same car, to have the same interests and views and to shadow the boss's good or bad opinion of others, I have even seen worse than this that would make you want to vomit believe me. Political savvy can go further much further than any merit. Indeed having merit can be a drawback (beware if your CV is rather too powerful for its audience) given that you will be without a shadow of doubt of greater competency, wisdom and insight than the executive in a 'dynastic arse kissed to the top culture' where the top tier is infested with lazy, incompetent, unpopular people but who do have political savvy. Will they get caught out as being so, often no as they know exactly when to move, to get out before the good managers rumble them.

If the super effective worker were allowed onto the board then it would be tantamount to bringing a fox into a hen house i.e. bloodshed would ensue and it would be their blood. Success may just come about by selling your soul to the devil but that is a high price to pay. Companies that advocate these underhanded methods with relish can only underperform or worse fail. If I were the shareholders I would keep a close eye not just on the balance sheets but also on the culture – the balance sheet might look good but it could also look a hell of a lot better.

The 'Mad Hatters' Tea Party (ref. Lewis Carroll's character from 'Alice in Wonderland')

I was going to state *"you don't have to be mad to work here but it helps"*, but this is a phrase so overused in the UK that it has become annoyingly trite, like any unsophisticated humour its hackneyed use can leave you feeling depressed, but to those who haven't heard it before at least you will get the picture of how this applies to where we work.

Some companies are so mad that they live in a totalitarian world, a world where individual thought is banned, where there is no opinion only obedience, a world of acute delusional psychosis where what is wrong must not be criticised and what is right is a rarity, this is a world in perpetual pretence. Loyalty is never enough it is your duty to show an almost 'infatuative' erotic love for the company and for your job. Everywhere you will be reminded of this. The obligatory mantra *"I love my company I love my job"* comes to mind. Unsurprisingly this is possibly the worst psychology imaginable based upon a childish imagination a world conjured up in the imagination of fools.

Humans are not stupid, although some may be idiots, and when we have to continually pretend that something is what it is not, and we will know when it isn't, then reluctant compliance can turn to mild amusement that can turn to irritation that can turn to intolerance and that which is seen to be intolerable if pushed upon us can even turn to hate. The company that enforces such infantile ideology upon a workforce, comprised of adults, is heading for deserved ridicule and inevitable and spectacular failure – the good staff will start to look for the exit from what is a totalitarian madness. If a company seeks to get the best from their staff they are better placed to show respect for their staff as being intelligent adults and to be honest with them. Once what are lies are spun into 'truth' then the staff will know this, they are not fools, and the perception of the company's credibility will be blown to shreds. The moral here; is try not to alarm the staff, but don't treat them like fools either, be honest and share the truth and they will appreciate you the more for doing so.

Checking Out

We may be enduring a totally crap situation or we may feel that we could do better but we all get a bit lazy a bit afraid to 'bite the bullet' and go for a change, we hang on a bit longer and then a bit more hoping that things might change, they may very well do but often don't. Before we know it we have become institutionalised we have given into apathy and all of sudden realisation hits home and twenty years have just gone and we are still in the same place.

You may just stay because you feel secure and you may very well be but this is not as guaranteed as you might imagine as I have seen good people fired when business has been less than great and redundancy may have no reflection upon competency, hard work and having a great attitude. You may also stay because you fear taking that 'leap of faith' you have so little experience of the world of work outside of where you are that you end up losing your confidence to move into it.

If your work experience is dreadful then you may have nothing to lose if you take the plunge. OK there is always the risk that a career move may turn out bad, but you can always move again, however it is more likely to turn out better and if you stay the likelihood of it improving is probably slim to none. One thing that can hold you back where you are prepared to endure all kinds of misery is money, if it's good enough that is, but this is a false assumption since what is more important to you money and misery or a bit less money and happiness.

Life is too short to worry too much about money and enduring misery could be the very thing that not only compromises your state of mind it can compromise your life, you could earn more (per annum) but consequent ill-health or an early death that means you have been short changed including the money too. Besides moving to a lower salary may not be as financially bad as it may appear since if you can find greater happiness then your motivation levels will increase and that may just result in an unexpected promotion so you may end up happier and even wealthier by taking that bold decision.

If you are looking to go into business just give your business idea the cold eye, give great attention to what may go wrong and its level of risk just as you might look at what may go right. Get plenty of good advice and research well. Remember that just because you might be interested in something doesn't mean that there is a market out there that is sufficient or sustainable enough to put food on your table. And one vital thing is that when you go into your own business you must never think it will be easier than working for someone else that you can relax back; to make it work well and get the rewards you seek you must be prepared to work hard sometimes very hard. In the end there is no easy option but you could make a great go of it and succeed beyond your wildest dreams if you go about it the right way.

Coping with Redundancy or Retirement

In the animal kingdom the female will select a mate who is of greatest physique this being a necessity for protection and fitness of the offspring and this is wired into our thinking in order to survive a primitive existence. In the human species of modern, and not so modern, times this doesn't apply where perceived fitness or success is now dependent and measured upon status, thus an ideal male suitor will be perceived along lines of many other characteristics than just, even instead of, physical strength or apparent physical fitness.

To be the most successful in the modern world depends not on size but on competence, intellect, an ethic of hard work, resilience and confidence, hence competition for success is no longer subject to physical strength – women take note as here is your opportunity onto a new career ladder. Anyone who has worked in a business organisation can see it that the higher your competence (and networking) the greater your chances of promotion and the greater your promotion the greater your confidence will become.

Essentially, and since confidence is a factor of well-being, then status and well-being are intrinsically linked by this formula. However, there is a down side to this in that the higher our status, or self-perceived status, the further we might fall when the inevitable comes i.e. when we retire or when we are made redundant.

If it were so that you passed through your entire life without being made redundant then you are probably a very lucky person although there is another way of looking at that too. If you were to remain in one company and particularly one role for your whole life then many might view that as being unlucky since you may have had done a lot better in your experience of work and even your salary had you had moved on. It is a factor of human nature to fear change, to fear the unknown, although some thrive upon it.

We mostly prefer to stay in our comfort zone and stay with what we know and what we can do. Is it that we have become too laid back just too comfortable, is it that we have had any sense of adventure blown right out of us or is it that our confidence is too dependent upon something that we cannot let go of - let go of what we have, venture into pastures new and our confidence may fly away. This thinking is what can hold us back from a fulfilling career and a fulfilling life for that matter.

Now it is so that change is not always so easy and later in life it may, in some circumstances of what we might desire, become nigh on impossible. Transferrable skills you may have in abundance and so you will find other career paths that you can slot into but reality is that the openings available to you are not limitless, you may like to choose a career that is so different than what you have hitherto worked in though in reality is an unrealistic dream as this could compromise such imperatives as your commitments to your family and that of your mortgage repayments. If your aspiration is to change from a maths teacher to a lawyer then this is a path not so easy to follow.

Redundancy and for that matter retirement have certain similarities in that both require a discovery of new purpose and both present possible financial adjustments. Either way it may be the end of a chapter in your life but it is not the end per se it is also the beginning of a new chapter, one that may be unknown but without knowing the path ahead also comes some excitement of something new. Our loss of what we had known is much like grief, it is something that can cause anger, sense of loss, anxiety and depression and will take time to work through and time to adjust.

Redundancy is best and rightly looked upon with optimism as a new start and the faster you see it in those terms the faster you will be able to find something new since you will be fired up and motivated rather than crestfallen. And for those who have retired it's time to reset your chronometer back to the age of 30, just think of it again as a new start where you find a new purpose and discover you, it is a time to feel young again since now you have so much time to yourself so you can use it to full effect for a new beginning.

Perhaps retirement is a time to enter back into the world of education, now that you have so many questions here is the opportunity to find the answers or perhaps we can think about passing on our skills to others or undertake voluntary work or is there something you always wanted to do but didn't – these are all things that can bring back a sense of purpose and with it some sense of status.

Unemployment Hell and How to Cope With It (but just don't get paranoid about it)

In the modern world it is highly unlikely that we could remain in the same employ for the rest of our lives, something that would have been realised in not so earlier times too. Albeit that we live in a more unstable world in these terms but the upside of this is the benefit of variety and opportunity, perhaps we could say that life is certainly less boring. This being said, having been thrown from employment to unemployment can be hard to cope with particularly if we are without work for an appreciable length of time. The world of work amongst its other benefits also provides structure a reason to rise every morning and at the same time and without this structure without reason to get out of bed can make us feel pretty miserable.

If we think about that then we need to maintain structure we need to find beneficial things to do and make the most of this time and enjoy it, even enjoy the challenge and effort of finding another job. So if you are between jobs, perhaps even retired, then you need to stay busy and get up early i.e. you need to maintain the same schedule as you would if in the world of work, this could also be a good time to acquire new skills and it's amazing what you can learn in even just one month that can give you an edge over others.

Be mindful too that the search for a job takes time with the natural path of the many null responses, rejections, close opportunities that fall and then eventual success, so stay patient and stay resolute. But during this time take breaks since constant obsessional attention to searching for a job, or for that matter in doing anything, may just drive you into nervous exhaustion; something that certainly won't help you find a job, so get out and enjoy life too this is something that you really must do.

To maintain momentum you may also have to delude yourself into thinking *'I've got a job I start next month'* this being a far better delusion (a positive one) than thinking *'I'm never going to get a job'* which of course is another delusion but a negative one. In effect we must visualise a successful outcome to precipitate a successful outcome. And if your search fails then perhaps it is meant to be perhaps your destiny is elsewhere perhaps you deserve something better something new, a change.

Finding a job can be something of a balancing act, if you (your CV) are good enough to be noticed it could also be that you are too good where a prospective but inadequate employer might see you more as a threat than an asset (you might then need to dumb-down your CV to circumvent their inadequacy). In sales we all must put our best foot forward but being too good can scare those who are not too good themselves, the contrast of your competence to theirs is what they fear and this may make you appear a lot less an attractive candidate. So if you are rejected where you would have expected at least some chance of attention then don't take this personally that you may think that you are not even good enough for what is essentially beneath your talents, you may have been rejected but you are certainly not a reject.

You also need to stay mindful not just on what attracts you to a job but also on what doesn't to assuage any disappointment if you happen to be rejected. In essence you really are better off not working for demonstrably inadequate employers since if they are so incompetent to fear you so much then perhaps you would have experienced animosity in working for them and a role that would not challenge you might just feel like a job from hell.

Interviews have to be probing to verify that you do actually have the skills that you say you have, that you have necessary aptitude to be able to adjust to the role, that may be very different from what you currently perform, that you are suited to the role in all of its nuances and environments, that your personality would fit and contribute to the company culture and its staff etc.

But it could also be that the person sitting opposite you in the interview could have issues; uninspiring, sour, defective personality, complicated, egomania, patronising (always with a smile), unresponsive and cold (the personality deficient zombie) – there being no reaction at all to all the good stuff you utter, pathologically envious, they are socially unintelligent, having a perverse dislike of anyone who happens to have a personality or confidence, have a complete inability to conduct a good interview, they may ask the most stupid of questions, they may be mean spirited, they may even want to make you feel worthless in some kind of game of dominance (where a feeling of power is more important than a feeling of happiness! – peculiar isn't it), they may even ask you questions that they know that no-one but them can answer (but for what purpose), are fastidious about esoteric requirements that are in reality relatively easy to acquire but yet they make such a big issue out of it or who are completely blind to, or unwilling to consider, your excellent transferrable skills and some interviewing 'techniques' can even border on the disgraceful.

Such behaviour, particularly in this forum (the candidate may be wracked with worry at being without a job) is not exactly nice and is not exactly classy and the person that you behave so badly to may one day be sitting across the other side of the table interviewing you in your moment of desperation to find employment, let's just hope that they are more charitable and more urbane. Being rejected might just teach you a lot more about who you are applying to, and their deficiencies, than what you are yourself.

If you are being rejected, as is now very common, on the basis of age then those who perpetuate such culture will inevitably become a victim of their own culture - their own children will face the misery from the severe difficulty or danger of ever getting a job and they themselves will age and face the hell of finding employment when redundancy strikes as it very likely will. Think on – whatever you do to others it will come back and bite you. Do not forget that the young can bring fresh ideas and the old have valuable experience, ideas and experience from which you can learn, these are things that can hotwire a business to its success but perhaps these are things that some will fear.

You may have massive skill and lorry loads of experience (and if you forget this, with waning confidence, then just re-read your CV and reflect on all what you can offer, never lose sight of what you are capable of) and you may be in no way an objectionable personality but to the inadequate you are a threat someone who they can't beat someone who could slaughter them in any disagreement and they know this. They will be quick to point out your shortcomings (all of us have shortcomings) but will they ever think about theirs, probably not.

It might be all too easy to become paranoid about the jobs market, however, there are great companies out there with great bosses who would value what you are and so you would be working alongside equals not those consumed by some inferiority complex. So just be patient and when someone shows an interest in you it is more likely that they match what you are and what are your expectations.

In the protracted process of finding another job a long wait is very much so not necessarily an indication of failure of inability to find anything at all and it is very easy very easy indeed to lose faith in yourself and in your ability to do anything useful which is the last thing you should ever do so maintain a 10,000% certainty in self-belief and maintain at least some faith in the rest of mankind. You may also encounter those 'helpful' (unhelpful) others, who may indeed be genuinely intent on helping you, who give 'useful' advice, negative advice, but who in reality have no idea what they are talking about, so don't listen to them, you can politely nod but don't listen.

If you doubt yourself then it is your self-perception that is faulty (and out of touch with reality) not you so you can stop that shit right now and instead think positive. Thinking negative, on anything not just unemployment, never does anyone any good; OK you may need to be aware of a negative situation in order to motivate action but don't obsess on a negative outcome and there is no such a thing as a destiny that is mapped out one that you cannot change.

I have great admiration for the Russian people for a lot of reasons but also for a very specific quality that they have in that they are immensely tough, they can endure, even as a civilian, a lot more than most. In the pushback in World War 2 the Russian army mounted a counter offensive at a little known place called Prokhorovka wherein around 1,000 tanks fought a fierce short battle in a small space tank-on-tank at point blank range and up to no more than 1,000 yards (approximately 1km). This is perhaps as fierce as battle can ever get, others might have capitulated but not Russians.

This is a lesson to us all in that to succeed, in anything, then we must never, and I repeat never, give up – we must stay goal focussed and goal driven and when seeking work or securing your future you need to do this and you cannot allow yourself to be distracted by anything else since your source of income supports everything else in your life, lose it and you may just lose everything else. If you feel that you can't take the heat of survival then think as a Russian.

So in the long wait don't lose your nerve just rationalise that perhaps you could be ideal but not quite as ideal as another candidate, that competition may be immense, perhaps your CV is too self-effacing where others would be gushing with confidence, hyperbole and even downright dishonesty, maybe your CV doesn't concisely list your key skills before anything else without which the practitioner of cursory appraisals will consign your CV to the reject pile without a second thought, you may be too good for the role or the organisation, does the job really even exist or could it be an employer who isn't just rejecting you but has some peculiar predilection to reject everyone (more common than you might imagine), perhaps your interview was on an off day or theirs, perhaps it's a bad time of year to look for a job (the summer holidays and before Christmas being particularly bad).

So don't lose faith never lose faith hang in there, take back command, stay focussed on what you can do not what you can't, you can get a job you can do it and keep that thought even when it's hard to think otherwise. It can never be that you are unemployable, no-one ever is (if, that is, they have a work ethic) and it is completely irrational, and mad, to think that you will never get a job. If you have come so far in this book you clearly have skills to do that, so think about that too.

Stay patient and put some trust in yourself and employers too (I reiterate that many are really very good) and having unassailable patience and faith in yourself is a valuable skill in itself but one day you will get that phone call or that email to say 'we would like to make you an offer' etc. and then your life in all of its potential glory can re-start, so just don't lose faith in you or the world of work. Hard as it may seem from where you are standing there is sunshine at the end of all of this, something will turn up but only if you never give up, you may be unknowingly just one application away from success.

If you are too stressed about finding a job, and in particular when it occupies your every thought (not just 9 till 5), then the best and only thing that you can do is to relax since stress will compromise your ability to present what you are and what you have, the alternative is that you end up ill and that won't do you any good.

If your anxiety is going off-scale then, as in all things, you can examine that anxiety and reclassify its terms i.e. instead of perceiving the immediate and obvious thought of being unemployed why not deconstruct what unemployment actually means into its constituent elements. Employment consists of financial security, activity, growth & prospects, social and status elements.

We perceive that unemployment has none of these, or does it. Look again; whilst unemployed you may have a financial cushion such as savings, pension funds, social security benefits or some casual work, you can keep active and you can learn new skills (lookout for free courses) from which you can set the seeds for growth and prospects, what is stopping you from still meeting others and on the question of status it has only diminished because you have imagined it to be so after all your current situation will change at some point, it's not you or your status that has changed, it is only your circumstances that have changed.

The Vulgarity of the Term 'Human Resource' (author's note)

To 'objectivise' someone is to perceive them as nothing more than a thing, an object, not as a person who we should value for what they are for what are their inner qualities and for their capacity for feelings; this is something that some men do to women (and other men!) and some women do to men (and other women!) and that politicians mostly seem to do to everyone. Typically if it's not about looks it's about money or it's about prestige.

Perhaps I am old fashioned but the term 'human resources' is a shameful, base and perhaps even fascist assertion of dominance to degrade the individual to be nothing more than an anthropomorphic machine, to be discarded when it is no longer useful, i.e. no greater than that of cattle. Could we ever imagine referring to our spouse as 'a resource of the marriage'? To refer to anyone in terms that are literally pejorative, and they are meant to be, is an act of division an act of stupidity.

Naturally as language develops over time we find new words and idioms but we are all well aware of foul words, in I would guess all world languages, and as used in the past that had divided our societies and that had stigmatized a race or group within a society possibly also in an act to assert superiority over them. What may appear natural at this time will be looked upon with contempt in years ahead. Let's show respect for one another instead of referring to others in what can only be pejorative terms, implied or otherwise.

* * * * *

Warning of What Is to Come (what should you read and what should you avoid)

The following chapters, save for chapter 12 ('On Destroying the Demons of Inequality'), are heavily political (or do have some direct and close relationship with politics) and so are here for good reason since much of our misery is at the hands of whom are often the foolish and/or corrupt. In the context of the aims of this book this subject is an unavoidable discussion, it is a subject of lamentable and repeated failure so must be discussed and must then be changed. However, such full-on reality may be too much to bear for those who are already weighed down with so much of their own issues. Politics, its ramifications and its consequences, is a depressing subject, perhaps this is why many politicians rarely look happy and if they do it is most probably for peculiar reasons, this being so the discussion of politics may just undo any benefit of a positive perspective hopefully gained from reading so far into this book.

It is for this reason that I warn the reader that if it is so that you have enough of your own troubles and at this time cannot bear the burden of the wider world then now is not the time to read or even listen to anything about politics, you are essentially better off not knowing at this time. If this is you then now move directly to and read chapter 12 but then move straight onto chapter 19 ('Just How Probable Is Our Existence') and then read on until the end.

Chapter 11

ON UNDERSTANDING AND MANAGING MONEY

(Elementary economics)

Politicians who are in complete denial of the economic woes of the world, would be indignant about someone like me someone who knows little about economics to question their management of the economy but let's face the facts that when in power or where they have been in power they make a complete unmitigated mess of it all, it was they who screwed up and continually do so not me.

However, it is a very odd thing indeed that despite our perception of being advanced that we still do not have an irrefutable standard model of how we run an economy, one that really does work but does so for us all, one that is fair but also that is not stupid. In the hands of politicians, national economics is often no more than a game one in which they still do not know the rules and a game where they must win and where we must often lose.

Some may argue that we could eradicate poverty with ease, we can't, we can only eradicate poverty through effort through work and there is no other option than that. We can of course redistribute wealth but wealth can only come about from work and it is an inalienable fact that those who work harder should be rewarded for doing so.

The Ugliness of Obscene Wealth

"There is nothing on this earth more to be prized than true friendship." – Saint Thomas Aquinas (Priest, Italy 13th century)

Are you loved for your money or for what you are as a person - money is worth nothing without genuine love.

Many of us work hard and long, we are stressed, our dissatisfaction with life can often be just about bearable and the reward for it all is not always as it should be, even so within our own societies some earn more than they deserve some less, this being largely through wrong choice, lack of opportunity or lack of our own confidence to do or to seek better. We survive and we have a few luxuries but our life is of no comparison to some at the very top, not the hard working business entrepreneur variety, who stoke and push forward our economic engines and who work incredibly long hours, but those who are the ostensibly 'ever so nice' 'sinecurist' who expends little effort and perhaps who just do a lot of smiling, and hand shaking, to justify themselves and maybe that big wide smile is less about sincerity and more to do with the cash being served up to them for doing very little.

Most of us struggle with everything, mostly we have just above a subsistence living standard, healthcare and pension. However, we might be able to count ourselves as lucky as many of our fellow human beings will have it far worse, they will live in dire poverty, enslaved to appalling work conditions and equally appalling salary, if you are ill and can't work you don't eat, and the very basic accommodation you may have may easily be lost, healthcare and education is at best rudimentary at worst non-existent, life is harsh and it is brutal. But for most of us our income is what we need to just about survive and maybe pay for the odd luxury, the odd moment of respite, from the toil and the stress. Our obsession our aim is essentially to survive.

In contrast some individuals and indeed some societies and cultures are obsessed with money, not in the context of its business precipitating and creative capacity but for the fact that it is something to flaunt in bad taste thus orientated in displaying the trappings of what money can buy (a very large house can be designed to look elegant, beautiful or architecturally fascinating but a design that is designed to do none other than to project wealth can look incredibly ugly).

The insatiable thirst for money for money's sake can become unquenchable. But to be fair though there are those who are fabulously wealthy who are also fabulously philanthropic who do help others and who are not obsessed with their wealth as only and all for themselves but in what they can do with it for the benefit of others less fortunate, so good for them and I commend them for what they do. Having fantastic wealth is not in itself necessarily obscene it is what that wealth means is what can become obscene.

Sadly a severe obsession with money creates victims and this includes most of the planet's population. Clearly, if someone is making vast amounts of money through a method of inadequately rewarding the toil of others, who may even have to work in awful conditions, then there is a dimension of moral consideration here, we therefore cross a boundary into what is obscene. There are those at the bottom of the pile who strive to make a very modest living and there are some at the top who are immorally syphoning of the toil of others close to the point of totality, but all is not so good for those who have self-congratulatory visions as being elevated, predicated upon wealth, above all others and not having a care on how they reach that position.

The wealthy obsessive seeker, or not, of wealth will often attract, often unwittingly, others who in the end just hang around them not for what they are as a person but for what they own. Such hangers on are shallow and can never be true and trustworthy friends, so a wealthy person needs to be extra cautious about the sincerity of their friends. Friends of a type can very easily abandon you like rats leaving a sinking ship should your financial status collapse. Never forget that you can make millions and you can also lose millions and on your way down you need friends to be there for you not to abandon you. To seek good genuine friends and to seek extreme wealth would often seem to be mutually exclusive, but it need not be.

To acquire a good living or to acquire reasonable wealth through hard work is by no means a sin and we need entrepreneurs to fire the economy, an economy needs doer's and go-getters, people who are driven and some deserve to be highly paid even very highly paid for what they do but beware when the drive is for money itself it is then that the desire for wealth can become ugly and even self-destructive.

What is Money?

This may seem a most odd subject to discuss, we all know what money is, or so we might think. It would be facile to think of money as nothing more than that paper stuff with the face of a dead person stamped on the back and a number indicating its purchasing power, that we have secreted into our wallets and purses or stashed deep within a bank vault. Some might imagine that it is something that a government prints at will and thereby are responsible for austerity or lack of wealth by limiting just how much of this stuff is to be disgorged from the printing presses. Print more of the stuff and we all become wealthy, we can pay off our debts and we can all live like Kings.

I remember a convicted bank robber who was quite perplexed that he didn't think he had done anything wrong *"all they had to do was print more money"* and the problem would be solved!!!

Money is nothing like this; money is a token of labour and is a necessary instrument in a modern economy, it has transactional capacity. Basically, if I do something I earn money for what I have done, if I don't do anything I do not earn money. The money I receive is a currency reflecting how hard and for how long I have worked, what work I have done and what skill and responsibility was performed in undertaking that work. Essentially it is a reward for what I have contributed to a society from which I can reward someone else with my money to provide something for me that I want, this being charged in relation to the skill and effort that has been imparted to provide me with the merchandise or services that I seek to purchase.

Imagine that I am a surgeon and that I save the life of someone who manufactures fertilizer, the only currency the fertilizer man has is fertilizer, something which is of absolutely no use to me, to me it might be useless but to a farmer it is absolutely essential for him to grow his crops. Now I may not want the fertilizer but I do want the produce from the farmer, however the farmer doesn't have any ailments so doesn't want my services as a surgeon, he might in future but not now. This is an impasse in that the payment (fertilizer) offered to me is of no use to my needs and what I offer to pay the farmer (my surgical skills) is of no use to him. None of us get paid so I refuse to operate on the fertilizer man and the farmer refuses to provide me with his produce.

We can break this impasse by using money, the fertilizer man pays me some cash for the operation, I can then pay the farmer and the farmer can then pay the fertilizer man. Through this method the surgeon won't need to transit sacks of fertilizer through his operating theatre. The economy can now move but note that all of these people; the surgeon, the fertilizer man and the farmer all have to work, if they do not work they do not contribute to the cycle, but not all can work and so cannot pay the farmer for food nor the surgeon for an operation, so what happens here is that the surgeon, fertilizer man and farmer must give some of their money (surplus) and thereby labour, for which they have worked, to the tax man who then distributes the money to those who do not or cannot contribute.

If we were to ignore the principle of money altogether then imagine that you wanted a home, which you cannot build, so another, a builder, would have to do that for you but this person is going to want something in return. Basically whatever effort you have received you will have to put in an equivalent value of effort in return.

What I have described is a very simplified depiction of how money works, in reality it is a lot more complex in that there are manifold ways in which money will move through a population, through an economy, and this is further complicated by the differences in reward for the diverse forms of labour. The surgeon, the fertilizer man and the farmer are all skilled in some capacity, the surgeon in medicine, the fertilizer man in chemistry and the farmer in agriculture but the surgeon requires the most training and surgery can be highly stressful, whereas the farmer works the longest hours and his job is the most physically demanding.

On this basis reward for work done is mostly dependent on perception of what the work is and unfortunately this is not always very equitable in that manual work is often undervalued and underpaid, there being no level playing field when it comes to reward for work. We all feel we deserve more reward but the truth is that some or many will deserve more than what you might imagine.

Is My Nation Rich?

It is very much a view of some idiots that wealth is a property of a nation by luck, not through effort, and that is it. In fact we are so awash with luck that we should give away a lot of our wealth, to others who don't have such 'luck'. I hear this mantra from the politically stupid, some of the famous and often wealthy, who like to be generous using other less well-off people's money, and from the attention seeking, scruffy, loud-mouthed, anarchist, 'ban the bomb' badged demonstrators who often don't work themselves and who seldom contribute to the wealth of the nation. Most of us work hard and have worked hard all of our lives and these people don't.

I think most of us would agree in providing help to all of mankind, whoever they are and wherever they are across this planet and who face natural disaster and poverty, I like most do so through our taxes and thereon international aid and I like many dig further to fund charities (many of whom are wonderful but not all are) and in the needs of international emergencies. But what I really take exception to are those hypocrites who, often aggressively, demand more when they are taking too much out of the pot for themselves and who may even have their self-indulgent disgusting sticky paws all over the charity supply chain and to indolent dropouts who do not contribute but set themselves up as professional protesters demanding an end to world poverty.

None of these people work hard enough to even feed themselves (we workers have to do that for them) let alone give anything to charity. The very thing that they viscerally detest 'capitalism' is the very thing that feeds them and that enables us to provide aid to others in need. They also fail to realise that in their idolised idealistic Marxist societies that if you don't work you don't eat and that would include them – simple as that.

Those who are so aggressively inclined to demand more are thus committed to galvanise their credentials of sincerity by relinquishing their own personal wealth and source thereof and give this to those who need, even better just get on a plane and go and help these people, cut out the 'capitalists' who you hate so much some of whom tap or tap into the aid gravy train, go and do something positive for those who you say you care so much for. Rioting and protesting never helps those who are in need but your own money and effort would. Can you act or do you just talk.

Some of these ideologists see Marxism as their holy grail, they seek egalitarianism amongst all, we are all to have the same experience of life, but are these people prepared to work the same since true egalitarianism requires not just to live the same but also to work the same and I wonder how many of these types would be volunteering to work in say a coal mine, like some who have to do just that, or for that matter to work at all. If they want communism they will see not the wealth divided equally but rank poverty equally shared amongst almost everyone, they will see militarism, secret police, they will see the death quotas, political imprisonment, torture, starvation and tyranny but perhaps this may seem utopia to these idiots. The very ideological system that they advocate would be the very ideology that would not tolerate the likes of them – in such regimes if you protest you would very likely be shot for doing so.

An economy can either get rich through having natural mineral resources, such as; oil, gas, iron ore, diamonds etc. that it can trade or that it is industrious in manufacturing and/or services. An economy that lacks these components is essentially an agrarian subsistence based economy, it will therefore survive on agriculture and agricultural derived products and if it can trade these products or can develop a tourist industry it can then raise international currency to therefore purchase essential supplies such as medicine, fuel and technology.

It is a natural state, that political merging of an industrial economy with an agrarian economy, somewhat analogous to having a joint bank account with a much less well-off neighbour, that an equilibrium will be realized where the rich will get poorer and the poor will get richer i.e. such a compact will always be to the detriment of the richer country and to the benefit of the poorer country and this is also true with excessive and often criminally siphoned off international aid. Entertaining such a move, in a moment of largesse or oversized altruism is madness in that the world economy depends upon having successful economic engines that drive growth elsewhere through opening up trade not through charity or through unwise international economic unions. Economic engines must not be burdened or diluted in power, let them run wild and then through trade they can help other nations to catch up.

But we do have to recognize, with a good deal of common sense and being open to the truth as it is, that some cultures, and thereby indigenous populations, do not aspire to anything more than having a subsistence based economy, some people are quite happy living the way they do and have no desire to work in factories or services and I do not blame them for thinking that way for in western society we have become too materialistic for our own good not recognising that any benefits of being totally materialistic are transitory. Also, some societies are so politically unstable that industry or services and therefore international trade can never get off the ground and so such places are often wracked with corruption, crime and sometimes civil war all of which leads a country inexorably to poverty.

For a nation to enter the economic engine club it must have rule of law, it must have economic prudence, a high skilled, highly motivated, industrious and well rewarded labour force, a unified, integrated and loyal population, it must be able to attract and nurture entrepreneurs and it must have sufficient capitalism of some form within which business has the right conditions to thrive and thus through work and the right conditions for business we avoid the misery of poverty.

If we need examples of outstanding economic success then look to China and Vietnam who have embraced the idea of a market economy (a pillar of capitalism). But in addition to this you need to maintain productive utilization in so much that you need low unemployment, a high efficiency workforce and you must keep the state burden low in that you do not employ millions of civil servants beyond need and that do not contribute to the wealth creating sectors of an economy. It is essential that we have administrators, those who run our system as well as others who do not produce but are critical to the functioning of a modern country, however, if we have too many in comparison to those who create the wealth then what we have is a low productivity economy that cannot pay its debts, cannot invest and may not even be able to afford the basic needs of its population such as a health service or welfare state.

If we continue relentlessly to bridge this gap i.e. to keep the services we want but with an inefficient low productivity economy then we are signing our own economic death warrant where <u>all</u> services are doomed to eventual collapse. If we want more we must have an efficient economy in which we work hard and ideally where all of us are employed in doing so.

The Deception of 'GDP' – but just what is GDP?

Ask any economist as to how they would rank the wealth of the nations of the world and they would use something called 'Gross Domestic Product' (GDP) as their benchmark. Put simply GDP is the annual dollar value of the goods and services that a nation produces. Typically so is that countries with extensive manufacturing industry, high technology (engineering and pharmaceutical), those with an extensive service sector including international banking and insurance and those with high mineral resources but also higher populations are most likely to be at the upper end of the GDP scale.

Essentially GDP is a measure of effort, knowledge, enterprise and resource. Using this indicator the UK is currently (as of 2016) the 5th largest economy in the world and has been so for a long time since even before its accession to the EEC (trade based), now EU (political based) and later will become the USE, the UK is also one of the most generous countries of all in terms of contribution towards international aid. In contrast if we look at the EU that, despite growth in population numbers, has fallen in its percentage of international GDP through the economic ascendancy of such countries as Brazil, Russia, India and China but also through its own economic stagnation and this is worrying for the continent of Europe. Even to stay where it is the EU will have to do better, a lot better and I hope it can.

So you may think that I would want to live where GDP is high but you would be wrong. If we were to consider the GDP of Luxembourg (GDP world ranking 75th) to that of India (GDP world ranking 7th) then you might assume that Luxembourg is a poor country but we all know this not to be the case. Clearly the wealth and therefore standard of living of the citizens of a nation does not relate to the total wealth of the nation (its GDP) as it also depends upon population. Less wealth certainly, but divided by a lot less people.

If we therefore wish to determine the available wealth available to the individual and in the sense of what individuals can contribute (aid) to others through disposable income we have to consider another term called 'GDP per capita' i.e. GDP divided by the population. If we now see wealth from this perspective then things are very different as now the UK ranks just 25th and Luxembourg now ranks 2nd. On this basis the idea that the UK is a rich nation is false, we are doing OK and our standard of living is pretty good but we are by no means rich, not as individuals, we are not in the top club.

I hear certain individuals, many of whom are in reality promoting their own self-interests, who contribute nothing or very little to our national wealth or are just very good at exclusively contributing to their own wealth, carp over what 'dismal' aid we give, really!!!, as a wealthy nation (based on GDP), that we should give more, despite massive incompetent distribution and criminal misappropriation of that aid. If they think at all like this then they really ought to stay quiet and dig deeper into their own pockets if this is what will make them feel good about themselves.

So should a politician loudly bang their drum about what the benefits of some policy or other has to a nation's GDP then they need to be questioned on what effect does this have upon the 'GDP per capita'. Benefit to GDP could turn out to be in detriment to GDP per capita and therefore what appears to be good turns out to be bad i.e. where the % increase in population is greater than the % increase in GDP.

If we come back to the miraculous success of China, it has become the factory for the entire world, and the nations of the developing world have caught on with this idea too, it is on the fast track to take the No.1 slot on world GDP ranking, although it's GDP per capita has some way to go but only a fool cannot see that China is working, the lives of its citizens have come a long way in a fairly short space of time. But how did they do it. China has the capacity to manufacture and does manufacture vast quantities of goods that the wealthier nations want, they do so with high quality but the main ingredient to their winning formula is that they can manufacture at low and so highly competitive cost.

Now some in the wealthier nations may complain that this is nothing other than oppression of these workers but if we didn't buy their goods then their economies would not grow and their standard of living would not have progressed. If we insisted on paying them the same as we do ourselves, so as not to 'oppress' them, then we would lose the incentive to buy their products we would instead manufacture these products ourselves. The 'oppressed' as some may define would have remained in poverty. Perhaps 'exploitation' is a necessary evil to get onto the path to work your way out of poverty. The exploitation phase, a phase not exactly unfamiliar within the history of wealthier nations either, is perhaps unavoidable for any economy to be able step on and move up.

The Deception of 'Deficit' – isn't that the same as 'debt'?

If you want to make the next government unpopular its easy, just rack up eye-watering debt with impunity, bucket loads of incompetence and dishonesty and the next poor mutt has to pick up the mess and then fix it usually with cuts, higher taxes or even more borrowing. You can then sit back and point the finger but the real culprit is you. Running a business in a likewise manner and you might just land yourself in jail but in politics anything is allowed to happen.

Imagine that you owe £100,000 to the bank, you have gone out and had a blast with money that you do not have and you have lived beyond your means. Now you may want to borrow to invest in your business or to buy a house both of which have or in themselves are sellable assets that can be marshalled if things should go 'pear-shaped' (idiom for 'bad'), but to borrow incessantly and long term on things that you could or must learn to do without is madness.

Many of us, but not all, are very tuned into doing what is sensible, unfortunately our governments are not. Governments will not dare live within their budgets, they will not dare to cut their overstaffed bureaucratic burden or cut those benefits that are often ill targeted or may even be over generous (where benefits are often much greater than the individuals earning capability, who complain they can't afford meat but strangely can afford cigarettes!) for if they did, albeit this would be prudent not just for them but also for us in the long term, in the short term this would be electoral suicide.

So we live with this debt but sooner or later the debt will be called in or at least the cost of borrowing will increase as a result of our economic mismanagement with ensuing and inevitable higher taxes to pay for it or the odd surreptitious raid on our pension pots, more taxes, surely they wouldn't, well they've done it before. Just like interchanging 'GDP per capita' with 'GDP' politicians have another card trick at their disposal - they simply replace the term 'debt' with the word 'deficit' and we might fall for one being the same as the other but they are quite different, in fact very different.

'Debt' is what we have borrowed, what we owe the bank i.e. our accumulated debt, whereas 'deficit' is the amount extra we borrow each year, it is in effect additional borrowing. Continuing with deficit, as some politicians often advocate, would be unsustainable it is economic suicide. Deficit is where we consume more than what we produce whereas debt is where we had consumed more than we had produced. We can be in eye-watering debt and instead of paying down our debt we still keep borrowing more but maybe this year we borrow a bit less than we did last year and we can therefore say with honesty that our deficit is falling.

Sounds good doesn't it only it isn't. Our debt instead of falling is still rising but perhaps at a slower rate, but it is still nevertheless rising. And if you think that is OK then at some point it will have to be paid off either through your children or grandchildren inheriting the debt, through austerity or that your bank account, house deeds and pension are commandeered by the state to wipe out this burden but at the risk, possibly inevitably so, of extremely serious consequences. So beware when a politician tries to paint a great picture based on falling deficit. The truth is that, unless we are borrowing to invest in industry or to reignite the economy from recession, then with massive debt we should be looking not for just a falling deficit but a negative deficit.

Do we have politicians who have the nerve to do the right thing or are they craven and will just wait for the inevitable catastrophe? Maybe we can ignore it but we all know what would happen if we failed to pay our mortgage or our rent. Our problem is that politicians have a very casual attitude to debt and just never seem to learn.

If we are ever going to borrow we should only do so in hard times where we borrow to invest but only invest in things that can get the economy back on the rails i.e. industry, technology, research to do otherwise we are just throwing more money down the drain. Many politicians, looking out for votes, demand more spending on everything – we need more investment on health, more for education, more for law and order, more for welfare, more, more, more. But put simply, where does the money come from. Perhaps what we need is to be realistic about what we can afford and just accept less, to therefore accept only what is equivalent to the work effort we put in.

The Deception and Dangers of 'Balance of Trade' – how to fool the public?

Let us imagine that there are two economic entities (nations or trading-blocks); 'A' with a large export market ($500 billion) and 'B' with a less so large export market ($200 billion) and that they trade exclusively (100%) with each other, they do not trade elsewhere. It is therefore clear that 'A' must be selling a lot more goods and services, a 'trade creditor' (the difference of $300 billion) to 'B', a 'trade debtor', than 'B' is selling to 'A', even though it's the same percentage of their individual export trade (100%).

The fact here is that albeit the trade either way is equally 100% the '$' value is not equal and so 'B' will suffer a trade deficit of $300 billion and 'A' will gorge on a trade surplus of $300 billion. As such there is an imbalance of trade in favour of 'A' and what will happen is that 'B' will get poorer and 'A' will get richer. In effect money will move in one direction as in from 'B' to 'A' but inevitably 'A' will depend, in terms of its trade, more on 'B' than 'B' will depend on 'A' and also in avoiding unemployment. So if 'A' no longer traded with 'B' then 'A' would be the overall loser.

So describing trade in terms of a percentage is therefore foolish in so much that 100% trade either way is not balanced trade in this scenario, on '%' terms we cannot see who is gaining from this arrangement whereas in '$' terms we can. In the real world any economic entity will trade with a multitude of other economic entities with the aim over time to balance out trade across all trading partners, if you don't balance out trade in your favour you will have to pay for that imbalance with money you don't have, you will have to borrow, or you will have to burn up your foreign currency or Gold reserves or your trade creditors, with the money you have paid them for their produce, will seek to buy up your national assets and infrastructure (industries, hotels, hospitals, transportation systems etc.), the last idea having some potentially undesirable political implications.

The important point here is that using percentages to measure trade is meaningless as what can be shown to be a trade benefit in percentage terms may be a trade deficit in '$' value terms.

However, politicians will repeatedly use percentage to illustrate the virtues of the importance of trade when they are very well aware that the real measure is '$' value. The fact also remains that if 'A' decided it would no longer trade with 'B' as in cut off all trade, a very, very, unlikely scenario except in war, then the nett result would be that the loss of $200 billion of export revenue for 'B' would translate into a gain of $500 billion extra revenue opportunity for 'B' to therefore provide such previously imported goods and services for itself.

In effect where there is a massive trade imbalance against you then you might be better off with no trade at all. And if there are any out there who believes that the defining factor is percentage then if they happen to be wealthier than you just offer to exchange 10% of their wealth for 10% of yours then let's see what response you get.

At some point a society that does not produce cannot continue to consume and if it uses its national assets to do so then what will it then do when those assets are exhausted.

This being said there is a caveat to all of this in that international trade is an absolute necessity in that there is no nation on the planet that is completely self-sufficient, in other words a nation cannot supply all of its goods that it needs from internal sources alone, for example high technology and certain climate dependant agricultural produce. But there is also another angle on this that free trade leads to world prosperity in that all nations would have opportunity to trigger growth within and without, markets for all sorts of produce would be hot-wired, in buying produce from others would enable them to buy your produce as in some kind of chain reaction. Given that we still keep one eye on the trade deficit then a good trading arrangement can not only benefit the producer but the consumer too and we can see this very much so with Chinese produce that has had significant influence on standards of living for everyone. Total protectionism where there is inefficiency or putting unreasonable demands on the terms of trade is much like putting a ligature around the neck of the world economy.

The Deception of 'The Average Salary' – surely it can't be that high can it?

You decide to throw a party, there are one hundred guests one of whom receives an annual salary of £1 million the other 99 guests earn just £20,000 per annum. This would equate, through who and how much, to an annual salary of around £30,000 but this doesn't sound very average, does it. What we perceive as average would be what most people earn i.e. in this scenario £20,000. So although the average is indisputably £30,000 out of our sample, the arithmetic, though not flawed, gives opportunity to portray something as it is not.

In reality our salary distribution sits on a curve with a large hump around the average salary (that's most of us), with fewer at the lowest wage and a very few at the very top end and for the UK only something like one quarter of us, not half, earn above the national average salary. Clearly given the sensitivity of highest salary upon the calculation of average salary, a government can easily state that average salaries have increased where in fact only a few at the top have done well and most of the rest of us have not. It could also be that average salary has increased when in fact the rest of us (99) have had a cut in salary.

The Distribution of Wealth

There has been substantial progress in respect of equality for what we are, however, and lamentably when it comes to wealth, there is still a long way to go, and not only that but in many parts of the world we seem to be sliding backwards in time. Agreed that many of us are a lot more affluent than where we once were but the gap between the super-rich often referred to as the top 1% and the rest of us has widened, there is in effect an inequality in the distribution of wealth. Now for most of us we are possibly very happy for being better off than we once were but the reality is that we could be a lot better off than that.

There is a theory in economics, though it baffles me how they arrived at it; that money trickles down – that if the rich get richer that they will then spend their surplus wealth on more products and services provided by those a lot less well-off, i.e. those who do most of the work, that's mostly you and me.

The theory goes that this increase in demand for merchandise will in turn provide more employment and prosperity for the rest of us. That's fine as a theory, but it is complete nonsense since the super-rich, who are just a few, have so much surplus that they cannot spend it as fast as they make it albeit they may try hard to do so, so the only options they have is to hoard it or to invest it in property, this being money that could have otherwise have worked its way through the economy providing even more employment and more prosperity for all.

And when it comes to property investment, with a view to 'buy to let' and so the greater pool of money in the hands of the super-rich is available for their purchase of such property, then in the process property from this demand is then taken out of the reach of average workers affordability leaving them no option but to rent and to rent is typically a lot more expensive than to buy with nothing to show for it at the end. And when you retire if you don't happen to own a property then you may land up living in poverty since your pension must now also cover your costs of renting and therein can be a real financial problem.

Conversely, those nearer the bottom end of the scale mostly earn very little above a subsistence wage, they have only just enough to live on and not much more. They have almost no surplus to spend on the merchandise that they might fancy thus they are in effect precluded from the demand base and in doing so the market potential is clamped to a size much smaller than it could have otherwise been. In effect the few super-rich spend a much smaller fraction of their wealth than those lower down the scale, the many.

If we were to redistribute wealth by increasing the tax threshold, the point at which we start to pay tax and couple this to a modest increase in taxation for the super-rich, but that would also not dissuade investment, then much of the money stuffed in banks and not doing anything is released to the workers and so the 99% of the population would now have surplus cash in their pockets much of which they would spend on products and services and in doing so this would massively increase demand and thus invigorate the economy. In effect you need to get the money out of banks and property and into purchasing products and services and thereby create employment as only the lower 99% will have the capacity to buy in any great volume.

For my business to succeed I need a market, I need demand for my goods but if my staff live on a subsistence wage then they have no money to buy the goods that they produce as manufactured in my factory, consequently the demand for my goods is less than it could have been and my business is therefore making less profit. What I might sell may only be affordable to 1% of the population but with proper redistribution of wealth, through fairer taxation, then my market might grow from 1% to 10% or even more.

Now this may sound the same tune that the 'great guru' Karl Marx would advocate but we need to be very careful. The concept of an egalitarian society can be extrapolated to where all property is owned by the state and where we are all paid the same irrespective of what we do or how hard we work. This may sound like utopia but it is economic suicide. For anyone who has ever visited a communist state that does not exercise a part capitalist based economy then what you will see is a failed economy where what is shared equally isn't the wealth, for there isn't any, but the poverty except of course for those at the very top.

In effect what you have is a crumbling economy where the top 1% will remain as the top 1%. Karl Marx probably couldn't see this as he was too busy daydreaming about his fanciful ideas that is when he wasn't being kicked from one country to another. In a pure communist state there is no incentive to do better, or to invest your own energy in being enterprising or inventive so why would I even bother. If I am not rewarded for my efforts there really is no point in making any. Furthermore, in a state where everything is state owned there is no incentive to create business. We shall be discussing communism a little deeper later.

Although capitalism may seem unfair to some but it does have at least some wealth to share around rather than none. Either way, pure communism and pure capitalism are economic constructs to largely serve the ruling class. The paradox to create the conditions to generate wealth but fairly distribute it is in reality not such a paradox, what is needed is to find the optimum point where we incentivise mass wealth creation and maximise the wealth for all individuals but where in the process we do not produce an unhappy society, something that often eludes economists being our desire to be happy and this also should be a consideration in how we steer our economy.

Regulation of Property Prices and Some More Economic Theory

Like most of us the most major financial decision of my life was to buy my first home and me being me did so with extreme caution; I had analysed my finances and my contingencies to the 'nth degree' but not so many months later the cost of borrowing went from a staggering 10% to an even more staggering 15.5% as a result of the UK joining an EU construct called the ERM (exchange rate mechanism) that was to be a prelude to the 'Euro' the common currency of the EU.

I remember then the stories of hundreds of thousands who fell into what was called negative equity where your home fell to a value lower than the amount that you had paid for it and I also remember those who lost their homes because of the effective 55% rise in the cost of their mortgage payments that they could no longer afford, I nearly became part of the same statistic. The anxiety level of so many went through the stratosphere. In the end the government exercised the only option they had and that was departure from the ERM. To cap it all house prices were far too high to begin with.

To explain ERM; the rule was that all members of ERM, of diverse economies, rich or poor, had to maintain the value of their currencies within a fixed band thus emulating a single currency. If their currency fell beneath the band then they would need to increase interest rates to attract foreign investment and thereby raise the value of their currency back into the band and if above the band then their interest rates would need to fall. The Euro is in effect the same as the ERM but without an emergency exit as once committed there is no easy going back. In practice this has been great for countries with a strong economy, e.g. Germany, who also use the Euro since the Euro value is weakened by its poorer members.

An economy with a currency that is low in relation to its economic strength will increase its export market (often technology and services based) but this is a disaster for the weaker economies that now have a currency that is too strong for them and so is in detriment to their export markets (often agricultural based) thus crippling their ability to pay off their debts. This raises the possibility that a poorer country with a broken economy may need to seriously consider departure from the Euro and to return to their own weaker but more competitive currency, consequently the cost of their produce would fall and this would increase exports needed to pay off their debts. In essence you can never achieve economic stability where there is one currency but different economic performances.

Land is a rather strange commodity it exists it is not manufactured yet our rulers seem to have assumed its ownership through our history, they then sell it on to those with enough money to purchase large swathes of it or they bestow its title, at no charge, to the ruling classes of times past. This land would then be sold on to developers who then sell it on to us usually with a house or apartment block built on top of it. This in itself is grossly unfair as shouldn't we have all had a free and equal share of this land. When I see an inexorable rise in property prices I lament for the young since I don't care about the value of my home its value is meaningless to me as to me it is my home not what I would see as an investment. However, upon inspection it cannot be the cost of building a house that has increased so rapidly but the value of the land upon which it is built.

To add to the misery there are too many of us looking for somewhere to live hence too much demand and so prices will rise accordingly. The cost to you of buying a home is not what it is worth but how much you are prepared to pay - a sort of legalised extortion. Basically, the more funds you can marshal the more they will demand. Imagine if say your local hospital had the same philosophy, there you are bleeding all over the floor and rapidly running out of the red stuff and the doctor won't treat you unless you give him all what you have in the bank, can you imagine the uproar. We are strangely quiet when it comes to property because there are so many in the same game at the same time and you have no option but to play by the rules, unfair as they are, if you don't you will never get a home. It's really nothing different than having a gun to your head, pay up or I'm pulling the trigger.

The simple answer is always that we could just build more properties but increasing housing stock in itself may not be enough to wipe out the extortionate practices and you would find that these extra homes would be snapped up en masse by the very wealthy who have now found even more opportunities to make their money work for them so we may just see more of us renting not buying.

Now an irresponsible bank can always loan you more money, you may never pay it off or afford a family and if interest rates go up or you lose your job you are in deep shit. Maybe the parents can chip in and increase the fund pot a bit more or a government scheme can in effect loan you some money too but all of this is to no avail. As earlier alluded to, the property market works in that the more money you have and the more who have that money (the demand) the more they pull up the ladder, in other words they increase prices as supply of aggregate funds increase.

So how do we get out of this impasse to reach a position of affordable property for all where our young won't be saddled with crushing debt? Perhaps we should consider this; we should restrict the amount we are allowed to borrow, restrict the amount we can put down as a deposit, buy-to-rent schemes should be closed down and where already invested they should be heavily taxed, we should restrict homes available to off-shore investors, we should not allow foreign investors to buy property that they do not live in and we should continue to build more homes where our economy has the surplus to do so.

We may even take this as far as some modest regulation of house prices, that bit about Marxism I would agree with when applied to property, in other words a government body will set the price of houses to a fixed formula not estate agents but this may in itself be impractical and if applied would require gradual not shock implementation. This may be government intervention but might be our only route to help the young afford the home that they deserve. Perhaps this is the way forward.

In the Hands of Fools Our Economy <u>Will</u> Collapse

In designing a nuclear reactor the pitch between the fuel rods requires careful calculation based upon a number of factors one of which being that as we increase the fuel pitch we increase the probability that neutrons will enter the preferred isotope of uranium but if we increase the pitch too much we then reduce the amount of neutrons available to re-enter the fuel. The question is, is at what point is the pitch optimum. Engineers determine how this is managed through the use of advanced reactor physics and some horrendous mathematical modelling and this is typical throughout much of engineering, there is in effect an optimum point that must be found but where is it.

This is an illustration of how engineering systems are optimized and controlled and any biologist or doctor will tell you the same is true in nature. Release of too much or too little insulin from the organ, the pancreas, would be a disaster, too much or too little adrenalin from the glands above the kidneys, too much or too little acetylcholine in nerve structures, in fact too much or too little of anything and we are in trouble, we like the nuclear reactor will start to malfunction and then malfunction permanently. As we increase what is of benefit, it will reach an optimum point beyond which the benefit will inevitably decline.

Now this concept applies to everything. Everything we do we instinctively know that we have to moderate it, we need to keep it in balance, or there will be consequences and this applies not only to government treasury departments but also to us, we have to live within our means, go without when need dictates and use our money wisely (take my advice and make use of spreadsheets, save well for a rainy day and a lot more to retire on).

Economies are no different and this is why our national banks have to increment interest rates with cautious sensitivity otherwise our economy could be irretrievably damaged, this is the same for quantitative easing (euphemism for printing money) to stimulate an economy though at a cost in our ability to pay off our debts for as we print money we reduce its value. When we manage our national and our personal finances we must do so wisely. If we are foolish, that we squander money and that we do not finely balance what we are doing then our economy will go out of control with disastrous effects.

We cannot spend what we haven't got and where we borrow we must do so wisely but at the end of the day if the economy can't afford it and we are not prepared to work harder then we can't have it and it's as simple as that.

How Can I Enjoy Life without Possession of Great Wealth?

Good friends are worth more than any riches, a friend will listen to your thoughts and pain, an expensive car may have style but it cannot listen it cannot give you any solace and it cannot share in your good times either, it is without life.

Contrary to common belief, having substantial wealth makes very little difference to your life experience in comparison to having just a reasonable living standard. Our life experience can be dire if we are poor, difficult if we earn below the survival threshold and reasonable if we have a western economy level average income but above that the quality and experience of our life plateaus. In other words above a reasonable but not excessive living standard our life experience does not alter much.

Let's put that into some context by rating some comparative experiences: how would you rate being with good friends at a lake taking in a sunrise whilst eating a cheese sandwich, I'm assuming that you like cheese sandwiches, and sharing a flask of tea compared with sharing the company of some very wealthy and perhaps rather conceited others in an extravagantly overpriced restaurant with a stuffy atmosphere, how would you rate owning a melancholic but original work of art compared with a second hand good book that gives you inspiration, how would you rate sitting on your own yacht berthed in Monte Carlo with very little to keep you amused other than yet another gin & tonic compared with taking a train to your nearest city to just walk about and admire the architecture.

"He is the richest who is content with the least, for content is the wealth of nature."
– Socrates (Philosopher, Greece 4th/5th century BC)

This is possibly quite unfair to many of those who are fabulously wealthy as many of them are not as shallow as I portray and some often do a lot for the less well-off and don't shout about it either. The line here is that we do not need to be wealthy to enjoy our lives really well and that having wealth often does not equate to happiness, indeed the rich are not immune from suicide, some may be so miserable that the only benefit of their wealth is that they can afford the very best psychiatric therapy to assuage the misery that their wealth has brought them.

But if you can afford that ridiculously expensive handbag and do find them too irresistible then why not instead spend that money on some good cause to make the lives of others better and you may also even feel better about yourself for doing so. It is after all essentially what we do for others is that which helps to make us feel happy.

"What greater wealth can there be than cheerfulness, peace of mind and freedom from anxiety." – Sir Thomas More (Statesman, England 16th century)

From the philosophical point of view a man can only eat from one rice bowl at any time, so if you have a dozen cars you can only drive one of them at any given time and if incessant shopping is your preferred therapy then what you buy will only give you temporary pleasure and temporary respite from what may feel a pointless existence.

Our lives should not be about consumption and all-consuming self-interest but should be aimed at finding contentment and at relieving our anxieties. If you are OK financially and even if you are poor you can still enjoy life through having a good outlook, having a constructive philosophy, good friends, having fun, having a community spirit and enjoying basic things of nature, like feeling the warmth of the sun, the cooling of the rain, the incredible changes of the seasons all of which money cannot buy. You do not need to own fancy stuff, we all have too much of this anyway, you do not need fancy holidays. If you can get to nature even for brief moments or if you are lucky enough to be able to access a library or that you do good deeds for others you can find heaven here on earth with or without substantial wealth.

Chapter 12

ON DESTROYING THE DEMONS OF INEQUALITY

(Culture, nation, perception, division & unification)

"We are all born equal without concepts of love or hate, these things we learn later in life." – Publius Vergilius Maro, 'Virgil' (Poet, Rome 1st century BC)

All Cultures Are Equal, or Are They?

Some will define the cultural measure of a society through its cultural contribution to our species, often from the distant past - this could be through literature, art, architecture, music, philosophy, science, law, cuisine, sport, language etc. It is important to recognize that such attributes are not systemic of a specific society as a whole though are mostly borne from the efforts of a few, attributes that may or not be taken up by, or typical of, the greater population or its leaders.

The culture we perceive as characteristic of a particular society may not be echoed in the cultivation of all of its individuals as from within. A society may also wax and wane through time in its cultural potential or yield – has anyone seen any great 21st century Greek statues or read any great works of English literature from antiquity. What we may define as a cultured society may had been so in the distant past but maybe no longer is, conversely we might define a society as lacking cultural heritage though could now be on the cultural ascendancy.

Given all of this we might postulate that societies that spawn culture in abundance must therefore have in some way nurtured the outpouring of this culture through systematically favourable conditions such as education of the masses, funding scientific research and the arts, construction of museums, theatres, libraries, art galleries and botanical gardens and therefore might be defined as culturally more advanced. However, what we may define as culture is not representative of the cultivation or refinement of a specific society; culture may therefore be nothing more than a veneer of what lays beneath.

For example; based on this superficial view, our cultural perception of Germany in the late 1930s would be exceptionally good – Germany a country of some of the greatest composers, philosophers and scientific achievers though a Germany of the 1930s ruled by the mad and infested with the depraved persecution of innocent minorities that eventually precipitated the deaths of millions. Germany is one example of many and when it comes to cruelty this is something that knows no borders and at various times in our world history has presented itself, albeit mostly of a lesser scale, in every society without exception.

What happened in Germany is by no means unique or a reflection of the German people; it is a reflection of a malignant sub-culture that happened to have taken root and this can happen anywhere, in any country and at any time and given the right conditions. It is a fact that many of us don't know what bad we are capable of doing it is just perhaps a question of motivation, just how far does our moral boundary stretch.

We may assume that such dark times are behind us never to be repeated and could never happen where we happen to live but that would be rank complacency. The existence, unchecked growth or worse still denial of malignant sub-cultures can only end in tragedy unless this is faced up to before it can take hold. Many could see and warned of where Hitler was going although most chose to ignore it and history has a very awkward habit of repeating itself.

Perhaps what we should define as cultivation is in how we behave and in how safe or unsafe we make our society, not by what music or literature that we have produced. On this basis it might be easier to define the antithesis in what is not a cultivated society rather than what it is: Is our society corrupt, crime ridden, where law is applied unequally, where there is persecution of minorities, or majorities, where our leaders are undemocratic and ignore the will of its people, where everyone is selfish, where everywhere there are people who agitate and seek to divide?

Some might argue that all cultures are equal and those that do are usually idiots who live in countries free from persecution or backward ideologies and who have never experienced such regimes. They might base their position upon some transitory experience, a statistically poor sample of evidence, cultural relativism where we are stridently instructed to tolerate even the intolerable (!) or upon impressionistic propaganda with appalling disregard for rational diligence.

Such idiots live in their own cosy little bubble completely ignorant of what goes on elsewhere. Their liberal views do not liberate the people suffering under a regime of a backward or repressive culture, in fact they are abandoning those people through their unwitting complicit vocal support for, or denial of fault in, such cultures – this in itself is depressing. History is replete with examples that cultures are not and cannot be equal. If we advocate that all cultures are equal would we then assume that Adolf Hitler or Joseph Stalin were culturally equivalent to Jesus Christ or the Buddha, does that seem in any way a logical proposition?

Albeit that a culture imputes its properties upon its population this is not to say that all people from an inferior culture are inferior but that it is the culture from where they came that is inferior. So an individual must not be judged upon the culture from where they came but by what they are as an individual. Even a hypothetical culture that is nothing but evil can yield those who are good just as a desert can yield an oasis. However, if a culture is deficient such that by virtue of its modification that it is converging upon perfection then what you have now is not just a different culture but a superior culture, ergo its earlier form was inferior.

If any of us were to look with honesty at our own nation we would recognise that its population consists of those who seek to do harm and those who seek to do good, the honest and those you cannot trust, the hard-working and the lazy, the givers and the takers, the experienced and the naïve, the truth seekers and the truth deniers, the sane and the insane, the joyful and the miserable, the cultured and the un-cultured, the honourable and the dishonourable, the moral and the immoral.

To insist that any population is not these things, that we do not see all characteristics, good and bad, of humanity within would be a gross misconception, or that we might be totally blind to the truth, and when I say any population I mean all populations everywhere. If it were that the negative human attributes never existed in any and all nations, as some might fantasize, then why do our national vocabularies even have words for these attributes, this is easily predicated along the lines that if a word exists then what it is describing must also exist.

Oddly enough often those who espouse that all cultures are equal also extend this assumption that those from within a culture are also all equal, that they are homogeneous, and from what we have just discussed this is untrue. However, some cultures are predisposed to specific characteristics i.e. we can attribute a characteristic as being quite typical of a culture for example; perhaps the most polite people on the planet are not the English, and I am speaking as an Englishman, but the Japanese would get my vote, perhaps the friendliest are the Canadians and the Danish, and perhaps the most spiritual are the Indians.

But no culture is entirely predisposed to good characteristics it may also have bad ones. Those with the greatest sense of humour may also have very high crime rates, those who are the most devout to their beliefs may not have just rule of law. The reality is that a population, though not an individual, may have cultural attributes, good or bad, that we will wrongly preconceive to apply to all but where we are not wrong to apply to some or even many, essentially we are weighing up probabilities. The moral here is that; be cautious but remain open as what you suspect may have some general prevailing truth although is not necessarily applicable to every individual.

Even more odd is that those who promote the notion that another culture is all good and that all of its citizens are likewise often denigrate their own culture as if all is bad about theirs and all is good about everyone else's. On this basis they have a self-loathing one often rooted in an hysteria of historical guilt for what had been done long ago which of course we are the only ones being guilty of such!!! They really need to read their history to see that no nation is without guilt of committing unjust war, enslavement, plunder or some form of ill-treatment of other nations.

Dig through history and you will find plenty of Hitlerian type monsters everywhere. For past sins not by us but by others, often long gone we must constantly flog ourselves in some act of atonement that must be total and irredeemable until all wealth is exhausted and the nation and any sense of nationality has been destroyed. To them patriotism, an essential element of any population to its mother nation – not necessarily its leaders, is an anathema, it must not be allowed it must be vigorously trodden into the ground.

What could not be described as anything other than patriotic is to be redefined as 'nationalism' in the guise of feeling superior over others rather than from what is really going on which is just to look after ourselves first. The misuse of the word 'nationalistic' is to corrupt the truth, defining something which it is not, what others want you to believe to make anyone who happens to feel patriotic to question themselves as being backward, bad and therefore made to feel foolish which of course they are none of these things.

Can we say with any sense of sanity that two cultures are equal or even only just different and therefore not unequal in for example; before women in the UK were given the right to vote and after they were given this right, that this is so in that before the American civil war where slavery, that has been a disgrace of our history where almost all nations have not been without guilt (just check out the Viking slave trade of Europeans into north Africa and the middle east), was 'legal' in the southern states of the USA though illegal after or that in the Crimean war that despite the availability of anaesthetics British army surgeons were instructed not to use them as they believed pain was an essential element of the healing process whereas Russian, French and Turkish surgeons took a more enlightened view. Or could it be that a culture is considered equal to another on the basis that, albeit consisting of outdated ideas or even cruelty, is otherwise enlightened and so on balance therefore must be equal despite having shortcomings in making the lives miserable of certain selected communities within – definitely not.

"We hold these truths to be self-evident, that all men are created equal." –
Thomas Jefferson (3rd President, USA 18th/19th century)

It is a measure of a society and thereby its cultivation through the way it behaves equally to all of humanity irrespective of race, colour, religion, orientation and gender and in the way how its individuals conduct themselves as being selfless, truthful, well-mannered, appreciative of the good actions of others, disinclined to conflict, industrious and law abiding. To suggest that we can define a culture as merely being culturally based on language and cuisine is fatuous, facile and naive. These things may define some elements of how a culture may appear although it is not exclusively what a culture is; I may live in China, speak fluent Mandarin and may eat exclusively Chinese food, however, this does not make me Chinese; that is my culture is not Chinese, i.e. I don't think like a Chinese person or necessarily appreciate the same things, noting that Chinese is not just a nationality it is also a race.

To be anything is more than just its superficial constituent parts. To establish my Chinese substrate culture would be predicted and predicated, albeit with some inaccuracy, upon my race, as would be confirmed through my DNA as where any palaeontologist would look to determine what I am or should I say what I was and thereby equally what had been my culture.

Do we now live in a decent world where all societies adopt enlightened and fair views of all? Where all are equal and where all individual behaviour is urbane - unfortunately no. Because we seek not to offend, or that we might be afraid to disagree with our dynamic group, we perpetuate those backward looking cultures and the ensuing misery that they inflict. Let us not forget those great heroes; Emily Pankhurst, Abraham Lincoln (a republican), Martin Luther King, Nelson Mandela, Mahatma Gandhi, Florence Nightingale, Mary Seacole, Václav Havel and Aleksandr Solzhenitsyn who had the courage to stand up to fight for what they believed and often endured years in prison for their belief – these people were not politically naïve nor stupid they were brave enough and prepared to challenge bad culture head on and change the world for the better.

You and I can either join them or take a liberal view that everything and every culture is equal and without need for change and should be 'celebrated' despite its foulness. To deny that not all cultures are equal is appalling ignorance and doesn't lessen the suffering of those having to endure the misery of having to live within those cultures that are oppressive and cruel.

Logic will always have its detractors and some will casually state that *"we all have a lot more in common than what is different about us"*. There is good intention in this as it attempts to bring people together despite what may be alarming differences in thinking but although we have a lot in common some cultures may pass specific thresholds of what we cherish of our own cultures as in social behaviour or values that are quite alien or unacceptable. It is at this point that what we have in common is irrelevant. How would we perceive the ardent religious institutions of the middle ages, e.g. 'the Catholic Inquisition', who would falsely accuse anyone at show trials (the 'auto de fe') of heresy with the intention of inflicting sadistic torture and then death, the ardent owner of slaves on a cotton plantation who inflicts misery on innocent human beings often with the whip, the obdurate male politician who refuses to yield to giving women the right to vote or the ardent murderer of Jews on an industrial scale, would we perceive them as having more in common with us than what is different I certainly don't. It might be argued that this is politics not culture although isn't it part of culture, of a failed culture, to look upon others who are just different as being inferior and so game for persecution.

All of these people were not suddenly ardent or obdurate anything, like all forms of rot they start from something that at first may seem quite innocuous, they grow with stealth and we may turn a blind eye to what is really developing to avoid causing offence or through our own fear, some may be so craven that they will seek to defend, excuse or even perpetuate another's failed culture than have the guts to face it down. Thank God that Winston Churchill stood against Nazism otherwise all of us may have ended up in a gas chamber. What may seem innocent if unchecked will develop and propagate just like any cancer and so bad culture must always be challenged, and to enlighten a culture it must also be challenged from within.

On a positive note, not all people are bad and mostly cultures are not bad either it is just certain factions will develop sub-cultures within that are bad by any sense of moral definition. If you look with discernment you will find good and bad in all cultures as not everyone within a culture will subscribe to what is bad and neither will some subscribe to what is good, this is something we just need to accept as this truth for what it is.

The Barometer of a Failed Society

We may all imagine that a failed society is one that suffers poverty and oppression, however, cultivation is not a component of wealth nor is it a component of political freedom. Despite what our economic or political state is we can still have cultivation we can still have a society that in its own right is successful and civilised, it has the potential to succeed in tackling poverty and rid itself of oppression if it were to have decent political leaders, right effort and commerce.

A good society is one where we are all honest and incorruptible, where we care for one another, where we all have a sense of duty and do our fair share of work for the greater good, where we have good manners, where we always do the decent thing and where we treat everyone with respect. A bad society is therefore one in which dishonesty, corruption, a care for only ourselves, a sense of having no duty to others, where we avoid work, where we are impolite where we do not do what is decent or where we show no respect for all others is what is prevalent. We may draw specious conclusions of other societies on where they sit in these terms of these cultivations but we cannot sensible deduce anything unless we live amongst a society for some time, and I don't mean an adventure holiday, you will need to go native to really know what is going on - sitting on a camel for a couple of hours on some excursion will not give you any insight into North African culture, you would need to live amongst its people and speak their language to get any idea of what their culture is really like. We like to think we know but we are just guessing.

However, from the world of a technically sophisticated media, from a remote position, there are certain factors that can be determined just how civilized or modern thinking a society is and that is through how a society behaves towards its minorities, does it for example, when we think of the Inquisition, persecute a minority religion or does it allow it to practice its religion within what is acceptable to just laws (human sacrifice would for example be a no no) but what is often the real litmus test is how does it behave towards its women.

In many societies women have achieved emancipation where for the same effort as a man they can achieve the same as a man they have equality in all respects where women, if they should choose, can enter any professional field in as much that the glass ceiling has been smashed. As yet we need to see more women, if they so desire, to take these opportunities that are away from their traditional and often low paid assumed roles as for example to consider the engineering profession where in the UK just 7% of its engineers are women yet oddly enough in countries offering less emancipation for women is where women are more inclined to take to these assumed male dominated and often better paid career paths. This being so perhaps we are still seeing women who are emancipated but yet not realising nor taking up the opportunity that it has to offer, so my advice is just go for it and don't hold back.

If you aspire to just go after those higher paying professions they are open to you too although the caveat to this is that they may be stressful in the extreme or even dangerous to the point that they are undoubtedly life limiting hence the reason for higher pay (perhaps men have less concern for their own safety given their hard-wired aggressive rather than compassion based traits). However, outside of enlightened societies there is in some places a long way to go as we are about to discuss.

Progress as just described is excellent but in some societies women are regarded as second class citizens whilst there is pretence by the men that they are just being protective. This is a lie. Where this is so women are often treated like cattle, they are enslaved, imprisoned in the home, savagely beaten, constantly chastised and humiliated, deprived of any kindness or care, sold as some commodity, they do not have any political representation, they are to do as they are told, they are to marry whom as they are instructed, they may be deliberately excluded from education and they may have essentially no protection from the law for what any man may decide to do with them and if they do not follow the rules their lives can be in mortal danger. Societies that are so obscene that they exhibit such pervasive misogyny do so because of a pathological male perpetuated culture in that women are to be perceived as nothing more than objects to serve men.

Along with this perception of servitude is one of power in that men are all-powerful over their women folk and with power there may also be some bizarre sense of entitlement in as much as a woman who they oddly believe falls short of what they believe they deserve, that they then feel justified to ill-treat, hence the appalling treatment women may face. If this describes what you are and you have a good wife then it is not you who deserves a better wife but it is your wife who deserves a better husband and this is perhaps why you also exert so much control for fear of your wife catching the eye of another and one who is a better man than you. You should count yourself as lucky if your wife is a good woman as many, in this world, live solitary lives perhaps never to find a good partner and if you do not change your ways you will only sour what otherwise could have been a wonderful union and experience of life. You can change everyone's life now, including yours for the better or remain living a wasted existence that is full of nothing but hate. Just think about it.

"As far as you can avoid it, do not give grief to anyone. Never inflict your rage on another. If you hope for eternal rest, feel the pain yourself; but don't hurt others."
– Omar Khayyam (Poet, Persia 12th century)

Some may argue that this doesn't happen but it does and if you find this just too incredible to believe then you might be interested to know what a lot of charities, their field workers and United Nations officials discover. Awful as this truth is we must accept what is true, to do otherwise is to abandon these women.

Let me make one thing clear to these 'types' that to treat women in such a way shows what they are, they violate any religious principles, they violate the rule of just law and they violate the rules of decency. They are essentially ignorant to behave in such a way to a woman who in no way is any less than a man and in no way any less than them, indeed their behaviour to women shows them to be the one who is inferior. And those women on the receiving end of such treatment who not only will refuse to condemn their ill-treatment but that they may even condone it only do so out of their own fear – just remind yourself of the artificial happiness you will see on the faces of those living in brutal totalitarian regimes, the rule being look happy or face imprisonment.

"How very little can be done under the spirit of fear." – Florence Nightingale
(Nurse - Crimean War, England 19th century)

Our women are our mothers who carried us for nine months and protected us through our early life and if necessary would sacrifice their own interests and even their life to protect us, they are also, our sisters, wives and daughters who with any sense of honour and decency we should protect, we should see that our woman folk do not come to any harm and we should give them equal latitude in all respects as a man, this meaning; the right to vote, equal access to education and to careers, are equally rewarded for equal performance and for what they do in their chosen career, to choose what they want to do and to whom they want to marry and to be equal under the law. No longer would a man be 'entitled' to a woman's affection, one that he arranges through family ties without consent of his future spouse, he would have to enter the competitive world in this respect and this might just motivate him to becoming a better person. This should not just apply to women it should equally apply to all, all shall be equal. If we as a world are to progress we need to complete this revolution where we are all to be looked upon equally.

If it is a religious perspective to believe that God made women inferior to men and therefore should be denied access to education then why did God give women an intelligence proven to be equal to that of a man. Today more and more women are successfully entering the world of engineering as engineers, in medicine as doctors and surgeons, in law as solicitors and barristers, as airline pilots and in many other professions and this movement is gaining momentum. They not only can prove that they can equal men but in many spheres they can surpass them.

Women are indeed equal to men and no more and men are indeed equal to women and no more. This book is some testament to women in that of all the many books I have read on countless subjects I find the best of all styles is largely dominated by female authors and I have certainly learnt a lot from them in how best to present my material. The only glass ceiling that is holding women back and the only reason why there were less notable women of the past was because men or culture held them back with outdated views, but things are changing.

The time of women worldwide is about to begin and I believe the 21st century will herald the dawn of a society worldwide where women are rightly valued at every corner of the planet. If you are a woman and don't see that this should happen it is only because you have been historically and culturally conditioned to think this way, if you are a man and don't see that this should happen then you are a fool. Indeed given our history it would seem that us men have somewhat screwed up many things so it's time to get out of the driving seat and let our women folk take over the wheel where they are the better candidate to do so so long as they do not try to emulate the arrogance of some men since arrogance is equally obnoxious, whether it be in the hands of a man or a woman.

There is evidence of female potential through investigating Neolithic civilisations as detailed in the writings of the great visionary psychologist Erich Fromm who postulated that a matriarchal structured society would probably be more peaceful and therefore more successful in certain respects, the female, that is not of a male emulating form, being more inclined to compassion and unity the male more inclined to aggression, conflict and dominance, at least this is the theory. If we were to have a matriarchal tilted society a woman should not try to emulate a man as in doing so she is depriving herself of the very qualities that the world so desperately needs. Perhaps with change we may now hope to envisage a new world order; one with less conflict where we could beat swords into ploughshares, where nations shall no longer lift up swords against other nations (an idea from Isaiah 2:4).

"I do not wish women to have power over men; but over themselves." – Mary Wollstonecraft (Philosopher, England 18th century)

I believe that what Mary Wollstonecraft was alluding to was that women must seek emancipation and no more as to seek more is to seek the very thing you object to i.e. inequality, the dominance of one over another and the loss of freedom, these very same ideas that led to the Suffragette movement of the 20th century where women would win the right to vote. But also remember that in the UK that neither did most men, working class men that is have any representation as in having the right to vote until well into the 19th century (the Chartist movement) until which access to the polling booth was essentially drawn along class lines.

Our Vision of the World

There are over seven billion human beings on our planet all of whom will think and perceive differently despite us thinking that there must be many out there who think exactly as I do although in actuality they don't. We may have a lot in common and we may have similar experiences but we are not the same, our journey through life would have brought us to different places of where we are as a thinking human being. However, more than this there are other things at play.

Psycho-linguistics would suggest that our language, our mother tongue, will make us perceive things differently to those who speak another, a word in one language may have identical meaning in another although the two words side by side have different sounds different tones and just how different music will elicit different emotions then so would the different sounds of the same word in different languages. I can communicate the same sentence to you in two different languages and you would understand what I am communicating as exactly the same although the different sounds will leave you feeling emotionally slightly different.

Further to this; we may share the same language though what we do in our life in our careers is markedly different, what a trauma surgeon must face is human suffering, death and work that is brutal, an engineer must deal with things that are based on logic rather than emotion and must face things often quite intimidating in scale and complexity, a police officer must face daily threats to their lives and deal with some quite unpleasant people or at least unpleasant in the state that they are in, whilst many other careers do not present any exposure to such harsh experiences, they may involve hard work although they are not exposed to anything particularly harsh.

What we experience inclines us in how we think and this is why certain demographic groups might be found to have certain political inclinations. We do not all vote the same in any particular group though how we vote or how we think can in part be predicted based upon what our life experience is through which demographic group we belong.

Perhaps all of this is based upon our vocabulary in the sense that if you lack a certain word you may be comparatively blind to its concept i.e. the greater the vocabulary the more adept we are at conceiving ideas as I mentioned earlier on - a word encases an idea. Imagine this that you may not have grasped the pathological implications of some around you until you read about 'sub-clinical personalities' as introduced in this book but now you have gained this connection in your thought patterns. No longer would you see someone as just very difficult you may start to see a connection into that which is pathological.

Later in this book I shall use a fairly rare word 'commutative' in a certain context and when you get there it may open up a new way of looking at what we expect to happen but a word gives this perception credence it galvanises it into the way how we think.

What all of this amounts to is that our life experience, our language, what we do as a career will markedly change the way how we think, it may affect how logical we are in our deductions or do we use emotion, whether or not we are resilient, whether or not we could mentally survive what other people have to do or have to face, whether we are obsessed with money or not, whether or not we are hard nose thinkers or perhaps a little naïve.

Further to all of this we have the human trait, or habit, of automatically jumping to conclusions based upon our own frame of reasoning, rightly or wrongly, or in failing to do so when our instincts tell us that we should. The actions of individuals from another culture may not be representative of that culture and so what they may do that is bad does not necessarily suggest that their culture is itself at fault, it could be that there are other factors that we need to consider or it may be that only certain adherents portray a corrupted version of their culture much in the same way as the Inquisition acted with such evil within a religion essentially based upon compassion.

Conversely, if we have identified a trend within a specific culture, and we have eliminated all other possible multi-variate causal factors as having any bearing, then we can only conclude that something is inherently remiss or at fault, we may therefore have good reason and necessity to confront those beliefs, interpretations of such beliefs or parts thereof. Thankfully though we continue to progress as a world society and as a species, although sometimes we may despair at the news, and we are a lot more egalitarian in our outlook than we might have been in times past, however, we still have a long way to go not just us but all of the seven billion inhabitants of this planet. So let's all pull together.

The Imperatives of Successful Integration in Living Alongside another Culture (are you or are you not in the team?)

As a 'parenthesis' to what is to follow: There is no problem with any society that is pluralist or at least there is no reason that there should be – different people different cultures should be mature enough to get along and mostly they do. But excesses of group identity, particularly 'agitative' group identity, or worse deliberately 'agitative' group identity, leads inevitably to friction to division to societal instability and that can lead on to who knows what perhaps to a hell that few could possibly imagine or ever expect. Who wins in this game? The answer is no-one.

The law may enforce tolerance, a political naivety, but this tactic can only build benign and then malignant resentment so is thus counterproductive. People cannot be forced to get on they must want to get on. But a society that has strong separatist cultures within that does not integrate is one that history teaches us, again and again, is doomed. To ignore this would be foolish in the extreme and our future can only look bleak if we are so stupid to not look or worse to fear looking.

It is therefore incumbent upon us all to seek cohesion in society, a common aim must pervade all who live within one nation; there must be something, something though that is very tangible and that even transcends imperative and demonstrable loyalty to the nation state and that is enthusiastically grasped by all, that pulls everyone together as one. An atomic nucleus would violently tear itself apart were it not for the strong cohesive forces within and society is no different.

We must learn to like one another and we must at all cost avoid having to be 'tolerated', we must avoid at all cost as being perceived as 'demanding'. The question is what can we find that will bind us together where we seek a common aim where we can live in peace where there is no need for suspicion or distrust where loyalty to all and by all is guaranteed. The hand of friendship can never be unilateral we are all in this together as one family one nation something that we must all strive diligently towards to make it work.

In our modern world we are on the move like never before and when we move it is critically important that we integrate successfully into the culture to which we are moving to. This does not mean that we need to abandon our cultural identity, since different cultures make the world a more interesting place, however in taking up citizenship in another country we are obliged to do several things, not just for being welcomed to our new home but also for practical reasons to integrate, we must; abandon our previous national identity and embrace our new nationality with pride, pledge our primary and total loyalty and allegiance to the country that we now call home, we must abide by its laws, contribute to its economy and we must be prepared to help defend the well-being of its people and nation.

It is a wonderful opportunity to be able to live in a new country of your choice, particularly if it is one that is open, relaxed and that has just laws and this at least deserves some reciprocation on your behalf i.e. your loyalty. If you cannot give your loyalty to your new home then you may want to question why besides any nation must be able to count on its citizens to stand together as one and this is particularly so where there is a crisis or in its need to strive for success.

By definition - it is not possible to become a citizen of a nation unless you are fully committed – if you don't fully commit to it then don't expect it to fully commit to you. If you want all of the advantages that it can offer then you must be prepared to give something in return. If we look at the USA, a nation with perhaps the most diverse population in race, ethnicity and religion it is particularly highly successful in one respect in that almost all are proud to identify themselves as Americans, they are quite rightly proud of their flag. You may argue that some things it does and has done are in error (the Vietnam war for example), but are there really any nations that are not without fault themselves and are we ourselves without fault, sometimes we do the wrong things for the right reasons but it is the intent that matters.

If anywhere on this planet and whoever they are is hit by a major disaster you can count on the USA to pitch in to help out, it always does. The USA may be the wealthiest nation on earth (GDP) though as individuals not all Americans are as well off as you might imagine and it does have its share of poverty but for the fact that it always does so much and often more than many others then we should all be grateful. This all being said the USA is a very successful nation and this in large part is thanks to its unity in the sense of being an American if all else is not equal at least one thing is and this is what binds the nation together to see a common purpose and loyalty.

If it is the fact that you have decided to permanently move to another country then you must have done so for good reason, you must perceive it, for whatever reason, to be better than from where you came and if you have the illusion that your new home must be the same as from where you came, that you cannot tolerate your new home then you need to ask yourself just why have I made this move was it the right thing to do. If it is your belief that you have been singled out and persecuted in your host country then ask yourself; are you treated differently under the law, are you denied healthcare, education or welfare upon receiving the gift of citizenship as afforded to others are you prevented from practicing your religion.

Conversely do you act as a model citizen who seeks to contribute to your new home? If where you live is not to your cultural liking then you need to ask yourself what am I looking for and where can I go that can give me the cultural life that I want. We all have licence to criticize, I often do so of my own country, however just don't overdo it and at least applaud it for what good there is but if you have aggressive designs to dramatically change where you are to what you want and that is against the common wishes of its people then think again as you might end up antagonising your compatriots and this is not a wise path to take since putting different cultures on collision course can only end in tragedy for all without any winners. If you cannot see this then just go and read up about history to see what lit the fuse in some appalling conflicts – different cultures that cannot live under one roof but could have done so if only they had applied some wisdom and worked together instead of against each other.

The obvious corollary from this is that if you don't like where you are and you are not prepared to change your opinion then don't act rash but first give it a chance and if after a few months you feel the same then your only real option is to consider to move elsewhere, there is really no point in staying in a state of misery. If you presume that everyone else should change to satisfy your demands then you are assuming that your needs transcends the needs of the many, a somewhat arrogant and counterproductive position to take.

If you were to think of the analogy of moving your job - here you would be in close proximity with others who often see the world differently to you but you need to make friends otherwise your time at work will be miserable and so we must do all we can to integrate with our colleagues not to isolate ourselves, you have to get to learn to like others of different persuasions and you will find that your life will be so much easier for it, you also have the opportunity to learn about another culture that you might discover to be better for you than what you had thought.

Life is a whole lot better if you set out to make friends not enemies. This is no different in moving where you live as in moving where you work. But think well on it since if you decided that you have no option but to move back to where you came from then you might just remember later why you left in the first place and you may bitterly regret what you have done.

The Unifying Properties of Culture – Different Cultures One Species

A long time ago I lived in London, London that is that is not as nice as it is now; I didn't enjoy my time there. Much of this was my fault as I was later, too late I add, to realise that my dislike was a lot to do with my own isolation - I didn't make the effort to explore to overcome my fear of the place a fear of not knowing or being unfamiliar. If only I had made the effort to look and to mingle instead of sitting in my room reading. It is an ineradicable fact that we often fear what we don't know or we may be too rash to do the opposite (absence of any fear of what we think we know). As in any judgment we should weigh up everything but to be fair on us all, wrongly perceived as bad or wrongly perceived as good, we should take a closer look and seek to find out what something really is but if we don't look we will never find out. We could be missing something wonderful. Now I know London so well I can't get enough of it. It's not so easy to love something or even like something if we don't explore and we don't mingle.

We are all the more enriched if we open our eyes to the rest of the world. As you read through this book you will note the international, intercultural and interracial sourcing of the quotes and individuals mentioned that I have chosen to include within. This was not contrived out of some politically correct gesture, since in doing so you just highlight differences that are not really there. What I chose to include was purely out of merit and what I felt was appropriate. If we were to discriminate in favour of one race, gender, nationality or whatever comes to mind over another then we have just discriminated against the other which is not exactly what it sets itself out to be i.e. egalitarian, besides I couldn't care a rat crap from what community someone comes from, I just look at them for what they are within what they are as a person, a simple way of looking at it is in just how good or how bad is this person nothing more, what is it that is in their heart what is their real motivation.

"My soul honours your soul. I honour the place in you where the entire universe resides. I honour the light, love, truth, beauty and peace within you, because it is

also in me. In sharing these things we are united, we are the same we are one." –
Indian proverb.

As I have said that not all cultures are equal although a lot of us wherever we are, are very much equal in so many ways. I have travelled much of this world and only in so much as my salary and career could take me though I would dearly love to have explored more. I have dabbled with languages, some quite exotic, but never got my backside in gear to learn one well since I have been too busy in my career to have done otherwise but seriously you would be very unimpressed with what I know.

I have spent much of my spare time reading the history and literature of much of the world though as in all of us we are just too limited in time to go as far as we would like. Unfortunately for me there are no cultural nuances to be had from working in engineering; working on the design of a power station in the UK is no different than designing one for Outer Mongolia. However, if we could find the time, do any of us make the effort to go and seek out the real flavour of another culture - to do so is a bit like peeling an onion down to its core or something like dismantling a Russian Matryoshka doll.

For most of us what we experience of another culture is from its architecture, its cuisine, in hearing its language, its 'tourist focussed' entertainment and in sampling the local 'hooch', which they are always proud to promote as the most potent stuff on the planet that you need to treat with the same respect as you would a blast furnace with a bad temper – this is the typical fare of the annual holiday abroad. We could dig a little deeper and examine its museums and history, we could perhaps try to make conversation with its people and we could listen to its music. If we go further we can study its language, explore its customs and we could even live amongst this culture we could go native.

Much of what we understand of another culture is in the main superficial we just get to the first base and no further. The further we go and if we are invited into their homes the more we see that in many ways people from different cultures are more like us than what we might imagine, they have the same emotions, they have many of the same problems, the same faults – they may not be exactly like us but they are very similar in many ways.

Now for most of us our finances are limited as is our time such that we may never get to afford to travel to or go native in exotic places such as India, Japan, Peru, the Caribbean, Egypt, Namibia, Malaysia, Vietnam or Bali though what we have is that fantastic invention the internet. We have effectively the whole world in one place such that if I can't get to the rest of the world I can at least bring the rest of the world to me. In our logical universally mutual interest in the cohesion and coexistence of humanity we need, as a first base, at least some appreciation of international cultural, since for the world over when it comes to culture we are often quite parochial; we know a lot of our own but very little of others.

Without the 'smorgasbord' of international culture we are missing so much and losing opportunities to learn and share ideas but also for the fact that as we care to see what others really are like then we see that they are in many ways not that unlike us, look more closely and we all have very much similar emotions and you can recognise joy and sadness the world over. The more we get to know others the more we may get to admire the positive elements of their culture and although we may have intractable difficulties elsewhere we may at least have a better chance to coexist as a world community rather than being in constant political or military conflict. Perhaps if we were to see that other cultures we know little about can evoke amazement, admiration and joy and in doing so perhaps this can bring down the walls of perceived differences.

If you can find the time, and believe me it's well worth it can you just spend a couple of hours on the internet exploring foreign culture through music and dance videos using my list below that pretty much circumnavigates world culture and the human race at its very best:

- Riverdance the final performance – Irish dance/music
- Som Sabadell flashmob – Spanish flashmob (music)
- California Dreamin' cover by The New Love Generation – German musicians
- Pirates of the Caribbean 5 Tribute Performance – Polish orchestra
- Naomi Wachira Africa Girl – Kenyan music
- Perlice Pata Pata – South African music (Miriam Makeba) with dance
- Sırnaşik Sevgili Ebru Gündeş – Turkish music
- Flash Mob Moscow Putting on the Ritz – Russian flashmob (dance)
- Katyusha Marina Devyatova and Katya Ryabova – Russian music
- When We Were At War Elena Vaenga – Russian music
- Für Elise in different tastes Maan Hamadeh 2 – Lebanese musician
- Hanine Arabia – Arabian music and dance
- Nari Nari – Arabic/Indian music/dance
- Kishore Janjanam (Noziya Karamatullo, Mara Karda Faramoush) – Tajikistani music/dance
- Lal Dupatta – Indian music/dance
- Chale Jaise Hawaein – Indian music/dance
- Hong Kong Festival Orchestra Flash Mob 2013: Beethoven's Ode to Joy – Chinese flashmob

- Chinese-Style Shuffle – The Most Amazing Dance in China's Cities – Chinese dance/music
- Zhang Chun Li Square Dance The Good Flower and the Moon – Chinese dance/music
- Pirates of the Caribbean Rhapsody Philharmonic – Vietnamese flashmob (music)
- Brian King Joseph I took a pill in Ibiza – American musician
- Apartment Sessions – Everyday People (Sly and the Family Stone) – American music
- The Byrds 'Turn Turn Turn' (Rickenbacker 360-12) Buddy Clontz – American musician
- Leo Rojas El Condor Pasa – Bolivian musician
- Bellini Samba Do Brazil – Brazilian music/dance
- Katrina and the Waves Love Shine a Light – English music
- Apartment Sessions – Somebody To Love – English music (American musicians)
- Nicole Ein Bisschen Frieden (Fernsehgarten 15-5-2016) – German music

If you have explored the above then you may have changed your perception at least a little of what you may believe to be alien cultures. I hope that what you will experience, as I did with them all, a sense of feeling beguiled, impressed, enchanted and perhaps even moved. My selection was deliberately so to encompass joy, passion, fun, creativity and as a representation and admiration of true human talent. See now how more alike we are than how different we are when we view humanity at its very best not at its very worst. If we can all aim for these heights to excel at something good then perhaps we can gain more respect for one another and live together in a better world. Despite our cultures being different we can see and admire the skill and the joy across all cultures. Basically, what this represents is that most of us despite our faults are OK wherever we are on planet earth.

There is a sad fact that not all of our species are OK and some just don't like to see others happy, they are the misfits, who are full of hate precipitated often from envy or through their own failure, who agitate and cause so much trouble and destruction and if they can't grow up and join the rest of us then they can never find the true value of life. However, to them I say it is never too late to cast aside hate and make the most of your lives, why throw a life away when you can work to find a better outlook. Why seek out hate when you can seek out joy. Hate doesn't bring happiness but joy does but it requires all parties to sign up to this idea. If you cannot seek peace then you will only seek your destruction and isn't that a waste of your life.

We are all one species and one family although we are a long way from a one nation and a one government world though I guess that we will have to wait for at least another millennium for it to be sensible to even contemplate this ideal. Our nations have different economies, different political ideas, different aspirations, different problems, may work less or more hours, retire earlier or later and some may have a cavalier or disciplined attitude to productivity, debt and taxation and some may have different perspectives of law that as yet are not aligned with that which is just or sensible.

These factors are evidently nebulous in the world of economic theory but are critical in the world of economic reality, a reality that can only be fully realised by looking beyond economics. In economic models we ignore such unquantifiable factors albeit that they may be highly significant in the conclusion, this we do at our peril. What we don't understand what we cannot quantify we are rather too inclined to dismiss as irrelevant. We should therefore not be too rash in forming politically as one without borders, as we say *"move with haste and repent at leisure"*, though we should aim to an ultimate end, perhaps far into the future, of a one nation world through collaboration and economic capacity convergence not foolish and corrupt political ambition and expediency. But if we look at us all through a prism of enlightenment we can identify just how alike most of us are and the seeds of working as one are already there we just need to cultivate them, be sensible and be patient.

Chapter 13

'UNZIPPING' THE MIND OF THE POLITICIAN

(Politicians, democracy and the obsessive craving for power)

Be kind to yourself by getting wise about the politically motivated, by doing so you shall be better informed at the ballot box and we hope that the political classes will then do what they must do for the good of all rather than for the good of themselves.

In politics almost every stone you turn over there is something horrible something pathological that crawls out.

Books are wonderful things they give us material to cultivate the mind from which we can think. Read enough of them and there is potential to construct completely new ways of perceiving the world such that we can then create new ideas and explore the unexplored. When it comes to the classification of politicians, to delve into their psychology and motivation, there is very little material to go on and if there is it's buried deep but speak to enough people and what you get is a consensus on how the public perceives or interprets its 'political masters'. In this sense this chapter is not so much written it is a construction of the insightful views of many.

Sad to say I hear a lot that is bad and not so much that is good. What politicians believe we cannot see is actually not hidden as well as they might imagine. This chapter may be excoriating of the politicos but they are often very bad people who do very bad things. Indeed we might be a whole lot better off without them.

I hate politics, I even hate to have to write this chapter, diatribe is not really in my nature, but it is after all a somewhat depressing subject though it shouldn't be so, a world which is largely corrupt, dishonest and largely a game of manipulation can be nothing other than a miserable existence but we cannot avoid the unavoidable when it has such dramatic effect upon our life's experience, so here we are in the world of politics and crawling around in the minds of those who seem to love it so much.

We all have good reasons to feel proud of the country we call home, despite its faults, and nowhere is perfect, and we can build a narrative around that idea, just imagine how would you promote your country on the world stage, but first I shall speak of my home.

The nation of my birth, the UK, is a great nation and for the fact that so many seek to make it their home and then stay attests to this fact they are qualifying this fact. The UK has substantial scientific and cultural achievement and it punches way above its weight in its sporting achievements too. It was here, where the industrial revolution began, that life changing inventions and discoveries were made including: penicillin, the jet engine, the television, the telephone and the internet, all of which have so much impact upon our lives. Modern drugs, ideas and inventions still pour out from this country. Just imagine that every time that you need an antibiotic that its existence, and so its saving of your life, is there as a result of painstaking research undertaken in the UK. Here we have a strong economy albeit with issues but then who doesn't, a hard working highly skilled workforce, a population who are generally polite, are generous and don't take themselves too seriously and we have the rule of law where all can feel safe, we even have a democracy, although of sorts as we shall discuss, but you can be sure that you won't be arrested for criticising the system. We are egalitarian, possibly as near to egalitarian as can be (mmm), given consideration of existing alternative socio-political systems.

Binding this all together we have a single and highly expressive language, that of the great bard Shakespeare, that will soon be spoken by everyone on Earth, at least as a second language if not a first, and we have London the most amazing city on our planet although I might be being a tad biased here but is there anything wrong in being patriotic. We have world class companies and we have world class Universities. The UK and its flag is a recognised brand. Geographically the UK is also a delight although if only we had a coast more like that as typical of the Caribbean and an interior something more like that of Austria or New Zealand then it would be perfect. It has its faults, everywhere does, but reality is that other than the not so great climate, yes it could do with a few extra degrees C, there is very little to moan about except of course politics, that which affects us all and is probably one of the main topics of conversation anywhere across the planet - politics; the inescapable ever present irritation to us all.

Despite my country being, in my mind, as something quite special I hear so many of my compatriots speak ill of it, they incessantly harp on about its faulty history, its economic fragility and that it is no longer great all of which is nonsense, hyperbole, disloyal and in some cases, especially if from the mouths of our political class, is treason as is collusion with those who we compete with. I often hear this from those who don't put in any of their own effort to make my country great, from those who play political games and from those who are unwilling to accept that a history, that is not entirely good, is not exactly unique to the UK that bad things have been done by all nations and all cultures not just by us.

Politics could in theory be all wonderful, so it is with great regret that I am compelled to write this, in the world of politics all is not good, so much so that for most of us our life potential is degraded and for many even destroyed. Some members of the human race are so low they are like vermin, they could crawl under the belly of a sleeping snake whilst wearing a top hat and the snake would remain undisturbed. Welcome to the squalid world of politics. It is quite depressing that surveys, of who we trust and who we don't, that the political class doesn't come out very favourably, though of any of us it is so important that they should since they have the power in their hands to do so much good but unfortunately also so much bad. Thankfully not all are alike and there are some good ones in there too, and across most of the political spectrum, but we need more of them, we need more good people in politics.

Imagine what the human race could achieve if we could forever be rid of the bad and replace with those of competence, honesty, prudence and good intent. This dream is not beyond possibility. But if I the author have got it all wrong then I'm just wrong, the consequences of which would be insignificant but what if I am right then what sits in government as endorsed by us may just be destroying our life's potential including yours. Perhaps it's a question of who can you trust the most.

Why Would We Want To Discuss Politics?

"One of the penalties for refusing to participate in politics is that you end up being governed by your inferiors." – Plato (Philosopher, Greece 4th/5th century BC)

Pretty much all of us would acknowledge, incorrectly, that we can do very little as individuals to change this world, we see ourselves as politically emasculated and politics is also a subject that few of us are that interested in. However we cannot escape the pervasive and massively substantial effects that politics has upon us, politics can and often does destroy lives, so the subject of politics is unavoidable in a book that is dedicated to the subject of our life experience. All this being said is there really any point in discussing politics when it comes to exploring how we can improve our lives. We are where we are and politicians just exist somewhere else out of our reach and beyond our influence. Or are they?

Politicians, many but not all, seek to manipulate and many will regard their electorate with intellectual contempt as if we are a flock of sheep. Many talk too much and just can't stop talking; they keep doing so until we are worn down, until we capitulate. We are 'brow beaten' into submissive compliance by the corrupt, the stupid and the psychopathic aided by 'competent experts'. To them it is something of a game to secure our patronage at the ballot box and then to renege on what they had promised. The ever so pleasant incessantly smiling, and occasionally obsequious, politician is not necessarily a nice person they may be a complete scumbag and the one who speaks with earnest and with a wise countenance may not be as intelligent and reflective as we may think, they may just be a complete idiot and often are, either way such types do not respect you or I.

Often, and even who appear to be the most sincere and friendly, are highly incompetent, dangerous and even insane, they can destroy an economy, a society, inflict misery and debt, engage in illegal wars and even murder. National and international problems don't just come about by accident they are through failure to think, failure to accept, failure to predict, failure to act or to know when not to do so, or to do what is right when it's too late - all of which falls into the lap of the political elite. They will go wherever their whim takes them without concept of moral boundaries; they only seek, often ridiculous, ideology or personal gain.

All that goes wrong with society happens under their watch. They cannot even fulfil what they promised and possibly had no intention of doing so. They will deny all of this although the evidence sits before us all, as we say *"if it looks like a duck, walks like a duck and quacks like a duck then it is a duck"*. If we are dead honest just how often do we find ourselves discussing politics and moaning about it?

Centre (this in reality being indefinable), right or left; there are many politicians who have very little respect for us, they look upon us as inferior beings, they are the elite, the masters, we are the servants and we should not have the audacity to question and we should do as we are instructed. But what if they knew that we were one step ahead of them, that we could see right through their act that we had a more incisive understanding of them than they might even have of themselves? What if they knew that we could recognize their every move and their techniques of manipulation for what they are, what if they discovered that they have been rumbled?

If we could capitalize on being able to surgically open up their act then they would have no other option but to speak the truth, they could no longer manipulate the facts and the statistics, they could no longer pretend just how wonderful they are for us. We would become more informed, we would seek out hard logical facts rather than be drawn by emotions, we would be more adept at questioning them and we would become intolerant of the way how they evade answering those awkward questions. Perhaps we could aim for a better world one where politics is beyond corruption and incompetence.

"What experience and history teaches us is that people and governments have never learnt anything from history, or acted on the principles deduced from it." - Georg Hegel (Philosopher, Germany 18th/19th century)

If we could do all of this we could change politics for the good, where the political traction of a prospective or existing political representative would no longer be based upon their abilities at manipulation and spin but on being credible to the electorate i.e. they would have to speak the truth and they would have to be good at what they do. To become electable, to an enlightened electorate, out would go all of the smug incompetents and liars, and in would come those of capability and honour. The government bubble would collapse and the bad would be driven into the sea. If we can do this our politics would be pulled from the sewer and all of our lives would be better for it. We could precipitate an enlightened form of government and as for the bad guys well they can go and get their arses nailed to the gates of hell.

> *"Stand up for what is right even if you stand alone."* – Native American Indian proverb.

To feel less alarmed about life to button down the hatches and turn away from that which may worry us doesn't do us any good. We can delude ourselves that our politicians, of our favoured political inclination, are all good, without exception, or that they just make mistakes, ones that could end in war, economic failure and collapse of law and order. We must be prepared to accept that not all politicians are good that some are indeed pathological liars, psychopaths, self-serving, incompetent and lazy. If we can't face this then we are stuck with what we have and then maybe that is what we deserve but in reality we all deserve a lot better.

The Political Landscape

When I was a lot younger, without the benefits of an old head on my shoulders, well-worn ears and a mind that could detect bullshit at 500 yards, I naively viewed politicians as a bunch of people who were perhaps at least moderately competent, who would mainly strive to improve the lives of their countrymen and women and they would strive with a high aspiration to improve the happiness of the nation. They would do the decent thing. And there are some that do. But it was the contention of Thomas Hobbes, the English philosopher of the 16th/17th century that the political class should be left alone to do exactly that without challenge since the alternative might be just too unthinkable (noting that Hobbes had lived through the time of the English civil war) but only to challenge the political establishment only when a point of intolerable misery had been reached.

However, like Hobbes I would like to hope and to think well of them all although what I have seen has led me first to despair and then to despise. To even the casual observer there are so many holes in the management of our nation that it begins to resemble Swiss cheese.

I looked back at our history a history largely replete with poverty, disease, war, misery, inequality, religious insanity, unenlightened thinking and generally very unfair where you had your station, you knew your place and you were never going anywhere except for a very fortunate few. This was the lot of most of us and would be so for you and I had we had lived then and for many of us across planet earth this remains so even now and this in itself is a disgrace. Our rulers were mostly cruel despots who with their acolytes would not strive to make the lives of their 'subjects' better but to not only have made their lives worse but would do so with glee. They took everything, they had it all, they wanted more and they took it all with a smile. In my university years, and with the backdrop of a working class background, I naively convinced myself that the way out of this mess was communism.

To me then communism looked so neatly wrapped so full of ideas, perhaps even 'intellectual', that which is different always does appear, though actually is not necessarily, 'intellectual', so I had a brief affair, probably more like a one night stand with its ideas; the romantic idea of the common man and woman struggling to gain an egalitarian utopia where all would be equal, although with more reading of history, not politics, I was to realise that communism and its ideological sibling 'socialism' could only spell disaster. I had thought communism might have had it all and then I would have caught it, something what you might diagnose as a sort of political syphilis.

Communism, a politics that is exclusively socialist, was full of ideas but thin on solutions or should I say devoid of solutions but steeped heavily in human tragedy. Perhaps my attention was drawn to those who seek attention or who shout the loudest thinking that they must therefore have the best of solutions without thinking, and without thinking that the quiet, self-effacing, centre ground of politics that seeks to maintain and to conserve what good things we have is where my attention should have been drawn. What I had realised, in the generic sense of political criticism, is that politics only teaches us ideological ambitions whereas history teaches us their consequences; a manifesto may often pledge what we may believe to be great ideas but never tells of the real consequences, and what is on offer seldom has any relationship to that which will be delivered.

The reality is that the route to better lives for all would not be through sharing out the poverty across a thought policed demotivated workforce and a nationalised, anti-business and indebted economy but through a brand of politics where there would be opportunity and wealth for all; a sort of politically central egalitarian capitalism one that would create wealth and then share that wealth fairly although also with prudence.

Yet somehow, despite all of the faults of politics, our lives are better than they were in the past but how did that come about; largely so through questioning the existence and then through conflict overthrowing the ruling classes of the time, through the development of rule of just law, enlightened thinking of a few that became enlightened thinking of many, good politicians (they are not all bad), through cheap energy, through economic growth and through scientific and technological discovery the result of all of this being that we have progressed everywhere. There is however a vein of goodness in that the human race had capacity for kindness, philanthropy and altruism. We had essentially the seeds to evolve and to move on. This being said our ruling classes have not entirely moved with the times. This sounds quite a pessimistic view but let's look at this in some more detail.

Our political class is really and often no more than a mirror of the lowest elements of the society that it serves and our society, the human race, does have, amongst some of us, the most awful characteristics (the scum, the stupid, the sinister, the sadistic, the spineless, the scheming, the selfish and very much the soulless) and we could ask; what therefore motivates someone to become a politician in the first place, was it a calling to do good for the people or was it a need to control to manipulate or for self-gain and we can explore this idea through attempting to classify politicians.

On reflection we could probably categorize politicians into broadly four archetypes: the competent political philanthropists - those who promote improvement of all of our lives and who do what is fair and right (although beware of any politician who makes this claim, some who have a hidden agenda of imprudent largesse) and who are competent to achieve this aim, the deluded incompetent - those who also have political ideals but based upon irrational, ill thought through or even twisted ideology, the career politician - those who have limited career options within their skill set and who see politics as a route to a comfortable living that otherwise life would not offer and then there is the psychopathic politician - those who sadistically delight in controlling or indeed destroying others, these you may also describe as Machiavellian or unscrupulous. Further to this, politicians may exhibit clear characteristics across these groups such that they could be incompetent but also psychopathic etc.

Political history and indeed recent history is replete with such examples that would fit into these categories. Without exhaustive research we cannot determine how these classifications are distributed on an individual basis such as who falls into what category/s. However, it would not be unreasonable to make some educated guess through observation, a guess that of course the politicians would challenge after all who would admit to being a deluded incompetent idiot with a psychopathic personality although we might live in hope that at least they might be honest, some hope! See if you can spot what archetypes the politicians, who are often in the public eye, fall into.

It is beneficial for us to attempt to classify politicians as this will show that they have been rumbled and that in doing so we become wise to the devious ways that they operate. Hopefully this will flush out the bad ones and they will be voted out at the next election. If there is one ambition of this chapter it is to facilitate the triumph of good over bad when it comes to those we elect to serve us in government.

One way how we could empirically establish allocation to a category is in examination of how politicians present themselves in interview, in how they avoid, how they obfuscate and how they say something that anyone with any reasonable wit can plainly see is a lie. You will also note that the most slippery of politicians will deny that they said something; *"oh it was meant in a different context"* or they simply will not answer even the most closed of questions with a simple 'yes' or 'no'. You may have no idea whatsoever of what they have just 'clearly' said but neither does the person sitting next to you, neither do I and neither do any of us. If you observe the body language of the interviewer; the irritation, frustration and annoyance of not getting anything like a direct or honest answer is very obvious indeed.

The Competent Political Philanthropist (The Wise – Specialist Subject: Truth)

Life teaches that the corrupt, incompetent and lazy are often not very nice people, and don't be fooled by the ones that smile, they are also adept at putting the blame onto others and whatever they do they mess up in the end although unfortunately are not found out until it's too late. However, competence and philanthropy do not by any rule mutually co-exist as in some cases philanthropy can be a characteristic of the deluded politician, using your hard earned money and often wastefully so i.e. philanthropy in not promoting what is good but promoting what is stupid.

As I have said this chapter's aim is to lift our politics from the sewer through us gaining insight into what is really going on with our political system and through an enlightened and astute electorate forcing the hand of the ruling class to do what is right. This being said we do have a modest though significant percentage of politicians who are excellent people, an example to us all, they do have the sense to know what is right and what is wrong, they are discerning, clever and highly competent and they do work hard for us and if you ask me I could name some of them. They are our example they are what we should look to for whom we should elect again and again but if you are one of those politicians who are the deluded idiots, the nasty lying bastard or unemployable then don't delude yourself into thinking that I'm talking about you here - I'm not so don't try to fool yourself like you try to fool us.

The Conceited Deluded Incompetent (The Fool – Specialist Subject: Stupidity)

Some people have no idea what they are on about; someone once said to me that 'A' level maths is easy, I asked him what grade did he achieve, he replied 'E'! I somehow doubt that he ever became a professor though strange things happen in this world, and some professors do seem to be quite thick, I wouldn't trust their 'data' or their judgment even in their own speciality, but it isn't beyond possibility that he had entered politics. Here I am not alluding to his competence in maths, I couldn't care about it, but I am alluding to his capacity to judge and from then decide what is to be done for the best. I wouldn't trust his judgment would you.

There is a saying that 'empty vessels makes the most sound'; perhaps this is very apt here where absolute power in the hands of an equally absolute non-entity with distinct deficiency in reasoning skills, an oversized (XXL) fast moving mouth, very small ears and perhaps even a 'semi or supressed hysterical' bad temper. Whatever you do don't ever give them a gun.

These politicians have a malignant and crippling incapacity to discern, they live in a world of fairies, they love using words such as 'progressive', 'proud' and 'celebrate' for ideas or situations that are not at all as they describe. They use words to fool us into perceiving something bad as good. 'Progressive' is the euphemistic annunciation of 'piffle', i.e. to defy logic even to invert logic, what is right must be wrong and what is wrong must be right. 'Progressive' might mean for example that we shut all prisons such that criminals are not punished and so never learn of the errors of their ways, although there will always be some academic out there who will propose this as the only workable and humane solution, it might also mean that those who have no desire to ever work deserve a life experience equal to those who do have the desire to work or do work or it might mean that the rich should always be vilified and the poor always perceived as good, that anyone and everyone who says that they are in need must be so, of course they are all telling the truth, aren't they.

They will be 'proud' and will 'celebrate' things that to most of us we would find to be quite offensive or worrying. Deluded politicians tend to be the pseudo-academics who have some grandiose and childish belief of feeling superior above all others since all others fail to grasp the value of their 'progressive' politics and are therefore to be regarded as ignorant. They tend to not be very bright whilst thinking that they are the very brightest – indeed the only thing that is impressive about them is their cringing and breath-taking stupidity.

They probably don't know anything about anything and will often lack a useful skill, are essentially unemployable outside (and, oh dear, also inside) of politics and often have never worked in the real world that could have given them some insight into the plight of their people and the workings of a modern economy. They will excuse their incompetence by not explaining their own errors but by referring to what someone else in the opposing party had done wrong. They can be so corrupt that they are even dishonest to themselves and even when faced with irrefutable facts they are not going to listen. They will not change their view because they are always right and to challenge them is an affront to their intelligence an intelligence that they are bereft of. They will also have a very select clientele, doing not what is best for the greater good, for everyone, but just for those loyal groups from whom they can procure votes at the price of misappropriation of tax revenue and therefore the toil of others.

If we were to imagine that anticipation and ability to adapt denotes intelligence then our political incompetents fail miserably; how often do we find ourselves in difficult national and international situations, I should rather ask how often don't we. Faced with difficulties they have no idea what to do despite having masses of often highly capable advisors around them whom they will often choose to ignore. They can talk a lot about it all although we seldom see much action. In the world of business they most probably wouldn't survive.

The Conceited Career Politician (The Opportunist – Specialist Subject: Greed)

Ever wondered why politicians are so defensive. Just watch what happens when a politician is cornered by an adept political interviewer. Just watch them squirm and wriggle with horror like a maggot on a fishing line, they don't like being caught out, those awkward questions they can't or don't want to answer. For the rest of us in our careers, if we didn't know the answers or refused to give a straight answer we would probably get the sack or we would say to ourselves clearly this is not for me and we would seek alternative employment.

But for a career politician it will just not do to give up a much better than average income for a lower than average performance, or capability. It is this that is the nub of it all, they often have no work experience outside of the government bubble, can you call the government bubble work experience I hear you ask, they may have all gone to the same schools, same universities and have pretty much studied within the very narrowest bands of subjects. Many are bereft of any real hard nose capability.

Surely you would think that to govern an entire nation, an 'astronomical' responsibility, requires those with education, skill, experience and most of all rigour, competence and honesty. Would we not expect that our government representatives should possess skills that are in some way congruent with that of its nation's citizen's skills and thereby are equipped to do what is best for what the nation's citizens do and therefore what the nation's interests are? In the UK we have world class science and engineering and we have a world class manufacturing base but what representation is there of these professions in our parliament.

We strangely seem to be over represented in biblical proportions by people who have limited cognizance of what we do and what we need as a country. It is as if, and analogous to a neurological homunculus, that our government capabilities are inconsistent to the proportions of what our national utility demands. Surely this lack of quantitative representation is in itself anti-democratic as well as lacking any sense. Some career politicians may cite their business experience credentials as making them suitable for government and indeed that may very well be so but some of those are businessmen/women who might aggressively run businesses for entirely their own interests to the exclusion of their employees and so might just do the same within government i.e. run it for themselves, and their kind, not for the electorate.

Career politicians I perhaps loath the most as they will do anything to stay in power. If necessary they will squeeze their head between the buttocks of their superiors to engage in the toadying sport of arse kissing but then stab their superiors in the back at the opportune moment to gain even more power, but what they won't do is upset the status quo at the wrong moment, that would be like stepping out of line, like being a maverick, they won't rock the boat.

Rule no.1 is to keep their job, after all what would they do what could they do in the real world. Most of them can't really do anything useful and they know it. However in order to keep things going as they are, and for their own interests, then they must acquiesce, they must fit exactly with the political zeitgeist of the establishment or they are toast, they must follow rules, rules that have never been written but are nevertheless understood in how to maintain power over the people not for the people as democracy might otherwise suggest.

The problem is that to keep in favour with the establishment they have to be adept at telling lies but the problem is that in telling lies you must have an excellent memory and you have to be able to seamlessly stitch some logic into a false argument using what is often very twisted logic. At the hands of the expert interviewer, they are not good enough at this trade, time and again they are caught out and under insurmountable scrutiny you see the ever so friendly cuddly politician start to look like a cornered animal or a spoilt child, it will get tetchy, petulant, indignant; anger and panic will ensue, lies will begat more lies.

The Conceited Psychopath (The Devil – Specialist Subject: Power and Its Abuse)

Have you ever been perplexed by what politicians sometimes do, that they do something so reckless that it is totally against any sense of sanity and that can only bring harm to their and our nation. Have we ever contemplated the unimaginable, some might say fanciful, idea that this may be deliberate that the act is a deliberate act of destruction. This all sounds rather far-fetched the stuff of conspiracy theory but what if this is exactly what is happening.

As we shall discuss later some can have such visceral hatred of life, often covertly behind a 'benevolent countenance', in that they are motivated for revenge against any target, valid or invalid, but what if that sickness pervades through the mind of a politician, someone who wields power. Then what, perhaps what we may call an enactment of political terrorism within a nation where people's lives are destroyed not from bombs and bullets but from political insanity and stupidity. Do not mistake this, but there are some who seek to destroy from within just as there are those who seek to do so from without and this happens right under our noses, we see it but we don't know its true source of motivation.

You may want to cast your thoughts back to earlier discussion on this subject where we discussed that the desire of the psychopath is to control and to destroy. Why would anyone want to destroy their own nation, a sort of scorched earth policy, well complete destruction would be the ultimate gratification of control, it's the stuff that psychopaths love; chaos also seems to assuage their boredom.

This desire for control and seeking to make other's lives a misery is mutually inclusive i.e. to have one you must also have the other. That may not be immediately apparent but if you imagine that if a psychopath gave you what you wanted i.e. what you might wish to vote for, even if they recognized it was to your benefit and to all of mankind, the problem here is that you have arrested control from them. It cannot be allowed that us, the electorate take control and this is clear with the lack of referendums on offer on major issues or the palpable contempt and even anger if the electorate just happens to vote 'the wrong way'. It is as if they must destroy your life or at least compromise it in some way for them to feel powerful for them to feel good. Such politicians are therefore no less depraved in thinking than that of your common mass murderer. In the psychopathic world the politician has no responsibility to its electorate, it will see the population as dispensable as a means to get what it wants; the population doesn't matter only they matter.

How Do We Define a Democracy – Does it really exist?

A true democracy is a specific form of government that through its representatives is elected to enact the will of its people on the basis that all of its citizens have an equal voice. In order for a democracy to function at the ballot box with any practicality it must do two things above everything else; it must determine and accept, without question, the will of the majority and second it must present unambiguous (simple 'yes' or 'no') options, options that therefore cannot later be challenged through legal nuances, semantics or through the will of any system of government procedure or body. 'Yes' means an unequivocal 'yes' and 'no' means an unequivocal 'no', there is no 'maybe', no middle ground, no room for interpretation. A question is presented and an answer is given; *"will you marry me"* or *"do you want a divorce"*. There is no middle ground.

The will of the people must be respected and not put to question as doing so would be to subvert democracy. A government must therefore enact a decision in accordance with the decision of the electorate, what they like to call a mandate i.e. in what the majority had voted for.

There is no point in asking for an answer and then questioning its validity. Any questioning would be a clear indication that the electorate is not respected, it is seen to have not arrived at the desired answer, it is seen as inept or even worse, disgustingly so, accused, often semi-hysterically, of being uneducated or not cognisant with the facts, noting that the elected representatives of government are no more adept or educated than the people they represent, often they are much less so. The people are asked a simple question, they have gone away and have thought through the arguments, they may even have rejected their normal party allegiance where they see that it had morphed into something not exactly good, weighed up the pros and cons of what is on offer and they have made their decision.

For me I may not always agree with what the electorate votes for but I would vigorously defend the democratic rights of the people, whether or not I agree with the result, for if we ignore the will of the people we really are heading for trouble, there will be a severe backlash, for where democracy ends tyranny begins and this can even lead to civil war.

"Did not permit government, by the consent of the governed, in which the people, through their representatives, were the source of power and authority." – (prosecution) statement from the Nuremburg Trials (1945-1946)

For the record; the term 'populism' means nothing more than 'representing the interests of the ordinary people' i.e. this is what the majority have voted for, it is what we would define as democracy. Where democracy is practiced then the resulting vote is a representation and mandate of what the people want - ergo it is democracy. Now; where the ordinary people happen to not agree with the 'elite', or their acolytes, then they are to be labelled as 'populist' that is now re-invented as some abusive colloquialism that does not suggest democracy but now suggests being a contemptible or repugnant character.

This stance is not just insulting to just those who voted against the elite's wishes but it is also an insult to all of the electorate, in other words whoever you are you must always vote in accordance with our instructions otherwise you will draw our contempt - it is as if the 'elite' defines the threat to democracy as democracy itself. If this is the respect that the elite have towards the electorate why then bother with a vote at all perhaps we should just sit back and let them have their totalitarian state where we all do as we are told. However, we need to beware of this since in politics something that looks innocuous can turn nasty. Contempt today can turn to authoritarian rule tomorrow.

In the UK system, within which I live, we pride ourselves on our democratic prowess, we believe without question that our system is amongst the best in the world, albeit we acknowledge that it does have its faults, and I believe it possibly is amongst the best in the world although in reality we are a world away from what can be described as a democratic utopia, far from it. There is the idea that the system affords equivalent representation in proportion to the population and by members who represent all walks of life, it doesn't, that the policy options on offer reflect what the public require and demand, often referred to with derision as being 'populist', it doesn't do that either, that if elected the mandate (the manifesto) is a legally binding contract, which it isn't and that there is no way through constitutional recourse that an unelected body, i.e. the Supreme Courts, the House of Lords or additionally the European Court of Justice, can quash the intended actions of the elected body i.e. the House of Commons, but it can.

If we quantitatively define a 'democratic utopia' as having a 'democracy quotient' (DQ) of 100% then I would guess that the reality of the DQ for the UK may be as low as 20% or even less since we have so many hurdles to jump over to move from what the electorate wants to what it actually gets. To frustrate the process even further, UK political parties have their special voters, those of whom they have special favour for who must be looked after under some pretext, the reality being that votes are effectively bought. Our so called incorruptible system also works such that the Westminster bubble is accountable to itself and not to the law, an MP or Peer who acts outside of the set rules of parliamentary ethics will be required to explain themselves not to an independent jury but to other parliamentarians.

This is democracy UK style and albeit one of the best in the world it is rather an affront when we accuse foreign governments of corruption of their democratic process. And for those who will jump for joy at my implied advocacy of proportional representation then beware, you may think that you will get what you want but the tectonics of democratic change could shock you. The percentage of support you have is very fragile and under such circumstances it will evaporate to other fringe groups albeit your fantasy view is that you would be preparing for government, in reality you might need to prepare for oblivion.

Duty of the Politician and Government (the social contract)

Put very simply our political system is put there by us for us and none other, hence the primary reason for its existence is to its own people, why else would it be there. To elaborate on this, in its simplest terms, it must ensure that the will of the people, without any hindrance is carried out, it must be accountable to the people, that our borders are protected and adequately defended, that we have self-determination of our laws and that our legal system must be based upon moral authority and not political power, that all citizens are equal, are free and have equal opportunity, that our citizens are protected from crime and, in as much as the economy can provide, will provide health care, education and prudent welfare support and where we deal with problems expediently rather than look the other way.

Furthermore, it must not embark on international misadventures, it must seek the best for the nation but must also behave ethically in all of what it does, it must be a democratic example to all other nations, it must not live beyond its means, it must be prudent with the nation's wealth and it must exercise efficient and independently verified administration. It must be accountable to the people and not the people accountable to it.

However, there is a caveat to this with respect to its democratic obligations in that where a nation is in complete disarray where the rule of law has broken down, where there is chaos then democracy cannot work. Under such conditions governments may have to operate under emergency measures and invoke even as far a martial law to restore order, to some this may be appear as an outrage although it is often of practical necessity.

Awful as it may seem but some nations are in such a mess that democracy could never work and forcing democratic principles too early can lead to a national disaster. There is a warning though for those who have such designs and where you use false excuse to do so and where you stand against the will of the people, you should be mindful that a clock is ticking to your very likely ultimate destruction. If your ambitions are for your own gain then beware as this could bring about your own demise and you may think it won't happen but maybe those at the Nuremburg trials who were later to hang thought that too.

Exactly What Is a Professional Politician?

"People who know little are usually great talkers, while those who know much say little." – Jean-Jacques Rousseau (Philosopher, France 18th century)

I once heard with some amusement a member of the UK parliament with a fly-weight intellect describing themselves as a 'professional politician'. But what is a professional politician? I get it that a doctor or a lawyer may describe themselves as a professional in that they have received very extensive and specific training and that they have a formal qualification but they must also demonstrate an impressive level of competence in their stated field – in other words in their professional situations they must predominantly make the right decisions, even the most competent can at times make mistakes, and that they have the ability to implement their solutions with skill. To engage in a field at a professional level is based upon study that is mandatory for the role it is not based upon time served.

I could learn how to set fractures, I could learn how to remove an appendix and a whole host of other things and I could successfully practice in this capacity for years, however I cannot call myself or delude myself into thinking that I am a doctor because I have not received any formal training in medicine in which I must be well versed in every minute detail of the extensive biological and chemical operation of the human body and so there will be massive gaps in my knowledge. If faced with a fracture or an appendix issue but with a complication then I would not want to be the patient under my care - the patient would most probably die. The problem here is that not only do we not know all that we need to know we also don't know what we don't know.

So what of the professional politician is there any formal study are there any exams, do they present to us a consistent approach to the same problem to arrive at the same logical and effective conclusion, can they exhibit competence as a practitioner of politics. The answer to this is no. Basically, the analogy here is that politicians are not in the true sense professionals, albeit that some, and I say some, can bring substantial skills to the process of running a country. It is a sad fact though that as in every walk of life that those who are promoted in politics are not always the most skilled but just happen, willingly or unwillingly, to share the same views as their leader, views that they must adhere to, come what may, for their political survival, and through obedience they can manipulate their way to the very top.

If it were that we could outline a prospectus in the 'profession of politics' for most then what might the course structure be, we might accurately predict it to be as follows: semesters 1 to 6 - fiddling expenses and not getting caught, kissing babies, how to smile and look normal, well almost, insincerity and manipulation, the deceptive properties of graphs and photographs, bullshit, how to make the honest look like liars, advanced bullshit, the political value of fear, the political value of national guilt, how to talk the nation down the toilet, how to destroy an economy, how to ignore the bank balance or lack of, maths without maths, how to twist logic, evasion and obfuscation in interviews, idiotic ideology, idiotic ideology with mass murder, how to maintain the establishment at any cost, the anathema of real democracy, techniques in disloyalty, the disadvantages of conscience, morality and truth, redaction and misrepresentation of critical data, political jargon, available punitive techniques to use against a non-compliant electorate, 'us and them' and the irrelevance of the electorate, amusement in the demise of others, the advantages of sewing discord amongst the electorate, pathological self-belief, narcissism and glory, how to be smug without shame, how to f*** everything up and still feel no shame, blame avoidance, the politicians oath to the club, how to steal the cream out of milk bottles.

Pretty much all of us out there must be able to perform our jobs well, if we don't well there goes our livelihood, we must therefore have competence in what we do – we are trained and experienced to that level of competence. In the political world you can do anything but being remiss of any relevant competence. This I find frightening and the results as we see are as you can only expect. Put someone inexperienced or worse an idiot or worse than that an idiot who is corrupt in charge of a large government department; the treasury, the home office, the foreign office, business, education, health etc. and what result would you expect. Perhaps it is time that we changed the system where a politician cannot be elevated to office through political ambition or promise but through being time served i.e. they must have successfully worked for some considerable time in the real world totally away from politics and in careers that are relevant to the activities that government departments must undertake. If we need professional results we need professional people to manage the country those who know exactly what is required to optimise what we have and so to work for us all.

The Thirst for Power and the Establishment

I once started a club in something that would be completely politically innocuous, at least that's what I thought, although life teaches you some odd lessons - everything was just great when the committee was just me, my interest was focussed on the activities of the club and getting the best experience for the members, you could sort of call this a benevolent dictatorship. However, our affiliation to a greater national body meant that I could no longer continue this way, the club, as dictated by national rules, must have a committee. I had already recognized the dynamics of the membership I knew most would not be interested, however a few I could see would be eager to promote themselves for election to office and when it did happen it reminded me of the excitement of a bunch of vultures tearing at a carcass.

What I saw and what I was to see more of, was the thirst for power with all the mad consequences, it became like being in the court of Henry VIII; one false move, one moment off-guard and you would lose your head. As a result of the political infighting I decided to walk away from it all in disgust and not long after the club fell apart. This lesson taught me that there are those who thirst for position who will exert power or play power games in the most bizarre and seemingly innocuous of places and I wouldn't be surprised that even stamp collecting could be tainted with power games, this is the way of the political operators.

Power is a strange thing and I have seen some change mostly for the worse when they have power over others, this can be through promotion at work, in the seemingly irrevocable cementing of a relationship, achieving some qualification, sometimes a uniform can do the same and of course politics. Power can become all too much like some parasitic organism that is all consuming upon the personality thus can be borne the megalomaniac. The experience of untrammelled and ultimate political power can often lead to a messianic self-belief, a God complex, that so disrupts attachment to reality that we enter the world of the pathologically deluded of the mad of the dangerously insane.

When we believe that our wisdom transcends above all others and on every subject, where we meddle, where we are secretive and thus conceal our true intentions and where we are manipulative, then we need to worry – it is perhaps more likely that we are much further from wisdom and much closer to insanity than what we can possibly imagine. If we seek or assume absolute command over others then now is the time not for office but to seek out a good psychiatrist.

So what in the hell is it where certain individuals crave power and must exert power over others. I do believe that a grounded balanced person who is at one with the world and themselves doesn't need to, or desire to, feel power over others although some of our fellow humans are only able to feel good or enhance the way how they feel if they can gain superiority, whatever that is, over others. It is an inadequacy syndrome; given that they are often elevated above those who they fear, they feel inadequate in some way perhaps they are possessed with pathological jealousy so must abuse their position to control or destroy what is in effect superior but not in authority over them. They have superior position although they are by no means superior, they are inferior and they know it. The reality is that in acting with superiority they will never find contentment, they have not dealt with the root issues within themselves i.e. their own inadequacy, they use their position of superiority like some plaster over a wound that won't heal.

A normal person seeks security and good friends but a power seeker lusts for power above all else; they are infatuated with the idea of power like some obsessive craze and anyone who challenges their power who stands up to them they will have a visceral hatred for. Their expectation is submissiveness in others and delivering fear and absolute control.

Ultimate power sits in the hands of a political elite an 'establishment', a self-perpetuating immovable power base, hence it is 'established' and to remain as such it must resist change or where it does change it will do so slowly and with great reluctance. The power in the hands of the electorate, the concept of democracy is no more than an illusion, it never existed, the power in planting an 'X' next to your politician of choice in the ballot box is where your power begins and also where it ends since once elected the manifesto, that is not a contract, is consigned to the waste paper basket and what follows is some form of charade that the manifesto is still being enacted according to its promise.

A charade in politics will also work like this in that; something that they don't want to happen will be engineered such that it can't happen, something that could have succeeded is engineered so that it can only become a failure, something that could have been successfully negotiated is declared as something that can only be capitulated, something that is plausible is engineered, with considerable effort of deception, to look implausible.

Truth is made to look false, votes and voters choices are made to look irrelevant, incompetent or illegitimate. Perhaps politics is less of a subject or activity but more of an illness a disease, just look at those who are intoxicated with it they are less in possession of a healthy mind but more in possession of a sick one. Those who vigorously defend charades must be removed from office, permanently, if they can't do what must be done then we should look to those who can.

An electorate must therefore not precipitate change and if it seeks to do so and then dare to think for itself, but then does not comply with the wishes of the establishment, then it is seen as a threat and is to be reviled. Democracy to the establishment is therefore an anathema. More recent events in the world shows that the passion that the establishment has to an electorate who votes against its wishes is not simply accepted as a democratic nuance but something more, something pathological, in other words you are to be pathologically hated for voting against their wishes.

The establishment is in effect a mutual benefit society that to gain membership you basically have to show total loyalty without any sense of moral rectitude. The establishment serves itself and as a member of it you have to serve the establishment and none other and you cannot in any way challenge it. The established power base must survive even at all cost and if necessary with recourse to conjured up fear. What is really odd is that those who espouse liberal views, ideas of democracy and often those with a career in some state of decay will often stand up for the establishment line and of course are 'doing so in the interests of the people and of democracy' although in truth they only seek their own survival. Their principles, if they ever had any, have been sacrificed to become associate members of the establishment club.

Democracy UK style is that laws passed through our 'democratically' elected parliament must then go before an unelected body of 'talented and honourable members' of the House of Lords, an outdated and yawningly traditional institution of the UK that should have long gone by now although probably will hang on in dishonour for some time. Although an unelected and therefore undemocratic institution it offers a lifeline for MPs who get the boot from their constituency come election-day since MPs who fail to be re-elected can walk through the revolving door and into another very well rewarded role.

Was democracy an idea that was already dead before it was even born?

Chapter 14

WITHOUT TRUTH WE ARE DESTINED TO FAIL

(The 'provocation' of truth, the mind can be easily fooled)

Aluminium foil is a rather uninteresting material to many of us, but to me when I was four years old (being under 30 so not fully developed in the pre-frontal cortex = impaired judgement of risk) I was fascinated with it, metal so thin that you could fold it but then I was inquisitive about its electrical properties so me being me, as I was then, I thought let's find out so I decided to shove a piece of it into the bars of an electric fire but using me as the instrument to measure the voltage. Instantaneously I found myself thrown across the other side of the room with an arm feeling like it had been kicked by a horse, a bad hair day and with smoke pouring out of every orifice. I remember sitting there thinking *"Adrian old son that was a bad idea"* but I had discovered a truth.

"The corruption of the best things gives rise to the worst." – David Hume
(Philosopher, Scotland 18th century)

Us humans do this a lot, we decide on what is true before we investigate through having too much self-belief (naivety) or we often decide what is true not upon what is truth but upon what suits us, to justify what we think, what we do, what we are (amoral motivation). Now that may seem OK since we find our path through life through also making mistakes, it is a necessary process of learning, but what if what we do or think has tragic consequences what then, just think that my foolish experiment with electricity could have meant no fifth birthday for me.

We are all far too casual with the truth and we are all far too obsessed with what we want and what suits us so our truth is not truth but truth that serves ourselves (a form of egoism) and with that danger will come. To avert danger we have to be honest with what is true and what is not. The question is, are we unwilling to see the truth or unable to see the truth or are we willing and able to find and accept the truth even though it is not what we wish to know.

In Defining Truth

Is it that everything that we read everything that we hear is nothing but a fabrication? Whatever to us is visual we believe more than anything else, we have seen it, this perception colours our view of what is written, it is written so therefore it must be true but really is it. Do we ever know what is true and what is not?

"You have lost your reason and taken the wrong path. You have taken lies for truth and hideousness for beauty." – Anton Chekov (Playwright, Russia 19th century)

A friend of mine of many years, a PhD student at Harvard, told me some very unusual facts that; did you know that 18% of stamp collectors are colour blind, that the Hippopotamus (being exclusively vegetarian, of course) is the safest of wild animals and that haemorrhoid cream if applied to the scalp cures 12% of baldness. When I heard this I thought this to be utterly ridiculous so I asked some expert colleagues to verify it all and they all confirmed it to be true. Given the evidence you would be a fool to disagree with this. Amazing what you learn isn't it. Did you know any of that, well neither did I and in fact all what I have just said is utter nonsense. Now your nose may have been twitching with suspicion somewhere in there but did you see how I may have destroyed your doubts, let's just dissect the paragraph to see what's going on in there:

A friend of mine of many years (so must be trustworthy), a PhD student (not an idiot) at Harvard (a highly respected institution), told me some very unusual facts (to shatter your suspicion that something is wrong) that; did you know that 18% (a credible sounding statistic) of stamp collectors are colour blind (doesn't sound too unbelievable so might be true), that the Hippopotamus (being vegetarian) is the safest of wild animals (to grab the bias of those who won't hear a bad word against animals, in reality the Hippopotamus can easily become very aggressive and is extremely dangerous) and that haemorrhoid cream if applied to the scalp cures 12% of baldness (gives hope so I want to believe it, you might not but I certainly would). When I heard this I thought this to be utterly ridiculous (you can trust me as I'm as suspicious as you are and also very open about my suspicions) so I asked some expert colleagues (plenty of valid 2nd opinions) to verify it all and they all confirmed it to be true (any doubts are now shattered). Given the evidence you would be a fool to disagree with this (a common ploy to get you to agree since you wouldn't want to be thought of as a fool). Amazing what you learn isn't it (now you've been hooked into this scam).

If I really wanted to impress the 'truth' I could have thrown in some 'cooked up' graphs since a graph gives a scientific edge, and so therefore adds further confirmation to prove a point of view that is in fact a lie. Another dimension in here is that in reading thus far into my book you may have gained some trust in me but do you really know me do you really know anyone, perceived trust is another dimension that the politician will also exploit to tell a lie. The political class is adept at making us believe something what it isn't, they even believe that they have some licence some God given right to tell lies.

Adolf Hitler used a tactic that if you tell a lie enough times and do so with absolute certainty then the public will swallow it without question – 'what I have just heard has been delivered with such certainty surely it must be true mustn't it'. Politicians do this en masse often using some mutually agreed hackneyed slogan designed to coax the public, you hear one use a manipulative expression then they all follow like talking parrots repeating *"who's a pretty boy then"*. Further to this even the most apparently cogent of arguments can equally be a lie. So now let's now look at what 'truth' really is or at least get as close to the truth about truth as we possibly can.

"Realists do not fear the results of their study." – Fyodor Dostoyevsky (Novelist, Russia 19th century)

A word that we would possibly never look up in the dictionary is 'truth' and if we did look it up its description is rather scant in that *'truth is a quality or state of being true, it is the opposite of false'*. I believe that the word 'truth' is the most important word to the human race and it is deserving of greater clarity and comprehension given how often this word is abused and replaced with not what is true but what I want you to believe to be true when I know it to be otherwise or because we are too attached to what we want to believe or have been led to believe.

Mostly we do all know when we are being honest, however we are not well equipped to know when others are not, we might believe the liar and disbelieve the teller of truth, even if we ourselves are honest are we telling the truth are we able to discriminate what is true and what is not given that we have conditioned minds. We know that to utter a truth is to utter something that is unquestionably correct and without any bias (now there's a challenge), that it is pure though may not be what we want to hear, it may be unpalatable, nor may we see it as fair but it is nevertheless true and so we must accept it albeit it is distasteful to our own thinking.

The truth is not at all what we want to believe but what we must believe. Truth is a wonderful thing something great to aspire to seek although, other than the fields of mathematics and logic, where truth is irrefutable, truth is essentially elusive, we just do our best, or some their worst, at telling what we believe to be true.

If we think back to our earlier discussions on metaphysics and epistemology we might conclude that we can never find the truth in almost, although not all of, anything. You could say that anything that has some uncertainty, i.e. if less than 100% true, is not necessarily an intended lie, which would be a good assumption. Given this we might have to propose a more practical definition of truth in that intentionally we seek to tell the truth or to tell a lie or that we unintentionally make a mistake and present something that we thought to be true, or what we thought was not far from the truth, as being true. On this basis we might propose that the 'intended truth' is that which is at least two thirds correct, that which is a 'conscious or intended lie' is less than one third true and that the middle third is a grey area that is both the truth but also a lie one which we could perhaps attribute a scale to. Given intent absolute truth is therefore elusive but an absolute lie is not.

The Card Trick That Anything Equals Anything Else

There is a certain mathematical function called the 'Kronecker delta' (represented by $\delta_{n,m}$) that works as follows: $\delta_{n,m} = 1$ if $n = m$ and $\delta_{n,m} = 0$ if 'n' $\neq$ (does not equal) 'm' for all values of 'n' and 'm', hence we could say that for all value of 'n' and 'm' whether they are equal or not then $n\delta_{n,m} = m\delta_{n,m}$. If we then divide both sides of the equation by $\delta_{n,m}$ then it follows that $n = m$ for all values of 'n' and 'm'.

Hence any number can equal any other number and so anything is equally valid and so truth (or falsehood) could arguable be equally proven as being equally valid. However, there is a massive flaw in this argument in that when $n \neq m$ then in effect you are dividing both sides of the equation by $\delta_{n,m}$ when it equals zero and dividing by zero is a fundamental no-no in mathematics, dividing by zero yields infinity, and so it is recognised as a corruption a falsification.

We could take this argument further, away from numbers and into logic, we could define a new term the 'Kronecker 'logos'' (logos = the logic that supports an argument). Here we could prove a conjecture that 'any point of view is equally as valid as any other'. But we now know the mathematical trick so since two different arguments can never be equal so then it must follow that at best only one argument can be true and the other one false or at worst they are both untrue.

Hence two things that are not equal cannot therefore be equally valid. The only way how two things can be equally valid is if they are identical, other than that equal validity would not be based on truth but on assumption of truth or perhaps a best guess and no more.

Cultural Relativism - The Confusing Post-Modernist Perspective on Truth - i.e. Catastrophic Stupidity

Some years ago I visited one of the great citadels of, certainly expensive and hypocritically 'capitalist', contemporary art, I didn't know anything about it so thought I was in need of some education, two hours and about eighteen double shot hyper caffeinated espresso's later, to keep me awake, my bladder was holding back Niagara falls, I needed the loo. When I entered the 'Gents' (toilet) to relieve the miseries of my urethral sphincter I did so as now an enlightened man; now deprived of artistic ignorance I could see the world in a different way, no longer was this a temple to the lavatory, in my mind I had entered another gallery in this esteemed institution.

No longer would I perceive the men sitting upon those thrones as having a crap, to me they were squeezing out works of art that would not look out of place in the other galleries that I had just visited. I could see that far from the human race being bereft of cultivation that in fact we were all fledgling artists, and we just didn't know this fact, we didn't know that this act of personal expression was art. Of all talents contemporary art is certainly the most inclusive of all.

It was a contention of Carl Jung that when we accept that which is false or that which is inadequate in truth then the result can only be neurosis (depression, anxiety, obsession or hysteria), hence when accepting that which is subjective or even a plain lie as being the truth then the result to us is catastrophic. To maintain good mental health and prospects of such we must be prepared to identify with honesty that which is false and then dismiss it for what it is.

Card 12 of the Tarot's major arcana is called 'the hanging man', fortunate for him he is not hanging from his neck but from an ankle and such lack of intuitive representation of the hidden meaning of the Tarot makes it all the more fascinating. So what does this card mean? The illustration on the face of card 12 points to the experience of life as being opposite (hence upside down) to that of reality, that our conditioning is what is between us and that which is truth and therefore to find the truth we must escape the shackles of what our life has conditioned us to think and be prepared to face ridicule and the wrath of those who prefer to not listen to what is reality.

The hanging man is a representation of those who are willing to look at life from a different perspective (hence his orientation) to that which is naturally within, to be committed to finding the truth and who have the courage to acknowledge what truth is whatever that may be. When this card is presented in its 'ill-dignified' form (upside down) then wisdom is replaced with foolishness, a life of meaning is replaced with suffering. Beware of the reversed meaning of the hanging man.

Have you ever read anything and thought to yourself that this doesn't make any sense. It could be that what you are reading is in esoteric language, ambiguous, or that the subject matter is just not so easy to understand and therefore requires further study to master it. If it is none of these then what you are reading may probably be a work of fiction i.e. something that cannot be proved external to itself external to what it professes itself to be. Much of what is academic endeavours to establish something for what it is, to understand how it works, how it might think or what it represents; from which we can determine a set of rules to enable us to understand our life, the universe and everything else, a set of rules from which we can live and where we can prosper.

"We are not afraid to follow truth, nor to tolerate any error so long as reason is free to combat it." – Thomas Jefferson (3rd President, USA 18th/19th century)

Now imagine that all what the great minds have established over millennia and what we have established to be clear accepted principles or truths, or as near as we can get to the truth that is, were to be challenged from an abstract philosophical school of thought. Imagine that what we have established is charged with being false on the basis that all what we adhere to is not the truth as we would arrive at through reason and logic but through bias i.e. through interpretation devoid of reason and logic, that there are no truths only interpretations. In other words all interpretations are equally valid despite lacking any credible empirical evidence.

Imagine a world where reason is perceived as a tool of oppression, where language is perceived as a construct not to communicate but to dominate to oppress or to exclude. Now you might be thinking that you need to see the optician but what you have just read was exactly what I had written. Now there are nuances on this as there is in everything but there are also reasonable limits in how we might perceive something. Absolute truth is somewhat elusive but here we take the ideas of metaphysics and epistemology into the abstract, to over define the errors in seeking the truth we have in effect eluded it even more.

"There are two ways to be fooled. One is to believe what isn't true; the other to refuse to believe what is true." – Søren Kierkegaard (Philosopher, Denmark 19th century)

Now there is very good reason to question history or rules that we have past established; what has been written down may have been done so through social or political bias, for instance could we ever say that a political autobiography is a document beyond question of its veracity and that what we had established as rules may very well have been correct then but are no longer so. But what if we were to take this rejection of truth beyond what is reasonable to what is bizarre and off of the map of reason, this being 'post-modernist' philosophy where would this take us. However, philosophy, like any other serious academic subject, should maintain rectitude of analysis and reason if it doesn't then it panders to the totalitarianism idea of 'rationally' replacing the truth with lies.

As in all totalitarian regimes the murder of truth presages the murder of the teller of the truth, out of necessity you have to lie to survive. Anarchistic post-modernism with its fervent dislike of that which is true and thereby accepted rules and so its fixation of 'oppression' by rules is therefore highly influenced by neo-Marxism, a carapace of totalitarian control. I might bash our political system here in my country but at least we have something to cherish enshrined in our culture that we have freedom as long as it does not bring harm or threat of harm to others; we can think what we like, read what we like, vote how we like we have freedom of expression and we have freedom to practice our religion we can even criticize without fear of persecution.

It's very curious that the very thing that post-modernists seem to hate the most, being racism of any form, is the very thing that they advocate, to them not only opinion but also the truth is something delivered from a 'social construct' and where reason is assumed to be for the privileged few but they lay the blame, of everything concerning the corruption of truth, squarely on the 'white-male' albeit that lies are subject to all cultures everywhere.

I'm right there with post-modernists on hating racism but to single out and falsely accuse white-males is nothing other than racism and sexism in itself and this is a disgrace. I could rattle off a long list of those of all races; achievers, great thinkers, great scientists and inventors, and those who laid down their lives in the interests of our hard won freedoms (including freedom for the advocates of post-modernism) who have made all of our lives so much better such that we are unhindered in having an opinion and many of these 'terrible' people were white-males. The white-male is the bad guy the one to be detested, outcast, ridiculed (often courtesy of TV adverts, odd marketing indeed).

To the post-modernist facts are to be obscured they are to be deliberately prevented from being known. The truth is to be replaced with nonsense or that which is fashionable as what a 'modern educated person' would think. Ergo the white-male must be uneducated in their view. If you seek the truth, if you do not ignore what is unpalatable, then you must be uneducated or so goes the theory.

If you might want to imagine the most dangerous scenario that the world could face you might think of nuclear war, total global economic collapse or pandemic penicillin resistant communicable diseases but you would be wrong. Faced with any of these catastrophes us humans would work out what we must do, we may have acted too late but at least we would have a chance to deal with the situation and perhaps pull society back together but to do so we would have to face the truth not some extreme philosophical version of it. Society would be rebuilt by those who follow rules that work – engineers, doctors, lawyers, teachers, builders etc.

A person in the post Armageddon job queue who cites their skill set as post-modernist philosophy would be laughed at – in effect they would be offering a 'skill' that is meaningless and that adds nothing to society in any way. Post-modernist intellectual stupidity at its very worst brings the world to a very dangerous and crazy place. Not facing the truth or redefining it so far removed from reality causes us to do some very stupid things and this alone could very easily bring us to catastrophe.

What we know of the truth is that what makes us wiser, and so by definition what we know or shall we say believe of distorted-truth, must make us dumber. In essence we pile in superficial academic effort into something that is in detriment to our intellectual ability – the more we learn the less we know. In its benign form, adhering to what is distorted-truth we are either looking for some pseudo-intellectual superiority in the sense that you just don't get it do you because 'you are not that bright whereas I'm ever so clever' or is it a retreat from reality that 'I cannot face up to what is true, to me it is unpalatable so therefore I shall redefine it as false' this being politicised pathological cowardice; not to fear what something is but to be unwilling to accept what something is because they lack the guts to face up to it, something what you might call 'truthophobia'.

If I had lived in the Soviet Union I might have rightly feared Stalin and use my common sense to not speak out against him, however I would still accept in my soul that he was evil and it would escape my comprehension as why those living in a free society could not even bring themselves to say such.

Oddly enough the post-modernist will not only ignore the truth but they even oppose the truth, even violently so. Rational debate must be shut down not because it is offensive but because they chose it to be so and furthermore they lack a willingness to explore multiple causes for any one observation. If they have sound valid reasoning why not state what this is rather than engage in threats, intimidation, assaults and expletives in order to silence others. If you have a point of view it might be very valid but at least put it across politely since doing so will invigorate good debate and might gain traction from others to what you believe. If you can't be polite then no-one will want to listen to you and being impolite doesn't add any validity to what you believe.

"A lie has many variations the truth none." – African proverb.

The great philosophers were right to question the concept of truth through metaphysical thinking but to postulate that truth is merely a social construct, rather than it is the ideas of truth that are social constructs, such that all socially constructed truths are therefore <u>equally</u> valid is both ridiculous beyond sane thinking and is dangerous. Post-modernism may be no more than an attempt at the stupid trying to look clever and do so without putting in any serious academic effort; it is what <u>they</u> believe to be the truth is what is the truth - they define it they therefore promote themselves to have supremacy, an authority which they detest, over what is to be regarded as the truth.

Read a book on post-modernism and suddenly they can criticise everything but yet are unable to actually do anything useful. It is very easy indeed to criticise what others have done and what I am unable and unwilling to do. If what they want is to look clever then go and study something difficult and useful not something stupid and useless.

Using the melancholic principles of post-modernism, in that all viewpoints are of equal validity, then it is impossible for any post-modernist to disagree with my definition of post-modernism, my definition merely determined from a different and therefore equally valid social construct, in effect my viewpoint, indeed anyone's viewpoint, is no less valid than theirs. Since post-modernism according to its own rules is fluid and can be interpreted from infinitely variant social constructs then the only conclusion to this is that post-modernism invalidates itself, it has like the Kronecker delta trick divided itself by zero it has proved itself to be nonsense.

This truth being established it is interesting to observe that it is the post-modernists themselves that have the most fixed views about what is right and what is wrong, they are the most vociferous about this yet in being so are the most hypocritical of its adherents. If I genuinely believed that all ideas of truth are equally valid as true then I wouldn't be so arrogant about disagreeing with others views that I am compelled with my ideology to accept as being equally valid.

"The roots of education are bitter, but the fruit is sweet." – Aristotle (Philosopher, Greece 4th century BC)

Having said all that the study of post-modernism does have its use in that perhaps what it really sets out to do is to whimsically deride that which is stupidity to explore stupidity and those who might be seduced by it. Is it just a parody of the truth or is its aim to take the piss out of its very self, if this is so then it is a very cleverly constructed piss take, perhaps its architects were thinking exactly that. Having said all of this, why would anyone want to study something of no value educationally or indeed for career advancement, perhaps its application is for comedic purpose and I can see that very easily, but why take it seriously.

What is observable is that some of the human race crave intellectual prowess, the idea that they are somewhat cultivated above the 'proletariat' appeals to them. They might take to some serious study but that requires hard work to achieve this goal but post-modernism is about as limp as education could ever get, read a book, acquire a fancy esoteric vocabulary, ideas that no-one else can understand not because they are difficult but because they defy common sense and you are starting to look like an intellectual. Just reading one book would be enough to bullshit your way through the exam. Perhaps this is the radical, rebellious and unhealthy 'fast food' equivalent of looking clever. Perhaps this is what the attraction is all along.

Since the rest of the human race has an intelligence that transcends that required of post-modernism then perhaps if you are studying this ignominious subject you might just save face by saying that you are actually researching how it needs to be criticised not extolled.

In Conclusion

It is axiomatic to suggest that nothing is perfect and that includes the truth, absolute truth is always out of our reach and absolute knowledge likewise, none of us can know everything but at least we should all strive to learn enough within our limited time and resources to establish at least some idea of what is right and what is wrong. If we set out on the path of logic and reason and avoid the path of stupidity we can at least converge nearer to what is true albeit that we can never reach it. At the end of the day truth wins, it must do, if it doesn't then we are all heading for trouble and we have no idea where that trouble might take us. Perhaps the truth does elude us and perhaps we have to go with what we have got no matter what shade of grey along the scale of truth that it is but at least we should know, for our own interests, just what shade of grey we are looking at.

If it is the fact that we choose the 'truth', 'a' 'truth', purely for self-interest to justify what we do and what we think, even if that may seem innocuous, then we are on the road to ruin and we can only hope that sensible others are there to guide us back onto the right path. 'Truth' that serves the self may indeed be the very thing that destroys the self.

Chapter 15

Don't Allow Yourself to Be Manipulated

(The game of politics & the lust for manipulation)

It's a very odd thing with politics that once signed up and committed to a political cause the individual can at times abandon all sense of what is right and what is wrong, they replace this with what is the party line and what is not. They cannot even bring themselves to dismiss the bad elements of what might otherwise be a good ideology. They have entered a seemingly irrevocable state of mentality of subordinate tribal allegiance where allegiance is to the party and not the truth or the people. The line is to stay fixated upon a position irrespective of the evidence but to then make up some 'logic' that supports that assertion, logic that is that would fail under any degree of reason and scrutiny, but let's stick with it anyway besides the public won't find out will they.

What is it that motivates them away from truth and what is in politics that motivates them to unquestionable loyalty to the party? One thing can surely be said is that with an unwillingness to face the truth and an unwillingness to adapt illustrates an unwillingness to survive, if you can't see the truth and can't adapt then you can't survive, the trouble is they take us down with them.

But one thing is for sure is that to get into the mind of the average politician we do not have to strap them to the psychiatrists couch, apply thumb screws or administer sodium pentothal (truth drug), it is for the fact that they are in the public eye so much that they give us plenty of opportunity to observe them, we can watch them almost all of the time and we can learn their ways we can deduce what are their motivations and peculiarities (especially in the personality department if it even exists). Observation from afar but nevertheless very valid and very accurate observation can be had.

I'm Going to Tell the Truth, the Whole Truth and Nothing but the Truth – What, Do You Take Me for an Idiot!

Political rule number 1 – you can say whatever you like, it doesn't even matter if it's a rank lie, don't even feel guilty about it, the public don't matter anyway but just keep up the pretence that they do. As they say *"bullshit baffles brains"*.

We are all too willing to listen to what is on offer to solve our problems even where with the most modest level of inspection we would find it out to be a lie. If we were told that to put our head in a crocodile's mouth would solve all of our problems we might just give it a go and this is more so if we face the politically manufactured attrition of anxiety and desperation. If you can worry someone you can manipulate them, politicians are well aware of the manipulative value of fear and they use it to full advantage. It is for this reason that politicians don't work with hard facts but work on our empathetic emotions and upon our insecurities.

It is the solemn duty of a politician to inform not to manipulate the electorate. They will assert that this is exactly what they do but this is also nothing more than yet another lie. The politician must sell you an idea that may often be false but that they want you to accept because it is what they want, but to sell a lie they must wrap it in even more lies and so it goes on.

Some of us imagine that truth is whatever serves ourselves to justify whatever we think or whatever we have done, this self-serving of truth in the end is not in our best interests though we may not see this as so. And the hooves of politics often stampede over that which is true, and that which is expressed as true is often so far from the truth that it is much like a joke but without a punchline, should we laugh at such things or should we weep for the consequences of a lie in politics is deadly serious. Telling lies can only lead to error of judgement and then often fatal consequence, this being the natural path of dishonesty.

If a politician is indignant about being accused of being a pathological liar then ask them if everything that the opposition party says is true, since we know that two opposing parties in government rarely seem to agree on anything. Now ask the opposition. There is only one conclusion from this act of iterative 'mutual discrediting' and that is that at least 50% of politicians must therefore be liars. In other words they can testify to their own dishonesty. Based on an approximation that the general public probably only fibs about 5% of the time, or less, then politicians don't seem to score highly on the scale of trust, therefore many of them are beyond our trust.

Now politicians will tell us either what they want us to hear, although what they don't believe themselves or what they want us to think, because they think that they are clever and that we are stupid or for the honest politicians, yes I did say honest, what they actually think irrespective of how unpopular this may make them. So the only thing that you can guarantee without any doubt about many politicians is that they can't be trusted, just ask any journalist. They may even go as far as to impugn the truth spoken by the honest politicians or others in as much that not being 'on message' with the majority of the political class, then you are the one to be accused of lying, not them.

A political party has a central core of its ideology which it will commit to at all cost, it won't even abandon this ideology if it is unequivocally proven to be in error and so the party must flagrantly lie to defend what otherwise would be an indefensible position. Truth, logic and reason must be thrown overboard in defence of what is a defective ideology and in order to secure their political careers when they are up for re-election. What is also amazing is that politicians believe themselves to be experts in everything – ask them a question and we never hear them say *"I don't know"* although to be fair none of us know everything or can have thought of everything, but to them this is irrelevant since they are 'all knowing' and this delusion will lead them to even more lies.

"He who knows all the answers has not been asked all the questions." – Confucius (Philosopher, China circa 500 BC)

They will *"pledge"* and then not carry out, *"did I sign a legal contract"*, they will *"invest"* although are actually throwing your money down the drain, they will be *"prudent"* but are actually undertaking acts of sheer stupidity, they will *"promise to make this nation great"* – oh not that one again. The promise being always more potent than what can be achieved and they know this. Imagine if they told the truth, just imagine if we had a proper appraisal of the state of our nation and what we really have to do to fix it. It would be seen as too unpalatable so let's pay off that debt tomorrow, not today, or better still borrow more and maybe pay it off decades later or let the grandchildren pay or why not rape the pension pot.

For these reasons we are partly responsible for the dishonesty of our politicians – they sometimes just tell us what we want to hear in order to procure our vote. A politician who promises just too much of everything is incompetent in the subject of economics and is most likely to lead their country to ruin and so voting for that promise is voting for ruin.

"A state too expensive in itself or by virtue of its dependencies ultimately falls into decay." – Simon Bolivar (Politician, Venezuela 18th/19th century)

This all sounds great doesn't it and I might have a bash myself: *"Vote for me and I pledge I will eradicate austerity and poverty, we will all retire at 50 on full pensions, the most advanced (and expensive) medical treatments would be available to all, free university education up to the level of PhD, income tax set at 7% and abolishment of VAT, a 30 hour maximum working week, an extra 12 days bank holiday for all"* what some might euphemistically call 'progressive politics'.

Sounds great and I would vote for all of that too but the reality is that it is impossible to deliver and it is highly irresponsible to make such false promises. My pledge is as hollow as what my political ideology is stupid. I am offering a lot more than what we are putting in, i.e. beyond the capacity of what our economy can provide. Basically the more we want the harder we or someone else, for that matter, shall have to work and that's a given fact. Now my scenario is clearly nonsense in the extreme, it flies in the face of logic and reason, although some propose scenarios that are also way beyond what our economy can provide, they offer what cannot be delivered. They may even say that *"the budget has been costed"* – it hasn't.

The fact is that the unreal politics, of what can only ever be a promise and what can never be a reality, is nothing more than a fantasy it is the politics of stupidity offered by the politically mad. You may vote for it with a wild hope but you would come to regret it. Put simply if it sounds too good to be true then it isn't true.

"Though shalt not bear false witness." – The Bible, book of Exodus (Christianity)

Saying all of that, politicians will tell 'porky pies' (London slang for 'lies') to gain our patronage to get us into the ballot box and put a tick against them not the other guy, but worse than this they will tell lies to get us to then do what they want. We have to be mindful of the fact that they also see us not just for our patronage but also as a threat. We are a threat to them and their kind. We are a threat to the establishment and to them having command and dominance over us. We are a threat to their personal ambitions, to their career and their livelihood.

Once voted out the high pay, easy living and the power have all gone. For their own political ambitions they will do anything and to anyone, almost without limits if they could get away with it. They, and their system, must at all costs be maintained intact. You, me and most of the rest of us, are nothing to them. They will despise us as if we are like some naughty child who doesn't do as it is told or that we do not believe what we have been told to believe. We are supposed to accept and on no account to question their lies. They have an ideology, patronage of a particular group of society, and a means to syphon wealth and power.

If they told us what was their real game is we would not only not vote for them we might just do a lot worse with reflection on what is the end for many dictators, so they have to lie to protect the interest of themselves and their acolytes. To do so they must manipulate the truth, they must play with words and I would say that they could not be trusted as far as their mistresses could throw them. If a politician can betray a decent and loyal partner then there is at least some possibility that they could just as easily betray their nation. Not just for politicians but for anyone we all need to ask ourselves that what we hear does it add up does it makes sense and I mean does it really make sense.

"False words are not only evil in themselves, but they infect the soul with evil." –
Socrates (Philosopher, Greece 4th/5th century BC)

Tactics and Theatricals (oh the subtleties of brainwashing)

Many politicians are great actors, they have to be, they will present an image that does not represent what they are but what they want you to believe, better still do it all on a friendly chat show and throw in some acolyte failed comedian (overt politically biased political satire or of ridicule of the electorate doesn't hang very well on a comedian and would instantly disqualify them from being such) who can make the politician appear even more normal, whatever that might be.

We might all get the idea that if they smile like someone who has just stolen your wallet, and they do tend to overdo this in the act, let out the odd giggle and kiss the odd baby or two, you may even get the odd humorous quip thrown in, then surely they must be nice, however all of these are contrived techniques of manipulation by those who are essentially rotten to the core. We might just get to like them, we may get this idea that Mr. or Mrs. Mendacious-Bastard is just like you or me but we would be wrong. Just like Adolf Hitler they will spend countless hours refining their act and what they lack in competence I must at least commend them on their acting skills, I would dearly love to hang a gong, or something lavatorial, around their neck as an award!.

In addition to this they can deploy other techniques of looking 'ever so concerned' or that they will speak with unswerving certainty to the point that we suck it all up. They sound pretty certain so it must be true. They are armed to the teeth with euphemisms that skilfully deployed will con you into thinking something is different than what is the actuality – *"it's right and fair we do this"*, *"we should be proud of what we have done"*, *"we should celebrate this"*. Get yourself a good enough backstreet used car salesman and he can sell a bag of shit for a bar of gold and make the buyer feel that they got a bargain.

Just look for these techniques; the nice guy, the ever so solemn concerned type, those who are dead certain about what they say but here is when your alarms should be going 'ding, ding, ding'. You are being pulled into a trap – the influence of words can indeed be very powerful. To be fair this may all be genuine but there is so much bullshit in there that it is difficult to sift through it to determine what is and what is not truth. Just who can we trust?

What I find is most amusing is the way how they influence using word play, the idea being that you would feel stupid or guilty not to vote the way they want e.g. *"I know the British public are not stupid"* ploy, *"I am voting this way because I love my country and if you love your country so would you vote the same"* ploy, *"the others are liars"* (and of course they are not are they) ploy, *"what we voted for is not what we thought we were voting for"* ploy, *"have you thought of your children/grandchildren"* ploy, *"anyone who votes that way is being selfish, backward looking or uneducated" or "surveys show that the opinion of the British public has changed"* ploy or somewhat out of politics – *"none of my friends can understand why you don't fancy me"* (a rhetorical response to rejection) ploy or *"this is a very sought after and most desirable property"* (the estate agent) ploy.

Just how treacherous can it get? Better than this plant 'sleepers' into the opposing view who miraculously change their mind at the right moment to favour a particular viewpoint that in itself has massive leverage. Miraculously their view doesn't just change a little it changes to the exact opposite position, now I wonder how that happened in a fully cognitive mind I wonder indeed.

What's more is they love it, to them to lie is a game. The ever so respectful countenance belies the disdain that they have for the average person in the street – that's you and me. Just look at when they are interviewed and observe their modus operandi; if they don't like the question that would require them to spit out the truth, then they will answer a different question that was not asked i.e. they go 'off-subject'.

If you can demolish their arguments (1+1 = 3) with irrefutable facts (1+1 = 2), *"how dare you confuse me with the facts"*, they will immediately ignore what has just been proven and revert back to the false argument that they peddle, they will keep banging that same drum or will say *"I have just answered that question"* or *"as I just clearly said"*, they didn't and it wasn't, sorry mate just more of their hackneyed phrases though underneath you will notice their anger, indignant tone and their squirming but the unblinking automaton will just keep to script without giving the game away. They don't even have the decency to look at least a tiny bit guilty when caught. Yuck indeed. I can see the interviewer wanting to bash the living daylights out of them.

What really 'takes the biscuit' (idiom for 'breathtakingly annoying') is to accuse those of telling the truth of lying when they are not and having later been found out of their lies and hyperbole will parry that with *"oh I wasn't being dishonest I was merely stating an opinion"* – so of course that's OK then!

Another neat trick is that a politician will procure more votes by attaching themselves to a cause or distastefully a disaster or the trump card - the badly managed NHS (the UK National Health Service), where they can attack or lay blame upon the opposition – anything to get votes anything and without any moral boundaries. Do this 'tearfully' on a party political broadcast (a cheap trick) and you can win another million votes. Just look for the emotive issues and exploit it, promise everything deliver nothing.

And Here We Have an Expert, An Expert In Airbrushing The Truth! (The High Priest/Priestess)

"The only true wisdom is knowing you know nothing." – Socrates (Philosopher, Greece 4th/5th century BC)

Politicians have a wonderful tool to manipulate us when all else has failed and where the electorate cannot otherwise be manipulated by their 'masters'. They will wheel out the 'impartial' expert from outside of the world of politics but who are nonetheless just as political as any politician. Wielding an 'impartial' expert, often an economist, who must be, by definition, an expert, is the betting equivalent of having a royal flush in a game of poker. If all else fails the 'punters' will swallow this one.

Unwittingly the electorate will be in check-mate and are all ears for the 'irrefutable' advice that they are about to be served and what they are about to digest, they are hooked just like a fish about to be battered and served up for dinner. Better than this talk up the expert as *"someone who the public trusts"*, their words not ours, and more so *"recognized as trusted more than anyone else on the subject"*, but also *"who's views are widely held in the 'experts' intellectual community"* – all lies. Once you hear an expert taking the line of the establishment, even someone who you may admire, you need to treat their 'facts' with some circumspection. Of course none of these, often gasbagging, experts are directly or indirectly in the pay of the establishment or its appendages nor are their livelihoods subject to how and what they pitch of their field of expertise!!

Some may also be intellectually crippled by their own arrogance of assumed intellectual supremacy over others which can often mean intellectual incompetence. Add to this the various 'respected' national and international institutions, with a distinct knack of getting it wrong and if they don't play the same tune then you can always edit out their research.

Me not initially a cynic, of what I am told but where experience has bestowed cynicism upon me I have concluded that when most of what politicians and their experts tell you is nothing to worry about it is actually something serious to worry about and that something serious to worry about is actually nothing to worry about. Given my appraisal of the political class as being mostly anything other than competent I have developed greater trust in what the minority think rather than what is the majority opinion although that isn't necessarily always correct.

If you want wisdom, just note that it is often only in the possession of the few when it comes to the domain of politicians. The nuclear war we were almost destined to have with the Soviet Union never came about, neither did the impending ice age and the irrevocable ozone hole seemed to repair itself, so wasn't so irrevocable after all and I have my doubts on certain other predictions. The EEC (European Economic Community, now the EU) that was sold to us as a free trading arrangement without any political ambition did the exact opposite and its promises of bringing prosperity brought stagnation, unemployment and misery for those on lower pay especially so in its southern nations. In amongst all of this we have seen the banking collapse of 2008 and many nations in near fatal debt.

All of this has happened on the watch of the 'greatest minds' on the planet, minds with highly questionable judgment, attending their lavish conferences and supported by the most powerful computers to be had. Come up with an idea to scare the public or to coerce them to the political will of the establishment and you can write your own cheque and the research cash will flow like a burst water main.

Humans are fallible and some are corrupt and some of these humans become experts. Does an expert never make a mistake does an expert always tell the truth or are some not so different than our politicians, ready willing and able to echo the 'truths' of the political establishment. The truth is that the causes, development and consequences of economics and certain areas of science are not held universally by all economists and scientists; you will find detractors everywhere and with good reason.

An impartial expert must be by definition impartial i.e. experts who are not in position to gain from their views, they are for that fact impartial, they will apply independent scrutiny to an idea and they often will disagree with the status quo but they seek the truth, they do not seek patronage of the establishment and they have nothing financially to gain.

Economics is not a science it is not exacting. If you ask a mechanical engineer to calculate the power that can be extracted from quantitative parameters of a specified flow rate of steam into a turbine at a specified density, dryness fraction, pressure and temperature and with certain exit conditions then he/she will determine a formula to do so and will then calculate the power. Give it to another mechanical engineer and he/she will arrive at the same figure and so would a hundred more. It is because thermodynamics is an exact science, the properties of steam are well documented, the physics is well proven by exhaustive laboratory experimentation and engineers are tested under examination to see that they can determine the right answer for which there is only one [viz. an engineering answer = a function of physical variables only].

In economics this is so different, it would be impossible to say determine what the expected retail sales figures would be at any given time based upon quantitative economic parameters such as inflation, exchange rates, productivity, employment, average salary, debt and interest rates and for that matter economists seem to have great trouble accurately forecasting growth or prospect of recession and furthermore cannot do so consistently and so can't agree with what the result would be amongst themselves.

So why is this – this is because there is a qualitative property in such things as growth and sales, these things depend upon us, how we feel, how we react, something that we cannot easily give a number to. If we feel enthusiastic (a positive emotion) or insecure (a negative emotion) we might equally work harder and growth increases, or maybe not, if we feel good about things we may buy more so sales increases or conversely we might still buy more when we feel bad to make us feel better, although this I don't recommend if we don't have the cash. Clearly economic performance is very complex and mostly we cannot determine with any degree of useful accuracy of what will be the outcome – as we say in engineering 'shit in = shit out', in other words if the formula is wrong or the input data is wrong then the answer has no chance of being right. As can also be seen from the chapter on understanding money that some factors in economics such as GDP are not necessarily as good as have been portrayed in what we present, what we deliberately fail to present and what is really going on.

Now the economic community may have excuse for their failings and have a fall-back position if they get it wrong unlike the poor mechanical engineer who will just face the sack. They can say that their view was an opinion or that there were some unexpected movements in economic factors and of course an 'objective' opinion as an opinion is going to be completely untainted by the political viewpoint of the economist!!! [viz: an economic answer/prediction/narrative $\approx$ a function of (economic variables + conjectured societal behaviours + the political bias of the economist)].

For the scientific community there is no excuse and they need to be extremely circumspect about stating that *"the science is proven"* (this is political language for *'shut up and don't question me'*) this is totally unacceptable especially so when there are detractors who may even be in a minority and if we are treated with such intellectual contempt then we are not exactly going to be 'all ears' to their ideas and concerns.

Unlike politics, science, provable science that is and most of science is provable, is not a consensus, and as Galileo had proven that it doesn't matter what the majority think, even if that majority is overwhelming, that what matters are the facts, the real facts, and the majority are often not in possession of the facts though they may like to think that they are. Often when the science is 'proven' it is anything but since later research reveals issues to be ironed out or that the hitherto theory was incomplete or just doesn't work properly under certain circumstances. Scientists are also not as omniscient as we might imagine, a scientific genius may be totally bereft of understanding what is and what is not good in politics.

Over the years we have learned of such things in science and engineering that we had never known before and that in absence of knowing people have died in aeroplane crashes or on the operating table, we have also seen many major disasters. Our knowledge is incomplete and never will be complete so can we ever say that anything is fully proven when we can't even test it through having control over its variables.

If we were to take the current and main topic of fear then I would fully warm to the idea of global warming (it's since been relabelled as 'climate change' – I guess warming must be no longer appropriate) if the presentation of the results showed scientific rectitude deserving of what they are opining as in; have we established that man-made CO_2 is the primary culprit, what of water vapour, cloud cover, that gives us those mild winter evenings, is it increasing CO_2 causing an increase in temperature or increasing temperature causing an increase in CO_2 consistent with temperature coefficients of CO_2 solubility in sea water where almost all of our CO_2 accumulates, where we see ice cleaving from the Antarctic ice shelf where it may be quite normal to do so at that location at that time of year but always looks good for the cameras, as does the odd raging forest fire, is our monitoring of temperature undertaken correctly and in a consistent way and in consistent locations to determine real change over time, have we determined why CO_2 was substantially higher, but then later declined, in prehistoric non-industrial, and in not so distant, times, why temperatures fell during our fastest period of industrial growth, what went wrong with the meteorological model to suggest that we were heading for an ice age in the 1970s and have we tested any of these theories under laboratory controlled conditions, do we even have any idea as to what is the optimum temperature of our planet.

I have even heard of a fear that malaria will move out of the tropics and into temperate northern Europe but yet not mentioning the existence of malaria in northern Europe in pre-industrial times for how is it that Oliver Cromwell contracted malaria in mid-17th century Ireland. Given all of this, have we also accepted that weather is notoriously difficult to predict despite massive research into this subject.

Why is it that with all of the satellite monitoring of our atmosphere and advanced computer thermal hydraulic modelling that we still can't predict to 100% accuracy what the weather will be tomorrow? Some will be spitting venom to hear my point of view but I am only advocating the same scrutiny that I receive when I as an engineer have designed anything, I have to prove that it works and that it works 100%. I have to prove my designs beyond any doubt and the meteorologists, being respected members of the scientific community, should do the same with their theories. Maybe they have a point, however they are by way of scientific method compelled to present all of the information <u>and</u> the reasons why they disagree with the doubts and so must present evidence on the conflicting facts that have been presented and that do not support their argument.

It is very unscientific indeed to dismiss something with such 'irreproachable' certainty that does not support their argument by using the mantra *"the science is proven"*, to me as a scientific thinking person to do such is woefully inadequate and you could say arrogant. Documentaries show the 'facts' as to what is happening with the mandatory videos to alarm the population but the cursory reason that it is all because of us humans and that we produce the greenhouse gas CO_2 is really not enough to throw into the debate, I like many are frustrated at the lack of detail, we need to know more - we need the whole thing, all of it, explained.

But this all being said we have a massive thirst for energy, something like 20TW (Terra Watts), and from my reckoning, from a very quick calculation, this equates to something like a staggering 3500 tonnes of CO_2 generated every second and further to this we have a very thin atmosphere so there is definitely something to be alarmed about in the way how we are affecting our planet and although CO_2 is not a pollutant, it is the 'oxygen' that plants breath in photosynthesis, it is nevertheless still alarming.

Although all of biological life (animal that is), and there is a lot of it, and volcanic activity, produces substantial CO_2, us humans, <u>at this time</u> would seem to produce a lot more through our demand for energy that underpins our modern lifestyle but the question is how and why does that effect our climate more so than that big yellow thing in the sky and what of the CO_2 we already have in our oceans and that moves in and out of our atmosphere.

So what is the truth what is really going on? And please don't say the *"science is proven"*. Can anyone categorically state just how much (%) of climate change is attributed to humans. Climate change, and I mean severe climate change, is not a modern phenomenon it has existed throughout the entire history of planet earth with or without us humans.

We cannot arrive at the truth if we use the classic political trick of presenting only one half of the argument, one half of the statistics (what's out but not what's in, what's up but not what's down etc.), we always must look at both sides. If it were so that climate change or indeed pollution (that is a known fact) is a real issue, and it <u>may</u> very well be, then this may point to over-population, where the population is becoming unsustainable given the finite resources of our planet (just look at deforestation), yet why are we not hearing political debate to perhaps discourage larger families, perhaps at the end of the day there are just too many of us.

If we are being serious about climate change then we must think about the over-population of our planet but perhaps that is a more contentious assertion of the truth something just too unpalatable to accept. Some may assume that we can sustain an ever increasing population but this is stupidity in the extreme, earth is of finite size and food and energy production are limited by this factor, there is therefore a critical mass of human life, a tipping point, and a time beyond which earth will run up the white flag – we need more plant life and we cannot rely exclusively on renewable energy sources alone, it would be nice to think that we can but we can't and that's that. Even if all of this is true we have to still accept the mortality of human life as there is an inevitability of the demise of us humans, a catastrophe will one day happen that will send our species into extinction, the question here is not if but when.

Either way on this subject I am not so pessimistic about our future but climate change is too enmeshed in politics to be devoid of political interference and political hyperbole the chalice of which is taken up with ease by those who constantly seek a cause and the circling political prostitutes on the lookout for an opportunity, who despite displays of desperate pessimism don't appear to look or sound so desperately depressed but seem to be more desperately far left and more desperately upper middle class (also never worked in a factory or down a mine), an oxymoron if there ever was one. Perhaps what we have here is 'white supremacy' in its quintessential form that shouts loudly about our 'terrible' world and the inequality therein and how their ideology will somehow solve it all but yet are strangely unwilling to relinquish their wealth in the name of their ideological belief.

"To find fault is easy; to do better may be difficult." – Plutarch (Biographer, Greece/Rome 1st century)

Some, often those hypocrites who lecture us on our wayward attitude to our home (planet earth), live in very large fuel guzzling mansions and travel around in private jets, may accuse me of irresponsibility in questioning why the concerns of the detractors have not been addressed but is it not irresponsible to waste such vast sums of tax-payers money and extravagant summits without presenting full evidence to the public other than telling us to 'shut up and listen', if they can't convince us then we should divert our resources towards fighting harder to eradicate poverty, poor education and the continuing misery of communicable disease.

Perhaps these things just lack glamour and so do not elicit the interest of the political community. Perhaps those who endure such hell in life are too far below the interest of those who are in charge. Perhaps the sudden alarm is because climate change is not just coming for us but it's also coming for them. Perhaps also there is no opportunity for money to be made with these issues.

The Ego and Demigods – I am not a politician I am a God

Isn't it a great shame that our politicians are not all competent people and that outside of politics there are some incredibly competent people who could make fantastic politicians but who are just too uninterested or too self-effacing to put themselves forward, but life is tough and to get anywhere takes more than competence it takes a lot of confidence too. But if there is one thing I can't stand, that annoys me more than anything is arrogance and arrogance is something that seems to be prevalent amongst much of our political classes, they have it by the lorry load.

Something I find odd, perhaps it even amuses me, is that they gorge off of their arrogance like they are some kind of low life parasitic organism like a leach with its jaws welded to a cows bottom. The arrogance of the arrogant politician is honed, it is absolute, it is noxious, it is breathtakingly obnoxious and it is indignant. I have met quite a few very arrogant people in my life although I do believe that mostly they would turn on the charm and at least try to look just a little self-effacing when selling themselves or their idea to others. So when our politicians remain unashamedly in arrogance mode when trying to sell themselves or their idea then logic would suggest that they perceive, us, i.e. you and me, as subordinate i.e. we are inferior to them, that they are our masters and that we are in their minds as but nothing more than perhaps 'revolting peasants'.

Their tone of speech alone reveals their rabid arrogance since every word is often delivered like a condescending thrust of a rapier that they articulate with force, no other voice must be heard above theirs and others must be cowered by their forceful display. Stand up to them and you are to be shot down. Surely are they not uncomfortable with themselves at such vulgar display – the hell no, they are beyond reproach, they are beyond the pale, they are not nice people, they are possibly so deluded about themselves that they have crossed the line into madness with an idea of being ever so powerful.

There is also another dimension to this arrogance and I find this most amusing too in that when they are proved to be wrong they just charge on hell-bent with the same line, they sidestep what has just been proved to them, it's as if I'm always right whatever you try to prove – yes they are smug, intoxicated and obsessed with their own vanity and their vanity must not be challenged, just watch when it is and you can see the hate precipitating, a hate that is quite palpable. Now this is what I would classify as pathological, it is disease.

Ordinarily this wouldn't matter too much if you encountered such in the pub discussing the price of coconut macaroons, however here we are talking of a politician who has authority to take major decisions that if wrong will have major consequences upon you, and I, and upon the national interest. They will continue, unstoppable, on a reckless path even though they can see what the outcome will be.

It is impossible for them to lose face to admit that they got it wrong, do any have the moral capacity to admit when they are wrong, mostly not. They will even tell us that the problem is too complex for mere mortals to solve; it is beyond the intelligence of us idiots, who make up the electorate, to work it out. Perhaps this is why, with their 'superior intelligence', that almost everything they touch they f*** up because they are so 'competent and clever'!!!! And if they have intelligence it is most probable that they would use it against us. We might see this with some amusing levity but these same characteristics are shared by equally unamusing individuals such as Hitler and Stalin.

"A fool thinks himself to be wise, but a wise man knows himself to be a fool." –
William Shakespeare (Writer, England 16th century)

To cap them we have the 'grand masters' of the 'self-appointed ever so wise (but aren't)' omniscient smug and arrogant ageing men and women of politics who we should show unswerving deference - their appearance to be so is contrived, *"I am the experienced, great enlightened sage"*, *"you should listen to me"*, they have a predilection to witter on, to babble, they love to hear themselves speak, the reality of course being that they are as 'thick as a plank of wood'. This is especially irritating with a retinue of, usually senior, ex-politicians who were known only to excel in their incompetence/ineffectiveness. What began with arrogance as a fledgling politician has morphed with decades of 'experience' into a belief of being full of turgid self-importance, even God like, indeed God is relegated to that of no greater significance than that of the electorate that they have so much contempt for, I guess they imagine us to be gullible, unthinking dopes, no mind of our own to be fed a diet of nonsense.

As I have almost always found to be true there is an odd and I mean odd exception in that the more arrogant someone is the more they overestimate their abilities just as someone who lacks confidence will underestimate their abilities. They will often sit there nodding in a display of dishonest affirmation and approval, a subliminal manipulation, at what the other idiotic clown is saying in attempt to give credence where of course there isn't any. What we have in this cabal is an arsenal of stupidity a self-congratulatory pact where stupidity begets more stupidity.

Political Extremes – The Mad Going Off-Scale (The Agitator)

Many of us would imagine that political extremes are a thing of the past and thankfully mostly they are but modern thinking believes that there is only one extreme this being the far right, a political position that deserves contempt and disdain. To just recap on our history of mid-20th century politics we can recall 'Hitlerian totalitarian socialism', what we would all agree to be the far right and 'Stalinist totalitarian socialism', what we would all agree to be the far left, the latter of which would seem infinitely more attractive being left wing surely it must be progressive, egalitarian and fair, mustn't it?

So from the historical perspective the difference between the two is; that one promoted persecution of minorities, the concept of racial purity, militarism, conquest, forced labour, mass murder, cohorts of informers, a secret police, political imprisonment, intimidation and the thwarting of free speech whereas the other promoted persecution of minorities, the concept of racial purity, militarism, conquest, forced labour, mass murder, cohorts of informers, a secret police, political imprisonment, intimidation and the thwarting of free speech. As you can see the difference is stark! The harsh reality is that in any political extreme it is a sure certainty that someone or other will be picked on. We shall return to this subject later.

In reality in Nazi Germany as long as you were not deemed, by their warped definition, to be 'racially impure' or had some disability and that you kept reasonably quiet about your opposing political views you were safe. In the Soviet Union no-one was safe, you would be killed to meet a death quota, you were killed for daring to utter the slightest insult of 'Uncle Joe' (a World War 2 epithet for Stalin, although Stalin was to be more menacing than avuncular) to your close relatives, one of whom would likely be an informant, you were even killed for having just enough to eat.

Often buried and forgotten is that millions of innocent citizens of the Soviet Union were murdered under the nightmare of Stalin mostly for no reason other than just existing, nothing more than a name on a list to be selected as if ordering death from a menu and millions more of innocent human beings were murdered on the orders of Hitler. Just imagine that could be you or me.

The fact is is that both of these monsters were indifferent to the suffering of their people and both were certainly insane, however both could present a countenance resembling normality, charm, affability and apparent reason, much like many of our politician's today complete with the obligatory smiles, joviality and kissing of babies which in themselves forged new depths to the appearance of madness. Politics of the extreme left is no less obscene and no less depraved than that of the extreme right. So much for the promised utopia that could, and never would be, realised.

Our Softened Society

For much of the twentieth century life remained difficult, we had experienced two devastatingly expensive world wars, in terms of human and economic cost, we faced, as it turns out much exaggerated, the cold war driven by post World War 2 paranoia, although perhaps not entirely without reason from both sides perspective, the existence of inexorably increasing nuclear weapons and by different political ideologies on collision course, in the mix we also had the odd bunch of crackpot and not so nice dictators, however medicine was advancing and epidemics of the likes of cholera, tuberculosis and diphtheria could finally be thwarted, we were not affluent, many were still poor and mostly we worked long hours in dangerous run down depressing old factories, in mines, on the land or far out to sea trawling for fish.

Those who experienced the twentieth century mostly did so with at least some or if not a lot of hardship although they did see change, things were improving and we were grateful for that improvement. As with all societies that experienced hardship, we would have no option but to look to our own, charity would begin at home and the home nation was all that mattered.

In the very latter part of the 20th century, possibly 1980's onwards although there is debate in there, more and more of us were starting to become affluent, we were taken out of poverty, not poverty as we might define today but what was sheer misery, many of us were taking clean office jobs as manufacturing moved abroad, we were living healthier, longer and we could all afford a decent holiday to some far flung exotic destination.

I remember as a 'baby boomer' of the 1960's a totally different world than that of today; mostly one of grim working conditions, no car, no phone, certainly no internet or even PC's, no central heating which was particularly awful and bad winters, the apotheosis of our home technology was an unreliable very low definition black and white television, food and clothing were somewhat drab and limited in choice, school dinners that a pig wouldn't eat, I never heard of anyone visiting a restaurant and coffee shops were almost non-existent, we had largely poor accommodation often furnished from second-hand shops, holidays would be confined to very basic UK coastal holiday camps, if we were lucky we might get a trip to London once a year, few could access higher education, you never heard of a gap year, a prom night or a wedding costing of the order of a year's income but all that being said I believe that we had a pretty good life as the music was great and so was the comedy and perhaps when living standards are not so great at least with joy and humour you could live well. OK you might have retired earlier then but your health and your life expectancy would have been somewhat diminished.

To the budding sociologists you can perhaps reach a greater insight into that period of history from the films 'The Leather Boys' and 'Up the Junction' what are described as 'kitchin sink drama's' that portray the grim conditions of these times so well.

As the later generations lost contact with the brutal reality of the past, that of grim working conditions, a near subsistence living standard, war and fatal communicable disease we became soft we have also become isolated from any serious threats that has given us a false illusion that there aren't any. This change in our lives has had dramatic effects upon us in how we think in that our perception of suffering has changed we have unconsciously redefined what we would call a calamity.

After a harsh childhood at the end of the 19th century a young man would every day face the distinct possibility of a horrible death or mutilation as a World War 1 soldier, his wife may be at home living in dire poverty nursing a child dying from tuberculosis and struggling to pay the rent on a hovel, by necessity this generation would become inured to a life at the extremes of suffering, they would have to, their measure of suffering would be commensurate with this hellish experience and just a few basic luxuries would give them a lot of pleasure, they would be grateful for very little.

Today most, but not all, of us in the modern world live soft lives, we have not faced suffering anything like that of the past generations, so what we perceive as the extremes of suffering is somewhat a lot less than in the past, indeed what in reality is extreme suffering is off of our radar, our lives are so cosy that we don't even reflect on just how lucky we are, we have come to expect too much and to endure too little. As a result of this our emotional reference frame will be scaled differently to that of the past, with a much narrower emotional exposure our emotional reaction will be amplified and so we have become prone to attacks of distress, hysteria and over reaction often to what previous generations might just shrug off or even laugh at.

The world has changed and so have we, perhaps we as a species are becoming more self-absorbed and self-centred and perhaps we shall see greater mental health problems that are centred upon the self, i.e. those such as histrionic and narcissistic personality disorders.

We have redefined poverty, we expect too much from life, with improved education we have become more hung up about who we are, what are our rights and what we 'deserve', we have become intolerant of our ideas being challenged and perhaps intolerant of wisdom itself, we fail to see the bigger picture we become self-centred. It is a modern affluent lifestyle that improves our lives in many ways but on a personal level the effect is catastrophic as we are now less able to form stable relationships as we are now so demanding in what we want from life and we are less able to survive real calamities, something very minor could mentally tip us over the edge.

I do often wonder if those of us who experience the modern cosy lifestyle could have survived the experience of past generations, although had we had lived then we would have been different than what we are now, so this is something we should reflect upon and perhaps have a sense of gratitude for what we have, and reflection on those who don't might just make us better more tolerant people.

However, another effect of living in an affluent society is that gone would be the ideology of helping ourselves first as we could now have the capacity in terms of wealth to help others, we had discovered altruism like never before. As with all human traits where we have opportunity to change we tend to overdo it. Altruism, if we have the economic muscle to do so, is a commendable virtue, one of our best and it defines us much of what we are, however, as in all human experiments, it can go too far (an altruism binge); just as society over indulges in drugs, drink, spending and sex so it is the same with our charitable intentions.

What is good intention can morph into exercising compassion and hospitality beyond the threshold of stupidity (paralytic benevolence) i.e. beyond our own sustainable economic capacity and to those who sometimes feign need and even to the unworthy, and yes they do exist. We all have our duties to the rest of our species wherever they are but largesse, particularly when we have to borrow more to provide it can just sometimes go too far and in the process we may cripple our own economies and our own future, what we should do is to help others within our means not assume that we have so much to give away when in reality we haven't - what we should be doing is to distribute aid equitably where aid should go to those who's need is genuine but none to those where it is not or is it that our motive is a need to feel that we are 'nice' and so we have to refuse to accept the existence of that which isn't at the cost of being taken for a fool. Along the axis of 'nice', some point will be reached upon which foolishness takes command.

Fact is that often international aid is pilfered to furnish the corrupt with a Mercedes or a fancy villa or systematically used on ridiculous projects but yet our own streets (just look in London or anywhere) you see the tragedy of those with nowhere to go and no one who cares and we see our pensioners who survive on an inadequate pension unbefitting to someone who has contributed so much to this nation, this in itself is an absolute disgrace. To those who think that our priorities should be to others first then you should experience the life of living on the streets or having to get by on nothing more than a state pension for even just a few days and then see what you have learnt.

Personally I would want to put a smile on the faces of those where need is desperate and genuine (e.g. abandoned children and facial reconstructive surgery in the 3rd world) but not to render a smile on the faces of those whose need is fake. The truth is that we deploy our aid with wanton foolishness at the cost of those who are in genuine need, we need to get real, get sensible and avoid ill targeted emotions and get to the real heart of the matter where aid is <u>really</u> needed.

In Closing

In my appraisal of politicians I may seem to have been a little unfair but many of them are deserving of what I have said, they are just as bad as I portray or even worse, some are not so different from that of the Sacculina parasite but a parasite with a smile. Can any of them admit to their incompetence or corruption, and being unfit for office, even a liability, can they do the decent thing, probably not. Do they not realise that we do not want them, probably yes but they really don't care much for that either, there is indeed a huge pull for a very high salary for appalling performance (and appalling dishonesty), indeed where else would they go, what could they even do?

As for us we need to be on guard and to not believe everything that we hear. Deft manipulation can lead us to trust the untrustworthy and disbelieve those who are really telling the truth and if you believe that you have worked out who is who you could still be very wrong. It is amazing that we believe, and allow ourselves to be manipulated by, the very same politicians who we should trust the least who often take but then seek to fool us others to be 'taken in' (cheated).

"One who deceives will always find those who allow themselves to be deceived." – Niccolò Machiavelli (Political Philosopher, Italy 15th/16th century)

However, thankfully we do also have many politicians who are highly competent, ideologically sound, compassionate where it is deserved, but also unafraid to use hard nose logic and who are also beyond corruption. What they do and what they have to do is not always pleasing to all but then again it never can be. If we as individuals live beyond what we as individuals put into a system then that system is unsustainable and this is something that we all have to accept. Maybe if our expectations were in proportion to the effort that we put in and if we were more enlightened to what is good and what is bad politics, and indeed who are and who are not good politicians, then we might just be rewarded with a better political system. It is in our hands to change politics for an optimistic future.

Perhaps what our world needs is an atypically political mostly non-radical/part radical political solution, not one of the left, centre or right but a solution based on common sense, being common sense defined by absolutes not as our traditional political class would like to define, with the additional qualities of imagination, innovation, perspicacity, prudence, real intelligence and honesty – most of which much of our traditional, embedded and intransigent political class fall short of. If we can make our economic engines work well, open up free trade with developing nations, invest in finding ways to combat disease, educate all and rid ourselves of corruption, politically insane ambitions and the desire to conquer others we might just make ourselves a better world.

In the 'kaleidoscope' of political opinion are any of us really qualified to judge what is or what is not rational in everything, yet we think that we are. What chance do any of us have of possessing 'omniscient rationality', can we really see everything as it really is, that we are endowed with a mind so intellectually acute such that we can home into the narrow band and purest form of the rational understanding of any of and of all subjects, can you and I really do this, I doubt that we can. Do we really know everything, how many of us are politically crippled in thinking that we do.

Politics is often portrayed as too complex for us 'simpletons' outside of the political bubble yet those within still don't understand politics any better than us, indeed hamstrung with arrogance, nastiness, vindictiveness, corruption and a tinge of inner hysteria it is highly unlikely that they really understand anything and so never will be able to acknowledge what is the truth and what must be the right course of action. If something is 'too complex for public consumption' then there is an onus on the politician to explain why, it is not good enough to just dismiss the subject, on the basis of its alleged complexity, as a means of avoiding it.

"One ought to look a good deal at oneself before thinking of condemning others." – Jean-Baptiste Poquelin, 'Molière' (Playwright, France 17th century)

It remains and always will that people will have different views and different conclusions in politics but you have a right to have your view and others have a right to have theirs, this is the essence of democracy. We should not have to conform to another's view as is expected, nay demanded, in the totalitarian mind. However, we see more and more rancour and bitterness in that there are those who cannot accept this principle they feel that any disagreement to their view warrants 'justifiable' harm to the opposition, the likes of death threats and even acting that out to its tragic end.

There is no excuse to harm another because they have a different view than yours, if they are not allowed their view then why should you be allowed yours. What may seem stupid and illogical to you may not seem that way to others or even to an absolute sane frame of reference – it might be that it is you that is wrong and even if you are right the other person is still entitled to their views. If you don't subscribe to this then you should experience totalitarianism where you and your view will be equally threatened and destroyed. OK there are politicians whose views disgust me but they have a right to their views and I would defend that right, let the ballot box do its work not violence, this is what we call democracy.

Chapter 16

BE AWARE, BE VERY AWARE, OF POLITICAL EXTREMES

(Be warned of what you may wish for, for storm clouds are gathering)

Some of us are motivated by selflessness, truth and in doing what is right and some are motivated by self-indulgence, agitation and the desire to control. Beware of the latter for they bring chaos and ruin not just to society but also to themselves. What they seek they end up realising the opposite result and will learn to bitterly regret it. Do we look within to be honest about what is our real motivation, are we looking for an equal society or a society where one individual or group seeks continually to agitate and control another.

Exactly why do we demand what we demand, what is our reason. Do we even know anything or enough about what we are demanding to justify those demands or are we making a huge mistake. Maybe others who oppose us do so because they know more about what we preach, and the dangers that lay within, than what we do ourselves.

Politicisation of Equality (self-imposed apartheid taking root)

Common belief is that if you are not a white-male then you belong to a minority albeit that there are more coloured-females on our planet than there are white-males. In reality we are all members of a minority of some form or other, I too am a member of a 'minority' and not one you would immediately think of; I am a bit 'deficient' in stature, I don't see it like this but I raise this merely to illustrate a valid point, yes unbelievable isn't it.

It's not just those of a different colour, race, religion or orientation who are on the receiving end of abuse, you will always find the odious and the pathetic who will target anyone for any reason to amuse their tiny minds - if you have a large bum, thin bum, knobbly knees, blonde hair, no hair, you walk with a limp, blue eyes, brown eyes, of this personality or that personality anything will do none of which is relevant to the value of the person, even if in their eyes you are perceived as perfect then they will look for something and if they can't find it they will invent it.

Perhaps their real motivation is pathological jealousy, something you have that they haven't, so on this basis any insult that they deliver you can take as a compliment as an insult is their manifestation of envy. In the eyes of the abuser you cannot win they will look hard for something to find something to amuse themselves with but it would have been easier if they had looked at themselves first as it is they who are the most deserving of ridicule, a person who seeks to abuse is not exactly normal by any stretch of the imagination, they are essentially experts in infantile stupidity. You would think they would have better things to do with their lives. You would think that they would grow up, but the minority clan of the pathetically inclined immature rarely does.

Now a very good and very wise friend of mine once asked me, without thinking: *"have you always been short"* to which my reply was *"no I used to be taller than this"* and we both had a good laugh, there was no malice such as intended ridicule in his question and my favourable perception of him was unchanged despite what he asked, I'm too grown up (and 'broad shouldered') to take offence where none was ever intended, I even makes jokes about myself this also being a technique of many British comedians.

But if it were that I had set out to make some political point about this and then incessantly played on it, demanding what he should and should not say, based upon some obsessive, 'shit-stirring', 'linguistic deconstruction', then my friend would have rightly thought that I had a psychological complex and upon continuance of my demands he might then have got mightily fed up with me, I would have lost a friend through my stupidity. I would also not be doing myself any favours by being obsessive.

However, I have in the past experienced abusive comments from some who's clear intent was to do harm but failed to do so since where they lacked maturity I didn't but in one instance this twit, who happened to also belong to a minority, was unhealthily obsessed about me and my height so much so that I had to have a quiet word with him in no uncertain terms to shut it. The truth is that albeit that you have nice people irrespective of their colour, race, religion or orientation you also have nasty ones as well; nasty people are well represented in all categories of the human race and in all minorities. But does this suggest that we are all oppressors and that we are all oppressed, no, since such a concept is a fantasy.

People don't pick on others because they are different what they do is solely because they are idiots. Now some scratch around in some pseudo-intellectual attention-seeking identity in that they can't identify with what they are as a person but what they want to raise awareness of, they actively seek victimhood, they want to be the victim and usually a demanding victim at that. What was nothing now has to enter the domain of politics and political agitation.

They and their acolytes, have found another cause, 'the ban the bomb' record has worn itself out so no longer do we see the demonstrations like we once did but without a cause the political agitators must find another attention-seeking platform, they might, the day after my book is published, decide to chain themselves together and shutdown Heathrow (London) airport waving banners emblazoned with 'short lives matter' or conversely even 'tall lives matter'. Yet another hate crime of 'heightophobia' or 'heightism' might suddenly appear, something else that you may then also need to be sensitive about where eventually we all dare not say anything in fear of offending someone, could it transpire that even comedy will also be banned or so confined that its essential comic elements must be censored. If I receive any insult, deserved or not, I can claim that it is because of prejudice against my minority status where the reality is that it may not be.

To the political agitators I don't matter and neither does anyone else; to them we are just an excuse (a sort of highly arrogant contrived semi-hysterical narcissistic paranoia by proxy) for them to draw attention to themselves and in doing so they are not helping anyone, they are doing the exact opposite, besides all lives matter not just mine. In effect the agitators have very questionable motivation; exactly what is it that they seek, for the motivation is not to stand up for anyone, it is to use an issue that really isn't an issue as a political tool a tool to cause agitation.

No society is ever perfect, and speaking of my own country, prejudice is largely, although not entirely, a thing of the past unless you have a hang up about what you are or perceive prejudice where there really isn't any. But what the loonies have done is that they have brought attention to their inventions of exploding definitions of minority where before there were really none or very few.

What I, you and others were not that conscious of, now everyone suddenly becomes conscious of, with the consequence of us all being labelled in accordance with some or other minority classification. No longer can I define myself as me I have to be defined by a minority status one that actually I don't want and the idea to make me 'inclusive' has just separated me from everyone else. Essentially we are bringing attention to something that isn't there and therefore manufacturing that attention.

There are those who once they have fought for and gained equality that that is still not enough, they don't just want to be equal they want to be more than equal, they demand prominence and demand special attention, hence they seek to control. The issue that has been quite rightly transcended must now become a political issue. Where we draw anything on political lines not on imperatives of equality in say for example colour, race, religion, orientation or anything then we are not uniting society we are dividing it and if we push too far for special treatment, for positive discrimination or other special demands and that may even negatively discriminate against others then what was acceptance by the majority can turn to the exact opposite.

If we continue to provoke others, and with gleeful self-satisfaction in doing so, then what was sympathy in others can turn to annoyance and then to hate and we may have lit a very dangerous fuse. If we manufacture our own hurt or offence at the slightest thing then the issue is not with others it is within ourselves. Just because someone does not bend to our demands does not in any way suggest that they hate us, they may even be trying to help, but we should ask ourselves do they treat us as an equal or don't they, demanding anything beyond being treated as an equal is too much to ask and is in truth an intent to seek control over others a control that we have no right to ask of and would be unwise to do so.

"Abuse if you slight it, will gradually die away; but if you show yourself irritated, you will be thought to have deserved it." – Publius Cornelius Tacitus, 'Tacitus' (Historian, Rome 1st/2nd century)

The Communist Spectrum

Extreme (or radical) left wing socialism is constituted within the core principles of Communism/Marxism/Maoism/Neo-Marxism each of which are not much more than variations on the same theme; some may have varying degrees of aspiration of world domination, covert political infiltration or even insurrection and some may have concepts of oppression, class structure and globalization from that which is real to that which is sheer fantasy. What may be dressed as socialism may be far left socialism and so is therefore communism.

A notable and topical angle on a left wing variant is that neo-Marxism with its depressingly obsessive paranoid pseudo-idea that if you are not an oppressor then you must be oppressed despite the fact that the so called 'oppressed', particularly so in modern societies, are accepted as equal, have equal opportunity and have freedom of speech, but to the neo-Marxist anarchist this is never enough. Life can be a bastard but this is not always anything to do with oppression.

What is often amazing is that neo-Marxists are usually not oppressed in the globalized sense of poverty and hardship, they may even be just immature, privileged and/or bad-mannered, and so would not curry favor with the 'great guru' himself, but who seek to vociferously demand too much and thereby in effect reversing roles from 'oppressed' to oppressor. The one who seeks dominance, who demands more than just being equal are redefining themselves as a new elite and so it is they who now become the oppressor.

Those who choose not to work and who are supported by the state, or through family wealth, or that are lucky enough to get to university are hardly oppressed and in the world of communism might get shot for having membership in either of these two categories.

The Economic Utopia of Extreme Left Wing Socialism

An exclusively, though extreme, capitalist society operates on the basis of free, not centrally controlled, market economics, where prices are unregulated and unlimited profit is permissible, where workers can be exploited for the benefit of the wealthy (bourgeoisie) and where the state provides nothing for its people (the working classes i.e. the proletariat) who are taxed principally to support a feckless and indolent ruling class and its military adventures. This economic position was particularly so during the $18^{th}/19^{th}$ century as a result of the industrial revolution and its concomitants of concentrations of large scale production and rapid growth whereby workers, in usually urban areas, were ripe for exploitation.

In theory communism was a solution to urbanised industrial scale exploitation. The manifest injustices of the capitalist system became even more manifest at this time from which the ideas of pre-Marxist socialism were spawned. The hitherto system was grossly unfair where you could be worked to death and receive very little in return, so things had to change and to be fair communism offered a theoretically viable (?) political alternative appropriate to that time, it had good though naïve intent, but what of now.

The economics of communism is quite the opposite to that of capitalism in that all individual ownership of property and the means to produce wealth is considered as theft and so the state, the common collective of the people, must then own everything (a sort of 100% tax) and collectively run everything (albeit impractical to do so), this not only applies to all factories, farms, machines and tools but also to your home, although consumer goods like your radio, refrigerator or the shirt on your back you would be allowed to own. All production and distribution would be state owned and state managed and so everyone would be employed by the state and furthermore on a basis that your value to the state was not measured by what you did or on what you had produced but on how many hours you had worked.

The centralised state would control everything including the pricing of all goods and all services and would collect, like some gigantic accounts department, all revenue for subsequent 'equitable' redistribution of all wealth and all food, the tenet being *"from each according to their ability, to each according to their needs"* although Lenin was later to revise this to *"to each according to their labour"*. Such an administrative machine would require a gargantuan but inevitably impossible to manage and inefficient system of governance.

Oddly enough we humans seem to believe that if one political system doesn't work then the only thing that will work must therefore be the exact opposite, a middle path just doesn't come to mind, and this is no different with the 'panacea' of socialism. We also all yearn for ideas, often what are impossible ideas that are offered to solve our problems even if we suspect it to be a lie, temptation to find that dream is just too much to resist. We are also inclined to compare what we have with what is a utopia, one that will always be out of our reach, instead we should be making comparisons with the miserable conditions that our ancestors had to endure and observe our experienced general improvements in living standards, we have somehow forgotten just how lucky we are today despite the stupidity and mendacity of much of our political class.

Pure 100% capitalism doesn't work but what of socialism, it promises utopia, often with five year plans, change and revolutions, so does it have a chance. However, there are two very immediate and very obvious major problems with socialism. First is the fact that large government administration systems are inefficient, even at the very best of times, they lack ability of response demanded of a crisis and even then the wrong decisions are often made – in a fully centrally planned system this can only be a lot worse. Secondly, there is the catastrophic issue of incentive, or should I say lack of. If it is so that you can never own anything and that whatever effort you put in will not gain you any more, then there seems little sense in working hard or working to any decent standards of quality.

As a result of all of this is that distribution is so inefficient that goods, services and most importantly food fail to be delivered and the lack of any incentive kills any chance of a viable productive economy and so commerce will not take off thus resulting in poverty and a lack of vital goods or services being available for distribution all of which leads to shortages, corruption and poor quality. This collapse into poverty, often accompanied with the deaths of millions, is a repeating fact of communism, a fact ideologists seem to want to ignore. I keep burning my hand every time I put it in the fire so I'll just have another go and see what happens!

It is very telling that the socialist and ex-socialist nations of China, Vietnam, Laos, Russia, and the eastern European and Asiatic ex-soviet satellite states, with the obvious notable exceptions, have abandoned much of their socialist economics and have embraced what is essentially a mixed economy one that doesn't totally abandon one (capitalism) for the other (socialism) but selects what is the best from both and combines this into something that works for all. Surprisingly, is that that great major practitioner of socialism Lenin also toyed with this idea of enmeshing some capitalist ideas, granted on too small a scale for its efficacy but nevertheless capitalist, so perhaps within that ideological mind of his was some pragmatism after all; Lenin was therefore acknowledging that utopian socialism was somewhat less than utopian and so in pure socialist terms he was something of a revisionist.

Surprisingly then is that perhaps the best of both worlds is to take ideas from both ends of the political spectrum from both right wing concepts of capitalism and left wing concepts of socialism, not for one to have totalitarian grip on a nation but to reach a middle path one of consensus i.e. one that does not silence the detractors who may actually have a point and so should be listened too rather than arrested or shot.

History, a subject many of us neglect and could do with reading a lot more of, has moved on and so has the plight of the ordinary person, OK the gap between rich and poor is obscene and has grown but poverty, and I mean real poverty not what some might describe as poverty but isn't, is on the decline and so the root politics, not its application, of the hard left, that absolutely made some sense 80+ years ago, has had its day.

Also our definition and therefore application of 'capitalism' has changed; what although may not be socialist countries, now have softer but fairer and prudent forms of socialism enmeshed in their governments systems, what they have is a welfare state (a concept that pre-dated communism and Marx) that is as good as can be afforded, and in some cases better than can be sustainably afforded, but afforded so because of the wealth production of mass business enterprise (a capitalist idea) they also have adopted increasingly fairer employment laws, where the worker is less likely to be exploited or unfairly treated.

Perhaps all that remains of the hard left are the 'intellectual sentimental fantasists' who in reality wish to satisfy their hunger for power by using a false premise of being the champions of the working classes, now often morphed into highly skilled middle classes, who they would claim continue to be dreadfully ill-treated, a problem that they claim that can only be solved by hard left solutions that in theory may had worked in the distant past, but in practice never did and would do the exact opposite of what is promised if applied now. The abandonment or severe watering down of hard left economics by former or even extant communist states is self-evident of this failure.

Granted that communist systems provide free healthcare and a welfare state of sorts but in a broken or combustible economy these things can only be of poor quality and trying to maintain any sense of high quality here is economically unsustainable. Communist regimes will often pride themselves on having armies of doctors but at the dearth of sophisticated drugs, high tech scanners and medical instrumentation and this together with a poor diet compromises life quality and life expectancy. However, communism does provide work for all but work that is poorly paid or often not paid, is tedious and often where all are expected to undertake manual work; can you imagine humanities graduates being forcibly enlisted, often at gun point, into working down coal mines or in factories - so much for the utopia.

The idea of equal wealth for all doesn't work, it destroys incentive ('profit' is not an evil word when it's fair) and so destroys the ability to manufacture wealth and without wealth there can only be poverty. The simplest way out of poverty is through acquiring useful education and through, though economically productive, hard work that is undertaken in a mixed economy.

However, what is amazing is the significant number of economists who advocate such extreme left wing economic ideas, ideas that have been proven, with such great human suffering, not to work. This in itself is evidence enough that economics has a very tenuous connection with science and thereby is clearly subject to personal political bias. Of course, despite the misery caused there are always those, the insanely self-deluded, who believe that the ideology can be different under their guidance, really!!! I suppose we could gamble the lives and livelihoods of millions of people on that premise but given the data I would rather not take that gamble indeed it would be foolish to do so.

OK So Extreme Socialism is A Rank Economic Disaster but At Least It Is a Political Utopia, Right?

We are mostly all on the same page when it comes to Nazism as something that is to be reviled but the word 'Nazi' seems now to be taken all too casually, it is often used as a stock political insult or accusation and in doing so we have watered down its actual meaning. If I want to make something look bad I can do so by attaching it to something that it really isn't. Having concerns of such things as economics and crime that to the far left are perceived as right thinking then you are to be labelled as a Nazi, not that you are, but its intent is to deceive and to manipulate perception. We need to be cautious of the misuse of a word that associates with terror and disgusting thinking. If those right of the far left who have perceivable moderate right wing views are branded 'Nazi' then what do we call the real Nazi's who believe in self-superiority of race who seek to murder those who do not conform to its 'racial type or norms' as self-defined.

To really exemplify what Nazism is about then my recommendation would be a visit to the Holocaust section of the Imperial War Museum in London where it is also interesting to gauge the reaction of everyone, including my own; all seem to be stunned into silence as a result of shock and disgust. It is here or a visit to the concentration camps in Eastern Europe where you will find the truth and if you can't do either of these then I would recommend the book 'Auschwitz' by Laurence Rees. We are all very aware of the extreme far right but what of the far left surely they must be very different being the polar opposite. That would seem a logical deduction and must make sense, surely.

The extreme right does exist as does the extreme left but in the hands of either anything that does not conform exactly to the same thinking is deliberately perceived as the extreme opposite; a left of centre thinking person perceived by the extreme left as extreme right and a right of centre thinking person perceived by the extreme right as extreme left.

Many of us would perceive the politics of the extreme left is one that is anti-racist and therefore tolerant of minorities, is anti-capitalist, egalitarian where wealth and opportunity is equally distributed amongst all and that provides a generous welfare state - it is an economic and political utopia. All sounds rather wonderful right? No wrong, very wrong. We have already discussed economics but now let's turn our attention to politics.

Under the utopian dream of particularly 1930's to 1950's Soviet communism, racial minorities that lived under the boot of the Soviet Union were robbed, raped, beaten, murdered – starved, tortured, frozen and shot in their millions. Minority ethnic groups, Kalmyks and Crimean Tartars were uprooted and deported to the other end of the empire to inhospitable places like Siberia, they were sent there to die indeed 50% did. A similar fate was to be metered out upon many of the inhabitants of the Baltics and Poland. The 1956 Hungarian uprising was put down with the deaths of tens of thousands – oppose the system, demonstrate or even utter the wrong words and you would be destroyed. The 'wealthier' (!) 'peasants' the Kulaks who didn't starve were enemies of the state just because they happened to have enough to eat, if you looked like someone who might live then you were to be murdered.

Large numbers of army officers were also to be 'rubbed out' because of obsessive suspicion and paranoia that they might try to overthrow the 'utopian and benevolent' regime. Millions would die in the Ukraine because of famine as a result of economic mismanagement and the Cossack culture was effectively wiped out. Millions of Russians were also to be murdered based on death quotas or simply because they had a different political view which incidentally was constantly changing at the whim of the masters. Religion could not be tolerated since there could be no God, no higher authority, than the first secretary (the boss) a quietly spoken, affable but menacing psychopath who was often four parts pissed i.e. comrade Iosif Vissarionovich Dzhugashvili who would later to become Joseph Stalin and who surprisingly, despite his credentials of ethnic hatred, was himself of an ethnic minority, he wasn't Russian he was Georgian just as Hitler wasn't German but Austrian.

The Soviet Union, as it was then, could be credited, in my view, in contributing the most towards the destruction of Nazism given that on D-day the western front compromised of 30 German divisions whereas the eastern front comprised of 150 and given the terrible suffering endured by its citizens throughout World War 2 (the great patriotic war), but this achievement was in spite of Stalin not because of him.

During the soviet era the media; the newspapers, such as Pravda (ПРАВДА)(meaning 'truth') and Izvestia (ИЗВЕСТИЯ)(meaning 'to inform' and so suggesting telling of the truth) etc. would have had no option at that time but to be 'strong-armed' under duress and no doubt life preserving compliance into feeding the population with reality checks as dictated by the soviet central committee, all media then, as in everything, would be under total state control – every institution, activity and individual would have the option to conform or to be destroyed.

The presentation of the Soviet Union as being some peaceful utopia was a lie since it is axiomatic that extremes of <u>any</u> political flavour and for that matter <u>any</u> religion too always precipitates violence, often euphemistically renamed 'struggle' or 'social revolution', and always leads to failure. If, you are seeking clarity on the true nature and horror of soviet style totalitarianism then you should read Aleksandr Solzhenitsyn's 'The Gulag Archipelago'.

Still at least the Soviet Union under Stalin was egalitarian and progressive, well not exactly, as they were the most elitist of any political system given that to get to the top you would have to be very well connected within the party and tellingly it is seldom for communist states to place women into positions of political significance. What is also most interesting is that often the advocates of socialism are not shy about seeking extreme wealth for themselves after which their ideas of shared wealth seems to elude them; they find ample argument to share out your wealth but not their own.

If you were at the top you also received privileges on par with that of the wealthy in capitalist economies, privileges that were unavailable to the proletariat, the proletariat were after all not individuals, thinking of oneself as an individual after all is a crime, but were units, instruments of labour, nothing more than cogs in the socialist machine to serve the central committee, the state must always come first the individual is nothing. Incredible as it sounds Hitler's opinion of Stalin was that he was mentally ill!!! It is also very telling that Stalin's successor, Nikita Khrushchev, was highly critical of Stalin's leadership and legacy, the Soviet Union was now on a path to enlightenment, the system was beginning to be questioned from within, especially so by virtue of its last leader the great luminary Mikhail Gorbachev, and in 1991 it finally collapsed and moved onto a better future.

But this is of course socialism soviet style, but surely other interpretations of Marx would be good wouldn't they. Communist countries seem to have a fetish for steel (even Stalin's name meant 'man of steel'); steel is one of the communist fanatical yardsticks for success and in the China of Mao Tse-tung the obsession with steel went off scale, farmers would be forced into manufacturing steel, unusable steel at that, whilst millions would consequently starve to death in addition to all the other millions who were to die.

A perhaps lesser well know country for its communist past, Cambodia, was to be run under a regime the Khmer Rouge of Pol Pot, a particularly nasty man who turned his entire country into a cemetery, even children were not spared from his brutality and if you were an academic or even a classical dancer you were destined for the mortuary slab. If you do not believe me then I suggest that you read the book 'When Broken Glass Floats' by Chanrithy Him then you might get some idea of what extreme left wing socialism can do. Nasty as Hitler was the death toll of extreme right wing totalitarianism was in the millions but the death toll of extreme left wing totalitarianism was in the tens of millions, this is not to say one is preferable to the other, no, they are both equally morally repugnant.

Marx and his philosophy advocated the overthrow of alternative systems to communism by means of violence if necessary, with of course the terror and the mass murder that goes with it, but the violence was mostly directed towards those who communism was supposed to help the most but in reality never could and perhaps never intended to. Perhaps, as in all extreme political ideologies, the real attraction for the politically ambitious was not ideological dominance but dominance through ideology or even dominance irrespective of the cost or consequences, in socialism egalitarianism may be the sales pitch but destructive power in the hands of a few is the real goal.

If we add it all up it would seem that other than guaranteed poverty the only thing that this ideology excels at is oppression this being the very thing that it claims to put a stop to.

Totalitarian states are very easy to spot; there are uniforms everywhere, curiously that can often raise a sense of self-confidence in the individual at the cost of being an individual, and with uniforms everywhere you will also see enforced conscription, excessive military spending, with a fetish for great military parades, overbearing national buildings, that are often adorned with political motifs and vain iconography, and oversized and endless statues built in homage to the great leaders; all of which is a need to impress and to remind the population of what they would face if they were to dissent, a one party a force much greater than them and a one party state by definition cannot tolerate dissent, and this is all to the inevitable detriment of its citizens. The inevitability of poor economic performance under communism coupled with military ambitions leaves very little for the welfare of the people the promised utopia is therefore nothing more than a sick joke overseen by the mentally depraved.

Most of us acknowledge that there are faults with our current political systems, there always will be, but extreme versions of socialism and for that matter anything extreme is not the answer. What may seem appealing in theory history teaches us that it is anything but. Perhaps what we have now is not as broke as some would like us to believe but nevertheless it could do with some modifications and that would certainly get my vote.

Totalitarian politics (hard right, hard left or hard who knows what) is a strange thing it suffers from scope creep. In its early stages it works upon a movement of dissatisfied individuals (some of whom live in a world of naïve intellectual fantasy), who may or may not have any real reason to be so, it manipulates them. It falls foul of the current system which it seeks to overthrow but the current system lacks the moral courage to face it down – the likes of Lenin and Hitler would use democratic freedom for their own ends and once they have arrived at that end they would then destroy democratic freedom. As the monster grows it will purge its elements of reason to seek purity in its madness, there is no room for the impure ideologist here. It will look for the means to gain power usually through wild undeliverable false promises of utopia or by vilifying that which opposes them.

Once power is achieved then the horror begins. What you thought you were supporting becomes something else it emerges to reveal its true identity its true aims. Now we are at the stage, the point of no return, where no-one dare stand up to them since the answer to dissent is prison, torture, murder and it might be you, even if you are a disciple, who is next to be arrested in the middle of the night, handcuffed, to be beaten, to face a show trial and imprisonment – three months, no ten years. You think it can't happen, surely intelligent humans wouldn't would they, think again.

Perhaps latching onto extreme ideologies, from cursory study or susceptibility to peer pressure, is a phase of adolescent rebellion (if that is you can afford to do so) many of whom who will move onto adulthood but some who will remain in perpetual adolescence, rebellion that will morph into a lifelong grudge with unbearable desire to 'teach' the rest of us a lesson, a lesson that we certainly don't need nor do we want. That which challenges everything, even challenges that which is OK, might satisfy the political hunger of those who were not listened to as frustrated but over-confident fledgling adults keen to make their mark on this world rather than keen to look for the truth. The world may seem broken and in many ways it is but a vase that is broken into a hundred pieces can then still be broken into a thousand more.

Change does not always mean change for the better it often means change for the worse. The world cannot be fixed by those who have read a couple of books, who are bereft of real privation or who have never known a hard working life, who are smug and all-knowing and who protest by means of economic disruption and criminal damage (there are other ways to be heard), all that must be repaired by those who do actually contribute to society, the quiet but competent majority of us humans. Actions speak louder than words and we can judge more from what actions that others perform than from the utterances of their motivations or to what they pretend to be their motivations - speech can often be drenched in lies and pretence actions are not.

But what is the attraction in extreme ideologies – could it be that in a world full of uncertainty, where some dare not face that uncertainty, that we look to those who offer us certainty who offer us everything and who are adept at convincing and seducing the vulnerable mind that will accept anything even the extreme on the basis of a promise on the basis of an idea – are we really that naïve to believe this.

Strong Sense of Identity the Cause of Political Fracturing (politically engineered disharmony)

How do you identify yourself and if you do how strongly are you attached to that identity? Depending upon our national politics, cultural heritage and level of freedom we can identify ourselves as either a citizen of a nation, a member of a group or as an individual or a combination of all three. For example British citizens would appear to have a weakening national identity but increasing individual or group identity. Identity is a continuum, if it is strong somewhere then it will be weak somewhere else.

A nation, where individuals identify strongly with the nation state, will often have national superiority that it may feel is constantly under threat and may be less tolerant of alternative identities or that alternative identities are just less apparent; the national interest comes first and so may have inclination to ideas of foreign conquest and thereby war or oppression of often minorities or even majorities within. In such systems the individual identity is unimportant and may even be a crime. Whereas a nation where its individuals are inclined to identify themselves as themselves first with no allegiance to the nation, the national identity is therefore weak and so the interests of all others is less important than the focus upon the self;

the individual may become prone to greater suffering or may become selfish, arrogant and perhaps inclined to commit crime, essentially a 'me first' culture.

In such a system the nation is weak and is ripe for foreign hostility, abuse and/or internal chaos since a nation to function needs at least a decent level of national identity i.e. a responsibility to the collective interest not just to ourselves.

But what of a strong group identity, traditionally drawn along political and religious lines, and what has often resulted in civil wars, but now incorporating such new identity dimensions as age, presumed education status and gender, that on occasion or often is no longer based upon a desire for equality, which would be the right thing to aspire to, but upon mischievous political pretexts. The question that we all mull over is what might be the consequences, as yet we can only guess as we lack any experience of how these new strong identities enmeshed with ambitions for political supremacy can take us, where will it all end I wonder.

Essentially where more and more dimensions of identity, that are very strong, precipitates a belief of superiority and self-excusing, often of what are disgraceful actions, we may see greater and greater politicisation and thereby division. It is not the identity that is worrying but it is the introduction of toxic political elements into that identity that is worrying.

Strong identities make a big thing about demand either from nation, individual or group. Not only is there demand but strong identity requires uniformity, all have not only to yield to the demands but must also join the collective thinking, everyone must be like them. Furthermore, even the idea of individual freedom can demand an ideology devoid of responsibility to others or to the nation. Freedom to exercise group identity often thwarts the same freedom for everyone else. Group identity with aggressive and/or persistent political posturing, beyond any utility for equality, reprehensibly demands what we all must think and even not think; this is the path to destruction of the individual it is the precursor to totalitarian ideology to terrorise those who happen not to think according to that which is enforced. If you are no longer in possession of the right to free thought then this is imprisonment of the mind, of the self, it is the murder of the freedom of the individual; your freedom of thought being on the line can very easily morph into your life being on the line – hyperbole, no history.

A group that engages politically, whatever its aim is a political force it is a political group, its real aim may not be what it pretends, who knows where it may go and what it may become. Political groups emerge because their different views are allowed, accepted and even nurtured by the mainstream, and often the mainstream will rightly defend their right of opinion, no matter its potential to offend (within reason), but this courtesy is rarely extended equally so to all, to those who may have an opposing view, and this in itself is unfair and unwise.

Often those who oppose the madness are the ones to be condemned to be vilified. Stand against the madness and surely you must be standing in the path of progress!!! We must never forget that both of those political monsters Herr Hitler and Comrade Lenin were very leniently treated even succoured by the state when espousing highly irrational views and not enough others were prepared to stand against them until it was too late, too many just accepted what they were told to do what they were told to think – result the death of millions. What starts as a group identity can end in totalitarian hell.

Our silence in the face of gestating totalitarianism (right or left) is what brings tragedy and it is not only our right to speak out and to speak up but it is also our duty. It is with consternation that we imagine that few stand-up to what develops when it is developing, gathering momentum, waiting to pounce and reveal its true identity its true nature, rather than act when it is too mature in its realised ambitions beyond the point where it is cannot be stopped or that cannot be stopped with other than blood or massive economic cost and reconstruction.

Perhaps for us all to stay equal and stay safe then what we need is national, group and individual identities that are neither strong nor weak but somewhere in the middle we have to find a balance to coexist and to survive.

And Back To Post-Modernism - *("I want power, give me my f***ing power")*

I am not comfortable with and I do have serious issues with the way how western civilisation operates, and our world can indeed be very annoying, but I am smart enough to recognise and to be adult in my consideration of tried, tested and failed alternatives and to come to the conclusion that for all of its faults that what we have in the west isn't anywhere near as bad as some may pretend, if it was then why do so many from outside risk all to get in.

But what alternatives do we have; we could of course look to the ideas dreamt up by the gasbagging, judgemental, bile-filled, resentful, miserable, skill lacking, disruptive radical fantasists, often spoilt and some perhaps mentally unstable, who themselves often have never experienced anywhere near a working class existence who, hard-left socialist, Marxist or post-modernist/neo-Marxist, often come from or are succoured from privilege or who exist in institution or rank of privilege and so are isolated from an experience of a hard world and hard labour. In the communist perspective do I see any Stakhanovites (a manual worker: factory, mining, agriculture etc. with exceptional performance) amongst them; well not exactly.

What if we throw away the garbage ideology, the attention seeking, 'anti-everything movement' (of arrogant but breathtakingly naive sheep), one that demands to be heard yet does not listen or even think, that must always have everything that it wants, that will condemn; those who generate wealth, who have worked hard, common sense, logic, reason, economic prudence, the rules, any rules and those who make the rules, those who act with caution, industry, science, pre post-modern art, anyone who challenges their ideas, even those who choose to eat meat; the same who obsess that all systems exist to oppress and who would rejoice at the collapse of western civilisation and in transporting all white-males into incarceration.

For an ideology that seeks to overthrow oppression they seem to do a lot of oppressing themselves. 'You must conform to what I want, get it'. Peculiarly what they seek is really what they condemn. What is it that is going on here, if all else if you believe that logic and reason are not designed to find the truth but to control to oppress then you have defined yourself as unfit to think. You may imagine how can anyone think like this, indeed how can anyone think like this.

Ideology is not a childish game within which we can feel power or intellectual superiority, it is a game of life and death often death, the death of millions. Let's not forget those who died and let's not allow radical ideology to do again what it always does.

The Bastions of Totalitarianism

We might imagine that the extreme far left and the extreme far right are the only political constructs that we need to worry about, that totalitarianism can only exist in these forms. The root signature of totalitarianism is subservience to the state, one that dictates, although in the wider context is subservience to any entity (a person or a collective that is also dictatorial).

Democracy on the other hand is about choice and freedom to choose and with that must be obligation of those in power to deliver exactly that choice, not to question it, not in any way to adulterate what has been asked for, to just do what has been asked and none other. However, what is very apparent is that democracies rarely seem to adhere to this definition of democracy since the politician is very well aware that you can achieve the same result, of getting what they want, but by using softer methods; the tools of deceit and manipulation are just as effective as the threat of the gun or the gulag. But I have just uttered a stupidity; no they are not the same they are in fact a lot more effective because with manipulation you may falsely believe that it was your choice and in this sense perhaps what is dressed as democracy is in reality totalitarianism.

You may imagine that this method is the new tactic of what we understand to be extremes but it is the practice of all flavours of politics; even what may appear to be soft and fluffy now operates along the same lines, it will also demand and dictate, just watch its aggression build when it doesn't get what it wants.

Concluding on Politics

The results and obsession in politics certainly gives us all anxiety and a lot of depression but we can't allow this, and I suspect that those within are not exactly happy either. Perhaps we spend too much time listening to the manipulators, perhaps we should listen less and just use our brain and to be more enlightened and free in how we vote. We can't avoid politics but we certainly can avoid it invading our everyday lives. Choose well and let others who are paid to do so do the worrying and do the right thing, if they don't we just need to get rid of them. Our absorption should be about us and ours not focussed incessantly on politics.

Chapter 17

TEARING UP THE DISGUSTING ROOTS
OF CONFLICT

(The anatomy of human conflict)

This chapter is dedicated to those who have fought and fallen throughout our 100,000+ years of human existence and to those who continue to protect us to this day in thwarting evil and to those who have been forced under threat of death to fight on the side of evil. We live as we do because we have those who stand on that line to protect us, between us and evil they stand so we must never forget what they do and what they have done.

Someone kills or inflicts suffering on someone you love and who is innocent of any bad deed, how does this make you feel? Yet this is exactly what you are doing to others if it is you that is the aggressor. Ask yourself and be serious in how you answer; is that in any sense right is it in any sense moral. If it is that you are confused by the meaning of the word 'innocent' then ask yourself *"did that person intentionally (and not by accident) and by way of their own hand target to kill or inflict suffering on me and mine, who are likewise innocent by this same definition, or had they instructed others to undertake such action"*.

If you are still confused then you need to take a long hard look at yourself and how you think, perhaps others are operating upon your susceptibility to manipulation or perhaps you need help. To kill an innocent person, to destroy what God has created is a very bad and stupid thing to do, it is a mistake for which you will no doubt pay.

"I revile and lament at the evil that takes place in your societies, the world is full of hate and destructive forces but there is extraordinary kindness amongst many of you and this I cherish and I am moved by this kindness." – 'Theoleptic spirituality'.

Be kind to yourself by being kind to others but where there is evil it must be stopped.

If you can find the energy to agitate and to provoke then you have the energy to help others, to work and to construct a better world not just for others but also for yourself. Ask yourself; what is the real root of your reason to seek conflict, do you really even know, search deep within yourself for the truth, what really is your motivation then question that motivation - is it dissatisfaction in your life, a need to feel power or importance, to seek attention, to vent anger, misdirected revenge or just ideology that brings you to kill, none of which is valid reason nor is it a moral one. You may be pissed off with life but this is no way reason enough to destroy an innocent life nor for you to arrogantly decide the innocent as being guilty.

A life is brought into this world it develops, it bonds with others, it gains education, cultivation, honour, refinement, gentleness, it undertakes good practices, it toils to provide for itself and for others, it faces suffering through its life experience, it endures and overcomes – all the things that the seeker of conflict is not. And then the conflict seeker destroys this life without a thought or without questioning of what they are doing. What sort of creature are they to do such things.

There are two types of people in this world – those who are civilised who act on the basis of truth and those who are uncivilised who act on the basis of want. To the latter such minds there is no wrong and no right, what there is, is what 'I' want and what 'I' don't want. It is all about them and what they want and everyone else must obey. They live in a world littered with a vocabulary dominated by 'me' and 'I' and where they cannot face any self-admission of dishonesty since honesty would get in the way of their irrational demands. This is where conflict exists in its gestation stage, from then on it moves on through various stages until we arrive at war.

Indeed the theoretical boundary state of those who are totally saturated in themselves and who are completely devoid of any morality or conscience is a capacity to do very bad things without limits. Saying this can any of these individuals stop and say to themselves *"I think that there must be something wrong with me to do what I do – why is it that I seek to agitate why do I seek to inflict misery and death upon others what is my motivation, why is it that I refuse to entertain the idea of reason"* or is it that they have made their minds up and don't want to be confused with the facts. If anyone believes that they are 100% correct in their viewpoint such that they feel justified in killing another without examining the truth then they are wrong and perhaps they should look at themselves first.

"There are three gates to this self-destructive hell: lust, anger and greed. Renounce these three." – The Bhagavad Gita (Hinduism)

Depressing as it is if we don't address this topic then maybe we will all have to live with it and within it since the only way how we can ever improve the future of our species in respect of conflict is to all have an understanding of its pathological roots and gain an appreciation of just how disgusting and futile the business of conflict is, maybe only then can we see an end to all of this stupidity.

Warning - Before Reading This Chapter

What is major conflict and why it comes about must be discussed from what it is, not from some different more palatable perspective i.e. what it is not. For the reader to see just how futile war is cannot be achieved by sanitising what it is, so some of what is to follow may be disturbing for some. Within there are very graphic descriptions deliberately so to evoke disgust though some may find quite upsetting. The political backdrop is also not so cheerful either and may evoke a fear for the future the same fear faced throughout our history by so many. If you happen to be in low mood or have sensitivities then I suggest that you skip this chapter, however if you can do so then read this at a later date when you feel ready to do so.

The 'Psycho-Philosophy' of the Origins of Conflict (the joyless who seek to inflict misery)

Some just love conflict it is what they live for, without it they would be nothing but with it they are without a soul. Conflict is often therefore a substitution for something that is missing in the life of the aggressor. To them, taking an innocent life is meaningless and sometimes they find disgusting amusement in this but some of us are made of clay and some are made of shit. The question is do they wish to stay in the cesspit of nihilism of worthless existence or climb to greater things to become a better person with new horizons for their future and ours. It is true that we can hate life through experiencing grief or just having too much to deal with but hatred through being selfish of an 'I want' mentality is what brings about conflict.

How many times have you switched on the news and hear that a high school student has shot up his classmates that someone has been blown up by a car bomb, that a mad dictator has brutally murdered someone just because they think differently to them – too many times. Is this an accurate or an inadequate indicator of how our society can be measured, how we could be defined as human beings and to where do such actions take us?

"From the deepest of desires often comes the deadliest hate." – Socrates
(Philosopher, Greece 4th/5th century BC)

Imagine that your life feels like hell it has fallen into the gutter, what may ensue is anger and then rage that is drenched in resentment and in some they cannot contain these emotions and they cannot see another way. For some their life may not be all that bad but still they obsess on something to the point that they see life as a life that doesn't amount to anything. Perhaps those who cannot see the real alternatives do so because they have a view that there are only two opinions in this world – their opinion and the wrong opinion and with this mindset that is closed to reason they then set a course for their own inevitable destruction. This you may believe can only happen to some in society, someone else but not me, but do we know ourselves what is deep within us, have we ever been pushed to the extremes of unbearable questioning of our own existence and at what point would we crack at what point could we do dreadful things to others who we rightly or wrongly believe or declare to be our enemies.

Of all hate there is none more dangerous than that of an embittered, paranoid, seething hatred of life itself, and perhaps therefore its concomitant hatred of the self, by virtue of possessing a pathological and unreachable, even obscene, expectation or demand that ends in failure, persistent disappointment and hopelessness, it is here that mankind can be driven to the greatest of depravities (acts that are certainly evil but the intent is rooted in the consequential self). As in anything, too high an expectation can result in crushing disappointment where our hopes for our own future come crashing down with an almighty bang.

When obscene hopes are thwarted, lame excuse, a fantasy, must be found to justify 'punishment' of the innocent by those who would be humiliated by the real truth behind their motivation of which they are very well aware. If only they were big enough to face and admit this truth is there any chance of preventing the suffering that they inflict and thereby also avoid condemning themselves for destroying that which God has created. Remember as we said earlier in this book that 'wicked people are not happy'. Adoption of such pretext and fantasies by all would unleash the destruction of the entire human race.

As for the rest of us who do not advocate such madness it may be so that we are equally dissatisfied with our lot but we are also decent enough not to expect too much either, we are too morally strong to be dishonest about our motivations, we are too civilized to go out and kill those who don't deserve such and despite our bitter view of the world we can still see that there is good to be found. How is it that I (the author) can connect with these inner feelings, it is because I have had such familiarity as do very many of us, the sense of bitter hatred of life is not shared by a select few, its transients are prevalent in many and also in those who are on the receiving end of its ensuing violence.

Those who are killed are in many cases no less disappointed with life than those who do the killing. This overwhelming sense of feeling a hatred of life can take us (some) to murder and destruction, to build walls around ourselves, to isolate ourselves or we can use the experience to learn and to enlighten ourselves to look beyond and to work towards a better happier ending.

On the assumption that those who are evil can find, granted warped, reasoning to justify their actions for example Hitler's hatred of the Jewish community then what would he have done if he were to find out that he was Jewish, what then. Whatever we preach or believe we must always consider its 'commutative' property i.e. what if the roles were reversed, what if those who are were to now decide on killing those who are not. What if your family were to be destroyed just as you have destroyed the family of another? Is that justifiable, the rule here being 'don't do to others what you don't want done to yourself'. The 'success' of Hitler, and his henchmen, only got them as far as the cyanide pill or the hangman, I wonder if they ever regretted what they did. However, it would be a natural progression to extend this commutative principle in that; if you believe that it is acceptable to kill anyone who happens to disagree with you, you therefore accept that it is OK for them to kill you if you happen to disagree with them – thus all principles must be equally applicable in all situations.

On reflection if you kill because the other person didn't see your point of view then you must have failed to prove your point either because you failed to articulate your argument or that you are just plain wrong, it is not always the case that the other person disagrees with you because it is they who are wrong.

My Personal Introduction and Fascination with War

Of all subjects I have probably read more on the subject of war than any other, it must be something like a couple of hundred books. Not only that but my dear dad, who has since departed this world, was deprived of six years of his life courtesy of a man with a bad temper and a funny moustache, so my father was clearly well versed in this subject. I learnt a lot from my father on war and perhaps asked him too many questions about it although he never seemed to mind he probably thought 'here we go again'.

War has a strange fascination with children; typically boys that is, possibly because the male of the species is too naturally inclined to aggression, destruction and spectacle. In my late pre-teenage years my fascination led me to bring home some unusual souvenirs from our holidays in Spain, souvenirs manufactured out of Toledo steel to serve the teenage market - I can see my father raising an eyebrow now. Some might have brought back a straw stuffed toy donkey or a sombrero, not me; a chain mace or war axe was the thing. Today you would never get within five miles of an aircraft with such items.

In my early 20s I joined a gun club and bought a Ruger 44 Magnum with enough ammunition to start World War 3. A 0.22 calibre would have done but no I wanted something that had a kick and was unbelievably loud. To own a gun you needed a licence but had the police known that my political ideology was based, albeit loosely, upon the ideas of Karl Marx and that, unbeknown to me then, advocated violence to overthrow a political system, that I was not a very happy young man at the time and without sense of purpose and that I didn't like myself, probably because I am a good judge of character, then the firearms officer would have probably refused my application. However, I would not have harmed anyone; this is not in my way of thinking and my religious belief was that to harm anyone then God would have sent me on an express elevator to hell for having destroyed what he had created.

As I grew older I could see that both Karl Marx and I had got it all wrong anyway. I was to lose my interest in politics and war as I became absorbed in expanding my engineering knowledge into electronics and initially medical instrumentation, a much more beneficial contributor to the human race, I had found a purpose. However, later my interest in war was to return although was to do so from a more enlightened angle; I was to pursue war from a desire to understand its psychological, philosophical and political perspectives largely looking at much of past history through written, photographic and newsreel evidence but specifically in writing this chapter to unravel reason, human behaviour and consequences using the backdrop and our experience of the two world wars of the 20th century, of the 'Thirty Years War' of the 17th century, precisely 1618 to 1648 and of the Catholic Inquisition of the late middle ages.

The very much lesser known thirty years war was a complex semi-religious (Christian v. Christian i.e. Catholic v. Lutheran Protestantism) war that involved different European nations at different times and that was to result in millions of casualties; the conclusion of which brought about a treaty that was to see the end to religious persecution from which all could freely practice their religions as equal citizens i.e. signalling the completion of the stage in history that we refer to as 'the reformation'.

What we know about the psychological, philosophical and political perspectives of war is as applicable now, in the 21st century, as it is for the 17th and 20th centuries - it is the same as it always has been. In my childhood I had read so much about this battle or that battle but now I wanted to know why war happens and what people experience from it. In reading and hearing from those who had had first-hand experience, and who had also since grown older and wiser, my fascination turned to disgust at realising that so much of war is without any justification and in disgust at what cruelty a man, mostly a man that is, can willingly do to another man or to a woman and even a child.

Why on the Subject of Conflict?

Do any of us know of any period in history where we were not in some way affected by human conflict? We may not even have been a combatant, we may not have lost a loved one or seen them endure a life with a life changing injury, we may not have been a displaced civilian, seen our homes or our country destroyed or been under the boot of a ruthless regime, but chances are we have, at minimum, experienced a depressed economy that lingers after such conflicts, often as a result of helping others where we may not had been or needed to be directly involved, for it takes decades to reconstruct an infrastructure for an economy to recover and naturally to regain trust and mend relationships with our former enemies. Even if it is none of these then all societies must labour to provide budgets for its defence, for it would be madness not to, budgets that would have been better utilized to improve the life experience and well-being of our race the human race though are a necessity to halt the mad aspirations of the tyrants, idiots or the just plain evil that did exist, still exists and always will exist.

> *"To secure peace is to prepare for war."* - Carl von Clausewitz (Military Philosopher, Germany 19th century)

War is very costly indeed, civil war even more so and where terror engulfs a society the rule of law breaks down and the human and economic costs are immense. Conflict is not so much just tragic but it is also a tragedy in that it is mostly avoidable, it is mostly unnecessary and it is mostly futile. 'Mostly' not from the perspective of the defender but of that of the aggressor for throughout history societies have had to engage in wars to protect their sovereignty, livelihood and their way of life and to thwart the ambitions of evil and powerful men but also in the protection and defence of others who cannot defend themselves.

In the roots of conflict is there any moral justification for an aggressor to presume a superiority over a particular race or against anyone who happens to have a different view to theirs, to exhibit a predilection for perpetual militaristic or ideological paranoia, to repress or inflict terror upon a population, to seek conquest or wanton destruction of others lands, resources and its people or in the enslavement or commandeering of the wealth from others toil – No, never. All of these things are crimes, war is a crime.

> *"There is nothing more inglorious than the glory that is gained by war."* – Sir Thomas More (Statesman, England 16th century)

We have to face facts that conflict against us humans is by the actions or inactions of other humans, it is there because some have evil intent and that many have failed to do anything about it until it is too late, they cannot face the truth for fear to offend or fear to confront an enemy and in doing so have an inevitable and much greater conflict to face. Conflict is often although oddly perceived, at times and by a few, as glorious, a distraction from life, a spectacle, a break from the mundane, a purpose, a stage where the psychopath or narcissistic fantasist can act out their depravities and control over others, conflict that invariably thwarts the potential to enjoy life for the aggressor just as it does to the defender too.

Does an aggressor not see that they may lose their life or that their life's potential can be utterly destroyed in pursuing this ridiculous path? Some engage in conflict with a smile but their imagination fails them in being able to see the destruction it will inflict upon them and that overwhelming forces will muster against them and overcome their sick pursuits.

For our own sake as a race and for ourselves as individuals we should be better informed as to what are the causes of conflict and how we have been manipulated into electing to destroy our own life for a cause that either is wrong or does not even exist. Conflict is caused by the few very evil, mean spirited and spiteful who manipulate impressionable malleable and gullible others to their evil ideology, who are too rash to believe what they are told and who's lives will be destroyed, any future any hope gone. It is very strange that whatever the cause and whatever the promises of even a glorious afterlife the evil men who co-ordinate all of this do not do the dying, they are usually the last to die. It is curious with all the promises that they make that they often don't seem to want a piece of the action themselves, it is that they hate civilized societies for prohibiting such things as conquest, rape and extortion so they convince others to do the killing, and the dying, for them to punish a society that happens to get in the way of their evil ambitions. The end result of conflict is not good for anyone least of all those who precipitate and then perpetrate it.

"Those who can make you believe absurdities can make you commit atrocities." – François-Marie Arouet, 'Voltaire' (Writer, France 18th century)

Evil others always work on the emotion of hate; they know this to be a most effective method to turn those who have intense dissatisfaction, disappointment or lack of purpose into killers. If hate can be well nurtured then the mind loses its connection with what is moral and what is repugnant so much so that hate can become directed indiscriminately against anyone for cooked up reasons, anyone is viewed as a valid target. In this state and in seeing that their own life is in ruins can easily bring the amoral to desire to bring everyone down to their level i.e. to ruin other's lives too and do so with some sadistic sense of satisfaction or amusement.

A desire to destroy others from irrational hate within the perpetrator is therefore a good indicator of a ruined life not a life ruined by others. To the perpetrator, blame must not be internally based but must be external, the perpetrator therefore has complete incapacity to ever blame themselves; blame must be directed even to those, as often is the case, who are blameless. Whatever moral structure for example through our culture or religion that we may have had it is now open to corruption such that we shall reinterpret our moral framework as endorsing hate where previously it didn't.

What provides some confirmation bias to all of this is that the victim will start to hate in return but did the conflict seeker really expect them to do anything other would you. Better still hate has a voracious appetite for collective approval, a community of hate must be a brotherhood one with a 'common cause' with much backslapping, smiling, praise and shaking of hands all part of the manipulation process; however there is a very dark side to your membership as once in you can never leave - as soon as your opinion starts to fracture where you become disillusioned with the 'common cause' then your 'brothers' will then turn upon you.

Defining Conflict to Evoke Disgust

As I write this it is the day after the 100th Anniversary of the commencement of the Battle of the Somme of World War 1, thus a time to reflect. As always these events are futile to any progression of our species, they do not gain us anything, all that war and terrorism contributes is death and misery and no more than that.

Fortunately, for most of us we do not live in time of war but unfortunately some do and we also live in a time of heightened terrorism and in some way it affects us all. In time of distant wars most of us would not know or would know very little of world conflict and we would mostly have had enough troubles of our own dealing with famine and disease but modern communications in media gives us all instant access to such events as they unfold. In the distant past if you had any experience of war it would not be through reading it in the Sunday newspapers whilst downing a cappuccino it would be an experience that would be close and personal.

Those who don't experience war have a very sanitized version of what it is like and therefore have no idea of it although will often discuss the morality of it. Oddly those who know least about it will often be the ones to moralise on what we should not have done to the enemy. War is ugly and unfortunately those brave souls who have had to stand against tyranny have also had to engage in unthinkable although necessary acts to counter the insane acts of others.

In my possession I have a small tin within which are my grandfather's (whom I never met thanks to the stupidity of war) World War 1 medals and 'dog tags' (identification tags) but there is something else something that unwittingly looks prosaic but is something most poignant and that tells me so much of this conflict. It doesn't look much it is just a lump of metal, ribbed and smooth on the one side and hideously jagged on the other and no longer than 1½" (40mm) by about ¾" (20mm) thick. This piece of shell, amongst others, tore into my grandfather at Passchendaele, another great spectacle of senseless carnage in World War 1, and was then cut out by overworked scalpel wielding surgeons and of course to make matters worse no anaesthetic.

The reality of war is dreadful beyond what most of us without combat experience can imagine, if we can project our mind into what the first day of the Somme was like, like many days before and many days to follow, we would sense fear like no other that death may be imminent and would often take you at a young age, you will never get the chance to live a life meet someone and raise a family but the psychological attrition from two years of war at a tender age would have brutalized the fledgling soldier into someone who would welcome an instant death to escape the horror and the fear of slow agony or of mutilation.

When the attack begins young men face high explosives that when falls upon you the explosion is incredibly and sufficiently deafening to rupture your ear drums and its shock wave could fatally damage your lungs, the shrapnel doesn't just hit you it tears into you and rips you apart releasing brain and bowel in the process and the blast will shatter and remove limbs. If that wasn't enough then you face an attack by thousands of the enemy who at close quarters will use the bayonet, club or flamethrower.

All about you hear the screams and the moaning of the dying for they often do not die quickly. The air is thick with smoke, with an odour of cordite (shell propellant), amatol (ammonium nitrate and TNT explosive), burnt metal, burning oil and wet mud but more than this there is the ever present acrid stench of rotting and burnt flesh, blood, vomit, urine and faeces. What you witness no human should ever see - bodies ripped open, limbs torn and shredded and entrails blown asunder, these images you will never be able to forget. You see this but what of those laying there dying or hideously wounded what is going through their minds is too painful to think of.

Many of the wounded having faced the horrors of battle will then face the horrors of primitive surgery as equally barbaric and in some sense more grotesque than that of the battle itself undertaken by surgeons who are equally horrified at the dreadful suffering that they inflict with some hope of saving a life, surgeons, despite our wrongly perceived assumption of their indifference have to incise, resect and amputate using arcane instruments that equally evoke horror are not indifferent, they like the injured soldier are just as human and will be emotionally traumatized at what they must do.

In all, of the three million men who fought in the battle of the Somme a staggering one million would end up killed or wounded, so let's hope that this sort of thing never happens again. War is hell beyond description it is no place for man or beast.

But even in hell you may still find acts of humanity as on a Christmas day the sound of shelling would be replaced by the calm sound of singing, the sound of 'silent night, holy night' from the British trenches and 'stille nacht, heilige nacht' from the German side and the two sides would meet in 'no man's land' the place between the opposing trenches where mortal enemies would on that day play football, share food and wine, share stories and show each other photographs of their loved ones - if this can be so then why would there be war. But tomorrow the carnage returns, the person who yesterday you shared a story or a joke with could be the person that today that you will kill. If it were so that you were marooned on an island with your enemy and your mutual survival depended upon each other's co-operation then you may even become the best of friends – strange things can even happen in conflict.

There are those who may be so mortally wounded and mutilated and beyond hope that the only merciful thing to do would be to end their suffering quickly with a bullet to the head. It is very easy for the liberal thinking to condemn such actions but it is not them laying there, torn to shreds, dying in agony, they may be shouting murder from the rooftops but the sanitized court room is a world away from the reality of war. If the judge or the political lobby cannot agree with this then they should volunteer to be sent to fight at the battlefront and enlighten themselves to the reality of war and perhaps infuse some common sense into their thick skulls.

This is a graphic image of war not to sensationalise it but to depict it exactly as it is. It is through disgust at such things that we can see what we, the human race, has done and so in doing so feel some sense of shame. If we lose any sense of disgust or shame we are more inclined to again embark upon this carnage and stupidity. Wars start and they end through the belligerents coming to the conclusion that they have had enough, not through some moral shame, they never had any, but merely because economically, materially, physically and emotionally they cannot take any more.

However, we bury our dead and then enter a period of peace and costly re-construction and as time heals and generations move on we come to forget the horror of war and the ideas and attraction of spectacle, adventure and excitement from what is possibly a mundane existence creep back into our minds and again we will find ourselves back in conflict, we learn this lesson and then we forget what we have learnt – this is history - times of peace, times of war, in a never ending cycle, or is it.

Human conflict comes about from a number of factors although greed, the desire to control others, boredom and the psychopathic lust for inflicting suffering would most probably be at the top of the list. What is it we gain or should we say - what is it that certain individuals gain. War that is rooted in political ambition essentially seeks conquest, typically of another nation or their territory or an assumption of that right and for material gain whereas terrorism essentially seeks to destroy for the sake of destruction in the name of some collective belief, it seeks to do bad things to good people, but war also seeks to check the wrongdoing of others – so war and terrorism must be met with war.

However, war mutates into terrorism in that in seeking military objectives property and civilians at times may become casualties through deliberate acts, or often just by accident, and terrorism mutates into war in that others have to organise and fight terrorism in order to thwart its destructive intentions.

Unchecked, war and terrorism would consume everyone, it would not stop. The sadistic thirst of the psychopathic few would seek to find greater means of depravity that they will relentlessly invent – they will kill, torture, rape and inflict the maximum misery upon populations and do so with a smile. The rule of law would be replaced by crime and eventually with no-one left to inflict suffering upon they will then turn upon themselves and they will find the slightest excuse to do so. Unchecked, war and terrorism would result in the total destruction of the human species.

Those Who Seek Conflict Bring About Their Own Destruction

The Hydra of Greek mythology was a monster with nine heads and the body of a serpent that had a CV (curriculum vitae or resume) that listed its job skills as instilling fear and terror, killing and destruction and with a breath so bad that a lorry load of peppermints would not fix. The Hydra had to be stopped before everything and everyone was laid waste. Heracles the son of the God Zeus would put a stop to the evil of the Hydra but as Heracles dispatched one head another would grow in its place. Heracles asked for help from his charioteer who using burning tree trunks burnt the neck stumps of the monster as Heracles yielded his scythe, only then was the monster defeated.

This may be mythology but literature of all forms can teach us so much. When we look at human conflict we might presume that if we defeat it enough times and particularly as we move into a more modern and presumably enlightened world that conflict just like that with the Hydra will fall never again to rise. This is not so because just as a dispatched head of the Hydra will regrow so will the pathological motivations for conflict. Given time and opportunity there will always be more psychopathic despots and crazed ideologists who seek to inflict suffering upon others and who will gain power through terror and false promises to a population eager to listen though less willing to question or even think.

At great human and financial cost we decapitate the Hydra but time and again we fail to cauterise the stumps such that the heads cannot regrow. A few years later

THE ESSENTIAL ART OF RATIONAL THINKING • 335

another maniac or group of maniacs emerge and conflict starts all over again in a never ending cycle of madness.

Why would the analogical Hydra's heads regrow? Mankind has a predilection for conflict, it is seen as an adventure, something to break from the boredom of what may seem a life without purpose or it is to feel a sense of success in a life that rightly or wrongly may be perceived as a failure, that given patience and effort could have been so much otherwise. In essence conflict is borne through feelings of inadequacy often with desire to instil terror in others.

Can a man be a man without having to swagger with a gun held to his breast; the gun being a symbol of strength, false strength, one that is designed to turn the unimpressive into the impressive but the man behind the gun may not have any strength at all. What we are seeing is a psychological compact of the ego with the gun. The gun is supporting the crippled ego like the crutch supports the crippled body. It is very easy for a bully or a thug to pull, any firearms instructor would actually and rightly say squeeze, a trigger; anyone can do it - it is nothing to be particularly proud of. *"Look at me I can intimidate I can kill"* - so what, is that really all I can do, can I not do anything that is magnificent, good and that contributes to society.

Intimidating or killing of those who are innocent is evil and of those who are defenceless is cowardice, to do so does not confirm strength it confirms inadequacy and insignificance. What is such a being without a gun? - Nothing. Killing feeds the ego in the maladjusted mind but what do they do when they have no-one left to kill, have they at this point found happiness, have they honestly found a constructive path out of their state of misery?

"I warn you against shedding blood, indulging in it and making a habit of it, for blood never sleeps." – An-Nasir Salah ad-Din Yusuf ibn Ayyub, 'Saladin' (Military Leader, Syria/Egypt 12th century)

Having a weapon even an impressive arsenal of such, an army, a will, like Shakespeare's Macbeth a delusion of being invincible and a strong and hot-headed rancorous belief in something brings about a psychological state, a militaristic ego, a projection of power, a display like a peacock showing off its feathers, in that the individual is impressed by what it sees. However, without any concept of industrial might or appreciation of the scale of the enemy, of what a nation can do, one where its population is industrious and technologically formidable then such perceived strength is an illusion a dangerous illusion.

The belligerents often get some sense of superiority but have failed woefully to measure their enemy. An enemy may appear to be passive it may live within the rule of law, this is why its society succeeds, and it may wish for what is normal i.e.

to live in peace, and this may give a false impression of it being weak and easily defeated, this is a very dangerous assumption. Look again and you might just realize that what you have is a sleeping giant with enormous potential to hit back a thousand fold of what your strength can muster.

Don't think that you can defeat it, use your brain and think about it, you may imagine that your presumed enemy will just roll over and capitulate – they won't. You may rattle your perceived enemy and they don't react much, you rattle them a bit more and you may start to feel that you have an edge, you rattle them a bit more and then suddenly what was passive can become a sudden avalanche of very ugly and very destructive retaliation – you have built a false sense of security you are not thinking as you would in playing a game of chess, think would you keep poking a sleeping tiger whilst you have your head in its mouth. Perhaps this is all what you want and if it is then you need to take a serious look at yourself.

Despite imagined strength, lock horns with a nation that has far higher industrial muscle than you and you will not find victory you will only find your complete destruction, for those of the enemy will include many who don't go around intimidating the unarmed and defenseless but have the courage to face those such as you and they will defeat you. Where there is evil there is no rule of just law, there is crime ergo there be the indolent and such societies never have economic and therefore industrial might to be able to prosecute a sustained war against societies that operate successfully in all respects.

In realizing all of this we should all of us avoid conflict, look for trouble and you will get it and you might be shocked at what you have awoken, don't forget this. We should all stop this nonsense of grandiose territorial claims, conquest, repression and terrorizing of our societies. There are times that we have to engage in war with brave men and women who in our armed forces are in no way inadequate, they use the instruments of war to defeat evil risking their own lives, they do not seek to intimidate or to kill those who are good who desire for peace and to live under a just rule of law, they seek to destroy what is evil.

All of us have a responsibility to each other to not look for conflict but to co-operate and to work at building better fairer societies. A life that is seduced by conflict is a wasted life one that will probably end in early death not one that could flourish given some decent effort. Don't waste this life. If all of us can look at our lives from a different perspective on this subject perhaps we can finally succeed in putting the Hydra into its permanent grave a world without any more destruction or killing.

I have often heard those who would disagree with how enemies have been dealt with in the past, we question the morality of our methods in order to destroy the military capacity and will of the enemy. It is all too easy to do so to look back and moralize but we didn't live then and we may have very little idea of what the enemy had done too. Some might prefer to ignore the truth that there aren't any really bad people but there are. Some might argue that it is better to capitulate with a false hope that all will turn out OK that in reality would be a highly unlikely outcome. Faced with psychopaths and psychopathic regimes there is no option other than to face up to them so somehow they must be stopped. Delay, appeasement or to do nothing will result in terrible regret.

A Freudian Contextualised Theory on the Conflict Seeking Personality

To understand the makeup of those who seek conflict we need to look at childhood development through the 'theory of personality' of the psychoanalyst Sigmund Freud a theory that does seem to make a lot of sense.

"Withdraw into yourself and look." – Plotinus (Philosopher, Egypt 3rd century BC)

As an early infant, a neonate that is, we are and we obviously have the 'moral' mind of an early infant, then at this stage in our development according to Freud we are devoid of any awareness of morality or logic, our world is narrow and of a view seeking to only fulfil our desires, we exist for pleasure and immediate gratification; if we want something we must have it without consideration of the needs of others since we are unable to consider others and so we do not know right from wrong. Freud labelled this stage of development as the 'Id' (the 'It') 'Id' being essentially our subconscious mind.

The 'Id' is what drives sex and aggression. Later, i.e. in our post neonate phase, what then develops is our 'Ego' our conscious mind where we realise that not all of our desires can be fulfilled we are thus able to think thus able to understand what is reality and what is rational. As we develop further we enter what Freud called the 'Superego' phase where we develop morality and understand the rules of society, our conscious mind has therefore acquired conscience we know what is right and what is wrong. It is here that we acquire the ability to feel guilt and where we may find moral perfection.

Between our 'Id' and our 'Superego' sits the arbitrator our 'Ego'; whatever we do is therefore under control of the 'Ego', it is the 'Ego' that ultimately decides our actions. The 'Id' reflects traits that we may associate with pathological personalities in its various forms and the 'Superego' reflects traits that we may associate with the destruction of the self as described early on in this book.

In essence the ideal mental state, a healthy mental state, is to have strong 'Ego' in its Freudian definition not the definition of ego that we are all usually aware of and as mentioned throughout this book. Therefore a mind saturated in 'Id', i.e. abnormal self-interest, or 'Superego', i.e. abnormal selflessness, is an unhealthy mind. A strong Freudian 'Ego' is that which provides us with our defence mechanisms from which we and society can survive and thrive within which we are reasonable about our sense of entitlement and not too hung up about being just too morally perfect.

The 'Id' alone would be predisposed to, indeed have predilection for aggression often excusing coexisting inflicting of sexual violence upon women it is also prone to other inappropriate behaviours and destruction. To develop beyond the 'Id' the early infant must learn from others that which are just rules and what is or is not moral in other words it needs to be nurtured in a mentally healthy not mentally unhealthy society. If its community within which it lives is unhealthy and so has culture devoid of morality and that systematically manipulates and nurtures criticism of anything but itself then there is little hope of developing beyond something that sets out to seek conflict, to kill, to rape, to inflict misery and to destroy. The individual becomes a product of a chaotic and lawless society one in which no-one including its own citizens can ever feel safe.

"In effect, religion, which should most distinguish us from beasts, and ought most peculiarly to elevate us, as rational creatures, above brutes, is that wherein men appear most irrational, and more senseless than beasts themselves." – John Locke
(Philosopher, England 17th/18th century)

Such individuals or societies that subscribe exclusively to their 'Id' will delude themselves that the rules that they have are in the 'Superego' - just ask any of the Catholic Inquisition of the middle-ages and they will find reason and justification to do exactly that - of course all of those men and women, who actually were innocent, deserved to be tortured and brutally murdered in the name of God, weren't they? They can't find an excuse so let's bring God into it – 'I did it because God told me to'; so that's OK then, is it?

What the Inquisition had, as do others of their ilk throughout history, are not morally justified rules instead they had their rules, rules remiss of any morality or they have equally outrageous and warped ideological interpretations, that they or evil others design to give licence to act out their depravities and to satisfy their sick desires - they have fake excuses made up by themselves; to them all of their disgusting actions are 'rationally' excusable. The Inquisition might describe themselves as quintessential Catholics but the reality was that they were psychopaths using Catholicism as an excuse for acting out their lust for inflicting misery although the reality was that most Catholics would not only fear them but would also detest them.

Without the reformation and its enlightened thinking the Inquisition may have survived where any other than non-Catholics would have been slaughtered into non-existence by decree of the Pope.

"Attack the evil that is within, rather than attacking the evil that is in others." – Confucius (Philosopher, China circa 500 BC)

Such people are in the 'Id' and they remain in the 'Id', there are no developmental horizons they in effect have a mind and value system not developed any further than that of a neonate and a very nasty neonate at that. The power of life, death, intimidation and destruction that they have over others is a false self-belief of toughness although it is anything but tough since this sense of power is through strength in numbers and as a result of being armed. It is the child mind, the mind of the immature, that of the 'Id' that cannot act responsibly with having power, with power it will smash anything it comes across, what others have invested so much effort to create they gleefully destroy, even culture a nations heritage cannot escape. Just as a child throws a tantrum then so does the immature adult; disagree with me, defy me, dissatisfy me and I will kill you. A tough person does not intimidate others or in any way destroy because they happen to be the one with the gun, a tough person is one who endures life and doesn't buckle to manipulation by evil others or from their own self-delusional obsessions, they rise above themselves and they rise above life, they make something of it and they protect others, they do not destroy. In absence of conscience and morality it is so easy to pick up a gun and kill someone but have you the strength to question yourself and challenge evil intent, can you hold yourself back from the edge of that black pit or are you just too lacking in moral strength to do so.

"If you would be a real seeker after truth, it is necessary that at least once in your life you doubt, as far as possible all things." – Rene Descartes (Philosopher, France 17th century)

If you were to become the minority, you were outnumbered in a community and the others didn't agree with your point of view would it then be acceptable for them to take your life when you have not inflicted any suffering upon others just as you may justify taking life if the tables were turned. No. You are entitled to a different view. Ask yourself what if everyone else subscribed to your view of justifying killing in other words they have the same moral frame of reference, what would happen? What would happen is that we would all die and for what; for what you have read and listened to (countless political ideologies) and deluded yourself into believing without questioning its rationality or interpretation, just think of the literary tripe of the suspiciously self-assumed God Adolf Hitler in his work 'Mein Kampf' (My Struggle) where did that get the human race indeed where did it get him and his cronies. We can only be thankful that the thinking and literature of

Hitler was never exalted to the status of a religion if it were we would all be doomed, all of us.

"You must hold every opinion with a measure of doubt." – John Locke
(Philosopher, England 17th/18th century)

In 1940 the victorious German 6th army would march through Paris with a sense of pride and no doubt feeling of invincibility, less than three years later it would be rotting in the ruins of Stalingrad (present day Volgograd) deep inside Russia and most of those who survived the onslaught of the battle were later to die from hypothermia, starvation and typhus. Of the 280,000 in the campaign only 5,000 were ever to return home, the invincible 6th army had been obliterated. Russia initially on the back-foot would later bring its huge resources to bear and turn the tide against the Nazi war machine.

Conflict seekers always make early wins since as the belligerents they have the advantage of the element of surprise but they forget that the enemy will strike back and it will strike back with all of its industrial might, can you really expect it to do otherwise – victory can be short lived as was proven at Stalingrad. As we say *"pride before a fool"*. Those who seek conflict seem to rarely think through the consequences of their actions not just for others but also for themselves.

"It is a greater man who can conquer himself once rather than conquer a thousand others a thousand times over." – Chinese proverb.

The question is does the aggressor have the courage to face what they are and to admit what they are. In this context there are two things a man must know, what he is and what he is not. If you sadistically kill then you are nothing but a murderer, can you accept this or does it upset you that someone would have the audacity to say what you really are, to speak the truth, or do you fear the truth. Are you open to reason for your own sake or are you like talking to a brick wall in that you won't listen or can you elevate yourself above this and make your life matter for the right reasons.

The 'Psycho-Political' Origins of Conflict

There are possibly as many causes for conflict as there are psychiatric conditions, and if you look in DSM that's a lot, but we could classify the causes of conflict broadly into political ambition or survival, thirst for power, an idiotic idea of glory, conquering another nation and its resources, pathological envy, sadistic lust for destruction and killing, opportunity to commit crime on a grand scale, criminal intent i.e. to overthrow the rule of law to steal, rape, torture and murder at will, to assuage inadequacy of the self, to assuage a lack of purpose or boredom in the indolent, for the self-outcast to feeling a belonging to a community or brotherhood, to arbitrarily punish an innocent society for the misery of the aggressor or for that which is not their fault and for which the aggressor refuses to accept responsibility, religious insanity or perverse interpretation of such, the 'fascist' assumption of religious or racial superiority, paranoid delusions or that they are easily wound up, fabrications of truth or simply because they don't like to hear the truth or finally to thwart all of the aforementioned. All of which, other than the last category, are enacted by the mad, the bad and the easily manipulated all who suffer from a pathological obsession or criminal desire.

Perhaps we can sum up the probability of conflict in all theatres not just in war from a formula as follows; the probability of conflict = a function of (perception of dominance over another x lack of morality x what I desire / what I have).

We might imagine in our cosy little world, one that affords us all with apparent safety and comfort that we believe that major conflict won't happen where I live and can't happen where I live; this is a complacent fantasy. A lot of our psychological negativity is rooted in the idea that nothing changes, essentially our lives will stay as they are – in the context of conflict this is a false and dangerous assumption, things can and do change, and we must all be alert to the warning signs. Just as what is bad can change to good so then what is good can change to that which is bad. Some very stupid actions or inactions by our leaders can change everything in the blink of an eye. The life that you have or imagine that you have in living a comfortable life where all is well can turn rapidly into a nightmare, into hell.

Imagine that where you live that the rule of law collapses that you have no protection that others can slaughter or rape at will, you have been separated from your family or they have been killed, that your home has been destroyed, that commerce has collapsed that you have no employment no money, there is no electricity, gas or fuel, the toilets don't flush there is no clean water there is no food, no longer do you feel safe or optimistic and you have lost any sense of enjoyment in life – your whole future is gone. This is the plight of the genuine refugee who must then seek protection elsewhere. One false move by our governments and this is where we may land up. Really does anyone deserve such hell?

In Understanding Fear and Hate, Their Causes and How We Can Stop It

There is a lot of fear and a lot of hate in this world there always has been and I suspect that unless we change our ways that there always will be. Indeed when we look at this subject and how it is presented here it is equally applicable throughout the entire history of our species. Fear and hate, and the reasons of how they came about, is an innate property of us humans. However, fear (phobias) and hate are two different emotions – you might fear something but that doesn't necessarily mean that you hate it.

I for example have a visceral fear of heights (acrophobia) but I don't hate tall buildings I usually look at them with awe and admiration but they scare the hell out of me. Oddly enough I have flown microlight aircraft at 5000ft yet no fear, the mind is indeed a strange thing. I might have a particular hate or loathing for someone, for example the more I read about that odious crackpot Joseph Goebbels (Hitler's minister of propaganda) the more I can't stand the man, if you were to listen to him you would realise just what a fool he was, however that doesn't necessarily suggest that I fear him, indeed he seems quite unimpressive.

Now if I were to put my hand on an electrical conductor I would get a shock, do it again what happens, then again and again. After a few shocks, my reaction to this is naturally one of fear but not hate. Now electricity can easily kill so whatever you do don't try my experiment. However, what we are alluding to is that to survive we will naturally instil fear within of something where there is a manifest emerging pattern, i.e. from a series of events that presents some statistical validity to what we suspect, this being part of our basic survival instincts – we learn from experience what to fear and therefore what to avoid. We may want to delude ourselves that fear is hate and therefore we should suppress our fear but if we do we are foolishly dropping our guard and as I said electricity at its worst can kill.

There is often good reason to fear and good reason to hate. Your fear can develop into hate where there is deliberate intent to do harm against you although hate can also be precipitated in a moderated form where you may just dislike, for example someone who doesn't pull his weight at work I might dislike but I would not hate. Fear of the depraved Gestapo (Hitler's secret police) could easily turn to, rational, hate if your family had been murdered in some Nazi concentration camp's gas chamber - this is a natural reaction. If it is believed that this is not so then at what point will hate be elicited within ourselves, we all have a threshold.

Some may preach that the answer is to love everyone, which in itself in an ideal world sounds very noble indeed, but they have no idea what they are dealing with, love wouldn't work with the pathologically selfish or the psychopath, they could test out this theory but it wouldn't do them any good and it might even get them killed, naivety here would be like gambling with their own life and for that matter the lives of others. But even those who preach universal love also have capacity for hate though they won't admit it and so how far could they be pushed for hate to arise, for the 'shadow' to emerge (ref. Carl Jung).

Not always does hate precipitate through harm just done to you as it is very easy to hate someone who has done harm to another person for example the rapist or murderer of a child and perhaps I'm not being very politically correct here but I could easily hang them myself.

Now we all might ask ourselves did I personally do something so bad as to deserve another's hate but an irrationality of hate is where innocent individuals are blamed for what their nation, race, religion has done or may have been wrongly accused of doing. Innocent individuals will be sought out and even sadistically murdered ad hoc for no reason other than this or just because they are different. This is a disgusting and very low point in humanity to be hated and then destroyed just because of whom you are and what you believe. The individual never did any harm but was singled out on some bogus excuse.

When this happens there is no rational reason for hating those who have been destroyed what we have here is in effect a psychopathic crime and the gas chambers of the SS are testament to this. When murder is carried out against individuals, murder after all is an irrevocable act against the individual, very much less so an irrevocable act against a nation as often wrongly perceived by the perpetrator, then the true reason for this lies in the abnormal mental pathology of the perpetrator who feels some gratification in committing such disgusting acts and will always find a bogus excuse to do so.

If we hate those just because they are different to us and if we are dead honest that they haven't done us any harm or planning to do so then this is what racism is in its true meaning. If we were then to add the dimension that we then desire to destroy, to murder then this is what you would call pathological racism in its quintessential form. Logically we can also conclude that that to hate an individual who without good reason has done us harm, and who happens to be different to us, is not racist.

However, history moves on and so must we. Under the regime of Adolf Hitler something like 40,000 civilians were killed in the bombing of London (check out the film 'The Battle of Britain'), Manchester, Liverpool, Birmingham, Newcastle, Coventry, Bristol, Portsmouth, Southampton, Glasgow, Cardiff and Belfast, many would also be maimed and the destruction would have been astronomical and as to Germany the consequences of World War 2 was to become even more severe in suffering and loss, millions of innocent Germans would die because of the stupidity of one man, and all of this was just under 80 years ago. Let us not forget that Hitler's final motivation was not in defence of Germany but in its eventual destruction.

After the war those who had lost loved ones would have been full of hate and this is understandably so and I have known those who lived through it and echoed those

THE ESSENTIAL ART OF RATIONAL THINKING • 344

sentiments. However, the German people then were not the Nazi party and we cannot blame all citizens of a nation for prosecuting a war and we cannot blame them all for the sordid crimes committed by a few in the name of a ridiculous and evil ideology. If we were to blame them all we would also to blame ourselves all of us that is, for all nations have something to be ashamed of.

As is often the case evil ideologies fall through the actions of those who chose not to ignore evil but to stand against it and those responsible for the atrocities would either die as cowards by their own hand or at the hands of the executioner, soon after to become nothing more than dust. This all being said we cannot bear a grudge for all time we have to move on besides none of us anywhere has a history devoid of injustice, once we have dealt with the guilty we must move on, we cannot continue to perpetuate hate and war until the human race is no more. At some point we must put behind us what has happened and we cannot blame individuals for what their nation has done often many decades or centuries past. History is history we can't just rake through it in perpetuity, so let's move on.

The Way Forward

Our species has enough challenges in struggling with poverty, famine, disease, debt and crime, we also have many personal issues to contend with and it is to these things that we need to put our effort to instead of diverting our energies towards manufacturing conflict. We should redirect our anger into doing something positive we should have respect and compassion for each other whoever we are unless the other of course is the implacable belligerent who we must deal with. War often comes about because politicians misread other nations instead of looking to build friendly relationships at all levels or from fear of offending those who are clearly heading in a confrontational direction.

Resigned to the idea that life is futile, that may have largely been so or appeared so of biblical/medieval times where few had opportunity but had hopes of a better life after death, but in the modern world there is hope in life, there is opportunity but what is required is effort.

If God exists we are all then products of God, it is therefore God's will that we are here in all of our cultures, races and religions. It was a contention of Oliver Cromwell that God is not partisan this being proven by the very fact that God never seems to take sides in conflict, those who believe God is on their side still lose wars and battles and if God was on their side why then did they lose. We may also wonder why those who look for conflict and who believe in God's approval of what they do never seem to find peace in their own lives, is it that God has abandoned them. We can either live in peace or remain forever in conflict until we are all gone.

We can grasp opportunities to co-operate or we can throw it to the wind. The question is what do we all want, what path do we wish to take. We can all do a lot better than this.

"To you, who are my murderers, punishment far heavier than you have inflicted on me will surely await you. The easiest and the noblest way is not to be disabling others, but to be improving yourselves." – Socrates (Philosopher, Greece 4th/5th century BC)

Make the best of your life for now, don't obsess about aggressive desires, move on make your life count for something good. This doesn't just apply to conflict but it applies to everything and to everyone. If your life isn't perfect (who's is?) or is far from perfect, if it isn't loved or it is unlovable then seek to perfect the self – to learn, to seek maturity, to seek magnanimity, to seek refinement and impress others with what you have made of yourself as a person. To destroy, to kill is not impressive to anyone of any quality since to destroy or to kill is something that any idiot can do, it's not difficult and it's not clever, it therefore doesn't reveal psychological strength it reveals psychological weakness.

Preferably, and I would hope, that those who may lack moral strength should endeavour to raise the willpower to go and find it to secure a better outcome for all including themselves. If you cannot do this for others then at least do it for yourself and seek to become a better human being.

"The life I have given you, do not waste it, do not take it on the path of ruin; use it wisely and to its full potential for good. Your life is precious and every atom within you is as dear to me as if it were my own. Do good and I will embrace you but I will abandon those who turn to evil." – 'Theoleptic spirituality'

And if you can't see a way out of this mess and for some inspiration check out the hymn 'Joyful Joyful' Royal Albert Hall, London. If this delightful hymn cannot move us away from a desire to destroy then I don't know what can.

Person to Person – Conflict on the Smaller Scale

You may be the easiest going most reasonable person on planet earth but it is very unlikely that you will go through life unscathed of someone who seeks, often without good reason or with an exaggerated reason, to take a verbal swipe at you. Is there a justified reason to do this, why did they escalate this to where we are or is the motive to dominate that in itself is a sign of a mind less healthy and perhaps more churlish shall we say.

Perhaps those who seek destruction or dominance subconsciously seek love and approval, even a hug, since our external false persona often describes an exact opposite and authentic inner self, one that we dare not reveal! Now it's very easy very easy indeed to aggressively fight back and sometimes we do have to do this but mostly this is a very unproductive approach in that to <u>unskilfully</u> challenge someone who may indeed be totally wrong in their belief of justification can often lead to expletive insults and even violence and some just cannot control what they will do. An argument over something as stupid as a tin of tomatoes can turn into murder if nothing else it ruins relationships.

Now I have already mentioned the following quote in the chapter on well-being but I believe this (and the whole poem) to be so profound that it's worth repeating, especially so here.

"If you can keep your head when all about you are losing theirs and blaming it on you" – From the poem 'If' by Rudyard Kipling (Poet, England 19th/20th century)

If we think about 'If' then perhaps there is a more skilful approach, one with a better outcome and lower blood pressure. Indeed to challenge an unskilful attack in a skilful way ('to keep your head') will catch your opponent off-balance. They have entered into the assault in a combative mode and they expect you to do likewise, they won't be expecting or prepared to be met with calm level headed reasoning. Once aggression is reached we lose ability to rationalise and to coherently make our case we may even be warming up our deeper darker and dangerous unconscious character within – who knows where that can go.

Perhaps if someone verbally attacks us then we should seek to defuse the situation, to stay relaxed to keep a cool head, perhaps to listen and just keep listening, let them talk themselves to exhaustion, and then to challenge their 'facts' with cogent discussion but not to ridicule or chastise the other person for what they are but you can challenge what they are wrong about you could ask: *"why do you think that"*, *"have you thought this"*, *"you may have misunderstood me, that isn't what I meant"*, *"let's look at this another way"*, *"I know what you mean but"*, *"is there really another way to look at this"*, *"what would you do"*, *"tell me more about why you disagree"*; stick to the facts, give them something to think about rather than something to act defensively upon.

Look upon an argument not as an argument but as a logical discourse of interest where you seek to discuss and to find out what is going on and where you aim to reach a point of agreement with the opposing argument even if that agreement is to disagree. Surprisingly you may even get your opponent to see your point of view you may even see theirs, who knows. Even when we are totally convinced that we are right we may be wrong. If reason isn't working and the other person is in 'all mouth, no ears, no reason' mode then there is no profit to be had with your words, listening and reasoning abilities instead it's time to use the legs and just walk away.

Chapter 18

THWARTING THE 'ATTRACTION' OF CRIME

(Law, crime, punishment and reform)

Law, that which is just, may exist in some remote place in the courts of law or within the hands of those who seek to protect us but it should never end there, it never must. Imagine if the apparatus of law enforcement were to disappear, would chaos then be allowed to fill the vacuum. It is the responsibility of us all to be law abiding but also that in all of our own actions, irrespective of the existence of law or not, that what we do and how we judge is based upon what is just and so what is fair.

Some judge others harshly, and those that do should judge themselves first using the same measure and then there are those who find excuse for the bad behaviour of others and so judge too leniently only to incentivize more of the same and those that do so deserve to be subjected to the same crime. Judgement should always be in a state of balance it should always be just and proportionate.

But there are also those, typically anarchists, who believe that all law, not just that which is unjust but also that which is just, is a political tool to oppress, but then they would wouldn't they. Taking that view, what would replace law, lawlessness maybe or perhaps law as now defined by the anarchists in as much that they then become the very class that they detest i.e. the ruling class, the new generation of oppressors.

Just law can only be achieved through the consensus of many of the wise and incorruptible but not the mob. When law is created by a select group of a few or select one it is often within a political dictatorship who define at a whim what is just though in reality that is not. This is law that serves the state rather than the interests of the people, often harshly even inhumanely punishing those who do no more than question the state. To question the state may be just enough to be sentenced to imprisonment or even death. If anything can ever judge the morality of a state then it is in its system of justice.

A state that administers unjust law, that abandons its fundamental legal obligation of protecting its citizens or that engages in unjust action outside of its borders is not a state that acts within the law. In reality all states and societies at various times through history have been guilty of illegal actions of some form or other but that's in the past, now we must move forward we all deserve it to do so.

"Wherever law ends, tyranny begins." – John Locke (Philosopher, England 17th century)

Jurisprudence - The Philosophy of Law

Modern society is fundamentally dependent upon science and technology but a decent successful society is fundamentally dependent upon the rule of law that is just law as not all law is just. Without the rule of law; as in being without rules and consequent retribution, the societal vacuum, without any doubt whatsoever, would be filled with crime, economic failure, tyranny, misery, poverty and chaos. A society without law is no different than a society that is economically bankrupt, it cannot progress it can only fail. Indeed without the rule of law, in some form or other, any chance of modern society to evolve would be undermined as would any chance of scientific and technological achievement. Society as we know it would collapse.

Why is this? Thankfully most of us are civilized and law abiding. In the absence of law we would continue to live our lives as decent citizens we would not embark on an orgy of crime. We would construct, we would show respect for others and we would build our economies through toil. However, we are not all alike – some in our society would take full advantage of the vacuum as soon as any administration breaks down and history is replete with such examples. Effectively crime would replace the rule of law. When this happens a society will be pulled into an abyss where everything fails.

With exception of economies who have substantial valuable mineral assets to trade (i.e. oil, gas, coal, metal ores, uranium, gold, precious stones etc., as is sufficient to sustain its population with its basic needs and expectations of living standards) then the idea of the criminal organization, governing along the lines of a mafia, that to take control of a state and plunder its assets will bring them untold and sustainable wealth and power is an illusion.

Nations without sufficient mineral wealth must create their wealth through manufacturing and services that requires even greater order and therefore that requires just law. As soon as crime takes hold of a wealthy though non-mineral-based, or insufficiently mineral-based economy, then its economic performance will rapidly decline. In other words to maintain a functioning economy requires work and order, something that is anathema to the criminal mind. For any society to prosper you need just law and good economic management.

It is by no accident that where we see that crime has replaced the rule of law or where the crime of tyranny and it is a crime, ensues, and that administers an unjust rule of law where its population is oppressed then the economic system is doomed, so poverty will ensue. With poverty a society cannot buy fuel, it cannot buy medicine and it cannot buy technology. Non mineral-based economies without law are unable to trade and are unable to maintain decent standards of living. There will be unrest and perhaps revolution so hence such regimes will oppress and inflict fear and severe and even sickening punishment for the smallest of misdemeanours, as are defined by them, in order to maintain its iron like grip over its population.

The point here is that an enlightened government that enacts enlightened and just laws will enable its nation to thrive politically, economically and socially. All, who are able and prepared to work, can live well, can be provided for, to have employment, good health and access to good education and all who need protection, those who are unable to work, are commensurately protected. Law is not always perfect though it does give us a framework to live by and for this we should be thankful.

The problem with any legal system is its relationship to that which is just. Legal systems often develop over time as for example from the 13th century legal document of the Magna Carta that introduced; that you cannot be unlawfully detained and that you have a right to a fair trial, this being the foundation of UK law within which it is still enshrined and in some instances is also referred to in US law. On this basis we can see that as our understanding of law develops then so does our legal system change accordingly, it is therefore never immutable and being so attests to its lack of maturity and so therefore it cannot be final.

Clearly something that must develop with time must therefore also lack perfection, albeit perfection being what it strives to achieve, then we can only deduce that our legal system cannot be 100% perfect and cannot therefore be 100% just. If anyone should state that *"if the law should say that it is correct then it must be correct"* can only be naïve at best. In the UK legal system we might for example have very good reason to state that contract law has achieved near perfection but when we consider divorce, human rights law or the concept of justifiable revenge or defence then perfection is somewhat questionable.

To put a stronger point on this; there are regimes who's legal system will imprison or even execute anyone who does none other than to speak out in dissent against the regime or who fail to observe ridiculous, freedom and joy depriving, rules, their ensuing punishment will be enacted within the law, their law, but a law that violates what is just and if you live in such a regime you need to think very 'very' carefully before you put you or yours in danger and it is often best to stay safe in silence. In a wider context perhaps we should define a crime, what a crime really is, not as is politically defined, in that it is an action that inflicts tangible harm upon another, not where another just disagrees with that action (or thought).

Where a regime or some other force of power, 'elected' or not, administers tyranny and injustice in that they inflict or promote major crime against individuals, a population or part of therein, a specific racial group for example, or who threatens the peace of other nations then there is justification for the international community to act and if necessary and where possible and prudent to destroy such regimes. The human race is after all one family and we all have obligations to one another. Sometimes it is necessary to destroy in order to prevent a greater evil.

Law is not necessarily just and for this reason it is the responsibility of the judiciary, where this is possible, to refuse, but only with very good reason to do so, to administer the law as prescribed by their governments particularly where it is used as a political tool and particularly where it is patently unfair. The judiciary does at least have at its disposal the means to interpret the law on a case by case assessment, they have discretional latitude and they have the means, in the UK, to take the legal system itself to judicial review where a law can be repealed if it is incompatible with a higher authority. All law is and should be questioned on its degree of being reasonable and just. Is it or is it not reasonable and just that is the question of its true and absolute legality.

Further to this, all societies suffer from some form or other of establishment corruption either in that; the will of the people or that law as desired by the people, who may see where the law is sometimes too harsh, elsewhere too lenient or serves the powers that be, is not enacted by an 'I know best' establishment attitude i.e. to 'lawfully' ignore the political mandate of the people, through traction to obtain the patronage of certain groups or individuals in a society, to sacrifice justice as a means to negotiate peace, transitory and unethical as it may be, to placate or capitulate to an unruly faction within a society or to protect from due punishment those who are in authority and hence part of the establishment club or its acolytes. This doesn't happen I hear, well it does and even in societies that we may deem to be ostensibly beyond corruption.

The law is therefore not applied equally and as such there are inevitable miscarriages of justice and any such corruption of the law in itself is nothing but criminal, this being so can only conclude that different legal systems, or interpretations thereof, cannot coexist with one society, to apply the law equally there can only be one law and only one interpretation of the law. Just as you or I can be an accessory to a crime then such known maladministration of the law, political expedience or not, is equally an accessory to a crime, by the state. All of us, whoever we are, pauper to head of state, and whatever consequences may ensue, should be equally subject to the law.

The rule of just law is the fundamental 'sine qua non' to a stable society, it is there to protect all equally and to punish where punishment is necessary, however as we become more liberal and 'progressive' so does our attitude to punishment; we identify the word 'punishment' with something crude and unrefined as commensurate with the rack or the axe of the middle ages. The bare fact is that without punishment there is no means of making the crime unappealing to the perpetrator who if had the moral will would have not committed the crime in the first place. A mere slap on the wrist and the offender will just go out and do it again.

Our modern societies tend to have an inclination to 'diametric reaction' i.e. if one idea doesn't work let's have a bash at the exact opposite. For example in the context of anything, if you are not able to show pusillanimous largesse then you might wrongly be labelled as backward looking rather than a realist, i.e. a realist being able to recognize something for what it really is rather than what we might like to think it to be, this becoming increasingly apparent with modern society in the persuasion of administering inadequate punishment.

'Progressive' thinking has become the new fashion such that anyone who happens to not be at the extreme and progressive end of the thinking spectrum is of course a person of unrefined thought a person who cannot think!!! We are all to abandon realistic and pragmatic thinking and to totally capitulate to the whim of whatever is the accepted intellectual zeitgeist, i.e. the current modern and 'educated' thinking for which anyone who is a detractor must therefore be stupid. Gone are the ideas that perhaps a middle of the road approach is best and this may not even dimly resonate in the minds of some politicians.

As with all daft experiments the progressive liberal approach will be found to fail and perhaps we will then swing to the other equally daft extreme and find that that won't work either. Having none is just as obnoxious and stupid as in having too much. Like all extremes, 'progressive' is therefore 'unprogressive', it doesn't work. As part of the rule of law as to what we define as to what is and what is not legal we must also define what is and what is not just, deserved and corrective punishment.

However, where we have a structured society it is the moral imperative of our government to protect us through enacting adequate and effective punishment, in effect to have a zero tolerance of crime, and if it is so that the law has removed your legal right to protect yourself then the law is obliged to do it for you and if they do not then philosophically you then must have the right to take back that obligation, in effect to do it for yourself and by whatever means that works in order to protect you and yours. If you are not protected then you have no alternative but to protect yourself though we should never have to arrive at this position and governments must never put us in this position to do so either.

A lack of adequate law is just as bad as the crime in itself, to see a murderer or rapist go unpunished or inadequately punished is obscene. The punishment, at the end of the day, must fit the crime and it is for this reason that I pour scorn on what I describe as, 'pusillanimous largesse' of the liberal thinking 'elite'.

The Efficacy of Trial - Judge and Jury, Roles & Responsibilities

Judges are very powerful people, and they know it and some know it rather too well. To administer the law a judge must be above any influence of government and therefore, by definition, cannot easily be removed from office. If they are in any way tainted by ego, arrogance, incompetence, political prejudice or they are irresolute then proper administration of justice and punishment will be compromised. In this sense to be good at administering justice requires outstanding competence, an incisive mind, unswerving diligence, procedural rectitude, ethical adherence, common sense, firmness but also humanity. This is not to say that a legal system is perfect, far from it, since law is commissioned by government with all of its fallibility, and often lack of wit, possibly often at the dismay of those who are at the front end of fighting crime. Hence, a judge administering the prescribed rule of law with fairness and impartiality may be administering a law that in itself is not fair and that is not impartial as has been directed by a government.

Where a crime is of sufficiently serious nature then in the UK system we have 'trial by jury' where the jury consists of members of the public, who are not representative of government in any capacity and are therefore independent of the government, who may be commanded to undertake this role, unless they lack legal or mental capacity to do so, and who must decide, not the judge, on whether the defendant is innocent or guilty. They may face challenges beyond their innate capabilities such as in trying to understand a complex fraud case or where they must put aside any prejudices that they may have.

Further to this they will be swayed by the defence and prosecution barristers ability, or lack of, to articulate, manipulate, dissect, present, circumvent and to theatrically entice. The judge who administers the process can advise the jury though the line between advising and leading a verdict may sometimes be very thin. Any procedural failure and that of the presentation and administration of the evidence can result in an incorrect verdict or a case acquitted through a technicality.

On this basis, with a highly adept defence counsel who can shred or cast doubt on solid evidence or who can elicit sympathy for his/her client, a dim judge, poorly processed evidence and presentation, a jury who is biased towards the defendant, a jury who may be swayed not by the verdict but by the ensuing punishment that they may revile or feel responsible for inflicting and a defendant of innocent appearance then a false verdict of innocence, or with opposite bias guilt, may ensue.

The issue here is also that no matter how adept they are, or the revulsion or sympathy that they may have for the accused, it is the legal duty of the defence and prosecution lawyers to undertake their role to their full ability, within the realms of truth, to ensure justice is done, that the defendant has been correctly defended and that they have been correctly cross examined and that all facts are correctly presented in order to establish guilt or innocence. The 'sine qua non' of a jury is that it must be totally impartial in that the appearance of the perpetrator, or the evidence in hand, may not necessarily suggest things are as they may seem - the 'benevolent' nurse who deliberately injects the patients in their care with a lethal overdose of insulin, the 'punk' who is caught kneeling over a stabbing victim though who had actually come to their aid.

The question is what is the objective truth?

A jury can be the architect of an outrageous miscarriage of justice. They may have a prejudice in favour of or against the defendant based upon for example race, colour, dress code, gender, religion, whether they are rich or poor. A specific crime to them they may wrongly perceive as acceptable behaviour or even something to be applauded or something they would blatantly excuse. As discussed they may also be biased in accordance with the punishment and may find a guilty defendant innocent because they are in disagreement with the punishment.

It is the purpose of the jury to determine innocence or guilt based upon the evidence only and this is a moot point that are all members of a jury capable of undertaking this task without bias, if they cannot then they are unfit to undertake this role. As a juror and in the interests of justice we should be occupied with one question and one question only in that is the defendant guilty or is the defendant not guilty it is as simple as that.

Incarceration - The System of Salutary Intent Punishment

If we were to go back one hundred years or more then crime would always be met with stiff and sometimes cruel and disproportionate punishment. It is true that if someone is inadequately punished for what they have done they will not learn their lesson and might just go out and re-offend (the recidivist), and this axiom militates for a need for at least proportionate punishment as an effective deterrent i.e. punishment that fits the crime.

It is also true that a harsh punishment would mostly, as many criminals still have the ability to rationalize, make someone think twice about committing a crime, and particularly so where there is a perceived high chance of being caught, and if that was not true then at what point (length of sentence) would many of us consider breaking into a bank vault. Fortunately, not many of us would or would even contemplate such an act as mostly we are moral beings but some live in a grey area where if opportunity presents they will not think with any moral argument. Their view is, if they want it and the opportunity presents then they take it. Oddly they may even believe that they deserve to acquire it even by criminal methods – indeed what a strange world we live in where reason seems to have vacated the building. For someone who doesn't think, more specifically who doesn't think about the consequences, then they should be made to think.

Prison can be hard with some institutions a lot worse than others and some are absolute shitholes. Imagine this - you are locked up most of your day in a claustrophobic cell with grey walls and a small barred window, you cannot feel the warmth of the sun or even see the majesty of a tree (you never thought about these insignificant things but you will now), you have lost your liberty; you cannot go down the pub with your mates (who may be the ones who dropped you in this crap in the first place), you cannot be with your loved ones, you cannot take a walk in the park, you cannot go shopping, there is no question of a holiday, you will sleep, eat and crap in accordance with instruction and permission, you do as you are told and you do it when you are told to.

The food is rank, your fellow inmates are often not exactly the nicest people on the planet and will not in any way help to rehabilitate you from your criminal tendencies, some will be dangerous, some will bully you, some will, in the morning, throw a potty of cold piss over you just for fun. You will encounter crazies too who will stab you or beat you to death just for the way you look, a real nut job might try to strangle you just because you are chirpy or that you have a pretty girlfriend on the outside. You will encounter loneliness, indescribable boredom and depression and you will have plenty of time to lament over what you have done.

The whole place stinks of disinfectant, body odour, urine, 'exhaust' fumes and that trash you are expected to eat, you might get very unwanted attention from someone in the shower block who is looking for a 'friend' and won't take no for an answer, I will let you fill in the blanks. You may think that you are a tough hard nut, you find such graphic description of prison amusing, you think you could handle that – trust me you won't find it amusing when that door slams and your freedom has gone and you are certainly not as tough as you might wish to delude yourself, even the toughest can crack.

If you want to avoid this punishment and want to avoid ruining your life then the simple answer is - don't do the crime. If you really want to know the 'glory' of prison then read the autobiographical novels 'Papillon' by Henri Charrière from which the famous Steve McQueen film was based and 'Inside Alcatraz My Time On The Rock' by Jim Quillen and one to watch, one of my personal favourites, is the film 'The Shawshank Redemption'; so if you are thinking of a career in crime then I would seriously study all of these first and then decide.

Some institutions are so severe that what you are will be broken, you will be destroyed. If ever you thought to embark on a career of crime then maybe you should do some research first into what are the other opportunities that this career may offer; other than a flash car and money or maybe you get fifteen years in prison, is that sounding attractive to you? If you are not sure why not seek advice from a reformed ex-convict and then see if that is the career you want.

But there are always those who will speak with pride about their villainous prowess, it may be their only 'achievement' in a wasted life, they might exhibit a casual humour to their plight as if 'a four stretch (that's four years) in the Scrubs' is like some holiday to look forward to, 'Scrubs' being an 'affectionate' term for the grim Victorian built Wormwood Scrubs prison in London. They are the same idiots who spend most of their lives in jail and delude themselves of having some criminal 'celebrity' status, worth what but in actuality worth nothing other than a badge of a failed life, perhaps all because criminality is the only culture that they know or aspire to. Such types are hard and I mean hard but their lives are ruined and lost to a meaningless existence and without having undertaken a life of decent work they will retire with nothing and if they have anything left of their mind they would look back with regret.

To many of us we may think that prison is just too inhumane but so is crime. Within the administration of just law those who are in prison are there because they have done something bad. Every crime has a victim, some innocent person may have been mugged, raped, robbed or murdered, these are not by accident they are not innocent mistakes though some may look upon it as such and have some sympathy for the perpetrator.

Even if the crime is just theft or destruction of property, society, that's you and me, still has to pay for the loss. I may have sympathy for the broken life that may have led them to where they are but my sympathy evaporates once they have crossed that line and enacted a terrible deed upon another human being. If you cannot imagine this then imagine that you are the one being attacked by an individual who does not value what you are or care about how you feel, they seek your loss and suffering and their own gratification, they often have limited or no boundaries of decency and none of remorse.

If you can't get inside of their mind then get inside that of the victim and imagine that the victim is you, imagine your fears as you are being pursued down a dark barely lit alley on a desolate wet winter's night, you perceive threat, who follows is more powerful than you, panic builds in anticipation of what you now know without doubt as to what is to come, your assailant is now right behind you, you then feel the sharp thrust of a knife puncturing your flesh, you defend as best as you can but it's too late, more thrust of the knife, to the assailant all this may even seem to amuse, you feel the agony of the trauma, your life is now ebbing away and no-one is there who can give you any comfort in your last moments, you are just thrown into a ditch, discarded, to die alone whilst overcome with the abject sadness of the life you are losing and of knowing that those who are dear to you - you may never see again. If you feel that punishment for the criminal is inhumane then think again you or yours could be their next victim.

If we adopt soft sentencing, as in short prison terms or ironical 'five star hotels', we have not only lost sight of the suffering of the victim but we are also encouraging crime and handing out shorter sentences will result in an inevitably large prison population. Liberal thinking is that to reduce the prison population would be through reducing the tariff (the length of sentence), however this is a specious, naïve and a very myopic argument, all you do is just make crime more appealing.

The sympathy that the liberal minded idiot apologist spouts will be seen by the criminal as a weakness, they will secretly despise such fools who they will manipulate to their own ends, they will give the impression that they have been hard done by in life and are ever so reasonable, besides prisons are full of those who say that *"they didn't do it"* and some will believe them.

However, an important point here is the rehabilitation of the offender. Whilst punishment is part of the learning process we do not want to release someone into the outside world who has become hardened, dehumanized, embittered, who has lost all hope of a future and who has not been equipped with the understanding of what is right and what is wrong.

Some may argue that systems focused on rehabilitation without punishment are highly successful, but all things are not always equal and it is very possibly so that different cultures have somewhat different perceptions of the experience of incarceration, a more affluent or educated society might be more easily deterred and more amenable to reform, and some societies may experience different types of crime than others, some predisposed to petty crime some predisposed to violent crime.

This being said prison can be an opportunity to reform to turn someone into a model citizen and to make them want to be a model citizen and it can be done.

Convicts may be where they are because they lacked the right guidance in childhood, were neglected or abused, have somehow drifted into the wrong company or have psychiatric issues. Some unfortunately are just plain evil and beyond ever being reformed and we have to accept that fact too and deal with that as needs be.

Our prison population may have always been high, and in the distant past even so with harsh sentencing, but this was not because the deterrent did not work, it was because so many lived in severe poverty or destitution such that many would risk such punishment just to feed their family. In modern society many of us do not face this problem and so crime is usually precipitated through greed, often precipitated through living in societies with manifest contrasting standards of living (note though that poverty itself does not precipitate crime given the existence of near on crime free but poor countries), idleness, delinquency often expressed in theft, spurious destruction or through a desire to control others.

If we were to consider the issue of prison population in a relatively affluent society, poorer societies may be quite different, then it is clear that at some point the aggregate of those who are convicted (where we also need to consider the attraction to re-offend) x the average length of sentence must follow some form of curve, a formula, where the prison population will be low for harsh though high for soft sentencing. The reasoning behind this is that in an affluent society harsh sentences would most probably stop almost all crime in its tracks except for a few who don't seem to care about the consequences of offending.

We may also consider that where there is no punishment or having capital punishment for all crimes, whatever they may be, then our prisons would be empty but this proposition is unworkable as we shall see later and the effect on crime statistics would be a moot point. It is also a moot point as to the comparative costs of different systems and as to where the optimum point is, all of which leads us thinking towards a middle path, given also that not only the sentence but also the crime, and its investigation, that costs society dearly.

In the ideal world, as near as can be, you would have a low prison population but you would also have a low crime rate so what is needed is an alternative solution where a sentence is sufficiently long and harsh to deter future crime, and therefore its ensuing cost, and to appropriately punish but that also can succeed in rehabilitation, hence a middle path approach. In other words we should aim to totally wipe out crime and do so at the least cost. This may seem obvious to all but sentencing is often based upon political ideology rather than being honest and realistic about what needs to be done and so hence woefully fails to deter. Furthermore, the political class will choose for us to accept crime as part of our life experience without any will or wit to do anything about it.

We should never resign ourselves to accepting what is unacceptable. All crime should be met with action, not endless discussion and trite stock condemnation. The litmus test in this respect is that are our leaders prepared to face what the truth is rather than pretend it is something else and will they have the courage to act decisively, if they don't then they are sleepwalking us all into inevitable trouble. These thoughts lead us to wonder if the policy of sentencing should be determined exclusively by professionals who are on the front line of fighting crime, often with their own lives in peril, but not by politicians who often can't seem to get their heads out of politics and into the world of reality.

Through history we have adopted different models none of which worked too well and the essence is really that to reform a human being into what is acceptable and to give them some chance of success after they are released then they must first accept their responsibility and be made to regret what they have done, the tables would have turned and they will feel the victim and only then is there really any chance of rehabilitation with genuine not fake remorse, remorse that can also be validated, otherwise if it can't then it is worthless.

To empathize with the victim you must first have at least some idea of how the victim feels through the experience of being a victim. But as the criminal remember that just as you would want someone stopped from doing something bad to you then you must also be stopped from doing something bad to others. On this basis would it not be a more enlightened system to have two stages of a punishment whereby we address the issue of responsibility and regret through harsh prison for all crimes and then at the appropriate point in the sentence transfer the prisoner to a different type of institution with the objective to not only contain but also to rehabilitate. Would this not be a better system? Some might say that we already have this system in place but do the punishment and rehabilitation elements adequately suffice in what they are supposed to be doing?

This all being said possibly the best way to fight crime is through prevention, *"prevention is better than cure"* as we say, so as a society we should recognize criminal tendencies in our young and deal with it in its incipient stages. This perspective of incipient resolution is of critical importance and not just in crime but also in everything we do.

Where it is indicative of behaviour in school, where there is emergence of anti-social behaviour or where sociological patterns in failing families present, perhaps as a result of parenting without instilling rules and responsibilities or that inflicts neglect or abuse, then we as a society need to deal with it then, not later. It may cost us to do so but isn't this better and more cost effective than locking someone up for 5, 10, 20 years and at least we could have another individual who becomes an asset to contribute to society and themselves rather than being a burden plus we would have rescued someone from their own irresponsibility to themselves and to others.

Administering Punishment Proportional to the Crime

In the last section we explored the idea of punishment versus rehabilitation. However, as punishment needs to be proportionate it must also be perceptively proportional to the seriousness of the crime in as much as that the perpetrator doesn't have any perceivable incentive to escalate what has been committed but furthermore is deterred from committing crime in the first place. Now that might be a mouthful so let's examine what this means. If we go back to the idea that harsh punishment for all crimes, such as execution, may for example; for someone 'lifting' a can of bake beans from the local grocery store, encourages them to escalate the crime to murdering the cashier knowing that for the lesser crime he will be executed, though he could, in theory, reduce his chances of being apprehended by killing the cashier for which the punishment is no different. On this basis the likely criminal must be made to see that by escalating a crime that there is a significant contrast of punishment and therefore incentive for him to not make matters worse for himself or for the victim.

Now this is quite a vexing problem in that how do you calibrate the sentence for different levels of crime to provide this incentive but as not to undermine the law in as much as then making the sentence an incentive to commit the lesser crime in the first place.

The question here is how do we pitch the sentence and should we, or how should we, tailor it to the individual as not all are equally receptive? Clearly society must arrive at a place where crime can be eradicated where sentencing can deter but also be proportionate i.e. the sentence matching the crime. Given those of criminal intent will know that when they are caught, and they will be caught, that they will suffer the same fate as their victim and so this should include capital punishment (execution) for murder, that can be proved beyond any shadow of doubt, and this is particularly so with child murderers and those who inflict appalling suffering upon the poor victim.

Is there any reason why someone should be spared the same fate as what they have inflicted upon an innocent victim, the victim didn't deserve what they suffered but the criminal had a choice so should be less deserving. With the capital punishment dimension added to the mix this immediately provides much greater latitude to the effective prevention of crime. Basically they would know that if they kill (but not in self-defence), as in murder (or as in the deliberate engineering of circumstances for fatal consequent self-defence), that they will be killed then certainly this would give them something to think about and would hopefully dissuade them from committing the crime in the first place.

We must also recognize that many victims of the lesser charge of attempted murder were not murder victims by virtue of some self-restraint of the assailant but only by virtue of the capabilities of modern medical science to save life, thereby murder statistics would otherwise be much higher. Some will no doubt argue that some societies with capital punishment may have high murder rates, therefore capital punishment doesn't work, but that is a very simplistic view since there are other contributing factors as to why murder may be prevalent in certain societies and it would be interesting to see what would happen if those societies were to abandon execution - more murder perhaps but very unlikely less, but who must die as the victim for the sake of a liberal experiment. Whatever the society the fledgling murderer will have something else to think about if he/she knows that his/her own life can also be taken. And to those who see capital punishment as distasteful then you may be surprised as to how little it would need to be enforced if it did indeed exist.

Realization and Rehabilitation

Though the punishment of prison is a necessity as a deterrent I would rather see no-one in prison as prison is a repository of failed lives and is furthermore a reflection of a failed society though failed because of the failure of individuals within and the inability of the system to thwart such actions, the not so irretrievably failing life has crossed the line to the point of no return. What was the planning or intent of committing the crime (the 'mens rea' – the guilty mind), has morphed into committing the criminal act (the 'actus reus' – the guilty act) at this point where 'mens rea' and 'actus reus' (or its 'transference of malice' to an unintended victim) is proven then a crime, by legal definition, has therefore been committed.

Not everyone in the human race is equal, some have standards or even cultural associated attributes that are well below that which is acceptable from any perspective of decency and to them what they do may seem perfectly normal and to some it may seem perfectly normal to take an innocent human life *"I can do what I like and I do not care anything of the victim."* We may try to excuse these actions for various reasons but the issue is that the obdurate criminal mind does not have a moral frame of reference, there are no limits no boundaries no guidelines, what matters to them is themselves. Some will be psychopaths and beyond reach though others may have some chance to rehabilitate, to recognize what they have done, to take responsibility for their actions, to lament on the suffering of the victim and the desire to change their life for the good.

So how do we rehabilitate someone who possibly has had no guidance on what is right or wrong, who over reacts to everything, who never stops to think of the consequences of their actions to them or to others, who lacks self-control in that a single punch, from a mind seized by anger, can lead to a life in prison a life full of regrets, or who are easily seduced by the evil manipulation of others, who do not understand that if you don't put anything into life then life will give you nothing back, who may have themselves experienced serious abuse.

What is the life story of this person to have brought them to this place? This does not detract from what they have done, many may seek what they see as an easier life, a route to their desires without having to work, in as much that others would have had to do the work for them, work that they won't do.

If you are the subject of this topic then you can either carry on as you are or you can reform, reform is your only salvation, it's your choice. You have the power in your hands to change your life, to turn your life around. Your destiny is with you. Stop blaming others and have the courage to start accepting your punishment and responsibility, and for once blame yourself for where you are, turn your back on crime – find a better way to live. Make your life count don't f*** it up, it may be the only life that you will ever have.

If you are currently 'doing time' give some thought to using your time wisely and avoid boredom; you can learn skills to help you back into the labour market upon your release, maybe even learn to play a musical instrument or learn a language, playing chess is also a useful activity as you will also then see the fun of rules, you may even find God but do something don't just sit on your bum for years doing nothing, even time in prison can be put to good use. Indeed one wonders if acquiring such skills, that will help to detract from criminal behaviour, should contribute to any consideration for early release. However, good behaviour should not be motivated on the basis of a desire for early release it should be motivated on a basis of the desire to become a better person. Good behaviour should not be used for self-gain it should be used for doing what is right.

If you are genuinely seeking to reform and have remorse for what you have done I do hope that these thoughts will give you some ideas, perhaps some direction for the good and so help reform you into a better human being and give you better chances for your future rather than just returning to prison and a wasted life. Change your life for the good make it happen.

However, if that doesn't 'cut any ice' with you then think of this, think of what you are doing to the victim, imagine someone doing to you and yours as equal to what you are inflicting upon another, just think. Imagine that it is you hit by that speeding car, stabbed or beaten up, the consequences of which you may be confined to a wheelchair for the rest of your life, your life being ruined just think how does that feel, did you really deserve that does any victim. Just imagine that you, an innocent person, were targeted for no reason other than some stupid act of amusement or greed. Just think before you do anything, think about the consequences always. Think first before you do anything that is foolish.

Chapter 19

JUST HOW PROBABLE IS OUR EXISTENCE?

(In search of the absolute)

I once heard that to find happiness that you need good friends, a skill that you can enjoy (e.g. dancing or music) and you need a faith or at least some sense of purposeful meaning to your existence. But what of faith is it real, could God really exist. Theistic religion of course says 'yes' and the theory of evolution would of course say 'no'. In reality we cannot categorically prove either, although many will claim otherwise, but let's at least consider the enormity of the difficulty of ever knowing for sure.

"Chance is a word void of sense; nothing can exist without a cause." – François-Marie Arouet, 'Voltaire' (Writer, France 18th century)

Evolutionary Theory

Science postulates that anywhere in the universe where there are the right conditions, where there is water and where basic organic chemicals are on tap then the building blocks of life are in place and evolutionary theory would suggest therefore that there is also a good chance for the existence of life. The materials to build us, i.e. the molecules from which we are made, are constructed from the atoms that our sun has given birth to. Thus every atom from which we are built has been manufactured from within the hellish world of a thermonuclear furnace with a core temperature of 15 million ^{O}C (Gold melts at just around 1000 ^{O}C), much as we would find within a hydrogen bomb explosion. Scientific reason would rightly suggest that, chemistry will combine atoms to form molecules and then onto more complex molecules from the ensuing chemical reactions.

Given time these reactions will form further complex molecules that, when present in the right conditions, so goes the theory, can form cell membranes, cell nuclei and the required support structures within, that would then progress to more advanced multicellular and heterogeneous organisms like you and me. (The biological detail of the design of a living cell is beyond the scope and intention of this book as our discussion here is in the evaluation of the possibility of life rather than exactly how life functions.).

The interminable debate that has troubled thinking minds for some time is that; in the theory of creation this all happens under the control of a higher being/s in that life was designed whereas the theory of evolution points to all of this development first coming about by chance formation of the requisite chemical precursors and then at some point jumping to a basic lifeform from which higher environmentally optimised and dominant lifeforms can evolve by presentation of adaptions, through available or progressing mutation, to survive the environment to which they are subjected to, what is referred to as 'natural selection'.

There is very good evidence and reason to concur with the theory of evolution to some extent on the bit about later evolution where natural history museums will attest to this fact, but the jump from chemistry to basic life is a gigantic leap indeed and something rather difficult to imagine just how, since life is not just chemistry it is also structure beyond anything chemistry can develop. Chemistry can enable the growth of large but simple crystal structures but cannot form complex shapes such as an eye and this is where evolutionary biology step in. The question is; how did even basic life and then complex biological structures come to be, given that nature lends itself to entropy and chaos.

At the core of the cell's existence is the DNA (deoxyribose nucleic acid) molecule which presents the code for a lifeform for its shape, size, structure, function etc. and has amazing replicating capability to enable the cell to divide and thereby produce offspring. It is our DNA that therefore defines biologically what we are and from which you could build a copy a clone. The structure of any lifeform, animal and vegetable, is based upon instructions encoded within separate strands of DNA (chromosomes, of which us humans have 23 pairs) with its molecular signature, and therefore code, within each DNA strand, being specific to the lifeform it creates. Errors in the code could result in a different form of life, potentially even quite strange lifeforms that we cannot even imagine, though invariably would lead to biological failure that would be unable to survive, albeit there is some latitude in departure from perfect code.

At this point we now need to digress - we humans in our quest for improving our life experience, and understanding, are forever indebted to much of the scientific community, for it is through their research and toil, often without proportionate reward or recognition, that we have everything we need to sustain us, from the production of the food we eat to drugs to defeat otherwise intractable diseases. When you think of the word 'hero' and you are not thinking of a member of our armed forces, emergency services, those who undertake arduous and dangerous work and those public spirited citizens, do not think of a footballer (!!) think of a scientist, for without science you and I would be living in the dark ages, our lives ravaged by poverty, lack of opportunity and disease. Four such scientists I wish to mention here, as it is because of them, their efforts and their ingenuity, that the mysteries of the DNA molecule were revealed (in 1953). So let's just pause a moment and remember those true hero's - James Watson and Francis Crick (Cambridge) and Rosalind Franklin and Maurice Wilkins (London). Their names and discoveries are indelibly etched for eternity and their research has laid the foundations to greater discoveries many of which are yet to come.

Getting back to our discourse - Along the length of the DNA molecule the instruction code is represented using chemicals called 'nucleotide bases' of which there are just four such chemicals (options) available namely; **A**denine, **C**ytosine, **G**uanine and **T**hymine. A code, or should we say the build instructions, to enable the lifeform to come into existence would therefore look like a story written with just four letters (i.e. **A**, **C**, **G** and **T**). It would be as if our 26 letter (English) alphabet was reduced to just four letters for us to communicate with.

However, such is the wonder of the scale at the molecular level is that just one gram of DNA can store as much information as 70 billion (4Gbyte) CDs (that's around 150 billion tonnes of paper) and that the build instructions for the entire human race could be stored in the equivalent volume of just thirty grains of sugar.

Over time the DNA molecule will mutate by apparent random changes since DNA doesn't have any intelligence in as much that it does not know what is good code neither does it know what is bad code. If we bring to mind that the difference of code between our specific DNA to that of a pig is only 5% (grass has 15% DNA in common with us humans), shocking as that may seem pigs and even grass as are all lifeforms are our biological cousins (ergo same origin or manufacturer), then on this basis a slight alteration in code, a mutation, would most probably have dramatic consequence that would then mostly, but rarely not, render a biological function defective.

Significant change therefore to the DNA molecule on its path to form a new lifeform is probably going to compromise functions that have been refined over time given that it will need to run the gauntlet of iterative mutations on its journey to finally produce a new but different fully functioning lifeform.

Therefore, we may successfully hit upon the correct code along the length of the DNA molecule for a certain type of, let's say, liver cell (function – chemical maintenance) but then we still have to wait to refine the code that creates successful bone cells (function – mostly but not limited to mechanical as in support, protection, anchorage and movement) at another site on the DNA. The problem is that when, through some iterative mutations of the bone cell coded part of the DNA, we strike lucky it is also possible that the liver cell code has also, through the same period of time, slightly mutated but mutated enough into a code that is now a catastrophic failure and cannot therefore generate healthy liver cells. To form even the most basic forms of life is indeed a fantastic miracle. But just how amazing is this miracle?

We might assume that good code, when encountered, locks and from then on is immutable though this would require intelligence or that the DNA is no longer subjected to any further mutations where defective code would also be locked. This thinking defeats natural selection in that albeit the survivors survive the continuance of mutation over time precipitates later failure. Agreed that the ones suited best to the environment survive and the ones unsuited die off but how did we ever get to the right code of the basic survivor in the first place, it didn't develop it existed in some incipient form along with the less able to survive but just was unique in its survival ability to the specified environment.

The Amazing and Improbable Miracle of Life

If we wanted to know just how amazing and probable, or has it happens improbable, life is then we would need to undertake some mathematical analysis that is a digression from the main purpose of this book but yet that nevertheless demands inclusion to support my conclusions here. For this reason, and for those who are otherwise curious, I have included an appendix (II) that outlines the mathematical theory and its results and for which I have made a gross assumption in favour of the natural existence of life (i.e. evolution) that all matter in our universe is DNA which it clearly is not and what is concluded is that:

1. The most sophisticated lifeform that could be guaranteed to exist in the lifetime of our universe, through random coding of DNA, would have a genome code of no longer than 155 nucleotides. This compares with 14,000 for the flu virus and 120 million critical nucleotides for us humans. It is very unlikely that such simple DNA of a length of just 155 nucleotides could even yield the most basic of organisms from which natural selection could then get to work.
2. To create human lifeform through random coding of DNA would require $10^{72,000,000}$ universes like ours or our universe repeated this number of times.

We need to pause for a moment to let the size of this number sink in in that generic, not individualised, human DNA requires 1 followed by 72 million zeros of our universe's to evolve. To visualize this further then imagine that this would be a number some 160 miles (250 kms) long if you were to write it down. Or to put it another way; just imagine repeating the word 'million' 12 million times and to do this would take about one month, day and night without stopping. Now that is nothing but staggering!

The conclusion from this is that the existence of life would seem impossible and that the odds are not just very bad they are unimaginably bad.

However, before we run off with the idea that evolution is almost completely impossible we need to revisit 'natural selection'. Natural selection is not that only the human being variety is open to possibility, as we have just discussed, but that a myriad of other possible and biologically successful lifeforms could occur, one of which could be what we, you and I that is, exist as, as you read this book and as I write it.

These lifeforms could be stepping stones along the path to the human form (or another) each of which, where offspring that are not rejected can advance onto greater things, has much greater probability of success than a presumed single leap from chemical to human but that instead is just in many steps. However, these discrete steps are not so easily defined or revealed, we just have enough information that is tantalisingly seductive to the idea of a universe bereft of a need for God but not entirely conclusive of such we also don't know what are all of the combinations of fatal code and what are not.

To calculate the massively enhanced probability of a step by step process is nigh on impossible, other than a best but possibly poor guess, without having some idea of what all of the steps are and what amount of code change is relevant in each step. This being said let us not forget the dearth of DNA and the hostile environment of our universe, so the odds of life remain poor indeed.

We clearly recognise that a species through mutation can adapt to its environment but what invokes that mutation or should I say what if that environmentally adapted mutation never happened in essence the species would face extinction and as we know many have and we also must remind ourselves that as random mutation that brings about variants that can survive then simultaneous random mutations elsewhere are in detriment to survival. Thus it is not the environment that brings about a mutation event it is the mutation event that brings about adaptation to the environment if that is it is your lucky day.

There is no systematic way how the environment can instruct DNA to change, mutation occurs randomly one of which will suit the environment and the one that does so will eventually dominate the population of the species within that environment. Do we know what is next for us will we mutate into a higher species of human or is it extinction that awaits us.

The Possibility of Life

As just discussed it is of course possible that you and I, by chance, could exist as a different lifeform to that of human and potentially there are a myriad of possible codes that could make us into such lifeforms, that are functionally successful and each of which possesses our level of intellect, emotions and awareness. However, in our calculation of probability we have been very magnanimous in our assumption that <u>all</u> matter in our universe is in the form of DNA where in reality the amount of DNA would be proportionately very tiny indeed, it is negligible here on planet earth let alone in the universe, and on this basis life like us in any form remains very 'very' improbable.

It could be argued that we are not fully accounting for evolution where successful lifeforms form fully and then progress onto something completely different, a different species, and not always just some environmental adaptation. So it cannot be true that the bits of the DNA that have achieved a successful code, to change the organism to a completely different species, then do not change, since if the imperfect parts of the DNA change then so must the perfected parts present significant probability of change too as we have already alluded to.

This all raises the point that life must be pretty much impossible, indeed infinitesimally so, and in the context of evolution we have therefore six possibilities to answer this question: 1. our universe is much larger than what we can imagine, 2. there are almost an infinite number of universes, 3. the universe has gone through an almost infinite number of reincarnations i.e. an infinite number of 'big bangs', 4. time repeats in a loop!!!, 5. there are hidden parallel universes to our own that follow different rules but in some way may/may not interact with us!!!, 6. that we are within something else again with different rules!!! Or could there be another possibility where there is a combination of those six possible outcomes or is it that we are just damned lucky.

Some in the scientific community describe life as being just 'beautiful', is that it just 'beautiful', where's the passion, for me, as an engineer with design experience and that of failure too along the way, that does sound a tad understated or rather dismissive, of evolution or creation, whichever you may decide upon, and I would have thought that an expression such as 'it is mind bogglingly f***ing awesome' is more appropriate, what it does for me is that I feel humbled beyond how words could describe.

But as a digression let's just put the scale of our universe into some perspective: our planet Earth is very small indeed, our own sun is around 100 x the diameter of our planet, our galaxy, the milky way, consists of over 300 billion stars some of which are like our sun and some are quite enormous for example the star Antares is about

800 x the diameter of our sun, our known universe contains around 100 billion galaxies. Our next nearest star would take 4 years to travel to at the speed of light that is at a speed of 186,000 miles per second. This is staggering indeed and what of other universes?

If the vastness of space and time is just so inconceivably immense such that anything can happen including the near impossible existence of intelligent life (us) then the concept of a creator, what we might refer to as God, is not beyond the realms of possibility either. You may postulate that faced with infinite time and infinite material that anything, imaginable or that which cannot be imagined, is also not beyond the realms of possibility perhaps even a life after death. Just as faith may be subjective, then in minds that are not devoid of bias, none of us are; then what we may believe to be reason may also be equally subjective. Anything may therefore be possible including the miraculous.

If we can believe in the theory of evolution with such infinitesimally low probability then we can equally believe in the theory of the existence of a creator. Far-fetched as it may seem but could it even be that given the nigh on impossibility of our existence that if there is a creator then could this creator exist in a dimension where evolution of intelligent life is realistically possible i.e. the material to evolve is not sparse as it is in our space dimension, may not even be anything like DNA, but is in huge abundance, here perhaps there is realistic chance for a creator/s to evolve and to then design us.

These conclusions sound pretty amazing and then we need to look at the survivors. Those that do survive will in some cases have improvements and advancements to their function, they will dominate over their siblings who are less improved or advanced as they will be faster, fitter, better equipped and more resilient. However, those that do survive will endure further mutations over time and again many will fall victim to bad mutation and some to good mutation, and again those that do prosper will go on to the detriment of those that fail.

What is good and bad is defined by what environment and what other challenges that the lifeform is subjected to. Therefore the same lifeform will be selected by how fit it is, or how it fits, for a particular environment. Those who are most suited to a certain environment will thrive and others, of the same species, less so, but change the environment and those at the back of the race with what is now the more suited characteristics can get to the front and so the tables are turned.

Now over time the single cell organism equipped with the most basic functions will start to form more complex multicellular organisms, for example a human being is made up from around 100 trillion cells from over 200 distinct types. However, these organisms have substantial complexity and heterogeneity to their construction and furthermore they have order. For example, why are our eyes in our head and not in our backside! I won't mention teeth and will leave that to your imagination, just imagine table etiquette! Maybe it is the same process as that from the natural selection of those with the best ability to survive; disgusting eating habits, pardon, and you will be ejected from that posh restaurant and won't get to eat, starvation may ensue and you are then no more. Seriously though, in our, just mentioned though not implausible example, therefore if we are sitting down eating lunch our eyes would not be able to see an approaching predator, so let's hope we have a great sense of hearing.

How is it then that this amorphous blob of cellular matter can develop highly complex heterogeneous ordered structures whilst it is undergoing cell division? How is this coded onto DNA and how does it command this structural order? We can imagine that cell division may experience other influences such as geotropism and phototropism such that a tree's roots are always in the ground and its branches head for the sky but that that a tree's shape is essentially somewhat random; one is totally different from another without having a fixed number or length of its branches or roots. This would be analogous to us humans in not just having different features but that we would alarmingly have more than two legs or two eyes and that may also be dimensionally quite different, although human mutation can sometimes yield a condition where we have other than five digits on a hand or foot (medically referred to as Polydactyly) and it is alleged that the second, though very unfortunate, wife of King Henry VIII, Anne Boleyn, had six fingers on one hand.

This also alludes to the architectural magnificence of the human form and if we were to look at the face, the hand or the foot they have very complex styling that would be some challenge for mathematicians to derive a formula and this alone is baffling in how cellular division can sculpt (as in intelligent aesthetic precipitation) such structures. Some may argue that chemical gradients in the developing foetus are at work but chemical gradients, notwithstanding gene activation, do not account for sudden and abrupt discontinuities where one structure suddenly becomes something else such as where bone is juxtaposed to muscle or where the gall bladder is juxtaposed to the liver but within the context of its three dimensional hyper-complexity/morphology. This change is not so much a gradient but it is a biological cliff face but how was it that it happened and exactly where it happened in the complex topography of the organism is a mystery.

How did these complex and different but symbiotic structures form can we explain this process in exacting rather than vague terms. Research into chemical activation (switches) may explain some of this but it looks doubtful that it will ever be able to explain all of it.

To further illustrate this point on structure, if we now look within for example the heart - it is a complex design of chambers (atriums and ventricles) and (bicuspid and tricuspid) non-return valves complete with an electrical initiator (the sinoatrial node) that enables de-oxygenated blood to be received from the venous system via the vena cava, our main vein, from where it is pumped to the lungs via the pulmonary artery, where carbon dioxide is exchanged for oxygen and then returned to the heart, via the pulmonary vein, where it is then distributed, via the aorta, to the 50,000 miles of blood vessels around the body. Not only that but it must undertake this process 2.5 billion times in our lifetime, pumping in all around 200,000 tonnes of blood (about the size of an oil tanker) and this is an organ not much larger than the size of your fist.

To add to this, our circulation system must accommodate different plumbing when we are a foetus in that our blood is oxygenated not by our lungs but through the placenta by virtue of a series of shunts being a hole (foramen) in the atrial-ventricular septum (wall) running down the centre line of our heart as well as a duct, the 'ductus arteriosus', both of which must close at the moment, the shock, of birth to transfer the respiratory process to our own lungs. Coupled with its function is its reliability that would impress any engineer in that it must perform, without mechanical failure, for not far off 1 million hours of operational life and do so without being serviced, so how does that compare to your car.

Like all things in life it is designed not beyond what its utility demands but is just the right size to pump at the right flow rate and the right pressure and will increase its output when required to do so.

I, like 10% of the population, suffer from a condition called Tinnitus. For me it is more of a nuisance than an ailment and I can never experience or enjoy silence. Unless my mind is distracted, usually from other background noise, I hear a hum in my head, always. Sometimes it's not so bad, sometimes it drives me nuts. As in all things you get used to it and the more attention you pay to it the more you hear it – well that's my experience of it.

Some can be less lucky with it and it can be just quite a bit more than a nuisance. But what is fascinating about this condition is something that I picked up during a seminar. Imagine this - you are in a pub having a pint, or a glass of wine, it's packed and everyone is in full blown chatter mode. You are right in the middle of this melee but yet you don't have too much trouble conversing with the person standing next to you, but why?

This is one of the clever things that the brain will do in that it will automatically filter unwanted noise but how does it determine what is and what is not wanted without the engagement of conscious thought – we don't stand there monitoring a myriad of different voice tones and one by one selectively decide *"oh I will ignore that one and that one"* but then only listen to the voices that we wish to. The brain will do this automatically. The problem specifically with Tinnitus is that the brain is unable to filter noise that is erroneously generated in the ear as a result of damage or ageing.

What is clever about this mechanism is that this automatic filter is also attuned to danger. If within the pub a tiger came through the door and it was lunch time you might subconsciously hear something not quite right and the brain will automatically channel the noise to the conscious part of the brain to alert you to danger. One would hope that you would run before thinking of finishing your drink – evolution might suggest that the alcoholic has then less chance of survival and not just for the damage to their liver. In effect in the evolutionary world full of pubs and tigers we would gradually lose the taste for alcohol.

So how do such structures, along with many others, develop from an amorphous blob of material into a machine of unfathomable complexity and elegance and this is something that still eludes scientists to anywhere near to approaching a satisfactory explanation though some might like to think otherwise.

Chapter 20

SHOULD WE REALLY WORRY ABOUT DEATH?

(We are more amazing than what we can possibly imagine)

Any student of classics can tell you that the life of a Roman legionnaire was not exactly soft; often heavily outnumbered in battle death must have been at the forefront of their minds but to them death was not something to be feared but something to be faced with courage. Is there a lesson in there for us, should we also add to this the properties of trust, hope, faith and wonder.

We have already established that the odds for the existence of life are looking pretty bleak but now it's about to get a lot worse.

Cosmological Implications in the Search for Life

In the last chapter we had made a very wild assumption that all of the matter in the universe is in the form of nucleotides, the building blocks of DNA, and therefore is available for the creation of life. We have assumed that for every hydrogen atom (of which 70% of the universe is comprised of), of atomic mass of 1 (i.e. a single proton), has been replaced by a DNA nucleotide of atomic mass of around 350. On this basis we are very much massaging the maths in favour of evolution.

However, there is something else that is of fundamental importance is that just where can life exist. Life as we know it, and we certainly have a lot of variety of it on our small planet, has a very narrow range of conditions within which it can survive. The conditions of temperature, atmospheric chemistry and pressure, gravitation, radiation and availability of water are critical. Unfortunately for life the universe is exceedingly hostile. Most of the atomic matter is buried within stars, such as our sun, a thermonuclear furnace with such high temperature, pressure, radiation and gravitation field that life could not survive. Black holes, postulated to exist at the centre of galaxies, have such enormous gravitational field that a person 6ft in height would be crushed to within 0.02mm.

There is a vast quantity of planets out there beyond our solar system but invariably life would have close to no chance, it would either be incinerated or frozen, crushed by a high gravitational field or atmospheric pressure, dissolved in acidic rain or volcanic larva, asphyxiated in a toxic or too thin an atmosphere, poisoned by ozone produced from violent weather conditions, destroyed by radiation, would have no means of adequate sustenance or would lack sufficient sunlight for vegetation to exist (an essential requirement at the bottom of the food chain).

We can further add to our consideration that not all universes are as ours and thus follow the same laws of physics and would therefore most probably be hostile or unable to support life, at least as we know it, or even to have allowed life to come into being. If we imagine that the big bang essentially spewed either atomic matter as we know it, or the precursors to atomic matter, from which we are made, and that along with this were the various constants and properties in physics to ensure harmony, that it is possible that the big bang could have done the other thing and produced something quite different or even weird within which life would be inconceivable or perhaps even where DNA, or some alternative, was so abundant that evolution theory would become a far more obvious conclusion.

Our planet is very special indeed and, other than the obvious, our planet's atmospheric oxygen concentration (i.e. 21%, most of the rest being nitrogen) is about right, too low (< 17%) and our mental and physical capabilities would be seriously impaired and eventually we would die and too high (> 24%) and our blood would become acidic also eventually resulting in death.

Atmospheric concentration of carbon dioxide is about 0.04% but increasing this to 3% and we are already in trouble, at 10% we are in deep trouble (you might need to buy a harp). If our ozone layer is too thick then we would receive insufficient ultraviolet light for us to produce the essential vitamin D, too thin and we would all die of skin cancer. Our magnetic field shields us from the intense nuclear radiation emanating from the sun and without this shield we would also die.

Given the exceedingly poor odds of life one wonders why scientists bother to search for extra-terrestrial life, it would almost be like betting on a dead horse.

Engineering Design Considerations in Biology (to design greater complexity always requires greater intelligence)

We switch on the television, make a phone call, make a cup of tea, fill up our car with petrol, take a flight for that well deserved holiday in the sun, when it's cold we turn up the central heating and we go and get that MRI scan to find out what that lump is under our armpit but do we stop and think how these things come about. We live in a world of technology and everything technological depends on the profession of engineering. Engineers design power stations, electronic equipment, aeroplanes and that scanner that you might have encountered at the hospital. Engineers are not those who, essential as they are, might rewire your house or fix the guttering. The world of engineering is something quite different, unknown, hidden and mysterious and is largely quite esoteric.

Engineers study physics and mathematics, and some branches of engineering also require a command of chemistry. The demarcation between engineering and science is very elusive as engineers also undertake scientific research and scientists do also work in engineering. A simple way to discern one from the other is that engineering design is made possible through scientific research and in the adoption of scientific laws. In the example of a power station engineers have to acquire intimate knowledge of thermal plant design, thermodynamics, fluid mechanics and stress analysis, nuclear reactor physics, combustion chemistry, electromagnetism, electronics and myriad of other scientific subjects. However, in any of those fields there is something quite remote from the understanding of biology.

Biology involves the understanding of biological function and its support chemistry. Biologists cannot design or construct any original biological organism although they can modify something that already exists and indeed this is very clever in itself. Conversely engineers are not equipped with any extensive understanding of the human body, or other biological organisms, without which an engineer just cannot perceive how difficult it is to design. To really get to the understanding of the difficulty in explaining life requires experience of engineering design and knowledge of biological function, so in this sense engineering and biology cannot have mutual exclusivity.

However, few of us really understand what engineering involves in that we see design from a perspective of shape and style but we do not see what really is going on in the detail as often the detail is impossible to see. We effectively mentally consign engineering to an assembly of disparate components; we perceive design though we are totally unfamiliar of the science within. What is not fully realised is that engineers don't just design something they have to know how to design it for maximum efficiency and compatibility and this requires the use of mathematics and physics, and in some cases this can get very difficult indeed.

Essentially the more complex something is and the more complex of what is within the greater the degree of intelligent design and thus intelligent thinking is required for it to come to exist.

If we consider something that we can all relate to then if you were to design the wing of an aircraft to be too thin then there would be insufficient lift delivered, too thick and there is too much profile drag and also flow separation. However, where is the right design point and how is it calculated. This is a subject an aeronautical engineer could write an entire book on though you might end up with a thumping headache reading it so next time you sit on an aeroplane just have a thought for the design of the wings, or the engines, and how was the design determined to enable the aeroplane to travel the furthest distance on the least amount of fuel and ensuring that the wings are strong enough to handle the load.

These components have exact mathematical shapes and dimension, determined through complex mathematical analysis, departure from which will be in detriment to production cost, aerodynamics, structural integrity, stability, safety and fuel efficiency. Without understanding the science and the right application of mathematics the aeroplane would most probably never fly and if it did it would be dangerous and inefficient.

We do not know everything of science so engineers progress designs based on the limitations of our scientific understanding as it is now, we still have new laws and new materials to discover so in this sense engineering is not perfect. For example, the very latest aircraft designs use new found techniques of manufacture and application in the use of materials such as carbon-fibre and plastics that circumvent the need for heavier materials such as aluminium and titanium in fuselage and wing construction.

On this basis we have lightened the load and the aircraft can fly the same distance though using less fuel. It is not that we have made mistakes in the past as we have optimized the design as best as we can with what we knew then and with the materials as were available to us – it is just that with time we discover more and we can then apply this thinking to even better ideas and better designs, in essence engineering designs evolve, they continually improve by refining previously acquired knowledge.

If we look at biology, its design is fantastic, beyond what words can describe, making engineering designs look positively primitive in comparison, however life is not absolutely perfect as perhaps a visual zoom function would render us less vulnerable to predators, our vascular system has what appears to be extraneous collateral circulation though possible deliberate in-built redundant architecture (ref. John Hunter, 18th century surgeon in the treatment of popliteal aneurisms) and we still remain vulnerable to disease and ageing.

If there is a creator maybe we should be less harsh in our criticism of Him/Her since as an engineer our creator may still need more time to learn and to perfect. After all the Wright brothers built the world's first aeroplane in 1903, they did not wait until they had perfected it to the level of Concorde, otherwise we might all still be waiting. The answer is; if you get a great idea, don't obsess on absolute perfection just get it into production at the earliest opportunity where it is adequately perfected for purpose – wouldn't this equally apply to creation of life just as it would to manufacturing aeroplanes. This does not suggest a lack of perfection in a creator though illustrates that all things take time and to achieve absolute perfection takes infinite time.

Was Life Engineered – The Theory of Creation

In our limited intelligence we can only think of one other possible reason for life in that if it didn't evolve was it created, therefore is there a creator. In that statement we have to realize that we are limited and maybe we do not have authoritative intellectual capacity and qualification to decide either way, and that goes for the evolutionary biologist, engineer, theologian or philosopher. In addition to this maybe there are other reasons why life came into existence. Although that statement might sound a bit like a fruitcake talking then consider the following:

If we were to consider our senses that us humans are bestowed with then let's just consider one of our species who was blind from birth and then try to explain to them what vision actually is. Difficult isn't it. Maybe there are other means of sense perception out there that we could not possibly imagine in our limitations as human beings. Maybe we are not yet at the top of the 'evolutionary tree' although we might arrogantly think that we are. In a creator's terms we might be like ants crawling on a rock. So maybe there are other possibilities for our existence that are beyond our limits of perception.

If we take the engineering scenario and we consider the complexity of life that not only do we have function we also have efficiency of use of our fuel, its conversion and storage. We have systems in place that constantly maintain our bodily functions through amazing chemistry (homeostasis) and that undertake repair and that all of our movement and co-ordination is finely balanced and stabilized.

What is really amazing is that for a species to exist at all then all of our plethora of collective interdependent functions would have had to coexist at the same time during the evolutionary process i.e. to evolve we would have to be fully evolved at a basic threshold to survive and further to this our species would also require simultaneous evolution of two genders. To survive we have to have all functions in place simultaneously and any precursor lifeforms to us would be dictated to in this respect in the same way. It would seem that we would therefore never get the opportunity to evolve.

If indeed evolution was the answer then the odds are so badly stacked against it that you might postulate that life would most probably only exist in one place in the universe, perhaps many universes, throughout the eons of time. Mathematically any occurrence, even the ostensibly impossible, can be given a finite probability or chance. However, if you are a tortoise crossing a road and every second a steam roller passes your chances are not really good at all so this in itself raises the possibility of the concept of zero probability. If you were never to contemplate rocket engine design, never to study it, never to read about it then what is the probability that you will understand it. We tend to imagine that everything has, in infinite time, at least some probability of occurring, but could it be that it has zero probability and therefore no possibility of occurring.

On balance, evolution and creation, is, and presents, something of a violent paradox that transcends human intelligence and so therefore are equally based upon faith. Neither can be proven in accordance with the standard scientific axiom:

"The results of scientific experiments and observations should form the basis of a theory from which these theories are to be tested by further experiment." - Galileo (Astronomer, Italy 16th/17th century)

It is therefore so that our formal, or informal, scientific experience in our lives may precipitate a theory, and in some cases a belief, in evolution or in creation, neither of which do we have an experiment that can categorically prove either one or the other. So in this sense both evolution and creation are equally subjective and therefore should equally be defined as a faith. Where we differ in our opinions is that formal science cannot acknowledge the concept of a creator as this defeats our scientific thinking (where is the proof) and 'informal science' (perhaps this is just our individual experience and inspiration from it) cannot acknowledge evolution as this defeats our religious beliefs. Because we cannot prove something or that it may seem illogical or even ridiculous does not mean that what is proposed is necessarily incorrect, just think back to the pre-enlightenment 'flat earth' thinkers and are we really that enlightened now.

Outside of the biological world we always relate order to intelligent design. If our telescopes were to identify straight lines or other orderly structures on the surface of a distant planet we would immediately claim the existence of extra-terrestrial intelligent life, we would have irrefutable proof, conferences would be called and television channels would be flooded with news flashes. Essentially ordered morphology would indicate intelligent design. Yet the development and structure of the most amazing thing, with order proved through perfection, in our universe is us but yet is there really no hand from intelligence in its design.

To put this into some context we could revisit the now quite well-known argument in imagining that a tornado passing through a scrap yard could assemble a fully working Boeing 747 but now we do so with a slightly different perspective. Biologists reject this scenario in that it does not account for natural selection but does natural selection account for success through mutation then turning into failure. If biologists believe it is that easy to build a 747 then maybe a transfer to the world of engineering would illuminate just how difficult it is to design such things. As an engineer I know all too well just how unforgiving engineering is; getting the fuel pitch in a nuclear reactor or the code in a missile guidance control system slightly wrong then what we have is something that just doesn't work and the idea that you can just 'cobble' something up won't work either as this will not be anywhere near clever enough to fix the problem.

The evolutionist will say *"but who created the creator"* and likewise the creationist would ask *"who wrote the code in our DNA because properly formatted code does not write itself"*. We now have machines and robots that can now automatically design and build, they create, do they not have a creator, they did, us, so maybe we also had a creator and the discovery of the existence of code does not suggest that we no longer require the programmer to write the code or that the programmer never existed, and how can you define the mechanics of self-awareness.

Maybe the answers to all of this lay in something that preceded our existence, or that is concurrent to our existence, but that we are unaware of, and is based upon laws of nature that we are unfamiliar with or that would seem quite alien or maybe it is all just mundane statistical chance. Could it be that if there is a creator who created us that He/She, yes our creator or God that is may indeed be female just as the head honcho in the bee hive is the queen. Could it be that this entity had evolved over essentially infinite time, given the believed plausibility of evolution, and that this may in itself seem a fantastic proposition but isn't our existence equally so.

If, however, there is life after death, then as an engineer, and after I have reconnected with my lost loves ones, I shall head straight for the celestial biological engineering department to find out just how the hell did they do it.

The Conscious Mind (an existence that is beyond articulation)

Our mind is like a universe it is incredible - there are something like 100 billion cells in the human brain, all wired up like some electronic circuit with 1,000 trillion connections, receiving simultaneous input stimuli from all of our senses; what we see, what we hear, what we can taste and smell, what we feel on our skin as in texture and heat or cold and we can feel pain or should I say that it is our brain that perceives pain based on some trouble alerted from some other part of the body, in essence it is our brain that interprets a signal as pain.

A crushed limb will feel painful though the pain, per se, is actually perceived by the brain not by the limb! Could this suggest that - just as pain does not reside in the injured limb, that equally possible is that our consciousness may not reside within our brain. Could it therefore be that the disparate parts of our brain are nothing more than transceivers for the disparate aspects of our consciousness and brain function? That may seem farfetched but is it.

We also have capacity to think and thereby develop capacity to learn and from that, capacity to react, adapt and interpret, unfortunately not always rationally as our electronic wiring may not always be ideal. The body is an exceptionally well designed machine however the brain is somehow left to itself over our lifetime to work out how to function in terms of thought and basic rules. In amongst all of this there are emotions such as the sensation of feeling joy or sadness, feeling surprise, disgust or revulsion, shame, attraction or admiration, fear or panic, enthusiasm or elicitation of interest or the more powerful feelings of love and hate that are possible embodiments of other emotions.

Evolutionists would argue that emotions are just facets of higher levels of survival development, we can see why evolution may engage mind development but we don't know how the post-natal mind physically develops at least in any detail to really understand what is going on, we know that it learns and that not everything is innate but how does it do that.

Given time and experience, our thinking changes, we may for example become more cynical, disillusioned or pessimistic of life or we may become more optimistic and hopeful, we may believe everything we hear from our social group or we may start to distrust others and even question what we ourselves think. Surprisingly, negative thinking is not necessarily wrong thinking – would you ever put your head in a crocodile's mouth, or take in a lodger of bad character. Lack of trust or showing caution is a sign of experience and ability to survive in anticipating the bad actions of others and in caution of what we might want to do.

"No man ever steps in the same river twice, for it's not the same river and he's not the same man." – Heraclitus (Philosopher, Greece 5th/6th century BC)

Every day we have new encounters and experiences, we may talk with the wise or unwittingly with fools and so every day we wake up essentially a bit different from the person we were the day before. In this sense what we are and what we think evolves and on that basis the different mindsets that we have had in our life; were they all bang on correct? – probably not, so you may land up disagreeing with your former self, I certainly have, if that is you then take advantage of the wealth of experiences and learning potential life has to offer.

If you lack capacity to disagree with your immediate thoughts, or even beyond, then you possibly have not had the experience to fully rationalize a situation, since you need to develop reasoning capacity by observing something from different angles, not just one angle, and reading one book on a subject or discussing with just one group of people does not, in any sense, make you wise. So what our brain does as an organ in terms of how and what it thinks depends on where we have taken it through our own experiences and learning through the unique experience of our own life.

With our inputs and our processing functions based on our logical, emotional and creative thinking we then output instructions to our body, the results of which can be constructive or sadly destructive. Our responses to input stimuli could be that we decide to cross the road here rather than over there, we eat meat or go veggie, we converse on one opinion or an opposite opinion or that we realise, in lacking critical information, that we cannot reach an opinion, we tell a joke or we discuss philosophy, we destroy or kill, we mend or heal, we make or reject relationships or we have to sometimes cast them aside.

If you believe the processing of these decisions/reactions is simple then let us consider the analogy of something that I have familiarity with in that to write software to remotely address and operate a (pipe) valve in a network of valves; to construct telemetry, instruct position, to read back status information and do so with communications error detection required over 1,500 lines of programming code but just one mistake in the code and the whole programme, not just part of it, could be compromised. Imagine the programming code you would require for the interpretation of sight; to detect and translate the colourless electromagnetic waves, of different wavelengths, into different colours and level of brightness, as in our brain attributing colour, and to then create an image that we can then perceive in our mind. But for this the brain doesn't use programming code but what does it use, how does it do it?

Things are just a lot more complex than what we might imagine. Could it be that the microprocessor is the wrong path to take to emulate human action and even thought? Do we need to use a new form of computing architecture yet to be discovered to take us to a new level, one closer to exactly how the human mind really does work?

What is really astounding with what we are is our capacity for emotion, for feeling and to be self-aware. To feel joy, to feel pain, to experience wonder, to feel enthusiasm, to be able to see, hear, taste, smell and feel - is this only our machine like brain at work here, are we just a cluster of atoms clinically processing instructions like some automaton, is that all we really are or are we something more.

Even now we only understand very little of how the brain functions although we do know about its structure as in what happens where. Through brain injury, neurological experiments and brain scans we have established that the frontal lobe is responsible for memory and behaviour, that the structure called the amygdala is responsible for our emotions and instincts and that the brain stem is responsible for regulating basic bodily functions. This being said we cannot reach as far as to how or why we feel emotions in what is essentially a processing engine, or so we might believe, much like the microprocessor in our home computer that we know exactly how it works as it is something designed by us humans.

We are essentially a machine but yet we have emotions we are a 'Cartesian duality' we have both body and mind as two distinct but interacting components. Some may argue that Descartes was just towing the line of the church out of self-preservation but to postulate the same is very different than to oppose the difference, to not do one would not cause you any trouble but to do the other certainly would.

'I think therefore I am.' – Rene Descartes (Philosopher, France 17th century).

It is conceivable that we may be able to construct a machine with 'emotions', however these would be nothing more than simulated emotions as the machine would not know the meaning of being able to actually experience emotions at all in the same way as we do. Like a human it may achieve progressive consciousness, from its birth, of its outside world, through experience and possibly aided by language, and then knit all of that consciousness together but it would not be able to achieve conscious thought, a robot can use its sensors to feel itself around a dark room for example but it is not conscious of its surroundings in the same way that we are, it would not know fear or excitement in anticipation of what it may find. Its emotional understanding would be very much a one dimensional analogy compared to our multi-dimensional experience.

To illustrate this point a simple sensor could, via a relay, stop a motor, what we would call 'an interlock', but there is absolutely no conscious thought in this process although from the outside observer's perspective the machine would appear to have made some independent decision – but this is nothing more than a simple electronic circuit within which there is no consciousness at all. The machine may act to survive by learning its spatial orientation and can do so with rudimentary programming but it lacks any conscious motivation to survive. Furthermore why do we even need consciousness, what is the purpose of consciousness that not only promotes survival but that can also create?

In terms of survival why would Shakespeare be equipped or need to be equipped with such fantastic literary capabilities, that of such higher mathematics in the case of Einstein or for the ultimate in Johann Sebastian Bach constructing his incredible Fugue in G Major, why did 'evolution' provide us such skills beyond what survival demands? The insect world seems to survive well without these skills so why can't we?

An insect certainly has motivation but it doesn't have such higher levels of consciousness although does have some capacity for basic conscious thought. However, given the lack of conscience and morality of the insect I certainly would not recommend getting close to a machine that has consciousness in its early developmental stages you may end up not just being deprived of your consciousness but also your life.

So many of us can understand how things work we understand the principles of much, not all, of science but to understand something is a huge gulf from being able to fully master it to be able to do it to create it. Any physicist might be able to tell you how a jet engine compressor works but they couldn't design one (its seriously difficult) at least not anywhere near the optimised performance as one designed by an aeronautical engineer, here you need a seriously deep and <u>exact</u> understanding not just enough to talk in vague terms about how it works but to master it so that you can create. In essence we can talk but can we also do.

Many physicists understand Einstein's theories but they are not in his league to be able to come up with such original ground-breaking and provable theories, they understand physics but they haven't mastered it in the same way that Einstein did. But what of our refinements beyond cold intellect, if we think of those who not only have intellect but who can create beauty then the likes of J.S.Bach are perhaps evolved beyond the likes of most of us including evolutionary biologists and yes engineers.

Perhaps our ultimate point of evolution is measured not by what we coldly understand and how we can incessantly talk about it and how clever we think we are but by what we are as humans in our higher senses of humanity, decency, creativity and in our good manners for it is qualities such as these that really show that we have evolved beyond ape.

Our ideas of what is self-awareness, being able to feel existence, might be based upon the foundations of having the capacity of memory, having awareness as to what is going on around us and to having an ability to perceive. However, there is also something quite elusive that we might call 'present realisation'; it is the combination of the overlaying flow of recent events and new ideas that accumulate within our minds, not just as memory but how we feel about those memories, that perhaps needs to be maintained i.e. a sense of what I am, what I value and what I feel about it – as humans we need to develop this. If we shut off the flow it would be akin to freezing a chemical reaction in time i.e. to think we have to keep thinking.

Is this something we are born with or is it something that develops i.e. when do we become self-aware and cross the Rubicon from machine to a fully actualized conscious human being – now that is some question. We may know what areas of the brain generate properties of consciousness but what consciousness is and how does it work will I believe, other than in broad sweeping terms, remain forever a mystery.

Before we depart this subject there are a couple of interesting related thoughts I wish to leave with you and what we might describe as paradoxes or in Tibetan Buddhism are called 'koans'. A 'koan' is where the proposition cannot precipitate an answer through discursive reasoning it cannot therefore be arrived at through reason or logic; essentially it is a riddle that cannot be solved.

Koan 1 – If we were to take you or I and using some machine we momentarily froze all of the atoms in our body so that their state was fixed and maintained, then disintegrated the whole such that all of these atoms would be dispersed from one another then we would essentially be classified as clinically dead. If we then reassembled them to the exact place from whence they came and re-ignited our life, then would you still be you and I still be me or are we just a carbon copy of what we were? Has our 'soul', i.e. consciousness, been maintained, lost or destroyed?

Koan 2 – On the basis of Koan 1; in that we maintain the belief that we are still who we were but if in this instance we take another group of atoms that constructs, atom by atom, replicating exactly you or I, so we now have an exact twin down to almost the atomic level, then would this person be just as valid as you or me i.e. is it another you or me or is it just a copy and would it have the same emotional value and attachments as you or I have. In essence, if it possessed emotion and attachment as you or I, it would be unspeakably cruel to reject such an entity as a carbon copy as it would think it was you or me just as you think you are you and I think that I am me.

In science fiction, that can often become science fact, there is presumption of technology to transport an individual from one place to another by destructing the person at one end, somehow transmitting this as a signal to another end and where the signal is reconstructed is presumably done so with different atoms. The question is: does the person being deconstructed, i.e. their conscious existence die in the process and if you were to ask the reconstructed person at the other end, would they then insist that they are the same person with the same memories and emotions though in reality they are not.

Could it be that not only our construction down to the atomic level but also the voltages maintained within our neurology in all of their places is what defines what we are? Take away these voltages and perhaps we die in more than just a physical sense, in that our soul dies, as if we have removed the state that we have arrived at through our life experience although our memory may remain intact. We are therefore more than memory we are more than just atoms.

Perhaps our consciousness has some relationship to what voltages are where. Is perhaps removal of the thread of our accumulated thinking experience the removal of our consciousness? Could it be that with time as we forget elements of our accumulated experience that we are gradually departing from our former self, in essence our consciousness could therefore become a different consciousness in other words our earlier self at some point will cease to exist, our soul being replaced by a new entity, a different person then exists. This being said we still cannot understand what is individual consciousness what is the soul what is it that makes us feel alive what is it that makes us feel aware.

But before we leave this subject let's just examine the shortcoming of the conscious mind. Could it be that the very property that makes us what we are is the very thing that inflicts our sense of suffering? A machine can neither feel physical nor psychological pain but we can. Could it be that for consciousness to exist also requires highly amplified senses, amplified that is beyond the self-preserving utility of the body, that which in its utility sense alerts us to danger requires even higher amplification to elicit consciousness with the unfortunate side effect of eliciting fear, anxiety and even depression. Is this a design fault or an unavoidable consequence of science in that consciousness requires high sensory amplification that unavoidably precipitates a high susceptibility to suffering?

In recognising this, could it be that what we perceive is not what we need to perceive and so perhaps what we worry about we should in reality worry less i.e. we compensate for the down side of our over amplified senses. Extending this further then perhaps it is for us to decide how we feel in that if we consciously decide to feel good we will feel good but to do so would be something quite amazing, but not beyond possibility, to master.

So What Should I Believe?

This chapter does not and cannot in any way prove the existence of a creator but what is important here is that we should be a little more circumspect of evolutionary theory being our final answer to the existence of life. Maybe by some amazing fluke it is the answer but as a scientific theory it is only partially proven and on this basis is not science as in the true meaning of what is, and what is not, legitimate science. Evolution is less of a scientific fact but more so a conclusion predicated upon clinical logic in so much as believing that creation doesn't fit with scientific thinking so therefore it must be wrong.

Perhaps therefore to prove that God does not exist, that we first have to assume that God does not exist and then go looking for the evidence of how life can be without God. Perhaps the way how the evolutionary biologist approaches this is not to determine how life came about but to disprove God and so must presuppose that God does not exist before then embarking on any science, in effect the possible 'smoking gun' may have been prematurely dismissed from the investigation.

With or without science we may never find out the answer. If I did wear the clinical hat of science then my view would be that the universe would be forever barren, no life would ever exist but yet it does and that is in itself beyond amazing. I strongly advocate scientific reason I believe that science, given time, can determine the cause of everything in the natural world but only if we know everything about science but yet we don't.

From the perspective of who created the creator and that life might have some possibility, albeit remote, through basic chemical reactions followed by biological evolution you might want to bet on evolution over creation. Indeed the chances of the existence of a creator would appear to be very slim and indeed from rational thought it is. Indeed it is possible that some are amenable to the concept of a creator from the perspective of fear as in *"I fear death"* (even though I may not be honest to myself about my belief in a creator) or from utilitarian reasons like *"I must worship God, and do so as my religious upbringing instructs me in order to secure a better afterlife"* (I doubt that in doing so for selfish interests would impress God,).

Scientifically we cannot prove evolution as providing us with all of the answers although we can observe that there have been apparent modifications of species and species jumps, but so far we have not been able to mutate one distinct species into another in our laboratories, we can modify a species but we can't jump to another of our design. This may even suggest that DNA has some distinct immutable property that might indicate that it is not easily amenable to evolving. We have to resign ourselves to the fact that science cannot answer all of our questions and so is therefore not the master of all, we may also be relatively in the dark ages of science with lots more to discover that as yet we are unaware of. We do not know what we do not know.

Indeed if science obsessively (especially the obsessed pathological iconoclast) dismisses creation as a possible reason for life, where the proof of evolution is so woefully inadequate, then it is in effect conceitedly appointing itself above God. Yet with our assumed franchise on intelligence (a sort of intellectual narcissism) we are unable to engineer life ourselves, it is beyond our capability. However, this does not exonerate religion in that creation and thereby the concept of God is also without scientific proof and the existence of religious texts is by no means credible evidence in themselves and to casually say that they are is not putting in the effort that this perspective deserves; we need to establish through more powerful theological reasoning, not dictum, as to the existence of God, if indeed God does exist.

The probability of evolution acting alone is poor indeed and it is also too slow to have 'baked the cake' in the time we have had. There is too much in evolution left unexplained and the concept of 'I', what am I, why do I think, why do I feel emotions is too much for science to cope with although unprovable theories will abound over time. Of course we shall continue to discover more of how our brain works, and we already have discoveries to hand, where thought takes place and where we feel emotions but we do not know the mechanisms within and maybe we never will and just maybe these structures in our brains are not what undertakes these functions and we may even hypothesise that they are merely a conduit to these functions much as your telephone links into an exchange – but an exchange as yet beyond scientific reach.

In reality both evolution and creation are subject to faith as we know so little and probably never will know all of the answers. However, with the best intentions, to err is still to be human and if God is indeed a forgiving entity He/She will not judge us harshly for getting it wrong. It is more likely that God will judge us not on man-made religious edicts, as written by the hand of mankind, but on our behaviour to others and on what good we have done and this does not include coercion of others into our own religious interpretations of God.

"Whatever I think of God I can only conceive of Him as a being infinitely great and infinitely good." – Joseph Haydn (Composer, Austria 18th/19th century)

If I were a betting man I would guess that if God exists then He/She would be very much disappointed with many of our species in how we can be selfish, aggressive, intolerant, cruel, indolent, dishonest, manipulative, arrogant and closed in our minds though He/She would also see good things too in that our species also exhibits some wonderful qualities such as compassion, kindness, creativity, a willingness to explore how we can do great things and to aspire to be better than what we are. Perhaps if we were to get closer to these finer qualities then we would be closer to God and His/Her intentions for us.

In closing this chapter, faith and in some cases religion can help you live a better life and can give some structure to what might otherwise be a disorganized society, it may impute morality where otherwise there would be none in a world where some are naturally moral, some are moral through fear of retribution (on earth or beyond) and some are devoid of any morality.

We consider ourselves to be civilized through our learning and our attitude to others and in the distant past societies only recourse to learning, and thereby aspiration to better themselves, may have only been through their religious experience. Sadly, as any student of history will tell you, that this is not always true as often societies have been, still are being and always will be manipulated by bad religious ideology or through the corruption of religion.

There are the lucky ones in our society who may have everything they want, their personal life and their careers may be successful and they may have reached some point of contentment, and they may postulate that we do not need religion but for some it is all they have and their lives would be empty without it. However, those who do need their religion need to ask themselves; does my religion make my life and that of others better or worse, does it give me a moral compass to do good and does it preach compassion for all and is it really what an all compassionate God would want.

To understand that question you need to study the scriptures yourself without the possible hand of corruption or misinterpretation of others and where you do depend upon scholars you need to read from different perspectives as in all religions, indeed as in anything, there are many subtle and sometimes different ways to look at the same thing. Could it even be that some of our religious edicts are something else that they are a test to see if we follow instructions that invoke evil actions for which we will be judged well not from following the instruction but in not following it. I may ask you to do something but that doesn't mean that I want you to do it, it may be a test to see what you really are and just where your morality will fail.

"I am ever present to those who have realised me in every creature. Seeing all life as my manifestation, they are never separated from me." – The Bhagavad Gita
(Hinduism)

To those who cannot assuage the pain of loss or who are alone in this world or less fortunate, then belief in God may help and if it does then why not believe in a God as it may be the only source of comfort to endure what may otherwise be a less than easy existence.

To question the existence of God may be to question the only hope some have of making any sense of this life and in finding a purpose in it and to challenge with total disrespect for such belief may be unwise where such belief is critical and solitary to an individual's self-esteem. However, the believer must also respect the view of those who have arrived at a different conclusion, had you had been them you would also conclude likewise and there is some validity in their argument just as there is some validity in yours. But it is very easy to dismiss what you perceive as fantasy when all is well in your life and that you feel you do not need God, but just remember those who are not so lucky and be mindful that one day your world may be destroyed by some bad event and you may then need to be a little more open and amenable to the idea of faith in order to survive. A good faith may be your only saviour and having faith in something may help us keep our sanity in a mad world.

"The Lord is my rock, my fortress and my deliverer; My God is my rock, in whom I take refuge. He is my shield and the horn of my salvation, my stronghold." – The Bible, Psalm 18 (Christianity)

Societies can be very protective of their religion, particularly when it plays a large part in their culture and life and so where they have become, rightly or wrongly, to depend too much on it then they will be far less willing to question it. You may not believe in God or you may not believe in evolution, either way that is OK but given that neither can be irrefutably proven then why not go with what suits you best go for what is best for your needs, if this is of course possible for you to do so. If you are coerced against your will by virtue of culture or peer pressure at least you can believe within your heart what you want to believe and keep your thoughts to yourself if needs be.

However, we should all try to learn to live in peace with one another as one society without the vociferous obsessive dogma of *"my God is more valid than yours"* attitude. Besides, if God favoured one faith over another, and is all powerful, then why is it that natural disasters and good fortune is never selective to adherents of any particular faith or alternative faiths? So just go a little easier on people who happen to think different to you, after all it may be them who are right and you that is wrong. You only think different to them not because you are right but because of the culture within which you were born into (think hard on this) or the educational bias to which you later experienced (ditto). It is not stupid to believe in God nor is it evil to not believe so we should all respect and tolerate different views. None of us are compelled to believe another's view, I am not compelled to believe what you believe and you are not compelled to believe what I believe.

When it comes to the subject of a creator science will identify with God as nothing more than a construct of tradition, superstition or religion and on this basis it will assume that God cannot exist, that God must be a myth, it must then seek out evidence to prove this position. However, neither science nor religion can conclusively prove creation or evolution and so all that is available to our reasoning is a best guess on both sides of the argument i.e. what is the most likely option based upon balance of probabilities. One thing we do know is that it is very unlikely indeed that the existence of just one universe as we know of could yield life. In the end it is down to faith and perhaps that is something we need a lot more of to see any sense to our existence.

If it is so that we do discover the exact science as to how we came to be this does not necessarily prove that God does not exist, all we may have done is unlock God's secrets. If creation is the answer then creation is the science of our existence just as any theory if proven becomes intrinsic and indelible to its subject.

"And to the presence in the room he said, what writest thou?, - the vision raised its head, and with a look made of all sweet accord, answered, the names of those who love the Lord. I pray thee, then, Write me as one that loves his fellow men." – From the poem *'Abou Ben Adhem (May his tribe increase!)'* by James Henry Leigh Hunt (Poet, England 19th century)

What do we decide upon, evolution or creation, this is something that I can't answer with any absolute certainty of proof but all I have is my faith and in my lifetime that will have to suffice for me. Scientists may yet prove that we don't need a God to explain our existence but that doesn't mean that there isn't one. I am not challenging the academic excellence of scientists in the same way that politicos bitch with one another like spoilt children in television debates but I am challenging the idea that the argument is anywhere near closed - blind spots will always remain in this debate and will perhaps remain so forever. Will we ever find the truth is it even within our intellectual power to do so?

If we really believe that we understand the origin of life then we must also make claim to understanding how the conscious mind operates, how we are self-aware, how we feel and if we are so advanced in this respect then what is holding us back from sketching out the design of a machine that can do the same. Surely what we have supreme understanding of, where we might suggest that the entity of God does not exist then we must be able to propose exactly how we would engineer the conscious mind with its concomitant diagrams, schematics, assembly drawings and specifications. If we can't do any of this then we do not possess any intellectual supremacy upon this matter, perhaps we are far too limited in intelligence to ever find out. Perhaps that in our quest for artificial intelligence within the framework of the microprocessor that we are looking in the wrong place to understand not the why (i.e. the stock phrase 'it's evolution') but the how and to this we may need to look in more detail at the drives for our most powerful of emotions and at the precipitation, or is it development, of consciousness in the neonate mind.

I can see both sides of the argument and I can see that religion (not God) has done some pretty appalling things throughout its history, but it is exceedingly bad mannered and uneducated to insult someone because they have a belief in a God that cannot be conclusively proven just as an opposite view cannot be conclusively proven, even though we may imagine that it can. If it is that they must insult those for choosing hope, or faith, over reason, as they see it to be, or reason over hope then why would anyone want to do that what is their objective.

What is the motive to crush another's hope in the interest of scientific 'truth' where that scientific 'truth' does not serve in any way those individuals who cling to hope, hope that may be the only way that they can tolerate this life, yes what is the motive is it to provoke, an ugly demonstration of assumed 'superior' intellect, a pathological jealousy of God or what? Atheists and creationists (including adherents to different religions) should be able to live alongside one another with some maturity and mutual respect not to sling insults or threats at one another and not to be constantly offended by light humour. There really is too much group identity in this world that may lead to bad things and we certainly don't need any more group identities than what we already have, there is certainly enough division in this world we really don't need any more.

Perhaps to a question that cannot be answered we should all instead focus upon our generosity and magnificence within ourselves and nurture these things, and whether you be atheist or a believer in God do check out the hymn 'Mine Eyes Have Seen The Glory Of the Coming Of The Lord', Royal Albert Hall, London; maybe this will penetrate through the wall of somewhat intransigent perception of the 'intellectually irritating' or 'irritatingly intellectual' hubris and hate that we see in this world. Perhaps it may even be that belief in God has a biological necessity or is programmed with deliberate purpose, will we ever know?

Luck is a strange thing since as I am ending this chapter I am also reading the Ivan Turgenev novel of 1862 'Fathers and Sons' within which are these words: *"entering upon that dim, murky period when regrets come to resemble hopes, and hopes are beginning to resemble regrets, and youth is fled, and old age is fast approaching"*, *"in that, in losing his past, he had lost his all."* Here is where as we get older we may reflect upon our condition, our regrets and our dreams that never came to fruition (something I advise against doing, so don't go there) but then again often with 19th century literature eloquently depicted despair of the human condition, or what I view as being a perhaps gross abstraction to give fiction its fierce bite, seemed to be the order of the day. But that being said this leads my thinking, as does anything we read, in that perhaps if we have lost all hope or maybe that our age wearies us then maybe faith is the answer maybe this is the time to grab the Bible, the Bhagavad Gita or whatever else to gain inspiration as to why we are here and where we are going; devotion to something greater than ourselves just may not be such a bad idea.

But if there is a God, then why make us, why are we here? A reward for some maybe and punishment for others, an experience from which to learn to develop to mature, a test, a component, a prototype, are we just passing through as observers yet to move onto greater things, is it just a potentially traumatic field trip where whatever we encounter we must remain untroubled in which we observe, take note and learn or is it for some higher purpose, a mission, for which self-interest can never serve. Why indeed are we here?

But one thing is for sure is that the human mind is far in excess of what it needs to be, than its self-preserving utility of the physical self, so is there something else going on here that we just don't know. We have purpose beyond the self and in there perhaps lays the answer as to why we are here.

In concluding; I have spoken with people of all of the major religions (Christianity, Hinduism, Buddhism, Islam, Sikhism, Judaism) many of whom are highly intelligent and who think deeply on this subject and I have spoken equally with atheists again many of whom are highly intelligent and who also think deeply on this subject, so perhaps what this points to is that to believe or to disbelieve is not an indicator of stupidity, or of evil, but just different views as a result of what is our cultural heritage, what is our belief within and what is our belief of ourselves. Whatever may be the truth we all have a common destiny at the end.

Chapter 21

A Cool Framework for a Calm Mind

(In the deconstruction of Buddhism)

In all religions there are followers who are good and followers who are bad and Buddhism is in no way an exception. We cannot therefore judge a religion from individuals who may be grossly unrepresentative of that religion and who often distort what it teaches, we need to look within, what exactly does the religion teach? Is it a force for good or a force for bad? If we see within ourselves a developing attraction to a religion we must first read it well and know what it is saying not listen to the words of others who may be just out to sell an idea and sometimes a political idea at that. If you find Buddhism attractive then don't take my word for it go and study it for yourself go and find out what it really is, don't just listen to me, you don't know me do you even know if you can trust me.

Why Buddhism?

Nothing is without fault but through observations and study, of all religions, Buddhism would probably stand a very good chance for election as the most rational and the most peaceful. Furthermore, Buddhism lacks any self-assumption of supremacy over others. If there ever was a fundamentalist interpretation of Buddhism the result would be world peace without any enforcement of belief, control or doctrine upon others. However, Buddhists are not fools; they will perceive and deal with threats just like anyone else if needs be i.e. being peaceful does not mean that you meekly capitulate in the face of evil but if you were to incur the wrath of a true strict adherent of Buddhism then you most probably have given them good reason.

In accordance to strict adherence to this religion a non-adherent would not be looked upon with contempt, they would not be persecuted for having a different viewpoint and they would not be forced or even persuaded in any way to convert. In the true Buddhist world everyone, of all cultures, races and religions would be treated equally, hospitality and care for one another would be equally offered whether or not you are Buddhist.

I once read an account of a group of Catholics who attended a Buddhist retreat and who afterwards had reached a consensus that the experience had made them better

Catholics but all had felt that the experience had also made them a better person, but yet they had no inclination to convert to Buddhism. As typical of the true essence of Buddhism there was no attempt to proselytize it really didn't matter who you are or what religion you followed, your soul would not go to hell nor would you be in any way condemned for being an unbeliever of Buddhist philosophy. The response of the Buddhist monk was not disappointment at them not wishing to convert nor was it anger at them for not having changed their viewpoint but was delight that they had gained something of good out of their experience – in effect they had each become a better person.

Because Buddhism does not threaten hell in the afterlife for refusing to follow its path, is respectful to other non-Buddhist viewpoints and that it offers practical ideas and compassion it is therefore an enlightened religion from which true wisdom can be born. It is for this reason, and for the openness of Buddhism, that it is selectively discussed in this book and for the reason that I believe it to provide a cultural imputation towards a better life. What follows is my personal interpretation, unique and fallible as any interpretation can only be, of Buddhism through having been a student of it for years and in as much as any of us might hope to accurately interpret a religion or philosophy our own or otherwise, but I believe that what follows captures the essence of what Buddhism is.

The Beginning of an Ancient But Modern Religion

Buddhism was founded in northern India around 2500 years ago. In the Buddhist calendar; our year 2020 is the year 2563.

Contrary to common belief Buddhism is not an atheistic religion, despite the fact that its founder never claimed to be a God, disciple of God nor a prophet of God, but neither does it deny the existence of God and in this sense Buddhism is a non-theistic not an atheistic religion. With absence of a God or devotion to a God this is unusual for a religion and perhaps for this reason it may be more appropriate to consider Buddhism as a philosophy.

The Buddha (the name meaning 'the enlightened one') was the founder of Buddhism ('enlightenment') - a philosophy that would introduce spiritual awareness and a capacity to gain deep understanding, through insight, and logical judgment, through reason as opposed to unchallenged tradition or dogma. In Buddhism there is no tradition or concept of religious authority and this is why Buddhism is quite relaxed about being challenged.

The Buddha, as he was to be later known, went by the name of Siddhartha Gautama who was born around 500 BC in what is now a part of northern India. In his early years the Buddha experienced a life of luxury but on a particular journey he encountered an old man, a dying man and a corpse an experience that troubled him profoundly and as a result of this experience he began to contemplate the dominance of suffering within life and thus he decided to go in search of the truth.

Siddhartha spent several years as an ascetic making the acquaintance of religious men and philosophers but was never fully satisfied with their answers and he never fully agreed with the current local religion of the time, Hinduism, specifically its caste system and also its polytheistic beliefs but what are essentially different manifestations of God. However, Hinduism, like Buddhism does support the ideas of karma and reincarnation and is likewise a fundamentally philosophical religion and if you haven't done so I do recommend a read of the Bhagavad Gita a very wonderful and inspiring religious text and one I just couldn't put down, so much so that I have read three different versions of it my favourite of which is the one by A.C. Bhaktivedanta.

The Buddha never intended his teachings, otherwise known as 'Dhamma', to be a religion but as a vehicle to achieve enlightenment and to then to dispose of such teachings when enlightenment is reached i.e. the paradoxical concept of non-attachment to the mechanisms of non-attachment! In other words once you have mastered Buddhism you might then decide to discard it, you have essentially reached the end of your journey.

This end of our journey of enlightenment or what we call 'Nirvana' is the main goal of Buddhism and is a form of non-existence where we bring to an end the endless cycle of birth and death and to achieve such depends on the assimilation of the philosophical elements as we are about to discuss. Once we reach Nirvana in essence we have also become a Buddha.

It was some time after the death of the Buddha that the followers of his teachings created what is known today as Buddhism. Since then many sects have arisen; Zen for example is widely known, however there are others such as Nicherin, Shingon and Lamaism etc. Broadly speaking these sects mostly fall into one of two categories namely; Hinayana Buddhism ('the lesser vehicle' or the traditional original teachings of the Buddha) otherwise known as Therevada Buddhism as practiced in Burma, Thailand, Cambodia, Vietnam and Laos, and Mahayana Buddhism (translates as 'the greater vehicle') as practiced in Tibet, China and Japan.

What is to follow in describing this philosophy is broadly common to both categories except that the more contemporary Mahayana teaching suggests that anyone can become a Buddha and proposes the existence of Boddisartvas i.e. mythical beings which protect others and take on their sufferings the most famous of which being Avalokiteshvara; a mythical being with eleven heads and a thousand arms where the heads signify the anguish from observance of the suffering in the world and the arms offering protection to all.

After several years of searching for the truth Siddhartha now at the age of 33 sat under a tree at a place called Bodh Gaya and after some time of meditation became enlightened to what is known as 'the four noble truths' and 'the eight fold path' thus the fundamental principle teachings of Buddhism came into being.

The Four Noble Truths

- We are all essentially dissatisfied with our life, our life experience is at odds with our expectations
- Our dissatisfaction is rooted in our sense of ego, our self-importance and in our desires
- Our dissatisfaction can be overcome when we transcend our own self-importance
- Our self-importance can be transcended by following the 'eight fold path'

The Eightfold Path

Right Knowledge - this is the knowledge and understanding of the four noble truths. It is also the understanding that our views are based on our conditioned perception and as such our views can never be totally correct, we are essentially all deluded from the truth, we do not see anything for what it really is. Our understanding of anything should not be seen as beyond question and we must not assume that possession of knowledge or experience presumes that our view is always correct. Wisdom is not attributed to our age or our education - we must first see that our views are based on our mind and not on reality, what is truth – to know this is the first step on the path to wisdom.

Right Attitude - or thought concerns mental attitude for goodwill and distancing oneself from desire and hatred. Assumption of self-perfection, self-righteousness or of intellectual superiority, over-assertion or abuse of power, being dismissive of others views, to be unbearably serious, to be without any humour, to be facetious or to lack diligence, self-control or discipline are aspects of bad attitude and are seen as aspects of an unenlightened mind. We should also all show humility and self-control.

Right Speech – dishonesty and useless talk is forbidden, instead speech must be wise and truthful. Speech designed to agitate, patronise, humiliate or disparage, or vulgarity, arrogance, loudness and indication of intolerance or impatience are prohibited. Speaking highly of one-self, piety or over expressed moral judgement is considered to be aspects of ego and is to be avoided.

Right Action - embraces all moral behaviour and therefore prohibits murder, rape, theft, destruction, lewdness, to deprive anyone who is genuinely in need of help, to break someone's will, any form of harm, malevolence or the deliberate causing of difficulty to others, whether physical or psychological, and cruelty to animals. Unjust or harsh judgement of others and self-justification of our own wrong actions is also prohibited. Ignorance of our own bad actions or their affects does not exonerate us. However, where there is evil then it is sometimes necessary to destroy in order to protect others – 'it is sometimes necessary to cut off a finger to save a hand'.

Right Livelihood - our occupation must not be harmful to others except where we have to stand in the face of evil or ill intent.

Right Effort - evil impulses must be kept in check and good ones should be cultivated. There is no excuse by way of our circumstances, of our position in society, of our relationship to others, in our work or our culture for causing distress or harm to others.

Right Mindfulness - or awareness means all views must be carefully considered and reflected upon, to seek out all that we do not see as well as that what we do as all opinions are all too easily influenced by our psychological and cultural bias and are therefore very much in error. When asking a Buddhist monk or nun a question they will often pause for a while without speaking as they are reflecting upon their knowledge and wisdom with intent to find the truth first rather than to express an ill-considered opinion. Right mindfulness requires quiet reflection. Awareness also teaches to expect the unexpected, to anticipate disappointment or loss and not to hold any craving for material objects or for that matter anything. On this basis we should also not build up too much hope as this may lead to disappointment and suffering.

Right Composure - this is achieved through deep concentration to keep our purpose in focus without distraction, externally or internally. It is also to maintain equilibrium, calmness and unassuming patience and to not lose these qualities even when outside influence may be a strong force to do otherwise.

Basically right speech, action and livelihood are concerned with morality, right effort, mindfulness and composure are for spiritual discipline and right knowledge and attitude are concerned with insight.

The Concept of Self

We all think of everything in terms of our own frame of reference i.e. in terms of our self, our opinions our sufferings our desires - everything is 'I', we see our existence as of ultimate importance. In its extreme this can be seen as delusion or psychosis represented in overbearing, egotistic, single-minded, unreasonable, judgmental, lack of willingness to listen to what may be the truth character traits. All these facets of personality are rooted in an unhealthy exaggeration of 'I'. The attachment to self-importance, to our ego, is largely why we suffer and although it is necessary to have a sense of self-esteem this must not be confused with pathological ego; our self should be seen with a balanced and realistic view.

In the Buddhist mindset all suffering and discord is rooted from the agitation within our minds caused by our selfish drives. If we can lessen the idea of the self we can lessen the suffering and the discord in this world. Division in this world is largely caused by an attachment to 'I', our ego, and therefore in what we believe being more important above all others beliefs, and if this is how we think then we can only foment trouble for us all.

Reincarnation

'We never began to exist and we shall never cease to exist'! The concept of reincarnation is one that may seem hard to accept although there is much to suggest that the nature of our life existence is far beyond what we know, what we believe by way of faith or what we are able to understand through logical deduction. Indeed to many the concept of life after death might seem irrational.

If we can see that there is a mind component that is not of a physical nature then this component cannot cease to function upon death of the body. It is the Buddhist belief that this component will therefore enter into another life or form part of something else. Hinduism would suggest similarly so but with the possibility of something quite different (union with God – Brahma Nirvana) subject to the mind's state of enlightenment. It is the Buddhist view that this component of our existence will reincarnate so we will all go through an endless cycle of birth and death with all the suffering that comes with it. Remember that as a sentient being we are not devoid of feelings so our existence cannot be without suffering. This cycle of continual birth, death and rebirth can only being broken when our mind reaches the state of enlightenment.

The Law of Karma

Every action or intention, physical, verbal or otherwise that we have undertaken is our own responsibility and for which we will suffer or be rewarded accordingly. The pay-off may either be immediate or it may even be in a future life. We may not see such life's retribution or reward but it is there. It is true to say that those who follow a path of evil can never find true happiness and their unhappiness is therefore as a result of their bad deeds. Further to this, unlike in Christianity, we cannot be absolved of our sins; what is done cannot be undone, we will always carry responsibility for what we have done - in this sense Buddhism shows no mercy.

The understanding of this principle serves two good purposes; the first is in that it precipitates a framework for moral conduct and moral intent and the second purpose is more practical in that if we see our suffering is as a consequence of this cause & effects rule we can then see that what we get in life is what we deserve. We can therefore accept what life has dished up for us and perhaps be less dissatisfied with the life we have as we know that what we have is what we deserve. Although, I would add the caveat that it is not always so that those afflicted with misfortune are experiencing such because they deserve it. Some of the nicest people as it would seem can experience the most horrendous misery by way of nothing more than bad luck.

The Concept of Impermanence

"I am destined to become old, there being no way to resist old age. I am destined to become afflicted with disease, there being no way to resist disease. And I am destined to die, there being no way to resist death." – An extract from the Buddhist scripture 'the five themes for recollection'.

In our ignorance we live our life without thought for the final chapter. We show day by day a lack of care with our lives and we can be inconsiderate to others, we obsess about things that really don't matter, we try to force our often ill-considered views upon others, we are arrogant about who we are and what we think we know. If we just stop and remind ourselves that our life and that of others will inevitably end and that our final day of this life could be today then perhaps we would show more respect for each other and we would not become so attached to or dependent upon the things that we will one day lose.

Everything is impermanent. For example we may be conceited about our appearance, mental capacity, wealth or possessions without awareness that an accident or change of fortune could take these things away in an instant. If we know this truth then we do not become so inflated with our own importance and when we do inevitably lose these things we suffer less because we are not as attached as we would have been in a state of ignorance of this truth. The awareness of death brings us into perspective of how fragile and insignificant we are.

In awareness of death we will realize that we should live life every day to the full, to appreciate those around us, to do our best, do what is right and to not cause difficulty for others, i.e. make the most of what you have when you have it. In understanding the impermanence of those around us we will also recognize the importance to take more refuge in ourselves, to become more self-reliant.

Meditation in the Context of Buddhism (the unattached mind) - Powerful

This is a practice that brings about what psychologists call an 'altered state of consciousness' the mechanism here being sensory deprivation where wild thoughts are discarded and where we bring the mind to a halt. If we observe our own mind, just have a look now, it is constantly busy serving what we perceive, our worries, our ego.

In the background it relates everything to our judgement system which is formed by our conditioning and our state of mind - the extreme of this state being 'rumination', where we just can't let go of something that troubles us that can even precipitate madness or at least severely degraded mental well-being. With this all going on how can we possibly have room for crystal clear rational thought? How can we see things as they really are? It is true that it is our opinion of our circumstances and not the circumstances themselves is that which we perceive. If we could change the way how we look at things then our lives would feel different.

So our mind in its normal busy state with its attachments to all of our psychological virtues and failings does not give a clear picture of what is going on around us. With this in mind how can we achieve clear and enlightened thought how can we rationalise anything? It is interesting that every day we attend to personal hygiene and yet our mind is neglected. We may selectively read and absorb huge quantities of information but none of this is of any value in a mind engulfed in worry or where we are unable to discriminate between good and bad.

Meditation is a process of emptying the mind and in its sublime form it is close to experiencing non-existence. It is in this state, if we can do it well where we can find tranquillity and we are more able to go in search for the truth without the 'I' getting in its way and we can cultivate a clear thinking wise mind that is unclouded by other thoughts.

The basic principle of meditation, usually practiced in the Lotus position (cross legged), is simple by allowing, but not forcing, the mind to observe and focus onto the breath, every inhalation and every exhalation, at its moment and none other and on nothing else but the breath; to become accomplished at this, where we can rid ourselves of all other contaminating thoughts, does however, take time and discipline.

If you lose control and other thoughts start to enter your mind and contaminate the practice then just bring the mind back to the breath, just be patient. For extra ambience I would also recommend burning some incense sticks since in attempting a state of sensory deprivation our mind may easily wander back to our senses and perhaps arresting this with the sense of smell may be the least contaminating of all or may even be a point upon which we can focus. If we have nothing else to occupy ourselves with and perhaps no-one to converse with we can fill that time, agonizing at times as it may be, if not with reading to expand the mind and put that time to good use then with practicing meditation. Bringing the mind to a place away from its boredom or even hell is of great benefit from which you can become energised and from which you can turn your life around. Meditation is possibly one of the most beneficial skills we can learn.

A slight though somewhat un-Buddhist variation on this is, perhaps very useful in moments of loneliness, overwhelming disappointment, despair, agitation etc., that instead of emptying the mind we visualise an unyielding torrent of water flooding through our cranium but entrained with the words of 'hope', 'purpose', the love of God, the wisdom of the universe or whatever you need to be thinking about that counteracts your negativity.

"My mind floats, it perceives nothing, yet it perceived everything, it can imagine beyond the limits of reality, it is self-actualised." – The human within (21ˢᵗ century)

If we were to apply the meditation principle to our thoughts or actions we bring the mind to one place, one subject and one moment for which we become aware of that thought or action and nothing else then we are exercising mindfulness where we are conscious of only one thing and one thing only and in doing so we are focussing the mind away from that which causes us suffering or confusion.

Mindfulness can be practiced in everything that we do from cleaning our home, shopping for groceries, reading, listening to the radio or a visit to the park. The question is do we wander through life looking lost and feeling lost within ourselves or can we focus the mind on what is going on around us and within us, do we look at how we really feel and explore it rather than just put up with it, do we observe all of our senses what we hear, see, taste, smell and feel. Get mindful and get another dimension on life one that you can enjoy and also use to bring your thoughts into a state of clarity.

Buddhist monks and nuns will spend much time on these practices, although this is on occasion accompanied with the chanting of Mantras, verses from the sacred texts. However, much of the time spent in the monastic community (the Sangha) is also spent reading not just on the subject of Buddhism but also on psychology and perspectives of other religions, teaching the wider community, receiving instruction and entering into dialogue on Buddhist philosophy all to gain spiritual knowledge and to attain the truth all that cannot be found in meditation alone.

And In the Final Words of the Buddha

"Hold fast to the truth as a lamp. Seek salvation alone in the truth. Look not for any assistance to anyone besides yourself."

Buddhism Gone Wrong

In my journey through life, many of whom I have encountered are what you might call 'natural Buddhists'. A natural Buddhist is someone who has a demeanour that is already spot on target in the context of Buddhism. If you were to meet with them without even discussing the subject of Buddhism you might suspect them to be Buddhist, they may even be adherents of other religions or none but you might nevertheless recognize that they have innate philosophical properties of Buddhism within.

These jewels are basically very good, decent, honest people who project a calm urbane manner and despite these qualities are manifestly self-effacing. However, this is not always so within the Buddhist community as at times you will encounter those who have a singular and very obvious but critically important gross misunderstanding of what it is all about. This misunderstanding is so fundamental that their claim to follow Buddhism couldn't be further from the truth.

A very fundamental axiom of Buddhism is that our suffering is rooted in our self-importance and this is well explained in the 'four noble truths'. Learning by rote, is not the same as understanding and if we have to recite from memory to recall meaning then we have not imputed that meaning in what we are, in what is our natural awareness. We may be able to accurately state what are 'the four noble truths', but do we really know what they mean. The more we have of ego, the more we are centring ourselves on the attachment to 'I', we have failed to understand the premise of attachment and so the more we shall suffer. We should learn to let go of our self-importance.

However, there are always those, a few though, who might say that they are Buddhist not because they are but because they want to be seen to be Buddhist, they want to wear it as a badge a badge of incorrectly assumed intellectual and cultural superiority given the fact that it is not mainstream and therefore but wrongly perceived as only intelligible to a few. Such people may also elbow their way into positions that they wrongly see as of authority in the group or they will assume greater knowledge of the subject where there may not be. This is not Buddhism this is the ego at work here.

If you attach to Buddhism as a property of your own ego then you are not Buddhist though you may think you are. You are missing the target and prolonging your own suffering. If you want to be a true Buddhist, in its quintessential form, then your ego is going to have to be discarded. Say 'goodbye' to the idea of self and 'hello' to happiness. Go and search for enlightenment.

Chapter 22

IN THE PURSUIT OF HAPPINESS

(To live – reaching for the opulence of life)

Perhaps more fundamental to us all is the search for a life that has purpose that has meaning without which life can seem just too intolerable to bear. Carl Jung would advocate this for sure and would no doubt extend these thoughts to a need for the individual to experience tangible growth and development, new experiences, wonder and creativity.

The human possessing remarkable intelligence requires something beyond its basic existence its basic needs without which life would just seem too flat. Our existence demands that we seek out that which is beyond our basic needs as an affirmation of why we are what we are and why we are here; it is for this reason that we humans thirst to explore to discover to learn.

It is foolish to believe that we can ever find contentment or even perhaps that elusive goal of ever-lasting happiness if we are weighed down by a motivation that is obsessed with destruction or with our own ego. If we seek a better life then first we must search within ourselves and be honest about what our motivations really are, is it that they are healthy and constructive or is it that we constantly seek to make the lives of others miserable and constantly seek a greater sense of our own feeling of importance or perhaps even superiority, these being traits that isolate us from genuinely good people and from genuinely meaningful experiences, in essence it may be our very self that thwarts our own life potential.

Life has a peculiar karmic quality in that whatever we do whatever games we play some way life will pay us back, to see this connection between what we do and what we get is critical in understanding how to make the most of what we experience.

> *"Who is wise? - He who learns from everyone. Who is strong? – He who controls his own impulses. Who is rich? – One who is happy with what he has. Who is honourable? One who honours everyone."* – Simeon Ben Zoma (Teacher, Israel 2nd century)

But today I feel f***ing marvellous, not necessarily about where I am but about where I am heading, does life get any better than this I ask, however reality might be somewhat different but perhaps if we fool ourselves into thinking that everything is great then maybe it will turn out to be just that, so why not remind yourself every day as you awake as to just how great life is.

The Perspective of Disappointment - Important

Consider this: what percentage of the population has a perfect life as can be defined by spouse, family, friends, great health security, a home, comfort, a wonderful childhood, job security, interest and satisfaction, well rewarded, confident, free of anxiety, boredom, fear, threat or anger, immediately liked by everyone, never ever received abuse of any kind, an optimistic future a past to feel great about a life where nothing ever goes wrong and nothing will ever change and where nothing will ever be lost.

If you think too much about your life you may be thinking a lot about what has gone wrong, lost time and lost opportunity that can never be recouped, what is wrong now and what you fear that can or will go wrong in the future. Thoughts such as these will tear you apart from constant rumination of comparing our experience to what it could be or could have been.

The difference between the life that we desire and the life that we have is a measure of our disappointment. If it is so that this disappointment is huge in our terms then in our terms we perceive life as a tragedy, tragedy that may even feel unbearable. The more tributaries that we are able to imagine to what we define as a fault free successful life the further we are away from that ideal. Indeed an admission on my part, as the author, is that in attempting to resolve some of life's many woes I have inadvertently opened up Pandora's box out of which jumps a paradox in that; the more adept we are at resolving problems the more problems we then perceive.

The saying that *"ignorance is bliss"* may then seem very apt. If we were less adept at imagining so many tributaries of success then we would suffer less and in theory if we could think of none then suffering would cease to exist. You may contemplate so many things in life and then come and think 'I/we don't have that' well neither do most of the rest of us and we must stay mindful of this fact.

Let's just look at reality. If you, your conscious self, exists as one of the seven billion human inhabitants of planet earth then you are very lucky indeed to at least exist as a member of a species that can at least realise something, albeit not everything, of a perfect life. But of the seven billion of us; the number who actually do experience the perfect life, as just defined, is exactly zero. Indeed human characteristics that could precipitate some of these aspects of perfection would preclude the existence of other aspects of perfection. You could say therefore that all factors of perfection have a mutually exclusive property; you may gain more of one but to the loss of another. Perfection is thus elusive.

We may be able to identify so many factors to reach perfection but here we should hold back and then consider not what we desire but what we are lucky to have. I may have something that you desire but you may have something else that I would rather have but don't. Essentially, we may have something in our support structure, environment or in the self that we are lucky to have and it is to this that we should focus our attention. The measure of a successful life should therefore be based upon what we have not upon what we haven't.

Dead Souls, Avalanching Rules and the Need for Change

I once offered the text from a much earlier incarnation of my chapter on Buddhism to a lost soul, but to one who was intransigent who believed that he did not need to learn anything, so he rejected my offer. As he was dying he lamented about his life. Don't leave things too late to learn, to be open, to do what is decent and to love others. He died as he was born not knowing how to live life, don't be like him, don't die with such regrets. You can either seek to make your life good or you just get left behind.

There are those who won't change when they need to, they are rigid and are unable to bend and as such they are unable to survive. The person who does not change who never did change has thwarted their own personality development where otherwise there could have been so much potential. It would be somewhat understandable if opportunity did not present itself or where life is full of privation or abuse, this could make any of us feel pretty pessimistic and so lose the will to do anything about it but yet not realise that all is not lost.

But what of those who are just unwilling to change, who may even had luck in their favour. Life they take too seriously they cannot lighten up and they abide by the rules to the letter. Life becomes a set of instructions to follow, *"I must do this" "I mustn't do that" "I have an image to keep up, an ego to protect" "I will not open my mind to anything"*. It must be a painful existence to follow and to be attached so much to rules and to ego. They may assume that they are happy although this is a delusion for they are not living they are just dead souls cast adrift and imprisoned in an ocean of self-inflicted isolation and misery whilst the rest of us who are willing to question, adapt and change are able to feel alive or have potential to do so despite the crap that we often have to put up with.

There are two types of people in this world those who are willing to explore change and those who are miserable. Any of us may die tomorrow and how might we sum up our life, might we say: *"I followed the rules"* or *"I made myself and others miserable"* (you can't have one without the other) or can I say *"I lived my life to its full potential and made a lot of others and myself happy in the process"* – these are our options.

And a note on ego is that contrary to belief it is not the same as self-esteem where we have a positive perception of what we are, instead we have desire to have a feeling of superiority one of self-importance. Once we clothe ourselves in self-importance we will suffer; it is the ego, the importance of the 'I', that finds all failure, rejection and social exclusion as agonisingly intolerable all of which become even more probable if we have ego. Ego gets in the way of where we need to go to get to the best experiences that life can offer.

It is unfortunate that in our modern world, with less manual work, that idle hands will find a purpose in imposing more rules or in demanding more rules, perhaps it is the only way that they can earn a living, they can't do anything else, they can't contribute any added value or do we impose rules and demands purely by our own volition our own craving. One of the main causes of misery can be bureaucracy, work place or government generated, too many rules so many in fact that mostly they either don't make sense and therefore have no material purpose or they constipate progress, they slow progress down or even prevent it. Give an entrepreneur a blank sheet of paper and they can invent fantastic business ideas; the unchained mind is free and full of limitless potential. However, what if we were to throw the rule book away what if we just follow rules as no more than guidelines where we do what is necessary rather than what we are told.

The successful business and the successful human being does best when it is prepared to do the unthinkable and to think outside of the box, if we didn't we would be without the marvels of modern technology, still living with the idea of a flat earth and we would be without equality for all. Those mavericks of the past who adapted rules to suit or who were prepared to think the unthinkable have changed our lives for the better not for the worse albeit that many of us rigidly refuse to row in the direction of progress.

If there is one rule, sense of duty or perhaps principle that humanity should have above all others it is 'what is it that you do for others' and if you sit there with an expectation that others, with this principle, should spoon feed you then you are not following the same rule.

"Kindness and good nature unite men more effectually and with greater strengths than any agreements." – Sir Thomas More (Statesman, England 16th century)

"I have given you the gift of life, do not abuse it, honour me by developing yourself in whatever way you can in the capacity that I have given you, strive to be good and

show kindness to others, if you do this you will be very dear to me." – 'Theoleptic spirituality'

Just as being unwilling to change thwarts our ability to feel alive so does a life that lacks change. To feel alive demands change, it demands new experiences, to go beyond, to go into the unknown and sometimes this requires risk to give a sense of exhilaration and adventure although we should always be mindful of the risk, is it just too dangerous and we should be mindful of how to prevent a disaster if things went badly wrong. We could sit in a chair for our whole life watching some nonsense on the television, yet more pulp entertainment, or for the price of a packet of cigarettes we could get ones arse up get out and explore by taking the car, the bus or train to somewhere else or we could buy a book that changes our whole view of things or we could meet up with a good friend we can find better reason to live and better things to do but just don't do the same thing over and over again; go and seek out new life enriching experiences and something to look forward to.

Even if you have no money you can still go outside and see the wonders of the world, if all around you seems ugly then look up to the sky (day and night), look at a tree, breathe in the air, even to listening to the rain (or a weir) has its delights or you could participate in say Tai Chi or something like Chinese line dancing. Even within your mind you can explore ideas and even places and discover new things and new experiences that bit by bit changes your perception of a dull existence and avoids the stagnation of the minds experience and thereby loss of joy.

The Questions That We Must Put To Ourselves

We may take interest in the world's problems and we may do our bit or may even be very active to alleviate them but are we trapped in endless anxiety, an anxiety that serves no purpose, about what is happening – should we lament and trouble ourselves so much or can we learn at some point that we must close the door on it all or otherwise go mad. Do we constantly obsess or exaggerate about things that in a wider perspective are really insignificant and do we put too much importance upon them and ourselves – should we not learn when to let go. Are we attached too much to our own ego, do we demand too much of others and of ourselves or can we not just sit back, relax and stay calm.

Do we look upon every challenge as a threat or something from which we have an opportunity to learn, to become greater than what we are. Are we able and willing to question ourselves when we have foolish ideas that will ultimately bring us harm, do we have this courage. Can we find a constructive reason to live or do we look only to destroy and so bring no good upon us. Can we look at life and live it to the full to make our lives and that of others so much better. Are we really making the most of the opportunities we have and making the effort to create those opportunities.

Do we perceive ourselves in terms of where we have failed or in terms of what is good, wonderful and special about us and also for the ambitions we have to improve upon what we are. Have we hotwired ourselves to live to our full potential.

What is it that we want, what path do we seek; a path to death of our soul or a path to feeling alive and making the most of the time we have here on planet earth.

The Journey So Far

Our liver, a rather and apparently boring reddish-brown rubbery organ about the size of a bag of sugar (1kg) is anything but boring; it has over 500 vital life maintaining critical functions ranging from protein synthesis, hormone regulation, metabolism of drugs, destruction of toxins, manufacture of digestive enzymes and is intrinsic in providing us with energy. Further to this it has a remarkable and miraculous ability to regenerate. Surgically excise 75% of its volume or inflict significant chemical damage to it and it will regrow to its original mass and it will restructure itself at the cellular level in its self-restoration. This is a stunning organ indeed. The liver we have is a complete functioning chemical factory and it was no different at our birth, it was effectively fully equipped as we entered the world.

Chemically we are designed to survive our environment very much by virtue of this amazing organ but we cannot say that we were equipped to survive life in so far as our mind is concerned. To survive life, that we mostly have to endure, can only be achieved through what we have learnt through experience for the neonate brain is not equipped with these survival skills.

"Life is not a problem to be solved, but a reality to be experienced." – Søren Kierkegaard (Philosopher, Denmark 19th century)

Now that you are coming towards the end of this book you have gone through a journey of philosophical awareness on the challenges that life throws at us and how we might be better prepared to deal with those challenges we have acquired some ideas to prevent or solve our problems and also those of the wider society within which we live and this in itself hopefully brings us to a better place but this in itself is not enough. Life is not just about survival it is about living about feeling alive. It is not good enough just to get by we need more we need optimism.

Goodbye Pessimism, Hello Optimism

Between reality and what we feel is our conditioned thinking, here we filter what may be good or what may be bad, we amplify it and we add to its narrative from which we can look at life with optimism or with pessimism. Further to this, much like a job interview, we don't always succeed from which we may assume ourselves to be a failure rather than having just failed in that moment of time, and opportunity for change may seem just too infrequent to yield any hope where in reality we should not be waiting for opportunity we should be going out and making it.

"To live without hope is to cease to live." – Fyodor Dostoyevsky (Novelist, Russia 19th century)

The world of pessimism is an unbearable world lacking hope without expectation of a good future, where we only look for fault and feel that we can't do anything about it, where we do nothing but criticize, where we obsess, where we incessantly blame others and ourselves, where we do not see the good that is around us. Given the difficulties that life present us with, and that the previous chapters elucidate to, then isn't it any wonder that most of us have pessimism to some or other extent; it could be said that pessimism is a natural state given the plethora of difficulties we face and have faced.

Some of us have been ground down by life or we are burnt out by it and many of us have a bad or sad story to tell. Whatever we have endured and are enduring we can lift ourselves above all of this by changing what we are we can become optimistic.

Pessimism destroys confidence, a belief of a positive outcome and so destroys motivation. In a nutshell pessimism doesn't work and if something doesn't work then what do we do with it – it's to go to the bin. Even when life throws the very worst at you and you have absolutely nothing left we can at least believe in hope and optimism and with hope and optimism this is where our life can be restarted we can find a new life and a reason to live.

When we are optimistic we have a sense of control over our life, we can plan where we are going and what we are going to do and we have an expectation that all will turn out good and if it doesn't it is not in any way that things have failed it just means that a different approach is all that is required. I can do something about this I am not the victim I am the master. The optimist is positive, full of confidence and motivated. The optimist is a survivor and will look beyond where they are and to where they want to go and they will put in all efforts required to do so.

If you are a pessimist it's time to change so let's get on the horse and charge into a new beginning. Saddle up now, don't wait just do it.

Maybe Contentment Should Be Our Objective

"It is my right to be happy" is a statement of self-importance, to elevate our rights above that of everyone else, do we even deserve to be happy or are we selfish in all that motivates us. Perhaps we should look at it from the perspective that it is the right of all of us to be able to find happiness.

> *"Happiness does not lie in happiness, but in the achievement of it."* – Fyodor Dostoyevsky (Novelist, Russia 19th century)

So much of our time we seek happiness and we believe that we shall be happy when we have achieved something only to then realise that we are still not happy it is like searching for that mythical pot of Gold at the end of the rainbow that isn't there. Just think of when you bought your first car, your home, what about when you got married, passed that exam, got that better job, went on that holiday of a lifetime, how did you feel; day 1 you would feel elated and after one week you still probably feel pretty good but what about in six months what about in six years. The happiness that these things bring you will decay, there will come a time that what fired you up no longer does, it's as if whatever we do our ecstasy doesn't last, we then have to find yet more things to make us happy, trade in the old car, another holiday, all that require work to earn these things, work that erodes away at our free time.

We can conclude that happiness is transitory and no more. Sustained happiness is not attainable and our continued searching and in particular our feeling of entitlement is what shackles us to a wasted cause. Happiness is an emotion that has a voracious appetite for change, to stay happy we have to keep changing things finding ways to rekindle that which extinguishes like any flame. To whatever place we come to, to wherever we have elevated ourselves and to whatever we have gained happiness cannot be fixed from that point on we will always want more or we will want better.

> *"The most common form of despair is not being who you are."* – Søren Kierkegaard (Philosopher, Denmark 19th century)

Perhaps happiness is not what makes us happy but perhaps what does is the never ending pursuit of happiness in striving and in changing in seeing constant development is what makes us happy but this requires constant input, investment of effort to which after some point our weariness from such effort will degrade how we feel. Can we therefore achieve happiness, though in some other notion of what it is, can we redefine happiness; a happiness without decay and without endless pursuit. What if we could change our view and just be happy with what we have and what we are; we are satisfied that everything we have is all that we ever want.

It is this feeling of contentment that can change our lives permanently. Let's go in search of contentment and be satisfied with what we have got.

But there is A Way to Find Happiness (avoiding 'I' and 'me' the pronouns of misery)

"Who is happy? This is a person, who has a healthy body, is dowered with peace of mind and cultivates his talents." – Thales of Miletus (Philosopher, Greece 7th century BC)

"Free from anger and selfish desire, unified in mind, those who follow the path of yoga and realise the self are established forever in that supreme state." – The Bhagavad Gita (Hinduism)

What may have appeared as me trying to deprive you of any hope of happiness, albeit that the intention of my whole book knowingly or unknowingly to you is to do the exact opposite, however all is not lost, there is a route to the primary objective that our life searches for. It is possible to be happy permanently but the trick to do so is very simple indeed. The pursuit of happiness is something to make 'me' happy is, dare I say, a selfish pursuit - I want to make me happy. From my own experience of so many others, that those who are selfish are seldom happy, they might like to think that they are happy but their happiness is very impoverished, they are 'happy' possibly through having a sense of power over others or that they have material wealth – the ego again.

"To love is to find the pleasure in the happiness of others." – Gottfried Leibnitz (Polymath, Germany 17th/18th century)

Here is the problem; our enemy our ego has pushed any potential of happiness aside. What could have been the pursuit of happiness has been replaced by the pursuit of ego and it is here that the very obvious conclusion can be made. If serving our ego the 'I' or 'Me' makes us unhappy then to become happy I have to serve the 'not I' or the 'not me' i.e. we have to serve others we have to make others happy in order for us to become happy. Confusing perhaps and not so intuitive but nevertheless true.

I have found time after time that the happiest people in this world are the ones who don't play power games, who are not materialistic, who are not awful to their fellow humans, who do not have ego. Much in the same way as I describe in the chapter on relationships as to what makes an engaging personality is much the same as what makes a person happier.

"Be good, be kind, be humane and charitable; love your fellows; console the afflicted." – Zarathustra (Prophet, Persia 6th century BC)

The happy person thinks about others feelings, they are friendly, compassionate, well-mannered and charismatic, they think about how others feel, they seek to make others feel good, but in addition to the personality precursors to happiness they also undertake acts of kindness focussed upon others though others who show sincere appreciation not as in some great reward but just a smile, and to see that you are making a difference to someone's life someone that is who deserves it, that's most of us although unfortunately not all. Such refinement of humanity cannot work without community. If we are the lone practitioner of this philosophy then we may just land up being used and abused so we need a society where there is fertile ground one where others appreciate what you do for them who likewise will extend you such similar courtesy. (Negative as it may sound but there are evil those who exploit charity and the good will of others, they are to be avoided as they not only bring ingratitude they also bring trouble.)

"Someday, somehow, I am going to do something useful, something for people. They are most of them so helpless, so hurt and so unhappy." – Edith Cavell (Nurse, England 19th/20th century)

The Paradise of Planet Earth

"I have become so great, as I am because I have won men's hearts by gentleness and kindness." – An-Nasir Salah ad-Din Yusuf ibn Ayyub, 'Saladin' (Sultan, Syria/Egypt 12th century)

Life can seem dull, however what do you see if you can get away from the humdrum of life; you can find the beauty of nature the wonder of creation. Just look at a flower, a tree, a forest, a river, a lake, the ocean, a hill, a distant mountain, the blue sky above, the clouds how they move how they change, the majesty of the heavens with all of its stars that stretch so far into an unimaginable distance and what of the beauty of life around, what is it that you observe what do you feel when you look at these things and have shut out all other thoughts. Can you also feel the warmth of the sun, can you feel and hear the breeze or the rain, can you hear the sound of mighty thunder, the waves crashing into the coastline or a running stream, the birds singing or the bees humming can you smell the fragrance of the flowers or of freshly cut grass.

Do you now feel nothing – use your senses just look at what you are missing what is there all around you. There is so much going on around us that we have lost sight of because we are too caught up in ourselves, we can't see it all not because it isn't there but because we have forgotten to look.

"What wisdom can you find that is greater than kindness." – Jean-Jacques Rousseau (Philosopher, France 18th century)

But it doesn't end there since where mankind has done its very best, and for which God has equipped us to do so, we have created literature, art, architecture, philosophy, music and dance and we have been given abilities to furnish our amazing home, planet earth, with such wonders. Further than this we see humanity itself in the most sublime in what we do for each other, the kindness, charity and compassion we have for our fellow human. We have ability to make heaven our place on earth. You may see the fools who do so much otherwise but their minds are beyond appreciation of what is really good - they cannot reach where the enlightened can and their lives can never be fulfilled.

"This is the best of all possible worlds." – Gottfried Leibnitz (Polymath, Germany 17th/18th century)

Philosophical Thoughts

"Live as if you were to die tomorrow. Learn as if you were to live forever." – Saint Isidore of Seville (Scholar, Spain 6th/7th century)

Opportunities do not just fall into your lap, you need to go out and find them and to succeed requires effort. Seldom is success through luck alone since if you put nothing in you will get nothing out but don't expect too much from your efforts so be happy with what you can achieve. Make sure that in all of your actions that you stay ahead of the curve of enlightenment but stay well behind the curve of stupidity since bad ideas or bad actions will bring you bad results.

Today may have been a failure and so may have yesterday but what of tomorrow, things can change and so can life since all things are impermanent and so even what is bad must come to its end. Failure does not map out your 'inevitable' future, there is nothing inevitable about it unless you allow it to be so, it maps out your need to change whereby you find out what went wrong and why and then you learn from the experience and adapt to suit. Just look upon every new day as you wake up as a new day for you a new life with new opportunities. What you do just make sure that it is decent and sensible where the outcome with all things considered is the right outcome.

We are here to learn not to destroy not to make other's lives a misery but to learn to grow and develop and in that process we shall help others on the same journey.

Every day make it your mission to make someone else feel happier and more optimistic about life and if you fail don't worry about it you can't win with everyone.

In Closing

You and I have both been through something of a rollercoaster in this book contemplating life's woes and its many opportunities. For me it has taken nearly four decades to think about and well over three years to write and for you some hours to read. I believe that every book I pick up I learn something new something that even in some small way may have challenged what I, to that point, had thought and that had then taken my life into a new and hopefully better direction for we are all constantly learning. It is my sincere intention to do the same with what I have written herein. Perhaps I have made some positive difference to your life, and I hope that I have, but if not at least you might question the life that you experience and what is beyond and look for ways in which you can improve things for you and for all those who you encounter.

Just thinking philosophically about philosophy; we must be vigilant in not becoming its slave, it is an advantage to gain wisdom but it is a distinct life consuming disadvantage to think too much in doing so, life after all is meant for living. The consequences upon life of not thinking can only be disaster but thinking too much can lead to self-torture and may even lead to madness.

But before we go we need to ask do we act responsibly and fairly to ourselves and to everyone else, do we do the right thing, but upon this philosophy alone we cannot live life. Is it that we seek the common but illogical seductions of power, superiority or self-importance to assuage our misery, a bad idea indeed with illusory success and in reality terrible existential failure, or do we seek to do the opposite do we seek fun, do we seek to be ourselves, do we seek to feel alive. Whilst I write this I cannot ignore a, such, apt allusion to the character played by Norman Wisdom in the film 'What's Good for the Goose' a hilarious but actually thought provoking story of personal transformation. If you get to see this film make sure you think about its real message, not that which is 'incidental' on its surface but that which is deep within.

Perhaps the answer to life is to know when and when not to use hard logic and when and when not to be light hearted, if we always do one without the other we will fail in our existence and we will fail in our reason to exist. Do not therefore waste your life, live it, be yourself, feel alive, live.

From this point on we need to go in search of the right path; and may your God, our God, look over you, be in your heart and help guide you to enlightenment. Whatever failures you may have had don't look back at your past, this is now the time to set a new course for the future a course that you must follow diligently. As for me I can go back to my own world and perhaps start on another book but definitely nothing more on this subject, time to close that chapter and move on. And in the words of Buddhism – *"Go in search of enlightenment go in search of the truth"*.

Each day brings a new beginning for a new life, one to explore, to learn, to create, to progress, to seek out self-discipline and to develop magnificence within, to stay focussed on success not on failure, to enjoy life and to help each other, to free the soul from fear and anger and to attain even greater heights of self-actualisation. Aspire for truth and reason and seek to leave each day in a better state than when you had entered it.

And now – a new start

APPENDIX I (THE ANXIETY LATCH)

Dissecting the Anxiety Latch

If it is that we have a serious perceived problem <u>AND</u> one that we also care much, perhaps too much, about, then we start to ruminate on the problem seeking out a solution. If we find a solution that is acceptable then our problem is resolved and we no longer ruminate.

If however we do not find an acceptable solution within a certain time by which our rumination is causing us considerable distress then we reach a state of severe depression, one that we cannot now assuage by any distractions often as a result of other damaging effects of the depression precipitating other but phantom perception problems. Our depression is latched, we are thus held in this dreadful state of hellish rumination never finding that ever so elusive solution, depression has compromised our ability to think straight ability to solve and rumination saps our emotional energy, we may even feel mentally ill. Further to this if we have an impoverished belief in ourselves and we believe all that which is negative then our ability to solve a problem is catastrophically degraded, even obliterated.

If we already possess unshakable self-esteem (as in 1000% 'military disciplined' belief in ourselves) and we rationally dismiss negative thoughts that deserve dismissal then we facilitate the process of finding a solution before depression has time to kick in but if we can only acquire these later, perhaps through some philosophical reflection, then we can reset (clear) the latch and rid ourselves of depression. So effective can this be that in finding the key to right thinking and we can destroy the foundations of our depressive thoughts in an instant, the cloud lifts and the hell is suddenly gone.

Some Further Thoughts

Think about the application of this in life, issues such as unemployment ('reset' might be a realisation that everyone is being rejected not just you), loss of confidence ('reset' might be a realisation to not obsess on your weaknesses but to reflect on your strengths), relationship failure ('reset' might be a realisation that it's not you it's just that you are making bad choices not just about others but perhaps also about yourself). 'Reset' may also be that you accept your lot and just move on.

Just drilling a little deeper then clearly avoiding the time limit for which the latch will set then we might need to think about our patience (change requires patience) and what we seek as an acceptable solution – if we are too picky, to demanding, then the solution becomes ever more elusive ever more improbable in the time frame that we unconsciously set – thus those more easily satisfied will be less prone to depression.

A lesson here is that although we need to optimise life we must not aim for the elusive holy grail of 100% perfection unless we are willing to forego ever reaching our goal, optimisation should therefore be framed in accordance with reality, effort and opportunity. When we consider the time aspect in this logic then it is very obvious that rapid progression to depression is precipitated if it is so that we are very much easily alarmed, too easily stressed and not laid back enough.

The question you must ask yourself is; do your negative thoughts control you or can you control them can you recognise crazy thinking believing everything that our mind conjures up or do we recognise spurious fatally paralysing parasitic thoughts built upon a substrate of life conditioned negativity. Are we naturally predisposed to being negative or even to be fatally negative and can we change how we think – not easy but not impossible either.

"The happiness of your life depends upon the quality of your thoughts: therefore guard accordingly, and take care that you entertain no notion unsuitable to virtue and reasonable nature." – Marcus Aurelius (Emperor, Rome 2nd century)

If your mind is predisposed to the negative and when it is trapped in a never ending cyclone of rumination then you really need to recognise that you are doing bad to yourself, granted that your situation may indeed be harsh, whereby your perceived outcome looks none other than hell when in reality this could be so far from what you can achieve and where your life can go. Life's problems are not so easy to fix and less so if we seek to solve everything, we should instead seek small victories that are within our reach as perceivable progress along the path to our ultimate goal.

APPENDIX II (THE (IM)PROBABILITY OF LIFE)

So How Amazing is the Miracle of Life

In consideration of the complexity of human DNA, there are around three billion (3×10^9) nucleotides in the human genome, i.e. our total DNA code, (a nucleotide consists of the aforementioned nucleotide base + a sugar + a phosphate component). Each nucleotide forms part of the code for a lifeform using the four nucleotide base chemicals. Some parts of the code, as we had alluded to, would instruct on the construction of liver cells and other parts would instruct on bone cells etc. Hence along the human genome there are 3 billion locations where we can place any of the four letters A, C, G or T.

However, in the human genome around 50% of the code is repeated of which only around 8% of that code has function and less than 0.5% of that is what makes us unique and individual within our human species.

On that basis there are 3×10^9 x 50% x 8% x (100% − 0.5%), i.e. 1.2×10^8 or 120,000,000 nucleotide locations that are critical to holding the code that defines us as being human.

If we were to consider that the first nucleotide location on the DNA molecule can accommodate one of four possible options (A, C, G or T), the second location can also accommodate four possible options (again A, C, G or T) and so on, then we can arrive at the number of possible combinations, i.e. how many different codes are available from such an arrangement or how many ways we can arrange the four letters along 120,000,000 locations.

Taking a very simple example, and assuming that we have an inexhaustible supply of each of our four letters, then how many combinations would be possible with our option of four letters to choose to fit into just two such locations; this would be 16 (from 4 x 4 or 4^2), the combinations being: AA, AC, AG, AT, CA, CC, CG, CT, GA, GC, GG, GT, TA, TC, TG and TT.

Three locations would yield 64 combinations (from 4 x 4 x 4 or 4^3) starting from AAA through all combinations to TTT. Taking this further, our 120,000,000 locations would present a staggering $4^{120,000,000}$ possible combinations using our four nucleotides.

In our analysis we need to re-acquaint ourselves in the use of (common) logarithms. A number such as 1,000,000 (i.e. 10 x 10 x 10 x 10 x 10 x 10 − note there are six

10's here) can in shorthand be represented as 10^6 where '6' is what we would call the logarithm of 1,000,000 i.e. **log 1,000,000** (i.e. **log 10^6**) = **6**. Another example would be that **log 1000** (i.e. **log 10^3**) = **3** and that **log 10** = **1** and so it can be deduced that **log 10^6** is the same as **6 x log 10** (i.e. 6 x 1) = **6**.

By replacing the constant '6' with the variable 'L' we can recast this formula into a more general rule such that: **log 10^L = L x log 10** and by then replacing '10' with 'N' then it follows that **log N^L = L x log N**, where 'N' is the number of <u>n</u>ucleotide base options, this is always 4 and where 'L' is the number of <u>l</u>ocations on the DNA molecule where we can attach nucleotides or we could call this the (nucleotide) length of the DNA.

Now the opposite of the logarithm is the anti-logarithm and this works as follows, in that if 6 is the logarithm of 10^6 then **10^6** is the **antilogarithm** of **6** (rule 1) i.e. it is the reverse process, also that the **antilog** of **log 10^6** = **10^6** (rule 2) where the 'antilog' and the 'log' cancel each other out.

In looking at our equation **log N^L = L x log N** then it follows that the **antilog** of **log N^L = N^L** (from rule 2) and that the **antilog** of L x log N = $10^{L \times \log N}$ (from rule 1), therefore our equation **log N^L = L x log N** can be re-written as **$N^L = 10^{L \times \log N}$**.

It also follows that by replacing 'N' with 4 (i.e. for our four nucleotide option) that **$4^L = 10^{L \times \log 4}$** and using tables of logarithms we can establish that log 4 = 0.6021 to be precise but we can approximate this to 0.6, so therefore it follows that **$4^L = 10^{0.6 \times L}$** and from this formula our $4^{120,000,000}$ combinations of nucleotides in human DNA can be re-written as $10^{72,000,000}$ (i.e. $10^{0.6 \times 120,000,000}$) this being the number 1 followed by 72,000,000 zeroes.

We can put this figure of $10^{72,000,000}$ (the possible combinations of human DNA) into a cosmological perspective by comparing it with the number of atoms in our known universe (i.e. of that which we can observe), this being around 10^{80} atoms (i.e. 1 followed by 80 zeros or 100 million million million million million million million million million million million million million) of which 70% of these atoms, by mass, are hydrogen.

Now hydrogen is our lightest atom at an atomic mass of 1 (it has just one proton and no neutrons) but a typical nucleotide has an atomic mass of around 350. For the analysis, and in wildly massive benefit to making life looking a lot more possible, we are going to assume that all of the material in the universe is fertile to generating DNA i.e. all atoms are replaced with off the shelf constructed nucleotides and therefore we are also assuming that we have 350 x as much matter as we actually have. Now these considerations should compensate towards the many but unknown quantity of lifeforms that could be achieved equally successfully with 120,000,000 nucleotides but that would not be human and for which most combinations by far would fail to create successful life.

We can also make a further comparison but with something a bit more down to earth in the 150 million million million (1.5×10^{20}, i.e. approximately 10^{20}) possible code combinations of the fiendishly 'unbreakable' World War 2 German 'Enigma' cyphering machine that as standard was fitted with just three rotors (26 settings) and a plug board. The DNA equivalent of the enigma machine would not be a 3 rotor machine but would require 50 million rotors [i.e. (72,000,000-20)/log 26, derived from the combinations of 'R' rotors that would be $26^{R-3} \times 10^{20}$].

Now an important consideration, is that just as a safe might require 1000 attempts to open its door if it has 1000 possible combinations, is that something with $10^{72,000,000}$ combinations may require $10^{72,000,000}$ attempts to hit the right code. However, how long does each attempt take at trying to open the safe and if we have lots of safes and lots of safe crackers we might at least successfully open one of these safes given enough time but how does this relate to our existence within the timespan of our universe and the material that is within it. We could of course be lucky with our first attempt but the probability of this happening is only $1/10^{72,000,000}$ so the odds are not good to say the least.

The Possibility of Life

Using exacting mathematical methods would make this task very complex for reasons I will not explain as they are somewhat abstruse so we shall make some assumptions along the way that simplifies the analysis and that happen to be in favour of success. Here we are using a rough analysis to just get some idea of the enormity of the problem not to achieve an accurate number that would be almost impossible to achieve.

We already know how to calculate the number of combinations of a DNA molecule of length 'L' nucleotides (i.e. 4^L or $10^{0.6 \times L}$) and therefore the number of times we must 'roll the dice' to hit lucky. But something else we know is that cells take typically around 10 minutes to reproduce where each reproduction may present a different mutation. The question is how do we calculate the number of DNA molecules that we can construct in the time of the universe where one of which will match the code we are aiming for – much in the same way as to how many lottery tickets do we need to buy to definitely win?

We have at our disposal a lot of resources which we have assumed to be 10^{80} nucleotides, so the number of complete DNA molecules that we can construct = $10^{80}/L$ where 'L' is the number of nucleotide locations along the DNA molecule.

This is analogous to how many houses can we build with 10^{80} bricks if each house requires 'L' bricks.

Now with our new understanding of logarithms we know that 'L' can be re-written as $10^{\log L}$ and so $10^{80}/L = 10^{80}/10^{\log L}$ or $10^{(80-\log L)}$ as derived from another rule that '$10^a/10^b = 10^{(a-b)}$'.

So with our 10^{80} nucleotides we can build $10^{(80-\log L)}$ DNA molecules of length 'L' nucleotides, at each attempt using all of our available materials, one of which we may strike lucky but we also have the lifetime of the universe to consider where this attempt can be repeated many times.

Our universe's existence is about 14 billion (14×10^9) years or in other words approximately 10^{16} minutes (derived from 14×10^9 years x 365 days x 24 hours x 60 minutes). Given the fact that cells reproduce every 10 minutes suggests that we have $10^{16}/10$, i.e. 10^{15} attempts, to try with all of our resources to match the right code in the lifetime of our universe.

Given that we have 10^{15} opportunities (that's every ten minutes in the lifetime of our universe) with in each opportunity enough material to construct $10^{(80-\log L)}$ DNA molecules, then in the lifetime of the universe we can construct a total of $10^{15} \times 10^{(80-\log L)}$ DNA molecules. If we were to assume more than one universe, say a quantity of 'U' universes, then we could construct a total of $U \times 10^{15} \times 10^{(80-\log L)}$ DNA molecules.

On the assumption of just one universe (U = 1), i.e. our known universe, then it therefore follows that to find 'L' the length of molecule that we can successfully hit upon is when the possible combinations of DNA equals the number of DNA molecules that we can construct then at this point $10^{0.6L} = U \times 10^{15} \times 10^{80-\log L}$. This we might call a 'life possibility conjecture'.

By rearranging this formula, where U =1, as: $10^{15} = 10^{0.6L}/10^{80-\log L}$ i.e. $10^{(0.6L-80+\log L)}$ then clearly: $15 = 0.6L - 80 + \log L$ or: $\mathbf{95 = 0.6L + \log L}$.

We now need to find a solution for 'L' that satisfies the equation in other words what is the length of the DNA that can be built in the lifetime of the universe using all material in the universe where one attempt to do so was a successful and exact match to a specified DNA code of the same length.

The solution for 'L' (through a process of successive approximation) that satisfies this equation is **155** and this is the maximum genome length that can be correctly matched by random sampling in the lifetime of our known universe and using all available material. So given chance, all of the material in the universe and all of the time in the universe then chances are that the most complex life form that we can construct has no more than 155 nucleotides compared to the common flu virus with

14,000 nucleotides, that is on the very edges of what you might call life, and to us with our 120 million critical nucleotides.

However, what if we considered our formula '$10^{0.6L} = U \times 10^{15} \times 10^{80-\log L}$' for us, for human life, where L = 120,000,000 such that upon rearranging and using the rules that '$10^a \times 10^b = 10^{(a+b)}$' and that '$\log (a \times b) = \log a + \log b$' we can calculate 'U' (i.e. how many universes are required to successfully construct us humans) as follows:

$$U = 10^{0.6L-95+\log L} = 10^{72,000,000-95+\log 120,000,000} \approx 10^{72,000,000-95+2+6} \approx 10^{72,000,000}$$

Therefore: U ≈ (approximately equals) $10^{72\ \text{million}}$. (Note that although the term '$10^{15} \times 10^{80-\log L}$' is a very large number it has very little influence on the perceived result because, although very significant, it is 'perceptibly' very small compared to the number of combinations, $10^{72,000,000}$, in the human genome.)

Bibliography/Further Reading

It would be impossible to enumerate all of the sources that have led me onto a path a direction in how I must think, not what, (literature of my own purchase and as studied in various libraries, lectures, documentaries, newspaper articles, conversations and debates, experiences and observations etc.) from which this book has been constructed.

I may also have indirectly alluded to the thoughts and/or achievements of the likes of Wittgenstein, Foucault, Adams-Keller, Vygotsky, Piaget, Adler, Mandela, Keynes, Curie, Laplace, Muhammad Ali, Garrett-Anderson, Tubman, Mendel, Edward Onslow Ford and to the countless unknown souls who also offer us insight into ourselves and others, they are in their somewhere as they are in my head but I couldn't tell you who, what or where, they are enmeshed within 'the soup' of what I have learnt from these explorers of thought, adventure and creativity.

It would be equally impossible for me to point to an exact source from which my ideas have been developed since all what you have read herein is a deconstruction, analysis, amalgam and then an eventual extrapolation of ideas with I add a great deal of agonising self-criticism in that 'does that idea make perfect sense' or is it flawed, but then again none of us, expert or novice, know anything with absolute certainty, for all of us we are always compelled to refine or even discard what we think we know. If I were to add all of this bibliographic detail then this book may easily have extended by another 500 pages.

Given this impossibility I have trawled through my own library to seek out what books are relevant to the subject matter basis not on a chapter basis odd as that may seem. Some publications may seem odd in their relevance but deeper study of each publication would reveal why they are not and in many cases the connection can only be gleaned through deeper understanding of each subject.

If it takes your fancy to study these publications in the context of this understanding then we are talking of perhaps 15 million words to digest this I would not recommend as this is not living take my word for it, it is not living and perhaps for me it's too late, with regret, having done so but at least this has brought me to writing this book.

But this being said some literature within will be very relevant to you or your circumstances and if you want or need to drill deeper into those areas then these books (and so many others not in my list for you to find yourself) I would highly recommend for further study and reflection.

Allusions to Philosophy/Religion/Spiritualism

1. *Buddhism, The Life of the Buddha and His Teachings – Abha Bhamorabutr*
2. *The Noble Path of Buddhism – Joseph Masson*
3. *Study Guide to Buddhism – Terry Thomas*
4. *The Teaching of Buddha – Bukkyo Dendo Kyokai*
5. *The Dhammapada – Narada Thera*
6. *Taming the Tiger – Akong Tulku Rinpoche*
7. *Watching the Tree – Adeline Yen Mah*
8. *Hinduism an Introduction – V.P. Kanitkar & W. Owen Cole*
9. *Bhagavad Gita As It Is – His Divine Grace A.C. Bhaktivedanta Swami Prabhupāda*
10. *The Bhagavad Gita According to Gandhi – Mahatma Gandhi*
11. *The Rider Encyclopedia of Eastern Philosophy and Religion – Rider Press*
12. *The World Religions – A Lion Handbook*
13. *Greek Mythology – Panaghiótis Chrístou and Katharini Papastamatis*
14. *A History of Western Philosophy – Bertrand Russell*
15. *Utopia – Thomas More*
16. *Joy, The Happiness That Comes from Within – Osho*
17. *A New Earth, Create A Better Life – Eckhart Tolle*
18. *A Journey in Ladakh – Andrew Harvey*
19. *On the Road – Jack Kerouac*
20. *The Tarot – Madeline Montalban*
21. *Fathers and Sons – Ivan Sergeyevich Turgenev*
22. *The Holy Bible Revised Standard Version – Collins Press*
23. *50 Paintings You Should Know - Kristina Lowis and Tamsin Pickeral*
24. *Da Vinci – Elizabeth Elias Kaufman*
25. *Caravaggio – Giles Lambert*
26. *On War - Carl Von Clausewitz*

Allusions to Understanding Logic (the potent precursor to rational thinking)

1. *The Darwin Awards – Wendy Northcutt*
2. *Lateral Thinking – Edward De Bono*
3. *The Code Book – Simon Singh*
4. *Algebra and Number Systems – Hunter, Monk, Blackburn, Donald*
5. *Understanding Digital Electronics – Gene McWhorter*
6. *Bletchley Park Demystifying the Bombe – Dermot Turing*
7. *The TTL Data Book for Design Engineers – Texas Instruments*
8. *Turbo C Programming for the PC – Robert Lafore*
9. *Safety-Critical Computer Systems – Neil Storey*
10. *What Colour Is Your Parachute – Richard Nelson Bolles*
11. *Mastering Business Law – Terry Price*

Allusions to Popular (and logical) Psychology, Personal Development and Inspiration

1. *Psycho-Cybernetics – Maxwell Maltz, MD*
2. *The Survivor Personality – Al Siebert, PhD*
3. *Stop Thinking Start Living – Richard Carlson*

4. *How To Stop Worrying and Start Living – Dale Carnegie*
5. *Crime and Punishment – Fyodor Dostoyevsky*
6. *The Stress Solution – Samuel H. Klarreich*
7. *It's All In Your Head, The Stories of Imaginary Illness – Suzanne O'Sullivan*
8. *A Guide To Rational Living – Albert Ellis PhD and Robert A.Harper PhD*
9. *The Motivated Mind – Dr Raj Persaud*
10. *Charisma – Marcia Grad*
11. *Laughing Matters, A Serious Look at Humour – John Durant and Jonathan Miller*
12. *No Dream Is Too High, Life Lessons From a Man Who Walked on the Moon – Buzz Aldrin*
13. *Admiral Richard Byrd, Alone In The Antarctic – Paul Rink*
14. *Robinson Crusoe – Daniel Defoe*
15. *The True History of the Elephant Man – Michael Howell & Peter Ford*

Allusions to Cognitive and Neuro Psychology

1. *The Brain – Jack Challoner*
2. *The Brain That Changes Itself – Norman Doidge*
3. *Microprocessor Engineering – B.Holdsworth*
4. *8080-8085 Assembly Language Programming – Lance A. Leventhal*
5. *Control Systems Engineering – Norman S. Nise*
6. *Why We Sleep – Matthew Walker*
7. *Jung – Anthony Stevens*
8. *Emotional Intelligence – Daniel Coleman*
9. *The Anatomy of Human Destructiveness – Erich Fromm*
10. *The Amazing World of M.C.Escher – Micky Piller, Patrick Elliott and Frans Peterse*

Allusions to the Theory, History and Literature of Psychiatry

1. *Psychiatry – Tom Burns*
2. *Madness Explained – Richard P. Bentall*
3. *Diagnostic Criteria (DSM-V) – American Psychiatric Association*
4. *From the Edge of the Couch – Dr Raj Persaud*
5. *Bedlam, London and Its Mad – Catharine Arnold*
6. *The Last Asylum, A Memoir of Madness in Our Times – Barbara Taylor*
7. *A Diary of a Madman and Other Stories – Nikolai Gogol*
8. *Psychopath Free – Jackson MacKenzie*
9. *Narcissists Exposed – Drew Keys*
10. *The Measure of Madness, Inside the Disturbed and Disturbing Criminal Mind – Cheryl Paradis*
11. *Jack the Ripper – Stewart Evans & Paul Gainey*
12. *Monsters, History's Most Evil Men and Women – Simon Sebag Montefiore*
13. *Auschwitz – Laurence Rees*
14. *The Dark Charisma of Adolf Hitler – Laurence Rees*
15. *Their Darkest Hour – Laurence Rees*
16. *No Country for Old Men – Cormac McCarthy*
17. *Talking with Serial Killers – Christopher Berry-Dee*
18. *The Divided Self – R.D. Laing*

19. *Parasite Rex – Carl Zimmer*
20. *Staying Sane – Dr Raj Persaud*

Allusions into the World of Politics, Corruption and Incompetent Power

1. *An English Affair Sex, Class and Power in the Age of Profumo – Richard Davenport-Hines*
2. *Patronising Bastards, How The Elites Betrayed Britain – Quentin Letts*
3. *The Prince – Niccolò Machiavelli*
4. *Thomas Cromwell – Robert Hutchinson*
5. *The Sisters Who Would Be Queen – Leanda De Lisle*
6. *Behind Closed Doors – Laurence Rees*
7. *The Sane Society – Erich Fromm*
8. *Communism – Leslie Holmes*
9. *Stalin and His Hangmen – Donald Rayfield*
10. *The Gulag Archipelago 1918-1956 – Aleksandr Solzhenitsyn*
11. *Iron Curtain – Anne Applebaum*
12. *Mao's Great Famine – Frank Dikötter*
13. *Nothing to Envy – Barbara Demick*
14. *When Broken Glass Floats, Growing Up Under the Khmer Rouge – Chanrithy Him*
15. *A Russian Diary – Anna Politkovskaya*
16. *Mafia State – Luke Harding*
17. *Elizabeth's Spy Master – Robert Hutchinson*
18. *The Fear of Freedom – Erich Fromm*
19. *Postmodernism – Christopher Butler*
20. *Green Hell, How Environmentalist's Plan to Control Your Life – Steve Milloy*
21. *Chemistry in Context – Graham C.Hill and John S.Holman*
22. *The English Civil Wars 1640-1660 – Blair Worden*
23. *The Gunpowder Plot, Terror and Faith in 1605 – Antonio Fraser*
24. *The Day of the Jackal – Frederick Forsyth*
25. *JFK, An American Coup D'etat – Colonel John Hughes-Wilson*
26. *With Malice Towards None, A Life of Abraham Lincoln – Stephen B. Oates*
27. *The Story of My Experiments with Truth – Gandhi*
28. *Three Cups of Tea, One Man's Mission to Promote Peace – Greg Mortensen and David Oliver Relin*
29. *Brilliant Negotiations – Nic Peeling*

Allusions to Non-Radical Feminism

1. *Sold, One Woman's Heartbreaking, True Account of Modern Slavery – Zana Muhsen*
2. *The Wonderful Adventures of Mary Seacole – Mary Seacole*
3. *Equal Opportunities A Career Guide – Ruth Miller*

Allusions to Economics, System Optimisation and Business

1. *Engineering Thermodynamics, Work and Heat Transfer – Rogers & Mayhew*
2. *The Great Divide – Joseph E. Stiglitz*
3. *How Do We Fix This Mess – Robert Peston*
4. *A Brief History of Capitalism – Yaris Varoufakis*

5. *Nuclear Reactor Engineering – Samuel Glasstone and Alexander Sesonske*
6. *Further Elementary Analysis – R.I. Porter*
7. *A Course of Mathematics for Engineers and Scientists Vol 1 – B.H.Chirgwin and C.Plumpton*
8. *An Introduction to Linear Analysis – Kreider, Kuller, Ostberg and Perkins*
9. *The 10 Day MBA – Steven Silbiger*
10. *Corporate Denial, Confronting the World's Most Damaging Business Taboo – Will Murray*
11. *Science, As Seen Through the Development of Scientific Instruments – Thomas Crump*
12. *Seven Wonders of the Industrial World – Deborah Cadbury*

Allusions to Social Conditions and Public Health

1. *London in the 19th Century – Jerry White*
2. *The Worst Street in London – Fiona Rule*
3. *If Walls Could Talk – Lucy Worsley*
4. *The Medical Detective – Sandra Hempel*
5. *A Short History of Disease – Sean Martin*
6. *Spitting Blood, The History of Tuberculosis – Helen Bynum*
7. *Typhoid Mary – Anthony Bourdain*
8. *Penicillin Man Alexander Fleming and the Antibiotic Revolution – Kevin Brown*

Allusions to the Experience, and Hell, of Warfare and Conflict

1. *All Quiet of the Western Front – Erich Maria Remarque*
2. *Birdsong – Sebastian Faulks*
3. *The Last Fighting Tommy – Harry Patch*
4. *Forgotten Voices of the Great War – Max Arthur*
5. *The First World War – Michael Howard*
6. *Forgotten Voices of the Somme – Joshua Levine*
7. *Blood and Guts, A History of Surgery – Richard Hollingham*
8. *Men of Steel, Surgery in the Napoleonic Wars – Michael Crumplin FRCS*
9. *Edith Cavell – Diana Souhami*
10. *The Nazis – Laurence Rees*
11. *Odette, Secret Agent, Prisoner, Survivor – Jerrard Tickell*
12. *All Hell Let Loose – Max Hastings*
13. *Nemesis – Max Hastings*
14. *The Blitz – Juliet Gardiner*
15. *Forgotten Voices of the Second World War – Max Arthur*
16. *Forgotten Voices of the Blitz and the Battle for Britain – Joshua Levine*
17. *Stalingrad – Antony Beevor*
18. *Berlin – Antony Beevor*
19. *Russia's Heroes – Albert Axell*
20. *A Woman in Berlin – Marta Hillers*
21. *Hiroshima – John Hersey*
22. *Inquisition – Toby Green*
23. *A Time to Die, The Kursk Disaster – Robert Moore*

Allusions to Crime, Law & Punishment

1. *Go Down Together, The True Untold Story of Bonnie & Clyde – Jeff Guinn*
2. *Born Fighter – Reg Kray*
3. *My Manor – Charlie Richardson*
4. *The Language of London – Daniel Smith*
5. *Inside The Firm, The Untold Story of the Krays' Reign Of Terror – Tony Lambrianou*
6. *The Great Train Robbery – Nick Russell Pavier & Stewart Richards*
7. *Infamous Murders – Verdict Press*
8. *The Rape of Nanking – Iris Chang*
9. *Forensics, The Anatomy of Crime – Val McDermid*
10. *The Rule of Law – Tom Bingham*
11. *Criminal Law – Emily Finch and Stefan Fafinski*
12. *Defending the Guilty – Alex McBride*
13. *Shadow of the Noose, The Story of Edward Marshall-Hall – Richard Cooper*
14. *Nuremberg, Infamy on Trial – Joseph E. Persico*
15. *Newgate, London's Prototype of Hell – Stephen Halliday*
16. *American Notes – Charles Dickens*
17. *Inside Alcatraz, My Time On the Rock – Jim Quillen*
18. *Papillon – Henri Charrière*
19. *The Krays The Prison Years – David Meikle and Kate Beal Blyth*
20. *Colditz the German Viewpoint – Reinhold Eggers*
21. *Executioner: Pierrepoint – Albert Pierrepoint*

Allusions to the Exploration of Evolutionary Biology and Theism

1. *Teach Yourself Genetics – Morton Jenkins*
2. *The Chemistry of Life – Steven Rose*
3. *Origin of Species – Charles Darwin*
4. *Life Ascending, The Ten Great Inventions of Evolution – Nick Lane*
5. *The God Delusion – Richard Dawkins*
6. *Adventures in Human Being – Gavin Francis*
7. *Biology, A Functional Approach – M.B.V.Roberts*
8. *Gray's Anatomy – Longmans press*
9. *The Knife Man – Wendy Moore*
10. *The Wonder of the Stars – Joseph McCabe*
11. *Elementary Analysis – A. Dakin and R.I. Porter*
12. *The Universal Encyclopedia of Machines – George Allen and Unwin press*
13. *It Makes Sense – Steven Gaukroger*
14. *Is God A Delusion – Nicky Gumbel*

Printed in Great Britain
by Amazon

45269999R00249